Transformations of Trac

Transformations of Tradition

Islamic Law in Colonial Modernity

JUNAID QUADRI

OXFORD
UNIVERSITY PRESS

OXFORD
UNIVERSITY PRESS

Oxford University Press is a department of the University of Oxford. It furthers the University's objective of excellence in research, scholarship, and education by publishing worldwide. Oxford is a registered trade mark of Oxford University Press in the UK and certain other countries.

Published in the United States of America by Oxford University Press
198 Madison Avenue, New York, NY 10016, United States of America.

Library of Congress Cataloging-in-Publication Data
Names: Quadri, Junaid, author.
Title: Transformations of tradition : Islamic law in colonial modernity / Junaid Quadri.
Description: 1. | New York : Oxford University Press, 2021. |
Includes bibliographical references and index. |
Contents: INTRODUCTION—1. PARTISANSHIP, TERRITORIALISM AND TRANSREGIONAL NETWORKS OF BELONGING—2. AUTHORITY, IJTIHĀD AND TEMPORALITY—3. COLONIALISM, TRANSLATION AND SEDUCTION—4. SCIENCE, PERCEPTION AND OBJECTIVITY—5. RELIGION, THE SECULAR AND LANGUAGE—CONCLUSION—BIBLIOGRAPHY.
Identifiers: LCCN 2020044148 | ISBN 9780190077044 (hardback) |
ISBN 9780190077075 (oso) | ISBN 9780190077051 (updf) | ISBN 9780190077068 (epub)
Subjects: LCSH: Islamic law—History—19th century. | Islamic law—History—20th century. | Islamic law—Interpretation and construction. | Islamic civilization—Western influences. | Islamic law—Europe—Colonies.
Classification: LCC KBP56 .Q83 2021 | DDC 340.5/9—dc23
LC record available at https://lccn.loc.gov/2020044148

DOI: 10.1093/oso/9780190077044.001.0001

1 3 5 7 9 8 6 4 2

Printed by Integrated Books International, United States of America

To my parents, for unending sacrifice

Contents

Acknowledgments ix
A Note on Transliteration xiii

Introduction 1

1. Partisanship, Territorialism, and Transregional Networks of Belonging 37

2. Authority, *Ijtihād*, and Temporality 59

3. Colonialism, Translation, and Seduction 101

4. Science, Perception, and Objectivity 133

5. Religion, the Secular, and Language 165

Conclusion 209

Bibliography 221
Index 237

Acknowledgments

This book has taken many years to write, but it could just as easily have taken many more given the richness of the material. In the time I have spent on it, I have accrued debts from far too many people to be able to do them justice in what follows.

I have been fortunate to be associated with a series of supportive departmental homes throughout my academic career. The early germs of the idea for this book were cultivated at the Institute of Islamic Studies at McGill University, to whose faculty I am grateful for an education that provided a solid grounding in the field, even as it remained attentive to larger intellectual questions animating the various disciplines that together constitute Islamic studies. I owe a special debt of gratitude to Setrag Manoukian, whose broad-mindedness and perspicacity are equaled only by his kindness and generosity. Wael Hallaq's intellectual presence has been a constant in my thinking, and it is hard to imagine what this book could have looked like without his many comments, discussions, lectures, and interventions. Rula Abisaab has been a continuous source of support and intellectual engagement. I thank also for their early interest in, and support for, my work Malek Abisaab, Sajida Alvi, Laila Parsons, Jamil Ragep, and Robert Wisnovsky. Dyala Hamzah served as a careful and demanding external reader. I owe a special note of thanks to Adina Sigartau and Kirsty McKinnon for their administrative expertise, and to the staff of the Islamic Studies Library for all sorts of support.

At the University of Illinois at Chicago, the Department of History has provided both an open and welcoming atmosphere and a supportive platform from which to pursue my intellectual interests. I am especially grateful to Chris Boyer, who has been a continuous source of wise counsel and encouragement since I joined the department, and was instrumental in shepherding this book to publication. Kevin Schultz has always been a reliable sounding board for matters both intellectual and professional. Laura Hostetler guided me through a hectic first year as an assistant professor with characteristic care and humanity. Marina Mogilner read the entire manuscript at a critical time and offered a number of perceptive suggestions on how to deepen the book's analysis. The work is stronger for those of her comments that I have been able to incorporate; those I could not address are but fodder for ongoing thinking and future discussion. Mary Parks and Linda VanPuyenbroeck, and now Hannah Landsmann and Jessica Hosley, smooth the way for us in the department. I am grateful also to Rama Mantena, Sunil Agnani, and Rachel Havrelock for their steady presence and continuous advocacy. Colleagues in the Program in Religious Studies have helped create a series of opportunities to explore shared interests in a world in which religion, when it is seen at all, is too often seen reductively. Ellen McClure read parts of the manuscript and served as a model of conscientious and thoughtful scholarship. My conversations with Sam Fleischacker on topics of shared interest regularly turn up insights. I am thankful also to Ralph Keen and Laura Dingeldein.

My interlude at the Qatar Faculty of Islamic Studies was a rewarding experience, and I am grateful to the many people who made my year in Doha feel like an extended workshop. I would be remiss if I did not mention the wonderful people at the Department of Philosophy at the University of Waterloo who first made the world of the academic humanities accessible to me. Brian Orend was an excellent mentor. E. J. Ashworth, Joe Novak, Dave Devidi, and Jan Narveson were all rigorous and supportive in equal measure.

For reading and commenting on my work over the years, or simply sharing in its preoccupations in the form of extended conversation in Montreal, Toronto, Cairo, Amman, Doha, and Chicago, I am grateful to Aun Hasan Ali, Emann Allebban, Ovamir Anjum, Alexandre Caeiro, Garrett Davidson, Sarah Eltantawi, Anver Emon, Ellen Etchingham, Bilal Ibrahim, Rizwan Mohammad, Yasmin Moll, Nermeen Mouftah, Nada Moumtaz, Michael Nafi, Nathan Spannaus, Emmanuelle Stefanidis, Daniel Stolz, Leonard Wood, and Florian Zemmin. In Cairo, where the bulk of this research took place, I was fortunate to have the company, experience, and guidance of Omar Cheta, Matt Ellis, Khaled Fahmy, Nathaniel Heisler, Gregory Hoadley, Ahmed Fekry Ibrahim, Aaron Jakes, Sara Nimis, Patrick Scharfe, and Alex Seggerman. In Amman, the staff and fellows of ACOR, in particular the Andersons, made the place feel like home. I am grateful also for the research assistance of the resourceful Muhammad al-Marakeby; and the editorial help of Ajapa Sharma, Avash Bhandari, and Zukhra Kasimova.

I would like to thank Cynthia Read and the staff at Oxford University Press for their work in bringing this book to light. I also wish to acknowledge with gratitude De Gruyter and Duke University Press for permitting me the use of select language from previous publications.

The staff at the following libraries and archives deserve my appreciation: the British National Archives, the British Library, and Palace Green Library (Durham University) in the United Kingdom; the Süleymaniyye Library and İSAM in Istanbul; Maktabat al-Azhar, Dār al-Iftāʾ al-Miṣriyya, Dār al-Kutub al-Qawmiyya (National Library), and Dār al-Wathāʾiq al-Qawmiyya (National Archives) in Cairo. I would also like to thank Dr. Ibrahim Negm of the Dār al-Iftāʾ al-Miṣriyya for his support and assistance. Muḥammad al-Rikābī is not affiliated with any institution, but his store of books in a makeshift office in the back alleys around the Azhar mosque was a *dhakhīra*. Ṣalāḥ Abū al-Ḥāj is similarly a treasure of knowledge pertaining to the Ḥanafī school, and it gives me great pleasure to acknowledge the immeasurable help he provided me in navigating the concerns of this book and Ḥanafism more broadly.

For financial support that made this research possible, I would like to express my gratitude to the American Council of Learned Societies, the Woodrow Wilson National Fellowship Foundation, the Andrew W. Mellon Foundation, the Social Sciences and Humanities Research Council of Canada, the American Research Center in Egypt, the American Center for Oriental Research in Amman, the College of Liberal Arts and Sciences at UIC, and the Faculty of Arts and the Institute of Islamic Studies at McGill.

Nermeen Mouftah endures more stress and worry observing my writing process than she does crafting her own. For her companionship, patience, and good nature, I am ever grateful. The Mouftah, Kamel, and Abdallah families give us homes away from home, both physically and spiritually. Omair Quadri and Sumaira Shah lighten my burdens; and Inayah brightens with her *raunaq*. For my parents, words will not do.

A Note on Transliteration

Arabic words are transliterated according to the guidelines proposed by the *International Journal of Middle East Studies* (*IJMES*), with two exceptions: I preserve diacritical markings on personal names, titles of books and articles, names of organizations, and words from the IJMES word list when they are used in compound or technical terms, for example, *Shaykh al-Islām* and *ʿayn al-sharīʿa*; and I prefer the usage of ulama, as in Merriam-Webster, to ʿulamaʾ.

Introduction

The Ramadan season of 1910 was a particularly eventful one for Muḥammad Bakhīt al-Muṭīʿī, then the head of the shariʿa court in Alexandria and later the Mufti of Egypt. Amid the fasting and festivities that mark the month every year, Bakhīt was called upon to offer his expert opinion on a matter of Islamic law that was proving to be a source of division for two very different Muslim communities. Each of these contexts presented its own specificities, but both were bedeviled by the question of how precisely to bring the venerable juristic tradition to bear upon a very modern problem, namely the evidentiary status of religious reports transmitted through the telegraph.

The first query came from the Khedive of Egypt, whose representative (*qāʾim maqām*) solicited the jurist's thoughts on a telegram he had received from Aswan reporting that the crescent had been spotted there on the eve of the thirtieth of Ramadan. Because the Muslim *hijrī* calendar follows a lunar schedule, this claim, after it had been certified by the local judge, was taken by Aswanis to signify the end of the fasting month of Ramadan and the beginning of Eid festivities.[1] The Khedive's office was interested to know from Bakhīt whether he thought it appropriate to rely on this telegraphic report to declare the Eid throughout the rest of the country. Bakhīt responded in the affirmative, his advisory opinion was subsequently confirmed by the Chief Justice of Cairo (*qāḍī miṣr*) out of an abundance of caution, and ceremonial cannons were set off to signal the beginning of the festival. This unfolding of events, however, troubled many of his learned compatriots who raised doubts about the legitimacy of legal reports conveyed via the telegraph, a new medium encountered only recently, and addressed only summarily, by Muslim jurists.

[1] Months in the *hijrī* calendar may be either twenty-nine or thirty days, a determination that, historically, could only be made on the eve of the thirtieth. On these traditional standards, which eschew the specification of a lunar calendar in advance, if the new moon (*hilāl*) is sighted that evening, the month is only twenty-nine days long, and the next day is deemed to be the first of the new month. If not, the month is considered to be thirty days long.

Transformations of Tradition. Junaid Quadri, Oxford University Press (2021). © Oxford University Press.
DOI: 10.1093/oso/9780190077044.003.0001

In the second case, Bakhīt received a letter from a prominent Egyptian merchant, Ḥasan Bāshā Madkūr, mentioning the experience of one of his friends in Medina who had traveled to a region of India, where he found the local community similarly occupied with the question of whether or not to accept "a report of fasting or ceasing fasting transmitted through the telegraph."[2] The Muslim scholars of the area, divided on the issue, subsequently sent along via this chain of contacts a detailed description of their differences and their respective justifications, seeking further guidance on the matter from the prominent shaykh. As Bakhīt would later recall, "They composed a petition and sent it to [the Medinan friend] in the hope that it may be presented to me, and that I would write upon the matter, illuminating it for them."[3] A little more than six months later, he did just that, penning a full-length treatise, which he titled *Irshād Ahl al-Milla ilā Ithbāt al-Ahilla* (*Guidance to the Muslims on Determining the New Moons*), that responded to both entreaties amid a comprehensive examination of a range of issues surrounding the determination of the *hijrī* months in an era of changed circumstances. It is this text, the context in which it emerged, and what we may learn about the history of Islamic law from the positions it took that constitute the centerpiece of our discussions in this book.

The practice of petitioning the knowledgeable for legal guidance (*istiftā'*) is, along with its complement, the learned jurists' furnishing (*iftā'*) of responsa (fatwas), a veritable institution of Muslim societies stretching back to the Prophetic era,[4] but these two incidences of it captured a series of modern anxieties that animated "traditionalist" ulama's confrontation with a radically changed—or, at least, rapidly changing—world. Historians of Islamic law have long noted that fatwas were a genre of legal writing closely connected to social change, existing as they did at the frontier of the juristic elite's engagement with society.[5] Driven by the concerns of social life, these questions and

[2] Muḥammad Bakhīt al-Muṭīʿī, *Irshād Ahl al-Milla ilā Ithbāt al-Ahilla*, ed. Ḥasan Aḥmad Isbir (Beirut: Dār Ibn Ḥazm, 2000), 17. The earlier edition of the text is Muḥammad Bakhīt al-Muṭīʿī, *Kitāb Irshād Ahl al-Milla ilā Ithbāt al-Ahilla* (Miṣr: Maṭbaʿat al-Kurdistān al-ʿIlmiyya, 1329 H). All page number references will be to the 2000 edition from Dār Ibn Ḥazm.

[3] Bakhīt al-Muṭīʿī, *Irshād Ahl al-Milla*, 18.

[4] Muhammad Khalid Masud, Brinkley Morris Messick, and David Stephan Powers, eds., *Islamic Legal Interpretation: Muftis and Their Fatwas*, Harvard Studies in Islamic Law (Cambridge, MA: Harvard University Press, 1996), 4. For a magisterial history of fatwa-giving in Egypt, see ʿImād Aḥmad Hilāl, *al-Iftā' al-Miṣrī min al-Ṣaḥābī ʿUqba ibn ʿĀmir ilā al-Duktūr ʿAlī Jumʿa*, 6 vols. (Cairo: Maṭbaʿat Dār al-Kutub wa-l-Wathā'iq al-Qawmiyya, 2010–2020).

[5] Wael B. Hallaq, "From Fatwās to Furūʿ: Growth and Change in Islamic Substantive Law," *Islamic Law and Society* 1, no. 1 (1994): 29–65; Judith E. Tucker, *In the House of the Law: Gender and Islamic Law in Ottoman Syria and Palestine* (Berkeley: University of California Press, 2000); Baber Johansen, *The Islamic Law on Land Tax and Rent: The Peasants' Loss of Property Rights as Interpreted in the*

answers often provide, therefore, rich and detailed accounts through which to understand the specific contexts in which petitioners found themselves. In particular, because these were matters everyday people felt ill-equipped to confidently resolve for themselves, fatwa responsa often addressed new and unprecedented situations (*nawāzil*) that required recourse to knowledgeable experts.

In the cases given here, the central question was how precisely to make sense of the presence of a new technology that had redefined communication. In particular, in a legal system that privileged oral testimonies and in-person transmissions of reports, and conceptualized the permissibility of written correspondences between judges as a concession to the practical needs of a growing empire, how ought Muslims understand the emergence of the telegraph and the set of procedures and protocols specific to it?[6] Disagreements over crescent sightings were not themselves a new phenomenon—narrations from as far back as the lives of the Prophet Muḥammad's Companions record divergent determinations of the months in disparate areas of the nascent Muslim empire and suggest differences of opinion among them over how to deal with discrepancies when they came to light.[7] In a world connected by telegraphic infrastructure, however, in which news that might previously take days to convey could now travel exponentially faster, the question presented a newfound urgency. Whereas the famous Companion of the Prophet ʿAbd Allāh b. ʿAbbās could simply set aside the news that Syrians had started fasting a day earlier than his community in Medina, summarily disregarding telegrams reporting events from the very same night seemed counterintuitive on its face.[8] And yet, if the Khedive's need to approach Bakhīt in the first place, Bakhīt's precautionary insistence that his opinion be confirmed by the

Hanafite Legal Literature of the Mamluk and Ottoman Periods (London: Croom Helm, 1988); Joseph Schacht, *An Introduction to Islamic Law* (Oxford: Clarendon Press, 1982).

6 Wael B. Hallaq, "Qāḍīs Communicating: Legal Change and the Law of Documentary Evidence," *Al-Qanṭara* XX, no. 2 (1999): 439.

7 See, for example, the famous hadith of Kurayb, related in the compilations of Muslim, Abū Dāwūd, al-Tirmidhī, al-Nasāʾī, and Aḥmad b. Ḥanbal. The text of the tradition can also be found in Muḥammad Amīn Ibn ʿĀbidīn, "Tanbīh al-Ghāfil wa-l-Wasnān ʿalā Aḥkām Hilāl Ramaḍān," in *Arbaʿa Rasāʾil fī Hilāl Khayr Al-Shuhūr* (Beirut: Dār Ibn Ḥazm, 2000), 106; Kamāl al-Dīn Ibn al-Humām, *Fatḥ al-Qadīr* (Beirut: Dār al-Fikr, n.d.), 2:314. See also chapter 5.

8 There is, in fact, an extensive jurisprudence on this issue that is framed around the question of "horizons." It treats the question of what ought to be considered a single jurisdiction, such that the determination of a crescent sighting in one area of the jurisdiction applies to the whole. Some have held, in contrast to the apparent meaning of the hadith given here, that the whole world is one "horizon" (*ittiḥād al-maṭāliʿ*), and a sighting anywhere is binding on all; while others have been content to divide the world into different jurisdictions (*ikhtilāf al-maṭāliʿ*).

head qadi ("the highest judge in the Egyptian lands") and the subsequent uproar are any indication, departing from the cumulative tradition of thinking and practice on this matter appears to have struck many as equally in need of careful deliberation and debate.

Figuring out how to grapple with the consequences of new technologies was but one of a series of challenges that confronted everyday Muslims in the opening decade of the twentieth century. A close reading of the two scenarios depicted above allows us to glimpse a handful of other salient features, laying bare the social and political terrain on which Muslim subjects now found themselves operating. To begin, the cases reveal the two overarching contexts that structured modern Egyptian Muslims' everyday lives: the first, the growing presence and intrusive involvement of the bureaucratizing and modernizing Egyptian state; and the second, the transregional worlds in which they were situated, formed variously by British imperialism, commercial connections, and networks of Muslim learning.

In the first case, jurists' engagement with the Khedive's petition is mediated entirely within the world of state officialdom. It is a judge in Aswan's central court (*maḥkamat al-markaz*, an institution set up and regulated by the Khedive) who certifies the claimed crescent sighting in the first instance; the *mudīr* of the district of Aswan then conveys the news to the offices of the Khedive, the Prime Minister, and the Interior Minister; the Khedive's representative approaches Bakhīt, the head of the Alexandria shariʿa court; Bakhīt's decision is then forwarded to the country's head judge in Cairo; and Egyptians are notified of the national decision by the government's sounding of cannons. This whole process takes place through official correspondences, and indeed, it is precisely this characteristic of the telegraph report that our mufti points to mudar explain his confidence in it: "it is an official report proceeding from the Egyptian government (*khabar rasmī ṣādir min ṭarīq al-ḥukūma al-miṣriyya*), and it is unlikely that the like of it is infiltrated by untruth."[9]

But the telegraph was from its inception as much an imperial institution as a national one. The famed Egyptian modernizer, Ismāʿīl Pāshā, had by 1870 laid down sixty-six internal telegraphic lines amounting to five thousand miles.[10] But the interest of telegraphy in Egypt was also

[9] Bakhīt al-Muṭīʿī, *Irshād Ahl al-Milla*, 16.

[10] See P. J. Vatikiotis, *The History of Modern Egypt: From Muhammad Ali to Mubarak*, 4th ed. (Baltimore: The Johns Hopkins University Press, 1991), 79; Eli M. Noam, *Telecommunications in Africa* (Oxford: Oxford University Press, 1999), 40.

spurred on by British strategic interests in using an overland Alexandria-Cairo-Suez line as a crucial link "on the road to India."[11] "The Eastern lines," as they came to be called, became the preferred route of cable communication to India: "because of their exemption from political surveillance and because of the greater speed and accuracy with which their messages were transmitted, [the Eastern lines] became the main artery of intercommunication system between West and East."[12] India and Egypt were, of course, two key zones of colonial influence and domination for the British, and indeed the importance of the connections between them was only underscored by the cross-fertilization of British officials and expertise—the British Consul-General for almost twenty-five years until 1907, for example, was Lord Cromer whose initial posts in imperial government had him shuttling between the Indian and Egyptian files.[13] The colonial presence of the British was, thus, an important supranational context that bore upon the politics of Egyptian society and connected it with other colonies.

But there were also older and more established Islamic networks that brought Muslim communities into contact with one another. The world of Islamdom is vividly represented here in the layered route by which Bakhīt came to know of debates within a far-off "region of India": via an Egyptian merchant whose associate in the sacred city of Medina had traveled to that part of the country, a chain that connects Muslim communities together through commerce and pilgrimage. Notably, in the Indian case, the appeal to Bakhīt's authority and expertise proceeds on an entirely different premise than it did within Egypt. Whereas the Egyptian chain of correspondence unfolded from start to finish under the auspices of a centralizing state, it is precisely the absence of Muslim rule and an established hierarchy of Muslim courts that motivated the letter from India. The questioners, aware of the peculiarity of their newfound political situation, ask how precisely to accommodate it:

11 Charles Bright, *Submarine Telegraphs: Their History, Construction, and Working* (London: C. Lockwood and Son, 1898), 62.

12 Halford Lancaster Hoskins, *British Routes to India* (New York: Longmans, Green and Co., 1928), 393. On the initial frustrations encountered by the effort to link Egypt to India telegraphically and their subsequent overcoming, see On Barak, *On Time: Technology and Temporality in Modern Egypt* (Berkeley: University of California Press, 2013), 44–49.

13 See Roger Owen, *Lord Cromer: Victorian Imperialist, Edwardian Proconsul* (Oxford: Oxford University Press, 2004).

> May the imam of a mosque take the place of a qadi in affirming [a sighting of] the crescent? Specifically, [may he do so] with the approval of the Muslims in lands where there is no Muslim sovereign or judge?[14]

Historians of Islamic law in India have pointed out that the disappearance of official Islamic legal authority was a recurring concern for Muslims in colonial India, with one influential solution being precisely the one asked about by Bakhīt's interlocutors.[15] Yet, despite apparent dissimilarities, this, too, was a shared anxiety. The contestation and reconstitution of the ulama's authority under modern conditions manifested differently in the two cases, but the stability of the Egyptian legal process taken for granted by Bakhīt was itself the result of a significant displacement of the power historically enjoyed by ulama in favor of state institutions.

The staying power of old (albeit reconfigured and reweighted) networks of Islamdom is also represented in these two vignettes in other ways. Perhaps even more fundamental than the connections formed by trade and piety is the shared universe of thought and debate constructed over centuries by ulama, Muslim learned scholars and jurists, across the Muslim world. The Indian imam who signed off on the letter is identified by Bakhīt as "Shaykh ʿAbd al-Ḥayy, the preacher (*khaṭīb*) of the 'Rankūt' mosque." This is a reference to ʿAbd al-Ḥayy al-Kaflaytwī, who delivered Friday sermons in the Rangoon mosque in Burma, then a part of the British Raj.[16] There is in Bakhīt's identification a typo or mistake in transcription—the replacing of *n* with the not dissimilar grapheme *t*—that gestures toward a distance and lack of familiarity between the petitioner and responder. But this misprint belies a deeper connection. Importantly, al-Kaflaytwī evinces not only a knowledge of his local community's social situation (especially their relative weakness vis-à-vis a British government he understands to be hostile to Islam) but also a command over the language of Islamic law—in particular,

[14] Bakhīt al-Muṭīʿī, *Irshād Ahl al-Milla*, 18.

[15] Muhammad Khalid Masud, "Apostasy and Judicial Separation in British India," in *Islamic Legal Interpretation: Muftis and Their Fatwas*, ed. Muhammad Khalid Masud, Brinkley Messick, and David S. Powers, Harvard Studies in Islamic Law (Cambridge, MA: Harvard University Press, 1996), 193–203; Muhammad Qasim Zaman, *The Ulama in Contemporary Islam: Custodians of Change*, Princeton Studies in Muslim Politics (Princeton, NJ: Princeton University Press, 2002), 29–31. Fareeha Khan, "Traditionalist Approaches to *Sharīʿah* Reform: Mawlana Ashraf ʿAli Thānawī's Fatwa on Women's Right to Divorce" (PhD diss., University of Michigan, 2008).

[16] I am grateful to Uwais Namazi for his help identifying this figure. For a short biographical entry on al-Kaflaytwī, see ʿAbd al-Ḥayy b. Fakhr al-Dīn al-Ḥasanī, *Nuzhat al-Khawāṭir* (Beiut: Dār Ibn Ḥazm, 1999), 8:1267–68.

the positive doctrine, evidentiary standards, and authoritative figures of the Ḥanafī school. The common idiom of the shariʿa has long been a glue that has bound educated Muslims from across continents. The fourteenth-century traveler Ibn Battuta, for example, could famously travel from his native Tangier and, based on his Maghribī training in Islamic law, work as a qadi under the Delhi Sultanate, trading on his knowledge and authority as he traversed the breadth of the Muslim world. In the modern period, the possibilities for transregional engagement proliferated as a result of the relative ease with which ideas and individuals circulated in an age of print and increased travel. These links were all the more solidified when, as in this case, the dialogue was had by two members of the same *madhhab*, or juristic school, a key frame through which Muslim jurists envisioned their allegiances, conducted their investigations, and carried out their craft.

The impact of new technology, the encroaching power of territorialized states, the persistence of older transregional networks of Islamic belonging and connection, the emergent presence of imperialism, the contested and unstable nature of legal authority—these are all themes that will emerge in this book as central to the manner in which Islamic law developed in the late nineteenth and early twentieth centuries. At its core, however, this book is a study of Islamic law's intellectual entanglement with colonial modernity. More specifically, it is an historical examination of the development of the long-standing, indigenous field of learning and praxis known as shariʿa or *fiqh* as a result of its imbalanced interaction with new European modes of knowing during, and in the immediate aftermath of, the colonial experience. I argue that central epistemological commitments associated with modernity came to be far more pervasive in colonial Muslim settings than is generally appreciated. Indeed, the legal discussions I treat in the chapters that follow give us reason to think that what is typically described as the "traditional" or "orthodox" sector of Islamic societies—the pre-eminent exemplars of which are the jurist-theologians of Islam (the ulama)—was much more accommodating of the entry of modernist epistemologies into its own conceptual thought-world than scholars have made it out to be. These findings, in turn, force us to reconsider, and trouble in new ways, the status and nature of Islamic law as a tradition in the modern world.

Taking Egypt in the late nineteenth and early twentieth centuries as my central case study, I examine the impact on Islamic legal thinking of cross-cultural encounters, social reconfigurations, and technological advances that made certain elements of modern European thinking attractive to Muslim jurists. In fact, I argue that in many cases the tilted power dynamics of a new political landscape—in which not only were colonial powers ascendant but French-trained intellectuals and modernizing reformers from the local population deftly used modern means like the printing press to contest the intellectual prestige and standing historically reserved for the ulama—placed significant pressure on "traditionalists" that made new epistemological commitments not simply accessible, but irresistible. In yet other cases, the penetration of new technologies like the telegraph, the telescope, the phonograph, and photography served to make available to Muslim jurists ways of perceiving the world that came to be understood as natural and uncontroversial, despite both their relatively recent origins and their foreignness to the sophisticated intellectual system erected over many centuries by the ulama.

These transformations of tradition appear most readily in the Ḥanafī legal school (*madhhab*) as represented by the intellectual output of the jurist we encountered at the outset of this introduction, Muḥammad Bakhīt al-Muṭīʿī (1854–1935; widely referred to by his father's name Bakhīt, rather than his *nisba* al-Muṭīʿī). Although relatively unknown in Western academia, Bakhīt was a towering figure in ulama circles of the period, remembered by one of his colleagues as "the undisputed *ʿallāma* of the Egyptian lands; the uncontested shaykh of its shaykhs."[17] As a leading member of the ulama often called upon to defend an older order in a rapidly changing environment, Bakhīt had a complicated relationship with colonial officials but regularly found himself at loggerheads with Muslim modernist intellectuals whom he thought to be disruptive bearers of foreign power and modern ideas.[18] As a result, he often figured in debates as one of the most ardent opponents of the Egyptian Reformist movement, earning himself a reputation among both his contemporaries and posterity as an arch-conservative or traditionalist par excellence. However, through close readings of his legal works, I show that Bakhīt had in fact absorbed some fundamental modernist ideals, commitments which at times mirrored and at other times exceeded what Muslim modernists were expressly agitating for. These findings only become apparent, I argue, when we shift our attention away from the politically charged turf battles that divided the ulama from their opponents (for example, reform of the law of endowments, which had for centuries been an important source of ulama income, or reform of the sensitive field of divorce

[17] Aḥmad Ibn al-Ṣiddīq al-Ghumārī, *al-Baḥr al-ʿAmīq fī Marwiyyāt Ibn al-Ṣiddīq*, vol. 1 (Cairo: Dār al-Kutubī, 2007), 195.

[18] See chapters 1 and 3.

law), and instead direct it toward unconventional sites like the jurisprudence of ritual.[19] Indeed, in couching these commitments in genres and language that had a distinguished pedigree in Muslim thought, Bakhīt often enhanced their respectability in ways that modernists who advocated for a conscious departure from the past could not.

My detailed reading of Bakhīt reveals the entry into the corpus of Islamic legal writing of a series of departures from the older tradition: (1) a historical consciousness that facilitates an upending of the structure of legal authority such that the findings of the medieval past are de-emphasized and the capacities of the modern jurist are valorized; (2) a scientific optimism which makes room for the findings of modern science precisely because of its "objectivity," often over and above long-standing genre-internal standards of perception, now castigated for their subjectivity and thus vulnerability to error; and (3) a compartmentalized notion of the concept of religion as including primarily ritual practices and private belief, which in turn forces an exclusion of those matters from the purview of the courts—a distinction between public and private that lays the groundwork for a certain type of secularity. Given how fundamental these shifts are, I claim that we are justified in asking to what extent they represent a radical transformation of Islamic law, and not simply a continuity of an older tradition.

Colonial Modernity and Islamic Tradition

In the last chapter of his widely acclaimed *Formations of the Secular*, the anthropologist Talal Asad offers his readers a particularly rich and nuanced discussion of shariʿa reform in colonial Egypt.[20] Redirecting our attention from the conventional tendency to either evaluate the Islamic authenticity of reformist arguments and personalities or to determine relative agency among the various political actors involved in the process, Asad invites us to consider instead the "new moral landscape" being constituted by the totality of social forces then converging to produce the phenomenon we call reform. "The basic question," for Asad,

[19] Bakhīt wrote three works on endowments and at least one on divorce law. See n77.

[20] Talal Asad, *Formations of the Secular: Christianity, Islam, Modernity* (Stanford, CA: Stanford University Press, 2003), 205–56.

> is not the determination of "oppressors" and "oppressed," of whether the elites or the popular masses were the agents in the history of reform. . . . It is the determination of that new landscape, and the degree to which the languages, behaviors, and institutions it makes possible come to resemble those that obtain in the West European nation-states.[21]

For his part, Asad focuses on three key, and interrelated, developments he takes to be fundamental to the reformulation of Islamic discursive tradition: a new salience given to the family unit, a strict demarcation between law and morality, and the production of new sorts of subjectivities which privilege the notion of an autonomous, self-governing conscience over that of an embodied moral agent. These "social and cultural changes," argues Asad, "created some of the basic preconditions for secular modernity."[22]

In a similar fashion, this book takes seriously the profound impact of the colonial experience, and the deep inroads made by "secular modernity" into Egyptian society and Islamic tradition as a result.[23] It does so by tracing the extensive penetration of what scholars have tended to see as "modern" or "Modernist"[24] intellectual commitments into the discursive tradition of the ulama, the class of Islamic jurist-scholars that has often been identified as traditional, conservative, and at times obscurantist. In centering my investigation on the ulama, my findings do not simply affirm Asad's observations about the widespread influence of colonial modernity but extend them to a domain of society that he and others have left relatively untouched. That is to say, detection of Modernist commitments in the writings of ulama figures

[21] Asad, *Formations of the Secular*, 216–17.

[22] Asad, *Formations of the Secular*, 235.

[23] An influential work that shows in detail how the colonial presence in Egypt restructured the political and social order of the country is Timothy Mitchell, *Colonising Egypt* (Berkeley: University of California Press, 1991). Drawing on Heidegger and Derrida, Mitchell identifies the colonial-modern device of "representation" as being at work in late nineteenth- and early twentieth-century Egypt. By "representation," he explains elsewhere, is meant "the forms of social practice that set up in the social architecture of the world what seems an absolute distinction between image (or meaning, or structure) and reality, and thus a distinctive imagination of the real." See Timothy Mitchell, ed., *Questions of Modernity*, Contradictions of Modernity, vol. 11 (Minneapolis: University of Minnesota Press, 2000), 17. The spread of this way of viewing one's surroundings, Mitchell argues, gives rise to "a new conception of space, new forms of personhood, and a new means of manufacturing the experience of the real." Mitchell, *Colonising Egypt*, ix. I discuss the impact of this conception on Muslim-Egyptian thinking in chapter 4.

[24] The secondary literature regularly calls the Reform movement "Modernist." This is a broad term, and it is not often clear what parallels are to be drawn to other Modernist movements in other fields. The central criteria for my interlocutors tends to be, as we will see later, the debate about the reassertion of *ijtihād*. Despite its limitations, I continue to find it a suitable appellation insofar as it denotes a conscious departure from the medieval past as represented by the culture of ulama.

demonstrates their pervasiveness to a greater degree than has been previously appreciated.[25]

This, however, raises questions about the status of Islamic law as a tradition. Since the landmark publication of Alasdair MacIntyre's *After Virtue* in 1981, scholarship has evidenced a renewed interest in the concept of "tradition." This shift in research orientation was presented to Islamic Studies most prominently in Asad's early work, in which he famously urged fellow anthropologists of Islam to reframe their analyses of Islam by "begin[ning], as Muslims do, from the concept of a discursive tradition."[26] This has been an important corrective in the field (by no means limited to anthropology), one that both eschews overly reductionist explanations of a complex religious tradition and displays a keen sensitivity and openness toward the intellectual claims of the very subjects of our scholarly research. For Asad,

> An Islamic discursive tradition is simply a tradition of Muslim discourse that addresses itself to conceptions of the Islamic past and future, with reference to a particular Islamic practice in the present. Clearly, not everything Muslims say and do belongs to an Islamic discursive tradition. Nor is an Islamic tradition in this sense necessarily imitative of what was done in the past. For even where traditional practices appear to the anthropologist to be imitative of what has gone before, it will be the practitioners' conceptions of what is *apt performance*, and of how the past is related to present practices, that will be crucial for tradition, not the apparent repetition of an old form.[27]

This early formulation captures rather well how Asad's category of tradition is at once circumscribed and expansive. Against a relativistic approach that considers anything a Muslim says or does as part of the social structure of

[25] Asad, for example, is content to restrict himself to the writings of Reformist-minded personalities Muḥammad ʿAbduh, Qāsim Amīn, and Aḥmad Ṣafwat, though he takes them to be influential representatives of a larger political and social shift. See Asad, *Formations of the Secular*, 228–41. Mitchell's interest in the ulama is restricted to brief discussions of the institution of al-Azhar, and traditional linguistic theory, and that, too, only inasmuch as they are useful contrasts to British conceptions of educational order and discipline, on the one hand, and modern theories of communication, on the other. Mitchell, *Colonising Egypt*, 80–87, 128–60. The lone author that seems to have taken up these issues at length is Indira Falk Gesink, but my differences with her project will emerge in due course. Indira Falk Gesink, *Islamic Reform and Conservatism: Al-Azhar and the Evolution of Modern Sunni Islam* (London: Tauris Academic Studies, 2010).

[26] Talal Asad, "The Idea of an Anthropology of Islam," Occasional Papers Series (Washington, DC: Georgetown University Center for Contemporary Arab Studies, 1986), 14.

[27] Asad, "The Idea of an Anthropology of Islam," 14–15.

Islam, Asad insists on some reference to a normative discourse. Yet that normative discourse is not so static as to demand only "the apparent repetition of an old form" to qualify as tradition.

In his chapter on Egypt, Asad stresses the latter of these two features, the openness to dispute and disagreement that characterizes traditions. With specific reference to the Reformists Muḥammad ʿAbduh and Muḥammad Rashīd Riḍā, who figure prominently in this book as Bakhīt's avowed opponents, Asad criticizes Orientalists who have thought the Reformers to be operating outside the tradition of Islamic law.[28] Rather, because they participate in a conversation whose starting points are "a theological vocabulary and a set of problems derived from the Qur'an (the divine revelation), the *sunna* (the Prophet's tradition), and the major jurists (that is, those cited as authoritative) who have commented on both,"[29] ʿAbduh's and Riḍā's "disagreement or difference is what makes it part of the tradition of Islamic jurisprudence."[30] In a recent article in which he revisits his theorization of tradition, Asad has reaffirmed, indeed intensified, this emphasis: "in principle tradition can accommodate rupture, recuperation, reorientation, and splitting—as well as continuity."[31]

More than thirty years after MacIntyre's and Asad's original contributions, however, we are justified in interrogating the limits of the category of tradition. In this work, I shift my attention to this concern. Where Asad finds the overlapping etymology of "tradition" and "treason" to evoke the ability of tradition to withstand even betrayal, it is instead their shared sense of something identifiable—a practice or belief, but equally a country—being "handed over" in a manner that preserves the object's integrity that principally informs my understanding of tradition in this book.[32] I do not deny that traditions change, but in place of the prevailing focus on tradition's expansiveness and enduring resilience, I inquire instead into its boundaries. How much flexibility and variance can a tradition sustain? When does a

[28] This line of argumentation is taken up in further detail by Samira Haj, *Reconfiguring Islamic Tradition: Reform, Rationality, and Modernity*, Cultural Memory in the Present (Stanford, CA: Stanford University Press, 2009).

[29] Asad, *Formations of the Secular*, 220.

[30] Asad, *Formations of the Secular*, 221. See also Haj, *Reconfiguring Islamic Tradition*.

[31] Talal Asad, "Thinking About Tradition, Religion, and Politics in Egypt Today," *Critical Inquiry* 42, no. 1 (September 1, 2015): 169.

[32] Asad, "Thinking About Tradition, Religion, and Politics in Egypt Today," 169. For an explanation of the Latin *trado* that explains this primary sense (shared with "treason"), see inter alia Peter Jackson, "Retracing the Path: Gesture, Memory, and the Exegesis of Tradition," *History of Religions* 45, no. 1 (2005): 5–9; Bruno Queysanne, "Tradition and Modernity in the Face of Time," *Traditional Dwellings and Settlements Review* 1, no. 1 (1989): 4.

claimed tradition become so different from previous incarnations that we are justified in speaking of it as having been transformed altogether? I argue that the sustainability and ongoing relevance of the concept of tradition demands drawing distinctions between a given tradition and other streams of thought—often traditions in their own right—as well as an account of when that given tradition ceases to be one. In the case of Islamic law in the colonial period, in particular, I argue that the Ḥanafism of the late nineteenth and early twentieth centuries experienced a shift from what MacIntyre might call a tradition-guided enquiry to one informed by key presuppositions of modernity: a progressivist history, a scientistic ontology and epistemology, and a new conception of religion.

Asad and MacIntyre have both had relatively little to say about the transformation or death of traditions.[33] As we have seen in the case of Asad, his latest contribution to the discussion has incorporated rupture itself within the meaning of tradition, a stretching of the plain meaning of the term that is in accordance with his spacious understanding of the concept. Jean Porter has posed the question of boundaries with regards to MacIntyre as well, concluding that "tradition" is "a term of the scholar's art" that has "fuzzy borders."[34] Whether or not one finds this satisfying, MacIntyre's extensive discussions of a number of traditions within Western philosophy provide us a base of historical material with which we can attempt to better clarify the substance of the boundaries that underlie his more direct formulations.

Central to MacIntyre's conception of what divides one tradition from another is the notion of internal standards, historically embedded, by which the rationality of a position within the tradition may be judged.[35] The respective standards of these two separate traditions render the traditions incommensurable in some meaningful way.[36] To take the case of two traditions that MacIntyre discusses at length, "the standards of truth and rationality to which appeal had to be made in order to debate them constructively were not the same for Aristotelians and for Augustinians."[37] Aristotle had a much

[33] Although MacIntyre does, in his first invocation of the concept, suggest that "traditions decay, disappear, and disintegrate." Alasdair MacIntyre, *After Virtue: A Study in Moral Theory*, 3rd ed. (Notre Dame, IN: University of Notre Dame Press, 2007), 22.

[34] Jean Porter, "Openness and Constraint: Moral Reflection as Tradition-Guided Inquiry in Alasdair MacIntyre's Recent Works," *The Journal of Religion* 73, no. 4 (1993): 518–19.

[35] Alasdair MacIntyre, *Whose Justice? Which Rationality?* (Notre Dame, IN: University of Notre Dame Press, 1988), 7, 348.

[36] MacIntyre, *Whose Justice? Which Rationality?*, 351.

[37] Alasdair MacIntyre, *Three Rival Versions of Moral Enquiry: Encyclopaedia, Genealogy, and Tradition*, paperback ed. (Notre Dame, IN: University of Notre Dame Press, 1991), 109.

more optimistic view of the intellect's ability to grasp all its objects, whereas Augustine believed in the fundamental incapacity of the mind. It is in terms of the mind adequately grasping those objects that Aristotle judged truth, while for Augustine, truth as an attribute of things is found in their relationship to *Veritas*, or God. Whereas, for Aristotle, the intellect is self-sufficient in arriving (or failing to arrive) at truth, both theoretical and practical, Augustine believed that the will is always a threat to mislead the intellect, and that "all intellectual error is rooted in moral defect."[38] As a result, MacIntyre concludes that "the Aristotelian philosopher and the Augustinian theologian appealed to rival and incompatible standards."[39] Despite their shared vocabulary, problematics, and points of reference, "each contending party had no standard by which to judge the questions about which it differed from the other which was not itself as much in dispute as anything else."[40] Here we have a way of distinguishing between two traditions which resided, for a time, side by side in an uneasy modus vivendi at the University of Paris.

One of my discomforts with Asad's formulation, then, is that "Islamic tradition" is too broad a category for historical purposes. Rather, individual streams of thought *within* Islam have put forward key defining standards that differentiated them from their counterparts. Muhammad Qasim Zaman has alluded to this in a rather astute, but underappreciated, observation. In discussing Asad's notion of a discursive tradition, Zaman writes, "But if Islam *in general* ought to be approached as a 'discursive tradition,' I would argue that particular facets of this tradition can be viewed in a broadly similar way. The *shari'a* is the preeminent example of a tradition and, indeed, of a discursive tradition."[41] This strikes as an eminently reasonable characterization. However, my own reading in this book is that traditions can be divided further, into even narrower groupings that more closely reflect the communal aspect of MacIntyrean traditions that allow adherents to speak of a common history. In the pages that follow, I consider the *madhhab*, the juristic school, to have such a claim to a tradition. In my view, it is through attention to the concept of the *madhhab* that we can most meaningfully delineate traditions, since the most defensible way of understanding what

[38] MacIntyre, *Three Rival Versions*, 110.
[39] MacIntyre, *Three Rival Versions*, 111.
[40] MacIntyre, *Three Rival Versions*, 111.
[41] Zaman, *The Ulama in Contemporary Islam*, 6. Asad has at times also referred to "the tradition of Islamic jurisprudence," though it is not clear how he theorizes the existence of this tradition *within* Islamic tradition more broadly. Asad, *Formations of the Secular*, 221. See also Asad, "Thinking About Tradition, Religion, and Politics in Egypt Today," 179n28, where he refers to "the *sharī'a* as tradition."

differentiates one *madhhab* from another, especially in their mature forms, is the expressly agreed-upon standards that define their discursive boundaries.[42] What distinguishes, for example, a Ḥanafī from a Shāfiʿī is the discursive continuity of the distinctive methodological positions explicated in works of jurisprudence (*uṣūl al-fiqh*) and exemplary cases found in works of substantive law (*furūʿ al-fiqh*) that together structure their respective approaches to the foundational texts, commitments that have come to be irreducible and defining postulates of those *madhhab*s themselves. Mere reference to the Qurʾan and sunna, I contend, is not sufficient to speak of a cohesive tradition. Rather, if, following MacIntyre, a constitutive element of a tradition is a clear sense of "critics and enemies external to the tradition,"[43] taking the usage of the Qurʾan and sunna as touchstones for reasoning to be the criteria for inclusion within the tradition does not leave much room for external critics that are recognizable within books of *fiqh*. The "constitutive others" with whom arguments are had in *fiqh* works are by and large members of other *madhhabs*, not non-Muslims who reject references to the Qurʾan and sunna altogether. As the example given by MacIntyre of the rival Augustinian and Aristotelian traditions indicates, the standards that divide traditions are much more robust epistemological premises.

No less important, however, is the corporate identities of these schools, embodied in a shared history that emerges from early figures vested with canonical authority. MacIntyre describes the originating moment of a tradition as follows:

> Every [tradition-constituted] enquiry begins in and from some condition of pure historical contingency, from the beliefs, institutions, and practices of some particular community which constitute a given. Within such a community authority will have been conferred upon certain texts and certain voices.[44]

[42] It is also worth considering whether Zaman's formulation does not itself raise questions. If *shariʿa* is a discursive tradition, for example, may we include Shīʿī juristic texts and communities as part of the same tradition as the Ḥanafīs in this work? It seems to me that considering the question in this way supports my contention that individual juristic communities' fundamental presuppositions and intellectual starting points are distinct enough to merit thinking instead of *madhhabs* as the proper unit by which to calibrate the term "tradition." For the characterization of Twelver Shīʿism as a tradition, see Aun Hasan Ali, "The Beginnings of the School of Ḥillah: A Bio-Bibliographical Study of Twelver Shīʿism in the Late ʿAbbāsid and Early Ilkhānid Periods" (PhD diss., McGill University, 2016).

[43] MacIntyre, *Whose Justice? Which Rationality?*, 12.

[44] MacIntyre, *Whose Justice? Which Rationality?*, 354.

In the case of jurisprudence, as I show in chapter 2, the eponym of the school functions more often as that contingent originating authority than the Prophet's sunna. Ḥanafīs are more often occupied with how to interpret the authoritative pronouncements of early jurists belonging to the school than they are with how to interpret Prophetic hadiths.[45] Thus, Asad's inclusion of "major jurists (that is, those cited as authoritative)" as part of the "specific material" from which the Reformists ʿAbduh and Riḍā reasoned seems to me to demand further differentiation. The jurists admitted as exerting some sense of authority over Ḥanafīs are distinct from those of Shāfiʿīs, and indeed from those of the Reformists.[46] If, as MacIntyre argues, traditions trace their origin to a canonical moment that cannot be repudiated without forfeiting membership in the tradition, within the domain of legal discussions, the intellectual work of the eponym is as eligible a candidate for that canonicity as is the life of the Prophet.

The feature of a tradition that most occupies both Asad and MacIntyre is its ability to adapt to new configurations of the world for which older instantiations of the tradition are no longer adequate.[47] A particular species of this developmental account, that of conscious reform, has been expressed in Asad's recent work in terms of the "purification" of tradition—the restoration of "an obscured origin that can then accommodate itself more smoothly to the real, progressive world."[48] Asad admits the possibility that this process means that "actual traditions, *descriptively so identified*, can disintegrate or implode."[49] But this reform, clearly applicable to the case of Egypt he treated in his earlier chapter, he identifies as an act of tradition.

My concern with this formulation is that it leaves no discernible room for an *outside* to tradition. This is not the case with MacIntyre, for whom tradition is opposed to both genealogy and encyclopedia. Asad has expressly disavowed the opposition of tradition to genealogy, but he has had less to say

[45] For the centrality of the doctrine of Abū Ḥanīfa to the Ḥanafī school, and Ḥanafīs' relationship to Prophetic hadiths, see also Behnam Sadeghi, *The Logic of Law Making in Islam: Women and Prayer in the Legal Tradition* (New York: Cambridge University Press, 2013), 128–41.

[46] Alternatively, Asad might be read as saying that the tradition of the Reformists is distinct from that of "the authorized exponents of the *sharīʿa*" whom the Reformists were trying to dislodge. This is supported by his emphasis on "*That* tradition" in the preceding sentence. This sits uneasily, however, with his inclusion of them as part of "the tradition of Islamic jurisprudence" toward the end of the paragraph. More consequentially, however, this reading would concede the point that these traditions are different and therefore incommensurable. *Formations of the Secular*, 220–21.

[47] For MacIntyre, see *Whose Justice? Which Rationality?*, 354–56.

[48] Asad, "Thinking About Tradition, Religion, and Politics in Egypt Today," 168.

[49] Asad, "Thinking About Tradition, Religion, and Politics in Egypt Today," 168, emphases mine.

about tradition's other Other, encyclopedia.[50] I hold that the proper frame through which to understand the Reformism of ʿAbduh and Riḍā is not as a movement internal to tradition, but rather as a movement away from tradition, if not an abandonment of it altogether. While it is true that thinkers in the Reformist movement continued to comment on topics of shared interest with traditional Islamic jurists, often by showcasing an impressive mastery of language and patterns of thought familiar to the *fiqh* tradition, they did so on different grounds, and with different standards. These standards more closely resemble what MacIntyre has referred to as encyclopedia, as against tradition. Pace Asad, who has doubted that Reformists make reference to universal reason, the hallmark of an encyclopedic approach, the notion of knowledge modeled on the scientific enterprise—progressive, teleological, and comprehensible by all—is central to Riḍā's conceptualization of the law. This stands opposed to tradition, which requires authority for its proper functioning.[51]

MacIntyre has suggested that when a viable tradition—the Ḥanafī *madhhab* in my telling—encounters a foreign challenge, it may go through an "epistemological crisis" in which there is a "dissolution of historically founded certitudes."[52] As a result, new concepts and theories must be invented to maintain the viability of the tradition. This is a tempting way to understand the contribution to Ḥanafism of Bakhīt and his influences, which I show to be importantly innovative. It is an open question whether Bakhīt's encounter with Reformism constitutes an epistemological crisis, in which a tradition fails to make progress "by its own standards of progress,"[53] or whether it is instead, more properly, a social struggle over capital, bound up in the politics of the moment which were in turn always conditioned by the colonial presence. More crucially, however, MacIntyre stipulates that a successful overcoming of an epistemological crisis must satisfy the condition that there be some "fundamental continuity of the new conceptual and theoretical structures with the shared beliefs in terms of which the tradition of enquiry had been defined up to that point."[54] Given the fundamentally radical

[50] For Asad's comments on genealogy, see David Scott and Charles Hirschkind, eds., *Powers of the Secular Modern: Talal Asad and His Interlocutors*, Cultural Memory in the Present (Stanford, CA: Stanford University Press, 2006), 233–34; Asad, "Thinking About Tradition, Religion, and Politics in Egypt Today," 168.

[51] MacIntyre, *Three Rival Versions of Moral Enquiry: Encyclopaedia, Genealogy, and Tradition*, 64–66. I discuss this at length in chapter 2.

[52] MacIntyre, *Whose Justice? Which Rationality?*, 362.

[53] MacIntyre, *Whose Justice? Which Rationality?*, 361.

[54] MacIntyre, *Whose Justice? Which Rationality?*, 362.

changes I consider Bakhīt to be advocating, I am doubtful that this condition is one that he fulfills with respect to Ḥanafism. It is less the case that he invents new concepts or theories, as MacIntyre envisions a proper tradition to do in the face of an epistemological crisis, than it is that he attempts—often in strained ways—to bring old debates and language to speak to new issues, all the while attaching those familiar debates and language to new epistemological standards.

Studying the Ulama

Because it relies heavily on the identification of discursive shifts in the specialized vocabulary of the ulama's intellectual tradition, this book affirms the conclusions of recent writers who have challenged historical characterizations of the ulama as reactionary and obstructionist, and their intellectual output as stagnant and mere hair-splitting.[55] In the context of the intellectual milieu of late nineteenth- and early twentieth-century Egypt, this conventional portrayal had made of the ulama little more than convenient foils against which Reformist efforts may be documented, even celebrated. Consider, for example, the value-laden account provided by Joseph Schacht in his entry on Muḥammad ʿAbduh, the famous Reformist leader, in the *Encyclopaedia of Islam*. According to Schacht,

[55] For a succinct statement of this general outlook, consider the words of Fazlur Rahman, by no means an uncritical historian of Islamic thought: "With the habit of writing commentaries for their own sake and the steady dwindling of original thought, the Muslim world witnessed the rise of a type of scholar who was truly encyclopedic in the scope of his learning but had little new to say on anything. This category of scholar-cum-commentator must be distinguished on the one hand from a very different type of a comprehensive thinker like Aristotle or even a lesser figure like Ibn Sīnā who welded a variety of fields of inquiry into a unified system and coherent world view, and on the other hand from the modern type of specialist whose knowledge has extremely narrow confines. The latter-day Muslim scholar I am talking about 'studied' all the fields of knowledge available, but he did this mainly through commentaries and was himself a commentator and a compiler. This type of scholar is, of course, not confined to the Muslim world but is also representative of many medieval European savants. One important but implicit assumption of this type is that scholarship is not regarded as an active pursuit, a creative 'reaching out' of the mind to the unknown—as is the case today—but rather as the more or less passive acquisition of already established knowledge. This attitude naturally is not conducive to original inquiry and thought, since it assumes that all that can be known about reality is already known except, perhaps, for a few 'gaps' to be filled by interpretation and extension or some angularities to be smoothed out. The view that mind is creative in knowledge is essentially a characteristic of modern theories of knowledge." Fazlur Rahman, *Islam & Modernity: Transformation of an Intellectual Tradition*, Publications of the Center for Middle Eastern Studies, no. 15 (Chicago: University of Chicago Press, 1982), 38–39.

> The *advanced* ideas put forward by Muḥammad ʿAbduh provoked the most vigorous hostility in orthodox and conservative circles, which manifested itself not only in serious refutations but also in attacks and intrigues against him, as we see from a whole literature of lampoons. But his teaching met with remarkable support among all *seriously minded* Muslims.[56]

Schacht's general attitude is representative of the literature of his time.[57] However, in recent years, the underlying theses of this outlook have been subject to significant pushback.

As an example, we may point to the emergent scholarly trend to focus on the role of ulama in modern settings. Works in this genre tend to attend more carefully to the writings, self-perceptions, and political positioning of the ulama themselves, rather than simply assigning them the role of the constitutive Other in a narrative heavily reliant on what Asad calls "a metaphysic of teleological progress."[58] The outstanding work here is that of Muhammad Qasim Zaman, who has demonstrated how ulama in South Asia were called upon to act as "custodians of change" in the face of rapidly changing circumstances in British India and post-Partition India and Pakistan.[59] The ulama, says Zaman,

> have not only continued to respond—admittedly, with varying degrees of enthusiasm and success—to the challenges of changing times; they have

[56] Joseph Schacht, "Muḥammad ʿAbduh," *Encyclopaedia of Islam*, 2nd ed., edited by P. Bearman, Th. Bianquis, C. E. Bosworth, E. van Donzel, and W. P. Heinrichs (Leiden: Brill, 1993), emphases mine. This coincides well with the assessment of Lord Cromer, the British Consul General in Egypt from 1883 to 1907, for whom ʿAbduh was "a very superior type to those of his brethren whom I have so far described . . . Sheikh Mohammed Abdu was a man of broad and enlightened views." Evelyn Baring Cromer, *Modern Egypt*, vol. 2 (New York: The Macmillan Company, 1908), 2:179.

[57] Restricting ourselves to the context under consideration, we may point, for example, to Farhat Ziadeh, who says that "In controversies that pertained to religious or quasi-religious matters, sharīʿah advocates tended to rigidity and reaction." Farhat Ziadeh, *Lawyers, the Rule of Law and Liberalism in Modern Egypt* (Stanford, CA: Hoover Institution on War Revolution and Peace, Stanford University, 1968), 58. Similarly, Ron Shaham, in his article on efforts to reform Egyptian family law, makes a strong distinction between Modernists, indebted to European culture, and conservatives, who presumably remained immune to these influences: "In Egypt, especially during the second half of the nineteenth century, European civilization influenced both modernist *ʿulamāʾ*, such as the Grand Mufti of Egypt at the turn of the century, Muḥammad ʿAbduh and his disciples, and Western-trained lawyers, journalists, parliament members and government ministers. . . . Replacement of traditional perceptions of the family by more liberal ones and modification of relations between the sexes became the focus of public debate between supporters of legal modernism and conservative ʿulamāʾ." Ron Shaham, "Judicial Divorce at the Wife's Initiative: The Sharīʿa Courts of Egypt, 1920–1955," *Islamic Law and Society* 1, no. 2 (January 1, 1994): 218. About Shaham's distinction between Modernist ulama and their conservative counterparts, see n105.

[58] Asad, *Formations of the Secular*, 216.

[59] Zaman, *The Ulama in Contemporary Islam*.

> also been successful in enhancing their influence in a number of contemporary Muslim societies, in broadening their audiences, in making significant contributions to public discourses, and even in setting the terms for such discourses.[60]

This has been an influential account, and a number of monographs devoted to ulama in other locales have since appeared.[61] One of the recurrent themes of this literature is that the ulama were participants in the emergence of modern reforms, often helping usher them in on their own terms. Far from being stagnant or irrelevant, they were required to be intellectually innovative in response to new political pressures, and the accompanying threat of the waning influence and relevance of older discursive commitments.

While this is a real phenomenon, this book shifts the focus toward another aspect of the encounter between ulama and colonial modernity, one which attempts to make sense of, and lay bare, the latter's "phenomenal power of replication and expansion."[62] In what follows, I argue that colonial modernity carried with it not simply political pressures which "traditionalist" thought accommodated, assimilated, and redirected but foundational cultural and intellectual challenges which placed discourse on a new terrain altogether, demanding of all pretenders to intellectual respectability that they work within its parameters to be taken seriously as scholars. As I show, newly emergent conceptions of time, science, and religion were important constitutive elements of this new powerful discourse and, as such, could not help but penetrate traditionalist thought, often in unconscious and imperceptible ways that are unaccounted for by the level of agency Zaman and others have attributed to the ulama. Whereas Zaman, despite acknowledging the deep rupture caused by the impact of Western modernity,[63] continues to position the ulama as bearers of a continuous Islamic tradition, I am more interested in their concessions to that modern rupture.[64]

60 Zaman, *The Ulama in Contemporary Islam*, 2.

61 Examples include Amit Bein, *Ottoman Ulema, Turkish Republic: Agents of Change and Guardians of Tradition* (Stanford, CA: Stanford University Press, 2011); Meir Hatina, ed., *Guardians of Faith in Modern Times: 'Ulama' in the Middle East* (Leiden: Brill, 2009); Gesink, *Islamic Reform and Conservatism*. Zaman himself has followed up with his *Modern Islamic Thought in a Radical Age* (New York: Cambridge University Press, 2012). For a different approach that predates Zaman's contribution, see Malika Zeghal, *Gardiens De l'Islam: Les Oulémas d'Al Azhar Dans l'Egypte Contemporaine* (Paris: Presses de la Fondation nationale des sciences politiques, 1996).

62 Mitchell, *Questions of Modernity*, xii.

63 Zaman, *The Ulama in Contemporary Islam*, 7.

64 Zaman, *The Ulama in Contemporary Islam*, 10.

This book, then, while acknowledging, and indeed foregrounding, the bitter intellectual partisanship of the period, identifies important points of commonality between Reformists and their "traditionalist" opponents, sometimes on substantive reform measures, but more importantly on some of the major epistemological premises underlying the logic of reform.

To demonstrate this, I draw on a wide variety of sources to trace the intellectual orientations—sometimes shifting, sometimes entrenched—of turn-of-the-century Egyptian ulama. The few previous works which have treated this group at all have tended to focus on writings of direct political import and controversy. Inasmuch as I take up these debates, I do so from a different angle. Whereas, for example, the relationship between the ulama and the state has often been foregrounded in the scholarship as a key focus of study, in the pages that follow, the state features as but one element of a background politics against which I examine intellectual debates and conceptual shifts. Indeed, one of the guiding principles of this work is that an examination of theoretical shariʿa works which seem, at first glance, removed from day-to-day intrigues may give us a clearer window into the social and political terrain of the time. That is, precisely because they remain at a safe distance from the direct, politically charged, and territorial disputes of the period, the writings I take up may allow us to better understand the intellectual commitments and struggles of the participants than if we were to limit ourselves to the polemical interventions upon which many previous authors have focused their contributions. As such, this project makes use of discursive legal monographs which treat seemingly unrelated or obscure *fiqh* matters, often found only in Bakhīt's personal library, now preserved as part of the collection at the Azhar Library; as well as fatwas, some still in manuscript form, and other archival material from the Egyptian and British National Archives, in an attempt to shed light on the intellectual milieu of the period.

The Transregional *Madhhab*

As is evident from my earlier discussion, this book takes the *madhhab* (juristic school) as a central unit of historical analysis. This choice in emphasis complicates two dominant approaches to the field: a national, or regional, approach which studies developments in Islamic thought as they unfold in isolated cultural zones, largely independent of their connections to other parts of the Muslim world; and a hermeneutic approach which prefers to focus on abstract textual argumentation without due consideration for the specific socialities and materialities of Islamic interpretation.[65] As it is usually portrayed by experts of Islamic law, the function of the *madhhab* is to act as a constraint, a regime of interpretation which defines both the outer boundaries of an established doctrine and the methods for deducing new legal judgments. Congenial to this view is the idea that in the modern period, when Muslim thinkers began to contemplate and advocate legal reforms, the *madhhab* suffered a downturn in fortunes. In other words, the modernization of Islamic law is linked to the process of breaking the fetters of Islamic legal tradition.

It is true, as I argue most forcefully in chapter 2, that the interpretive identity of the *madhhab* is transformed in the modern period. This book, however, also directs attention to a different feature of the *madhhab*, one which permits us to see it as an enabler, and not only victim, of legal reform in the late nineteenth and early twentieth centuries.[66] This is possible, I argue, when we construe the *madhhab* not only as an interpretive regime but also as a network of individual legal scholars constituted by nodes spread, in at least the Ḥanafī case, widely throughout the Muslim world. In the story I tell in this book, Bakhīt writing in Cairo occupies the bulk of my attention, but importantly I envision him as embedded within a web of influences that allows him to incorporate the work of jurists writing in places as disparate as Kazan, Lucknow, and Baghdad, cities which have been largely marginal to our conceptualization of Ḥanafism but were nonetheless important sites of Ḥanafī intellectual activity. Cairo emerges on this telling, then, not as a center exporting ideas to the rest of the Muslim world, as it usually does for intellectual historians of the period, but as part of a network distributed across the Muslim world, in this case *receiving* ideas that are then put to specific use within its local context. This conceptualization of Bakhīt's role is by no means meant to denigrate him as "merely" a passive recipient or to mitigate

[65] Thus, one of the classic statements of modern Islamic thought is the work of Albert Hourani, whose titular aim is to examine specifically "Arabic" (primarily Egyptian and Syrian) thought in what he calls "the liberal age." Albert Hourani, *Arabic Thought in the Liberal Age, 1798–1939* (London: Oxford University Press, 1970). In contrast, the prominent Orientalist Joseph Schacht's many writings on the modern period, including chapters in his *Introduction to Islamic Law*, tend to evaluate the success of legal argumentation as measured against the premodern Islamic tradition. Schacht, *An Introduction to Islamic Law*.

[66] My use of "legal reform" in this sentence differentiates it from scholarship in Islamic legal history over the past few decades that has successfully shown that Islamic law in its traditional *madhhab*-based form was amenable to the possibility of legal change, and not a fossilized artifact of some bygone era. In contrast, my argument that the *madhhab* supported, in this instance, reform and not just change is a stronger claim.

his intellectual prowess by charging him with a lack of originality. Rather, it helps us better understand the field of intellectual influences of the period, subverting the Cairo-centric focus of much of scholarship and pushing us to think more directly of its scholarly culture as one node in a network of transregional influences.

This approach, in turn, pushes us to interrogate the scholarly preoccupation with originality. Though I argue that Bakhīt is advancing legal argumentation that demarcates a shift in the history of Ḥanafism, his virtuosity lies precisely in his command of the tradition and in his ability to deploy a range of authors in skilled ways to effect this shift. It is not my position, therefore, that he is always making arguments that are completely without precedent, pushing views never before contemplated by Ḥanafī thinkers. Rather, I show how Bakhīt more often draws on strains (stray positions, anomalous opinions, overridden views, familiar concepts and language) within the corpus of Ḥanafī writing which he then exploits, amplifies, repositions, and recontextualizes in ways that sit better with, and reflect, the deeper epistemological commitments to which he has acceded. These shifts are significant enough to think about them in terms of a transformation, but they are not the product of pure thought, but rather the function of a particular historical moment in which discursive possibilities mix with social circumstances to render an intellectual option available and appealing. Against the bias of much writing in Islamic studies interested in pinpointing the first appearance of some position or another, I maintain that such shifts, too, demand historical explanation and attention.

In chapter 1, I show how the structure of the *madhhab* facilitated these shifts. While the salience of the *madhhab*'s better recognized role as an interpretive institution may have waned in the modern period, I argue in chapter 1 that its *social* role as an association of scholars who shared protocols guiding their interaction with one another and with authoritative predecessors continued to exert significant sway. These links—further strengthened in the modern period as a result of the relative ease with which ideas and individuals circulated in an age of print and increased travel—facilitated the reformulation of long-held positions through creative practices of citation that crossed regional social contexts, the calling upon of older authorities, and the excavation of dormant opinions put to new purposes in new contexts. For Bakhīt, this social linkage became an important mode through which to close ranks against the "modernist incursions" of reformist-minded Muslims; though in constructing this front, far from warding off modernism altogether, he instead naturalized some of the most central commitments of the modernist project, and indeed entrenched them by couching them within language and lines of argument that fit better with Ḥanafī tradition.

The Case of Muḥammad Bakhīt al-Muṭīʿī

To make my case, I focus primarily on the writings of Muḥammad Bakhīt al-Muṭīʿī, a leading and respected figure among the ulama of al-Azhar, the venerable center of Islamic learning.[67] An active Azharī scholar and the Mufti of Egypt from 1914 to 1920, Bakhīt was born to a family of laborers in 1271/1854[68] in the village of Mutiʿa in Egypt's Asyut governorate.[69] He studied at a local *kuttāb* (elementary Qurʾan school) in his hometown before traveling to Cairo to study at al-Azhar, obtaining the *shahāda ʿālimiyya* degree from there with first-class honors in 1292/1875. Although he was born to a family of Mālikīs, he became a Ḥanafī, perhaps to take advantage of the bettering fortunes of the Ḥanafī school in this period.[70]

[67] The biographical information that follows is taken, with modifications, from the following sources: Aḥmad Ibn al-Ṣiddīq al-Ghumārī, *al-Baḥr al-ʿAmīq fī Marwiyyāt Ibn al-Ṣiddīq*, vol. 1 (Cairo: Dār al-Kutubī, 2007), 195–209; F. de Jong, "Bakhīt al-Muṭīʿī, Muḥammad," *Encyclopaedia of Islam* (Leiden: Brill, n.d.); Cengiz Kallek, "Bahît, Muhammed," *İslâm Ansiklopedisi* (Üsküdar, İstanbul: Türkiye Diyanet Vakfı, 1991); Khayr al-Dīn al-Ziriklī, *al-Aʿlām*, vol. 6 (Beirut: Dār al ʿIlm li-l-Malāyīn, 2002), 50; Jakob Skovgaard-Petersen, *Defining Islam for the Egyptian State: Muftis and Fatwas of the Dār al-Iftā* (Leiden: Brill, 1997), 133–41; Zakī Fahmī, *Ṣafwat al-ʿAṣr fī Tārīkh wa-Rusūm Mashāhīr Rijāl Miṣr min ʿAhd Sākin al-Jinān Muḥammad ʿAlī Bāshā al-Kabīr*, reprint of the 1926 edition, Ṣafaḥāt min Tārīkh Miṣr 23 (Cairo: Maktabat Madbūlī, 1995), 501–4; Aḥmad ʿAṭiyyat Allāh, *al-Qāmūs al-Islāmī* (Cairo: Maktabat al-Nahḍa al-Miṣriyya, 1963), 284–85; Bassām Jābī, *Muʿjam al-Aʿlām: Muʿjam Tarājim li-Ashhar al-Rijāl wa-l-Nisāʾ min al-ʿArab wa-l-Mustaʿribīn wa-l-Mustashriqīn* (Limassol, Cyprus: al-Jaffān wa-l-Jābī, 1987); and ʿUmar Kaḥḥāla, *Muʿjam al-Muʾallifīn: Tarājim Muṣannifī al-Kutub al-ʿArabiyya*, vol. 9 (Beirut: Dār Iḥyāʾ al-Turāth al-ʿArabī, n.d.), 98–99.

[68] There appears to be some disagreement about the year of Bakhīt's birth. Skovgaard-Petersen, perhaps following Zakī Fahmī, lists it as 1856, but the majority of sources consulted agree on the 1854 date. A different discrepancy is introduced by al-Ghumārī, who relates that some of the scholars associated with the Azhar, perhaps his students and admirers, considered him to be over one hundred years old, placing his birthday around 1254/1838 or thereabouts. This does not seem likely because al-Ghumārī reports from Bakhīt himself statements to the effect that he was born "around 1270[/1853 or 1854]." This roughly coincides with the preponderant position of the secondary literature.

[69] The famous Egyptian statesman and encyclopaedist ʿAlī Pāshā Mubārak notes that the village was known at the time of Bakhīt's birth as Quṭīʿa, though "it is now called Muṭīʿa with a *mīm* at the beginning." Writing in the late 1880s, Mubārak describes it as "a town in Asyūṭ province on the Western banks of the Nile . . . approximately two hours away from [the city of] Asyūṭ . . . The majority of its inhabitants are farmers, though some of them are seamen, and others collect firewood from the *sanṭ* tree which grows in abundance there on the banks of the river." ʿAlī Mubārak, *al-Khiṭaṭ al-Tawfīqiyya al-Jadīda*, vol. 14 (Būlāq: al-Maṭbaʿa al-Kubrā al-Amīriyya, 1305), 103–104.

[70] See al-Ghumārī, who says, "His family was Mālikī, and he was the first among them to become Ḥanafī (*huwa awwalu man taḥannafa minhum*)." Al-Ghumārī, *al-Baḥr al-ʿAmīq fī Marwiyyāt Ibn al-Ṣiddīq*, 1:195. For the increasing privilege accorded to the Ḥanafī school starting in the mid-nineteenth

During his time at al-Azhar, he studied with the prominent scholars of the period, including Muḥammad ʿIllīsh, ʿAbd al-Raḥmān al-Shirbīnī, Ḥasan al-Ṭawīl, ʿAbd al-Raḥmān al-Baḥrāwī, Muḥammad al-ʿAbbasī al-Mahdī, Aḥmad al-Rifāʿī, Muḥammad al-Khuḍarī, Muḥammad al-Basyūnī, and al-Damanhūrī. Outside of his formal studies, he is known to have attended the philosophy lessons of Jamāl al-Dīn al-Afghānī, although he was perhaps best known for his opposition, often quite bitter, of Muḥammad ʿAbduh and Muḥammad Rashīd Riḍā, widely acclaimed as the inheritors of al-Afghānī's Reformist legacy.[71]

Upon the completion of his studies, he continued at al-Azhar as a teacher of *fiqh* (substantive law), *tafsīr* (Qurʾanic exegesis), and *uṣūl al-fiqh* (legal theory) until his appointment to a judgeship in Qalyubiyya province in 1297/1880. From there, he went on to a series of judicial appointments throughout the country, serving as a qadi in Minya, Port Saʿid, Suez, Fayyum, and Asyut, before serving in in the Ministry of Justice as shariʿa inspector, and then judge and head of Alexandria's shariʿa council (*al-majlis al-sharʿī*) for a number of years. After the reorganization of the shariʿa court system in 1314/1897, Bakhīt was relocated to Cairo and appointed to senior positions in the new system, most prominently the head of the High Shariʿa Court of Egypt.[72] During this period, he was tapped to serve as the Chief Justice of Cairo on an interim basis for six months during the illness of the incumbent, ʿAbd Allāh Jamāl al-Dīn. In 1907, he became the head of the Alexandria Shariʿa Court for five years, during which time he reportedly commuted regularly to Cairo by train to deliver lessons at the Azhar. From there, he moved to a muftiship in the Ministry of Justice, where he served until he was appointed to the prestigious office of the Mufti of Egypt in 1914.[73] He continued in this

century, see Rudolph Peters, "Muḥammad al-ʿAbbāsī al-Mahdī (d. 1897), Grand Muftī of Egypt, and His *al-Fatāwā al-Mahdiyya*," *Islamic Law and Society* 1, no. 1 (January 1, 1994): 66–82. Peters writes, "Following the Ottoman conquest of Egypt, the Ḥanafī mufti assigned to the Grand Shariʿa Court in Cairo . . . , with the title *muftī al-sāda al-ḥanafiyya*, came to be regarded as the highest ranking mufti in the country. To emphasize his position with regard to the other chief muftis, he was referred to, from the middle of the nineteenth century, as *muftī al-diyār al-miṣriyya* [the Mufti of the Egyptian lands] and, sometimes, simply as *bāshmuftī* [the head Mufti]," 75. This, of course, was the position Bakhīt himself would later take up. See also Kenneth M. Cuno, "Reorganization of the Sharia Courts of Egypt: How Legal Modernization Set Back Women's Rights in the Nineteenth Century," in *Law and Legality in the Ottoman Empire and Republic of Turkey*, ed. Kent F. Schull, M. Safa Saraçoğlu, and Robert Zens (Bloomington: Indiana University Press, 2016), 95–96, 100; Shaham, *Family and the Courts in Modern Egypt* (Leiden: Brill, 1997), 12–13; and *Description de l'Egypte*, vol. 18, 233.

71 For details on this intellectual competition and rivalry, see CO.P62–CO.P67 and chapter 1.

72 Ziadeh, *Lawyers, the Rule of Law and Liberalism in Modern Egypt*, 56.

73 On this office, see Skovgaard-Petersen, *Defining Islam for the Egyptian State*.

post until 1920, becoming known as an expert in *iftā'* (issuing fatwas) and for his mastery of the range of opinions among the four Sunni *madhhab*s (juristic schools). During his tenure, the fatwa that attracted the most attention was his condemnation of Bolshevism, which was eagerly taken up by the British—who were worried about the growing Bolshevik influence in their Muslim colonies—for distribution in other Muslim countries.[74] This was to become a problem for Bakhīt when he later joined the nationalist cause. Because his contribution was seen as being allied too closely with—and, all too often, simply a mouthpiece for—the British, his allegiance to the nationalist movement was cast into doubt in certain quarters.[75]

Bakhīt continued to issue fatwas even after his forced retirement from the official position of State Mufti. Although the termination of his term is attributed to the introduction of a mandatory retirement age, which he had already exceeded, his student Aḥmad b. Ṣiddīq al-Ghumārī speculates that this legislation was political payback from the Prime Minister Nasīm Pāshā[76] for a dispute stemming from Bakhīt's refusal to sanction government plans to appropriate land that had been endowed as a mosque.[77]

[74] The fatwa exists in the Dār al-Iftā' Archives, DIM register 17/#152. The British enthusiasm for this fatwa, as well as a translation, and clippings of Egyptian critiques can be gleaned from the folder in the British National Archives, FO 141/779/1. See also the discussion in Tareq Y. Ismael, *The Communist Movement in Egypt, 1920–1988*, 1st ed. (Syracuse, NY: Syracuse University Press, 1990).

[75] See CO.P63–CO.P66. At one point in his writings, Riḍā mocks Bakhīt's later attempts to make amends and restore his name by saying that the fatwa was not intended to repudiate Bolshevism, but rather to correct it by bringing it within the orbit of the shari'a. Muḥammad Rashīd Riḍā, *Maqālāt al-Shaykh Rashīd Riḍā al-Siyāsiyya*, ed. Yūsuf Ībish and Yūsuf Q. Khūrī, vol. 4 (Beirut: Dār Ibn 'Arabī, 1994), 1272.

[76] This supposition is strengthened by the two files of internal memos I found in the Egyptian National Archives revealing the keen interest of the Prime Minister's Cabinet in the Mufti's retirement and replacement. See the Egyptian National Archives, DWQ *Majlis al-Nuẓẓār wa-l-Wuzarā'* 0075-040582; 0075-040583. In contrast, the only document I found in the archives relating to his appointment was one formal memo from the Ministry of Endowments informing the Cabinet of their nomination of Bakhīt to the Muftiship and requesting official approval. DWQ *Majlis al-Nuẓẓār wa-l-Wuzarā'* 0075-046808-0001.

[77] Al-Ghumārī, *al-Baḥr al-'Amīq fī Marwiyyāt Ibn al-Ṣiddīq*, 1:199–200. The jealous protection of endowments (*awqāf*) was a major preoccupation of the ulama in the wake of Muḥammad 'Alī's confiscation of endowments (*awqāf*) and tax farms (*iltizām*s), which had been for years the major sources of "shaykhly wealth." See Daniel Neil Crecelius, "The Ulama and the State in Modern Egypt" (PhD diss., Princeton University, 1967), 85–146. That Bakhīt was no exception to this trend can be seen not only through this one incident but also his attempt while State Mufti to influence the decision to appoint Ibrāhīm Fatḥī Pasha as the Minister of Endowments in 1915. This memo can be found in the Egyptian National Archives, DWQ *Majlis al-Wuzarā'* 0075-046518-0001. Indeed, the status of endowments continued to be a point of central concern for Bakhīt. In 1345/1927 and 1346/1928, he delivered a pair of lectures responding to an earlier speech by the former Minister of Endowments 'Alī 'Alūba Pāshā to lawyers at the Cairo Court of Appeal. In his remarks, 'Alūba Pāshā had claimed that family endowments (*awqāf ahliyya*) were not specifically religious, but rather a civil matter, a point which Bakhīt felt obliged to rebut in short order. See 'Alī 'Alūba Pāshā, *Muḥāḍara fī al-Waqf* (Cairo: Maṭba'a al-Qāhira, n.d.); Muḥammad Bakhīt al-Muṭī'ī, *Muḥāḍara fī Niẓām al-Waqf* (Cairo: al-Maṭba'a al-Salafiyya, 1345H); and Muḥammad Bakhīt al-Muṭī'ī, *Muḥāḍara fī*

The prestige accorded to Bakhīt during his tenure as Mufti paved the way for his appointment to the chairmanship of a number of committees within the administration of the Azhar.[78] Although he continued to be held in high regard by the Azharī establishment after his retirement—he was in fact granted a salary by the *Hay'at Kibār al-'Ulamā'* (Council of Senior Ulama) to cover the losses he would incur as a result[79]—the influence he wielded in these circles seems to have diminished slightly. He continued to harbor aspirations to be appointed the Rector of al-Azhar (*Shaykh al-Azhar*) but these, much to his chagrin, did not materialize.[80]

As a result of his diminishing influence in more traditional forums, Bakhīt searched out alternate audiences in a Cairo that was becoming increasingly

Niẓām al-Waqf (Cairo: al-Maṭba'a al-Salafiyya, 1346H). Bakhīt's lecture drew on a treatise he had written on the status of family endowments earlier, Muḥammad Bakhīt al-Muṭī'ī, *al-Murhafāt al-Yamāniyya fī 'Unq man Qāla bi-Buṭlān al-Waqf 'alā al-Dhurriyya* (Cairo: al-Maṭba'a al-Salafiyya, 1344H). Family endowments were a major concern for colonial powers throughout the Muslim world because they were seen as a hindrance to economic progress. To discredit them, religious arguments were often advanced that endowments restricted to familial beneficiaries were not technically legal. The ulama, however, closed ranks on this issue and produced a number of responses. The same year as Bakhīt's lecture, a joint publication was issued by a number of ulama, *Ḥukm al-Sharī'a al-Islāmiyya fī al-Waqf al-Khayrī wa-l-Ahlī: Bayān min al-'Ulamā'* (Cairo: al-Maṭba'a al-Salafiyya wa-Maktabatuhā, 1927). Two years later, another response from Muḥammad b. Ḥasanayn Makhlūf was published, Muḥammad b. Ḥasanayn b. Muḥammad Makhlūf, *Manhaj al-Yaqīn fī Bayān anna al-Waqf al-Ahlī min al-Dīn* (Cairo: Maṭba'a Muṣṭafā al-Ḥalabī, 1347H). For a synopsis of the debate which concerns itself primarily with the arguments of critics of family endowments, see Ziadeh, *Lawyers, the Rule of Law and Liberalism in Modern Egypt*, 127–35. For a more extensive discussion, see Nada Moumtaz, "'Is the Family Waqf a Religious Institution?' Charity, Religion, and Economy in French Mandate Lebanon," *Islamic Law and Society* 25, no. 1–2 (April 3, 2018): 37–77.

78 Rather than list all the individual documents in the Egyptian National Archives that contain the minutes of these committee meetings, it might suffice to point to DWQ *Majlis al-Azhar al-A'lā* 0069-006873-0008, a resolution taken by the Azhar administration shortly after Bakhīt's retirement to gather together in one volume all the proceedings of meetings which had been conducted under Bakhīt's chairmanship.

79 DWQ *Majlis al-Azhar al-A'lā*, 0069-006869-0005. "A memo regarding the resolution of the Council of Senior Ulama to grant to His Eminence Muḥammad Bakhīt al-Muṭī'ī, former Grand Mufti of Egypt, a member's salary due to his retirement." On the *Hay'at Kibār al-'Ulamā'*, see Skovgaard-Petersen, *Defining Islam for the Egyptian State*, 146–50.

80 Al-Ghumārī says, "He remained hopeful [of being appointed to] the position of the *Shaykh al-Azhar*—and there was no one in his era who was better suited for it than him—but the times conspired against him in that [matter]. One of the oddities of the world is that his own students, like al-Ẓawāhirī and al-Marāghī, ascended to the position while he was still alive." Al-Ghumārī, *al-Baḥr al-'Amīq fī Marwiyyāt Ibn al-Ṣiddīq*, 1:200. See also the issue of *al-Siyāsa al-Usbū'iyya* on April 10, 1926, which recounts his attempt to position himself as a potential successor to the just-deceased Shaykh al-Azhar Salīm al-Bishrī, only to come away empty-handed and disappointed. "Al-Shaykh Muḥammad Bakhīt," *al-Siyāsa al-Usbū'iyya*, April 10, 1926. Earlier attempts are found in the head of the Bakriyya Sufi order Tawfīq al-Bakrī's entreaty to Khedive 'Abbās Ḥilmī II to appoint Bakhīt to the position instead of Muḥammad 'Abduh. HIL 1/21 ('Abduh was, of course, never appointed to the position either). Bakrī was involved in numerous intrigues against 'Abduh (see Aḥmad Shafīq, *Mudhakkirātī*, 2:35ff).

diverse, intellectually and politically.[81] This brought him squarely within the public debates, controversies, and intrigues of the day.

Indeed, the germs of this later active political participation may have been planted during his tenure as Mufti itself. Jacques Berque notes that Bakhīt played a part in the Egyptian revolution of 1919, in particular chairing the meeting at the Azhar which resolved to commence a national strike the following day.[82] This stance made him a natural choice to address a commemoration of the third anniversary of Saʿd Zaghlūl's demand for independence and to be selected to help draft a new constitution.[83]

Bakhīt also attended in 1923 the founding meeting of the Liberal Constitutionalist Party, which "consist[ed] mainly of rich landowners and a couple of well-known intellectuals [and] was to be the major competitor to the Wafd party throughout the next decade"[84]; and joined al-Rābiṭa al-Sharqiyya, "the focal point of the Islamic-Arab cultural orientation . . . [which held] that the culture of the Egyptians was Eastern-Islamic in origin, rather than a local Egyptian or a Western one, and, moreover, that this culture was an integral part of the 'Eastern civilization' of all the Eastern peoples."[85] However, his participation in both of these organizations was short-lived as a result of the acrimonious controversy that followed the publication of ʿAlī ʿAbd al-Rāziq's *al-Islam wa-Uṣūl al-Hukm* (*Islam and the Principles of Governance*).[86] This book, which argued for the essentially secular nature of

[81] An indication of his searching out alternatives is his chairmanship of a commemoration of the life of Muḥammad ʿAbduh, with whom he had disagreed sharply, shortly after his retirement. Muḥammad ʿAbduh, *al-Iḥtifāl bi-Iḥyāʾ Dhikrā al-Ustādh al-Imām al-Shaykh Muḥammad ʿAbduh bi-Dār al-Jāmiʿa al-Miṣriyya fī 11 Yūlyū 1922* (Miṣr: Maṭbaʿat al-Manār, 1340H). Rashīd Riḍā also records that Bakhīt spoke to him of ʿAbduh's piety and said that he regularly asked him to lead the congregational prayer due to his upright character. *Tārīkh al-Ustādh al-Imām*, 1:1043. These should be seen as political moves. Bakhīt continued to have a poor opinion of ʿAbduh, though he could not be open about this in public due to ʿAbduh's popularity among the Egyptian public and status among foreigners. Al-Ghumārī, *al-Baḥr al-ʿAmīq fī Marwiyyāt Ibn al-Ṣiddīq*, 1:209–10. On Bakhīt's opportunistic politics and my characterization of him as a *mudhabdhab*, see chapter 3.

[82] Jacques Berque, *Egypt: Imperialism & Revolution* (London: Faber, 1972), 309.

[83] Skovgaard-Petersen, *Defining Islam for the Egyptian State*, 135.

[84] Skovgaard-Petersen, *Defining Islam for the Egyptian State*, 135. For more on the Liberal Constitutionalists, see Marius Deeb, *Party Politics in Egypt: The Wafd & Its Rivals, 1919–1939*, St. Antony's Middle East Monographs, no. 9 (London: Ithaca Press for the Middle East Centre, St Antony's College, Oxford, 1979), and Afaf Lutfi Sayyid-Marsot, *Egypt's Liberal Experiment, 1922–1936* (Berkeley: University of California Press, 1977).

[85] Israel Gershoni, "The Evolution of National Culture in Modern Egypt: Intellectual Formation and Social Diffusion, 1892–1945," *Poetics Today* 13, no. 2 (July 1, 1992): 345. For more on the *Rābiṭa*, see I. Gershoni and James P. Jankowski, *Egypt, Islam, and the Arabs: The Search for Egyptian Nationhood, 1900–1930*, Studies in Middle Eastern History (New York: Oxford University Press, 1986), 255–69; and James Jankowski, "The Eastern Idea and the Eastern Union in Interwar Egypt," *The International Journal of African Historical Studies* 14, no. 4 (January 1, 1981): 643–66.

[86] ʿAlī ʿAbd al-Rāziq, *al-Islām wa-Uṣūl al-Ḥukm: Baḥth fī al-Khilāfa wa-l-Ḥukūma fī al-Islām*, 2nd ed. (Cairo: Maṭbaʿat Miṣr, 1925). This work has been translated into French as ʿAlī ʿAbd

governance and the purely spiritual role of the Prophet, caused a serious controversy among the Azharī ulama in the wake of the abolition of the Ottoman Caliphate. Unwilling to brook these ideas from one of their own, the Council of Senior Ulama eventually decided to strip ʿAbd al-Rāziq of his diploma and his judicial appointment.[87] In view of the influence exerted by ʿAbd al-Rāziq on both of these organizations, Bakhīt resigned from each, and proceeded to launch a scathing attack in a publication of his own, *Ḥaqīqat al-Islām wa-Uṣūl al-Ḥukm* (a play on words which can be read as either *The Truth of Islam and the Principles of Governance*, or *The Truth about [the Book]* Al-Islām wa-Uṣūl al-Ḥukm).[88] This response to ʿAbd al-Rāziq, who was widely perceived as critiquing the now defunct Caliphate at a time when its demise was being lamented by the ulama, may have been one of the motivations behind Bakhīt's participation in the Cairo Caliphate Conference. Indeed, at one point in the conference, Bakhīt insists on the traditional definition of the Caliphate and is keen to point out that "it is impossible to say that the Caliphate is merely spiritual, as the heretics (*mulḥidūn*) do, for they believe in parts of the Book [the Qurʾan] but reject other parts."[89] When the minutes were read back in the next meeting, some scholars objected to this harsh language, but Bakhīt adamantly refused to temper it.[90]

This was not the only current event on which Bakhīt offered his opinion. Indeed, he acted as something of a public intellectual his whole

al-Rāziq, *L'Islam et Les Fondements Du Pouvoir*, trans. Abdou Filali-Ansary (Paris: Éditions La Découverte, 1994).

[87] The decision was published as *Ḥukm Hayʾat Kibār al-ʿUlamāʾ ʿalā Kitāb al-Islām wa-Uṣūl al-Ḥukm* (al-Maṭbaʿa al-Salafiyya, 1344H). For details of ʿAbd al-Rāziq's arguments and the subsequent debate, see Souad T. Ali, *A Religion, Not a State: Ali ʿAbd Al-Raziq's Islamic Justification of Political Secularism* (Salt Lake City: University of Utah Press, 2009); Hamid Enayat, *Modern Islamic Political Thought: The Response of the Shīʿī and Sunnī Muslims to the Twentieth Century*, new ed. (London: I.B. Tauris, 2005), 62–68.; Charles C. Adams, *Islam and Modernism in Egypt: A Study of the Modern Reform Movement Inaugurated by Muḥammad ʿAbduh* (London: Oxford University Press, 1933), 259–69; Hourani, *Arabic Thought in the Liberal Age, 1798–1939*, 183–92.

[88] Muḥammad Bakhīt al-Muṭīʿī, *Ḥaqīqat al-Islām wa-Uṣūl al-Ḥukm* (Cairo: al-Maṭbaʿa al-Salafiyya, 1925). In response, the weekly *al-Siyāsa al-Usbūʿiyya*, which had carried ʿAbd al-Rāziq's views on governance, struck back with a front-page "biography" of Bakhīt which emphasized his opportunism (describing him as "covetous for positions") and his intellectual deficiencies and scholarly mistakes. ("Even the Ministry of Justice issued a publication once warning shariʿa court judges from following the fatwas of muftis. The Ministry was referring that day to none other than the disturbing fatwas that Shaykh Bakhīt issues.") "Al-Shaykh Muḥammad Bakhīt," *al-Siyāsa al-Usbūʿiyya* (Cairo, April 10, 1926). Other critiques by leading Azharī scholars include Muḥammad al-Khiḍr Ḥusayn, *Naqḍ Kitāb al-Islām wa-Uṣūl al-Ḥukm* (Cairo: al-Maṭbaʿa al-Salafiyya wa-Maktabatuhā, 1344); and Yūsuf al-Dijwī, *Radd Ḥaḍrat Ṣāḥib al-Faḍīla al-Ustādh al-Kabīr al-Shaykh Yūsuf al-Dijwī ʿalā Kitāb al-Shaykh ʿAlī ʿAbd al-Rāziq al-Islām wa-Uṣūl al-Ḥukm* (Miṣr: Maṭbaʿat al-Samāḥ, n.d.).

[89] Riḍā, *Maqālāt al-Shaykh Rashīd Riḍā al-Siyāsiyya*, 4:1891.

[90] Riḍā, *Maqālāt al-Shaykh Rashīd Riḍā al-Siyāsiyya*, 4:1894–95.

life, publishing a number of small treatises offering his takes on newly emergent technologies (photography, the phonograph, the telegraph) as well as political controversies, for example, waqf endowments, divorce laws, and insurance. This, however, did not distract him from a prolific career as a commentator in the more traditional genres of Islamic scholarship, especially for pedagogical purposes. His two most famous and impressive works are in jurisprudence (*uṣūl al-fiqh*): *Sullam al-Wuṣūl*, a supercommentary on al-Isnawī's *Nihāyat al-Sūl*; and *al-Badr al-Sāṭiʿ*, his gloss on al-Zarkashī's commentary of Tāj al-Dīn al-Subkī's *Jamʿ al-Jawāmiʿ*, both important teaching texts. He also contributed a commentary on the famous theology manual of al-Dardīr, *al-Kharīda al-Bahiyya*.

Bakhīt died on Rajab 21, 1354/October 19, 1935. Ten years later, his body was moved from its burial place to a mosque which bears his name in the Cairene suburb where he had lived, Hilmiyyat al-Zaytun.[91]

***

Something might be said at this point about why Bakhīt in particular is an appropriate figure to investigate for our purposes. There are two specific features of his life that make him a suitable case study. The first is his renown and stellar credentials as a leading member of the ulama class. Reference has already been made to his inclusion in the Council of Senior Ulama. Even among them, however, he stands out as an imposing figure, a teacher and scholar around whom an entourage of admirers and students developed, and who gained an international reputation. For example, the famous Ottoman scholar Muḥammad Zāhid al-Kawtharī remembers him as "the *shaykh* of the jurists of his era," and "the authority to which the qadis and ulama of the world turned... due to the wide scope of his knowledge of the *madhāhib* (juristic schools) and his extensive experience in teaching, judgeship and giving fatwas."[92]

Shortly after his death, the Azhar journal ran an obituary which made a point of mentioning that

[91] A plaque above the doorway to Bakhīt's grave indicates that his body was moved there at a later date. There is a certain irony to this turn of events in view of the numerous fatwas Bakhīt issued prohibiting exhuming graves (*nabsh al-qubur*) and moving corpses (*naql al-mawtā*), except in cases of necessity. Bakhīt's unpublished fatwas on this in the Dār al-Iftāʾ archives can be found under the following numbers: DIM register 11/#62, register 14/#43, register 14/#66, register 16/#249.

[92] Muḥammad Zāhid al-Kawtharī, *Maqālāt al-Kawtharī* (Cairo: al-Maktaba al-Azhariyya li-l-Turāth, 2009), 199.

> his fame transcended Egypt and [he was renowned in] the entire Islamic world. . . . He was known, may God have mercy on him, for his leadership in the field of jurisprudence. Leading ulama would make recourse to him with regards to issues that stumped them, and would find with him a solution for all their problems, as if he had encountered them before.[93]

According to al-Ghumārī, his dedication to learning meant he spent a good deal of time and money collecting books and building a library, in marked contrast to the practice of his contemporaries at the Azhar.[94]

The second feature of Bakhīt's biography that is of relevance to us here is stated most succinctly by the biographer Khayr al-Dīn al-Ziriklī, who labels Bakhīt "one of the staunchest opponents" (*min ashadd al-muʿāriḍīn*) of the Reform movement established by Muḥammad ʿAbduh.[95] As early as 1900, Bakhīt was responding to major Reformist figures. That year, he wrote an introduction to the new printed edition of the eighth/fourteenth-century Shafiʿite Taqī al-Dīn al-Subkī's treatise on the permissibility of visiting the grave of the Prophet.[96] Al-Subkī's work was a response to his contemporary Ibn Taymiyya's (d. 728/1328) position on the matter. Rituals associated with grave visiting had once again become a point of contention in Bakhīt's time, and so it was thought worthwhile to publish al-Subkī's authoritative work. Before moving on to the issue at hand, though, Bakhīt took the opportunity to attack his own contemporary opponents. In particular, he takes to task Qāsim Amīn for his permissive positions on the role of the modern woman, accusing him of bias, unscholarly conclusions, and transgressing the bounds of shariʿa.[97]

A mere six years later, Bakhīt and Riḍā engaged in a highly polemical and contentious debate, which did less to shed light on the substance of the disagreement than it did to make clear the animosity between the two parties.[98] These hostilities seem not to have abated with the passage of time. As late as 1921, Riḍā devoted an article to disparaging Bakhīt's political involvement,

[93] "Ilā Raḥmat Allāh," *Majallat Al-Azhar* 6, no. 8 (1354H): 583.

[94] Al-Ghumārī, *al-Baḥr al-ʿAmīq fī Marwiyyāt Ibn al-Ṣiddīq*, 1:202. Al-Ghumārī points out that the material he took an interest in included foreign works in translation, as well as the scholarly journals of the time. Al-Ghumārī, *al-Baḥr al-ʿAmīq fī Marwiyyāt Ibn al-Ṣiddīq*, 1:200.

[95] Al-Ziriklī, *al-Aʿlām*, 6:50.

[96] Al-Subkī's work is Taqī al-Dīn al-Subkī, *Shifāʾ al-Saqām fī Ziyārat Khayr al-Anām* (Būlāq: al-Maṭbaʿa al-Kubrā al-Amīriyya, 1318H). Bakhīt's introduction is Muḥammad Bakhīt al-Muṭīʿī, *Taṭhīr al-Fuʾād min Danas al-Iʿtiqād* (Būlāq: al-Maṭbaʿa al-Kubrā al-Amīriyya, 1318H).

[97] Al-Muṭīʿī, *Taṭhīr al-Fuʾād min Danas al-Iʿtiqād*, 5–6.

[98] For details, see the next chapter.

labeling it immature and opportunistic. In the spirit of nationalist fervor in which Riḍā was writing, calling Bakhīt "one of the country's strongest supporters of occupation when the British Protectorate was announced" was a particularly damning indictment. As Grand Mufti, Riḍā argued, Bakhīt had:

> served the occupying powers as they wished. It was his position, along with that of the Shaykh al-Azhar, to drop the name of the Ottoman Sultan from the Friday sermon, though the whole country acknowledged the Caliphate. Never has Britain found men of religion [as acquiescent as] these in its Indian domains.[99]

This, according to Riḍā, was before Bakhīt moved on to curry favor with the Egyptian nationalist movement.[100]

This sort of opportunism, Riḍā argued, was unseemly and irresponsible for men who "demand that they be followed (*yajibu taqlīduhum*) in politics, just as they demand to be followed in religion."[101] If they "desire to immerse themselves in the politics of their nation and the public benefit," Riḍā went on to argue, "they must prepare for this by learning about the history of contemporary peoples and nations, and their revolutions, both religious and civil; and about what the Europeans call separation between religion and politics, and the elimination of the power of popes."[102]

Nor did Bakhīt ever seem to make his peace with the Reformists. Although he appeared with Riḍā at certain events, such as the Cairo Caliphate Conference, and even chaired a commemoration of the anniversary of ʿAbduh's death,[103] he confided to al-Ghumārī late in life that "No one has corrupted the beliefs of the Muslims and introduced misguidance to the Azhar like [ʿAbduh] has. Before him, the Azhar was pure of deviance, heresy and the like."[104]

The personage of Bakhīt, then, is a particularly fitting example for this study for, as both an avowed rival of the Reformists and an elite member of the ulama, any indication of fundamental Reformist commitments in his

[99] Riḍā, *Maqālāt al-Shaykh Rashīd Riḍā al-Siyāsiyya*, 4:1268.
[100] See CO.P54–CO.P55.
[101] Riḍā, *Maqālāt al-Shaykh Rashīd Riḍā al-Siyāsiyya*, 4:1269.
[102] Riḍā, *Maqālāt al-Shaykh Rashīd Riḍā al-Siyāsiyya*, 4:1275–76.
[103] ʿAbduh, *al-Iḥtifāl bi-Iḥyāʾ Dhikrā al-Ustādh al-Imām al-Shaykh Muḥammad ʿAbduh bi-Dār al-Jāmiʿa al-Miṣriyya fī 11 Yūlyū 1922*.
[104] Al-Ghumārī, *al-Baḥr al-ʿAmīq fī Marwiyyāt Ibn al-Ṣiddīq*, 1:209.

work says volumes about the extent to which ideas thitherto foreign to the ulama's long-standing discursive tradition found their way in.

***

A point of terminological clarification may be warranted here. It is quite possible to object that many of the Modernist-Reformists themselves could very well be considered ulama, due to their training at the Azhar, and their procurement of positions within the religious establishment. Muḥammad ʿAbduh immediately comes to mind as such a figure.[105] Similarly, Rashīd Riḍā, though not trained at the Azhar, was remarkably erudite and received an education at the school of the Azharite Ḥusayn al-Jisr. I do not dispute the credentials or accomplishments of these figures. However, the literature tends to remember them as Modernists or Reformists, in large part because much of their innovation—and secondary scholarship's interest in them—lay precisely in the sustained critique they leveled against the ulama at the Azhar and their traditions. Thus, I use the shorthand "ulama" to refer to those who have been the subject of this critique, and were widely considered to be conservative or traditional. Because I will be disputing the latter characterizations, I have chosen not to use these adjectives to describe the main protagonists except when it is clear that they represent the assessments of others.

The Plan of This Book

This book is centered on close and focused readings of the works of Bakhīt, especially the *Irshād Ahl al-Milla ilā Ithbāt al-Ahilla*. I treat three separate aspects of Bakhīt's legal thought (chapters 2, 4, and 5), each of which reveal his strong reliance on epistemological commitments usually understood to be fundamental premises underlying central Modernist ideals.

[105] So, for example, Ron Shaham identifies him and his disciples as "modernist ʿulama," and groups them together with "Western-trained lawyers, journalists, parliament members and government ministers" for their European influence and support for "legal modernism." These are in contradistinction to the "conservative ʿulama." Shaham, "Judicial Divorce at the Wife's Initiative," 217–18. As Shaham points out, some Azharī scholars of a later generation have also been remembered as Modernists. Notably, these are often the same personalities on whom we have monographs in European languages. See, for example, Francine Costet-Tardieu, *Un Réformiste à l'Université al-Azhar: Oeuvre et Pensée de Mustafâ al-Marâghî, 1881–1945* (Paris: Centre d'études et de documentation économiques juridiques et sociales, 2005); and Kate Zebiri, *Maḥmūd Shaltūt and Islamic Modernism* (Oxford: Oxford University Press, 1993).

Paying careful attention to the social, political, and cultural shifts that laid the groundwork for the penetration of these new ways of thinking, I show in each case how Bakhīt's thought constituted a departure from the prevailing Ḥanafī juristic tradition to which he belonged and point instead to his operating within an intellectual world which, though it continued to draw on the legacy of the *madhhab*, had already assumed and naturalized Modernist epistemological commitments. Indeed, in some cases, Bakhīt can be said to be further entrenching these very commitments through his use of language and lines of argumentation familiar to the Ḥanafī tradition.

Chapter 1 sketches out the historical and transregional context of the project, examining two acrimonious episodes local to twentieth-century Egypt to lay bare the ever-present context of Muslim history and the larger Muslim world. Paying close attention to the social and political developments that dominated Egyptian intellectual life at the turn of the century, I examine two exchanges between Bakhīt and Riḍā to lay out the terrain of partisanship and territorialism that so heavily structured Cairo's intellectual scene in the early twentieth century. As a result of what Jakob Skovgaard-Petersen has termed the "Salafi Press," the previous monopoly on Islamic interpretation held by the Azharī ulama began to loosen, and the latter began to sense their authority being threatened. These resulted in bitter polemics, but also, I argue, a substantial reconfiguration of the intellectual landscape simply by virtue of the indefatigable onslaught of the Modernists, Rashīd Riḍā in particular. This state of affairs motivated the ulama to draw on resources that exceeded their specific context both historically and geographically, resulting in a certain rearrangement of authority that relied on older structures of the *madhhab* to create new networks of belonging and allegiance.

Chapter 2 traces changes in Ḥanafī conceptions of history by examining the manner in which authority is conceptualized within the school by both colonial-era writers and their predecessors. It locates self-representations of the school's history embedded within formal hierarchies of the relative standing (and authoritativeness) of Ḥanafī jurists. By examining Bakhīt's rankings of Ḥanafī jurists, I reveal his refashioning of *ijtihād* within the school and its implications for a new conception of legal authority mirrored in Reformism's insistence on an increasingly democratized and direct access to the primary texts of the Qur'an and sunna, unmediated by the ulama and the historical corpus of the *fiqh* tradition. I argue that this reworking of authority structures, in turn, relies on a new temporality, moving from one which sees ulama-subjects as inheritors of a tradition expressed through a continuous and organic history to one which displays a "historical consciousness," privileging the Prophetic generation so as to be able to downgrade the "accretions" of the medieval interlude.

In chapter 3, I consider what precisely it means to say that Bakhīt is a colonial figure. Given that this book places his ideas within the context of a modernity conditioned by the specter of colonialism, this chapter uncovers how colonialism figures in his writings. Examining his contributions to a new genre of literature that attempts to harmonize Islam and modern science, I argue that Bakhīt fits squarely within a colonial discourse premised on what Homi Bhabha has called mimicry. For Bhabha, mimicry does not mean a complete capitulation, but rather draws on an ambivalence and partiality characteristic of the native subject whose difference from the European always looms over the encounter. Bakhīt's writings, then, constitute a partial discourse in which he at once reaffirms the modern scientism of the colonizing power and asserts an independent Arab-Islamic civilization with an illustrious past that is available for reactivation.

In chapter 4, taking as a case study Bakhīt's discussion of the validity of relying on astronomical calculations to determine the month of Ramadan, I discuss Bakhīt's openness to the scientific enterprise from a different angle. In particular, I examine his shift from a procedural approach to this question that stressed the importance of methods and norms that were internal to the *fiqh* tradition to an *epistemological* approach that stressed the importance of knowledge as determined by science. The introduction of certain technologies to Egypt was accompanied by a new salience being given to science and particular notions of scientific truth. Here we examine the impact of the telescope in facilitating a view of knowledge, including *fiqhī* knowledge, as scientistic and representationalist, itself dependent upon a notion of reality best understood by what Timothy Mitchell has called the colonial conception of the "world-as-picture"—namely, the idea that the world is composed of the two distinct realms of image and reality, the second of which can be achieved through specifically scientific precision.

Finally, in chapter 5, I examine the impact of processes of secularization on Bakhīt's thought. Despite being strongly opposed to the encroaching influence of secularist arguments such as that of ʿAlī ʿAbd al-Rāziq, this chapter seeks to outline how Bakhīt comes to reformulate the category of religion in a peculiarly modern way. This question emerges from the problematic with which I opened this introduction: namely, the *fiqhī* validity of "religious reports" transmitted by new telegraphic technology. Whereas the prevailing

Ḥanafī tradition was interested in regulating, constraining, and guiding human sociality through the maintenance of procedural parameters within which knowledge-reports became "actionable" because they were circulated through the proper judicial authorities, Bakhīt is interested in emphasizing "religious matters" as intellectual entities, independent of the materiality of judicial institutions and new technologies. This stands in contrast to the integrated worldview which informed premodern shariʿa in which sociality and proceduralism were constitutive features of what it meant to do law.

1
Partisanship, Territorialism, and Transregional Networks of Belonging

When Muḥammad ʿAbduh died in 1905, his funeral was an official affair. ʿAbduh had been in Alexandria at the time of his death, having traveled there in the hope that a change in climate would help him recover from a stomach and liver illness, and regain enough strength to travel to Europe in search of medical attention. Upon hearing the news of his passing, the Egyptian Cabinet arranged a private train to transport his body to Cairo, where he was prayed upon in the Azhar mosque and buried in an area reserved for Azharites in the Qarāfa, the sprawling graveyard between the old city of Fustat and the Muqattam Hills.[1] In the first issue of *al-Manār* published after ʿAbduh's death, Rashīd Riḍā commented that the number of mourners who turned out to pay their respects in both cities was unprecedented, leaving those who joined the crowd with the impression that "there remained no inhabitant of either Alexandria or Cairo who did not attend and bid this imam a final farewell."[2]

Among the many mourners was Muḥammad Shākir, then the Shaykh of the Ulama of Alexandria, and later the deputy (*wakīl*) of the Shaykh al-Azhar. Some years earlier, Shākir had enjoyed a relationship with ʿAbduh that was beneficial for both parties. Shākir was an early advocate of reforming the shariʿa courts, whose insistence on narrowly ruling only according to the Ḥanafī school he judged to be an undue hardship to ordinary people. In this, he found common cause with ʿAbduh.[3] His suggestion to allow, in exceptional cases, recourse to especially the Mālikī *madhhab* was dismissed

[1] The details of this account come from Muḥammad Rashīd Riḍā, *Tārīkh al-Ustādh al-Imām al-Shaykh Muḥammad ʿAbduh* (Cairo: Dār al-Faḍīla, 2006), 1:1044–49. The text was first printed in two parts in *al-Manār* 8, no. 9 (July 3, 1905): 355–57 and *al-Manār* 8, no. 10 (July 19, 1905): 375–79.

[2] Riḍā, *Tārīkh al-Ustādh al-Imām*, 1:1049.

[3] On the history of "forum shopping" and "pragmatism" in Islamic law, see Ahmed Fekry Ibrahim, *Pragmatism in Islamic Law: A Social and Intellectual History* (Syracuse, NY: Syracuse University Press, 2015).

Transformations of Tradition. Junaid Quadri, Oxford University Press (2021). © Oxford University Press.
DOI: 10.1093/oso/9780190077044.003.0002

by his mentor Muḥammad al-ʿAbbāsī al-Mahdī, the first Mufti of Egypt.[4] But despite al-ʿAbbāsī al-Mahdī's disapproval, the student remained convinced of the soundness of his proposal, and when ʿAbduh took over the muftiship, Shākir presented the new Mufti with a report he had prepared suggesting concrete reforms for what he deemed a dysfunctional system.[5] After conducting an inspection of some of the courts himself, ʿAbduh prepared his own famous report on court reform, which agreed with many of Shākir's recommendations.[6] Shākir's biographer and son, Aḥmad (a prominent scholar in his own right[7]), speculates that the obstacles ʿAbduh faced in advancing his proposed reforms beyond this stage led him to seek a different tack: the implementation of his vision through the appointment of like-minded judges. One of his recommendations to the Khedive ʿAbbās Ḥilmī II, then, was that Shākir be appointed to the position of Chief Judge (*qāḍī al-quḍāt*) in the Sudan.

Not long after, however, Shākir had cultivated a direct line to ʿAbbās. When ʿAbduh's relations with the Khedive began to deteriorate toward the end of the Mufti's life, it was Shākir who was deputed by the Khedive, alongside foreign minister (and later prime minister) Buṭrus Ghālī, to approach the shaykh for the purpose of sowing dissension between him and his most famous student, Riḍā.[8] Through these two intermediaries, ʿAbbās offered ʿAbduh support for his attempts to reform the Azhar on condition that the latter distance himself from Riḍā.[9] ʿAbduh refused, citing Riḍā's intellectual

[4] On al-ʿAbbāsī al-Mahdī and the preference accorded the Ḥanafī school after the Ottoman conquest of Egypt, see Rudolph Peters, "Muḥammad al-ʿAbbāsī al-Mahdī (d. 1897), Grand Muftī of Egypt, and His *al-Fatāwā al-Mahdiyya*," *Islamic Law and Society* 1, no. 1 (January 1, 1994): 73–75.

[5] A biography written by Muḥammad Shākir's son, Aḥmad, says this report was deposited in the Egyptian National Library (*Dār al-Kutub al-Miṣriyya*). See Usāma Muḥammad Shākir, ed., *Min Aʿlām al-ʿAṣr* (Cairo, 2001), 11.

[6] Shākir's report was submitted to ʿAbduh in early 1899. ʿAbduh completed his own report in November of the same year and it was printed by Maṭbaʿat al-Manār in Shawwal 1317 (= 1900). Shākir, *Min Aʿlām al-ʿAṣr*, 11.

[7] For more on Aḥmad Shākir, see Shākir, *Min Aʿlām al-ʿAṣr*, 29–58; Ebrahim Moosa, "Shaykh Aḥmad Shākir and the Adoption of a Scientifically-Based Lunar Calendar," *Islamic Law and Society* 5, no. 1 (1998): 57–89; Ahmed El Shamsy, *Rediscovering the Islamic Classics: How Editors and Print Culture Transformed an Intellectual Tradition* (Princeton, NJ: Princeton University Press, 2020), 229–34.

[8] For the deterioration of relations between ʿAbduh and ʿAbbās, see Mohamed Haddad, "ʿAbduh et ses Lecteurs: Pour une Histoire Critique des 'Lectures' de M. ʿAbduh," *Arabica* 45, no. 1 (1998): 31–33; Mark J. Sedgwick, *Muhammad Abduh: A Biography* (Cairo: The American University in Cairo Press, 2009), 107–13. For a hagiographical account of Buṭrus Ghālī, see Muḥammad Ḥusayn Haykal, *Tarājim Miṣriyya wa-Gharbiyya* (Cairo: Dār al-Maʿārif, n.d.), 105–21. See also Arthur Goldschmidt, "The Butrus Ghali Family," *Journal of the American Research Center in Egypt* 30 (1993): 183–88, who mentions Ghālī's closeness to the Khedive (185) and his oft-reprised role as a "go-between" (185).

[9] The precise reason for the Khedive's displeasure with Riḍā is unclear from the latter's account, though he does mention that their relationship went through ups and downs (Riḍā, *Tārīkh al-Ustādh*

agreement with his project, his service as a mouthpiece for ʿAbduh's views, and his solidarity during the controversial Transvaal fatwa affair.[10]

On this occasion, Shākir seems to have been quite direct with ʿAbduh, relating the Khedive's request to him in a rather straightforward manner. However, the Khedive, convinced of ʿAbduh's loyalty to the British, made use of Shākir for other, less transparent attempts to thwart the Mufti's agenda. It is in a forlorn letter from Shākir in the aftermath of ʿAbduh's funeral that we discover the extent of these cloak-and-dagger tactics. The note, archived among ʿAbbās's personal papers under the title "A plea for forgiveness from the benefactor," was Shākir's attempt at preempting a rebuke from the palace after he caught wind of the Khedive's displeasure that some in Shākir's retinue had decided to join ʿAbduh's funeral. In it, he apologizes profusely to the ruler and attributes his own attendance to a misunderstanding.

> Forgive me, master, for your sincere servant joined the funeral believing that such was your desire, and that he was not transgressing the limits of your lofty commands. For, in the Qubba Palace, you ordered me to flatter the deceased and maintain appearances with him after his removal from [the administrative council of] al-Azhar al-Sharīf, so that he would not be in a position to oppose any of the beneficial plans you have charged your weak servant with. So, I flattered him until he died, and joined his funeral out of sincere devotion to Your Highness and obedience to your commands, which must be obeyed. The man has now died, and neither the attendance at his funeral nor the honors of the government will save him with God. Nor will the praise of those who praise (*madḥ al-mādiḥīn*) or the extolling of critics benefit him. Through attending the funeral, the servant of Your Highness cut short the tongues of the traitors who are quick to confrontation with your sincere servants and the close entourage of Your Highness. My good intentions in this [matter] are the greatest intercession before Your Highness.

al-Imām, 1:580), and that during this period ʿAbbās used members of his palace entourage to oppose (*muʿākasa*) Riḍā and spy on him. Riḍā claims he was informed of this by one of the palace spies himself. Riḍā, *Tārīkh al-Ustādh al-Imām*, 1:585.

[10] On the Transvaal fatwa, see Jakob Skovgaard-Petersen, *Defining Islam for the Egyptian State: Muftis and Fatwas of the Dār al-Iftā* (Leiden: Brill, 1997), 123–33. A translation can be found in Charles C. Adams, "Muḥammad ʿAbduh and the Transvaal Fatwā," in *The Macdonald Presentation Volume, a Tribute to Duncan Black Macdonald, Consisting of Articles by Former Students, Presented to Him on His Seventieth Birthday, April 9, 1933* (Princeton, NJ: Princeton University Press, 1933), 13–29.

> Forgive me, master, for any step I took towards other than Your Highness, or for any tongue by which I sought any mercy other than your gracious mercies, or for any face I called on other than yours. It is not proper etiquette or morals for a servant of Your Highness to vacillate between him and standing at the doors of traitors and thieves, for his is a noble religion that protects him from making the *qibla* of his religious hopes the face of an infidel, who believes not in God, nor His Prophet, nor the Last Day.[11]

***

Many years after the death of ʿAbduh and the end of ʿAbbās's reign, Aḥmad b. Ṣiddīq al-Ghumārī, scion of a prominent Maghribī family of Sufis and hadith scholars based in Tangier, traveled to Cairo to study at the Azhar. When he was setting out, his father advised him to attach himself to Bakhīt, whose scholarship and reputation seemed to have made an impression on the elder al-Ghumārī.[12] True to his father's wishes, Aḥmad studied *tafsīr* and the *Ṣaḥīḥ* of al-Bukhārī with Bakhīt, but more consequentially, formed an intimate personal bond with the aging shaykh whom he remembered as the "shaykh of knowledge in the Egyptian lands, rather in all of the East."[13] In a short biographical note on his esteemed teacher, al-Ghumārī writes that one day, on one of their many personal visits, Bakhīt decided to confide in his promising young student.

> One day, when I was alone [with him], Shaykh Bakhīt, may God have mercy on him, told me [something] with regards to Muḥammad ʿAbduh, which I understood could not be said openly because [ʿAbduh] was much loved and respected among the masses and especially the foreigners. He said to me, "No one has corrupted the beliefs (*ʿaqāʾid*) of the Muslims and introduced misguidance (*adkhala al-ḍalāl*) to the Azhar like [ʿAbduh] has. Before him, the Azhar was pure of deviance, heresy and the like. He [went on] to tell me that when the nationalist movement emerged, and

[11] ʿAbbās Ḥilmī II Papers, HIL 52/44. Compare to ʿAbbās's letter to Aḥmad Shafīq Bey in which the Khedive castigates Shafīq for not seeking the permission of the Palace before joining ʿAbduh's funeral, and concluding from that that all he sought to do was flatter the man after his death. Aḥmad Shafīq, *Mudhakkirātī fī Niṣf Qarn* (Cairo: Maṭbaʿat Miṣr, 1936), 2:71–73.

[12] Aḥmad ibn al-Ṣiddīq al-Ghumārī, *al-Baḥr al-ʿAmīq fī Marwiyyāt Ibn al-Ṣiddīq* (Cairo: Dār al-Kutubī, 2007), 1:55.

[13] Al-Ghumārī, *al-Baḥr al-ʿAmīq*, 1:196. Despite his enormous respect for Bakhīt's erudition, al-Ghumārī did think that his mentor was deficient in hadith scholarship "as is customary of great jurists and imams of the rational sciences." Al-Ghumārī, *al-Baḥr al-ʿAmīq*, 1:206.

> Egyptian Muslims and Copts joined forces, they began to enter the Azhar together and deliver political speeches. Among them were monks and priests. . . . One day, they arrived with a crucifix, and one of the teachers at the Azhar, Muṣṭafā al-Ghiyāthī, may God's curse be upon him, . . . affixed it to the *miḥrāb* (the prayer-niche), called out that both religions are one, proclaimed "God is Great" and prayed towards the crucifix and the *qibla*. Thousands of pashas present prayed with him.[14]

Al-Ghumārī adds that Bakhīt "mentioned this [anecdote] to me immediately following his comment about Muḥammad ʿAbduh and the misguidance he introduced to al-Azhar,"[15] making it clear to him that the two were directly linked.

***

The juxtapositions found in these two episodes are striking. In each, we have a very public spectacle—the throngs of mourners at ʿAbduh's funeral, the nationalist display of religious unity at the Azhar—contrasted with secret missives and backroom confidences that ʿAbduh's opponents felt could not be made public. Shākir's keeping up of appearances and insincere flattery, and Bakhīt's unwillingness to speak openly about his resentment toward ʿAbduh's influence both speak to the popularity of ʿAbduh and his ideals. As Shākir notes, the government honored him despite the Khedive's enmity toward the man, and people arrived in droves to do the same. Moreover, as both Shākir and Bakhīt observed, he was widely praised, beloved, and respected by the masses. The timidity of the two "establishment" scholars in these anecdotes speaks volumes about the extent to which they felt themselves losing ground to the personality of ʿAbduh and the new ideals he represented. Indeed, when ʿAbbās wrote a pointed rebuke to Aḥmad Shafīq, head of the Khedival Council, for having attending ʿAbduh's funeral—the same note which had raised Shākir's concerns in the first place—he made clear that ʿAbduh ought to be seen as an "enemy of the ulama."[16] This letter, too, however, is penned in the plaintive tone of someone who, despite his position, could not control the ascendancy of a movement he thought to be working, in alliance with the British, against Khedival interests. ʿAbbās

[14] Al-Ghumārī, *al-Baḥr al-ʿAmīq*, 1:209.
[15] Al-Ghumārī, *al-Baḥr al-ʿAmīq*, 1:209.
[16] In fact, ʿAbbās took ʿAbduh to be an enemy of not only the ulama but also God, the Prophet, religion, the *amīr*, Muslims, his family, and even himself. Shafīq, *Mudhakkirātī fī Niṣf Qarn*, 2:72.

admits, for instance, that he had no way of restricting the many journals that decided to publish laudatory obituaries of ʿAbduh. Even a journal like al-Muʾayyad, where his people tried to modulate those sentiments, "emptied its quiver" in praising the man.[17]

A key motif of the anxiety felt by both Shākir and Bakhīt is that of a corrupted *qibla*, the direction toward which Muslims pray. For Shākir, to betray the Khedive in favor of ʿAbduh is to direct himself away from the Muslim community toward those who disbelieve in its fundamental doctrines. For Bakhīt, the effect of the reform and nationalist movements, retrospectively conflated into one unified entity, is the defiling of a pristine Muslim space. To associate the direction of Muslim prayer with the symbols of Christianity is to sully it, and to then pray toward it is a startling and inconceivably blatant form of blasphemy. In both cases, the symbol of the corrupted *qibla* signifies the danger of reorienting oneself away from the predictable traditions of the older regime toward a new uncontrollable order. ʿAbduh's intellectual and social presence is perceived as forcing Muslims in a new and undesirable direction. Needless to say, there are good historical reasons to doubt that ʿAbduh was aligned unreservedly with either Christianity or Britain, but the challenge his agenda posed was experienced by the likes of Shākir and Bakhīt as a departure from the past: ʿAbduh was successfully directing society toward something foreign, and doing so in a manner that could not be contained by the familiar rules of older modes of belonging.

It was the threat of this perceived change in orientation that gave rise to the atmosphere of competition and suspicion, and the secret intrigues and public withholdings, that characterize both accounts. In the case of Bakhīt, this fostered an attitude of territorialism and partisanship that heavily conditioned his thinking. His written work, almost all of which was published after 1900 when ʿAbduh's thought was already a prominent fixture of the Egyptian intellectual scene, can only be properly understood against the backdrop of this context of antagonism and opposition. Indeed, in a short entry otherwise dominated by basic biographical details and a (partial) list of publications, the modern bio-bibliographer Khayr al-Dīn al-Ziriklī was sure to remember Bakhīt as "one of the staunchest opponents (*min ashadd al-muʿāriḍīn*) of the Reform movement established by Muḥammad ʿAbduh."[18] The remainder of

[17] ʿAbbās also included an addendum in the envelope to Shafīq which demanded a full report on an elegiac poem composed by an employee of the *dīwān al-awqāf* and published by the *dīwān* itself. Shafīq, *Mudhakkirātī fī Niṣf Qarn*, 2:73.

[18] Khayr al-Dīn al-Ziriklī, *al-Aʿlām: Qāmūs Tarājim li-Ashhar al-Rijāl wa-l-Nisāʾ min al-ʿArab wa-l-Mustaʿribīn wa-l-Mustashriqīn*, 15th ed. (Beirut: Dār al-ʿIlm li-l-Malāyīn, 2002), 6:50.

this chapter shows how the lines that defined this partisan territorialism were drawn by Bakhīt within the realm of Islamic thought, the domain in which he was most expert and therefore most threatened, and in whose language he felt most emboldened to express his criticisms. By examining two debates with Rashīd Riḍā, who understood himself to be taking on ʿAbduh's mantle, we will see that the rivalry between Bakhīt and Reformists, though animated by points of contention in early twentieth-century Egypt, was conducted on a ground that exceeded that immediate context both historically and geographically. It resurrected old debates from medieval Islam to make sense of Reformist commitments, and it recruited transnational figures into a network of belonging and authority that drew upon older structures like the *madhhab* to carve out new alliances that served the demands of the present.

Partisanship Made Explicit: Resurrecting Old Debates

One of the results of the intellectual displacement of the period was a reconsideration of figures who had previously challenged orthodoxies and upset prevailing intellectual orders. Perhaps the pre-eminent example of a figure so recuperated is Ibn Taymiyya (d. 1328), the fourteenth-century Damascene writer who sharply confronted the scholars of his time with novel views, scathing critiques, and often penetrating insights. In 1900, a group of Egyptians set out to reintroduce him to their countrymen. Among the efforts of this group was the publication of *al-Wāsiṭa*, a pamphlet-length treatise that Ibn Taymiyya wrote to address the practice of worshippers making use of intermediaries when praying to God.[19] It is unclear how close this group of patrons was to the Reformist movement, but the danger of falling into the cardinal sin of *shirk* (associating nondivine entities with God, by attributing qualities to the former that are the exclusive prerogative of the latter) was a key complaint of both Ibn Taymiyya and twentieth-century Reformists. Riḍā, in particular, regularly railed in *al-Manār* against the superstitions (*khurāfāt*) that pervaded Egyptian society, especially those emanating from vernacular expressions of Sufism centered around shrines and the saints buried within them.[20] Riḍā took the enterprising men who financed the

[19] Taqī al-Dīn Aḥmad Ibn Taymiyya, *al-Wāsiṭa bayna al-Khalq wa-l-Ḥaqq* (Cairo: Maṭbaʿat al-Ādāb, 1318 H [1900]).

[20] For but one example, see his review of Bakhīt's volume *Taṭhīr al-Fuʾād* (discussed later) in *al-Manār* 4:318–20, which makes explicit mention of shrines at 319 and is included under the heading *al-bidaʿ wa-l-khurāfāt* (innovations and superstitions). The presence of these innovations

publication of the book to be *fuḍalāʾ*, eminent personalities, concerned for the beliefs of the populace. Bakhīt, on the other hand, thought they were corruptors of true faith, deviant followers of Ibn Taymiyya's rejected beliefs and misguided opinions. The effect of this publication in his opinion was to awaken an old *fitna*, a seditious intrigue that had long lain dormant within the Muslim *umma*.[21] He felt dutybound, therefore, to respond so that the re-assertion of this long-discarded heresy could be staved off. Within the year, Bakhīt published a collection of works from medieval critics that together "comprised a rebuttal to the likes of Ibn Taymiyya."[22] The centerpiece of this collection was a text written by Ibn Taymiyya's contemporary and avowed critic, Taqī al-Dīn al-Subkī (d. 1355), titled *Shifāʾ al-Saqām fī Ziyārat Khayr al-Anām* (*Curing the Illness: On Visiting the Best of Mankind*).[23]

The most intriguing part of the volume, however, is not al-Subkī's text nor the particular mix of medieval authors published, but rather the revealing essay Bakhīt wrote and attached to the collection as a preface. He tellingly titled it *Cleansing the Heart of Impure Beliefs* (*Taṭhīr al-Fuʾād min Danas al-Iʿtiqād*). The *Taṭhīr* seems to have been the textual moment where Bakhīt's confrontation with Reformism was first made explicit in his work. Key to Bakhīt's preface was the parallel he drew between the deviance of Ibn Taymiyya, on the one hand, and the heresy of "the likes of Ibn Taymiyya" in the present day, on the other. Though he decries the "revival of the Ibn Taymiyya *fitna*," the modern publication of *al-Wāsiṭa* provided him with a hook on which he could confidently hang a critique that had a long pedigree, as well as an opportunity to analogize the circumstances of the fourteenth-century debate to the present threat. Bakhīt's critique is framed around the concept of *ʿulamāʾ al-sūʾ*, scholars of iniquity. These are those knowledgeable people, "no matter their era," who, despite their learning, fail to cling firmly to "what the Prophet came with," whose beliefs transgress the boundaries of the shariʿa, who give themselves free rein to disregard reason and

and superstitions among ordinary Muslims, and their licensing by the scholars of al-Azhar, was a preoccupation of Riḍā throughout his career. Toward the end of his life, confronted by a series of accusations put forth by the official journal of al-Azhar, *Nūr al-Islām*, he responded by accusing the Azharī establishment of supporting "*al-bidaʿ wa-l-khurāfāt*." The terminology is used on the cover page of Muḥammad Rashīd Riḍā, *al-Manār wa-l-Azhar* (Cairo: Maṭbaʿat al-Manār, 1353H).

21 Muḥammad Bakhīt al-Muṭīʿī, *Taṭhīr al-Fuʾād min Danas al-Iʿtiqād* (Būlāq: al-Maṭbaʿa al-Kubrā al-Amīriyya, 1318H), 13.

22 Bakhīt al-Muṭīʿī, *Taṭhīr al-Fuʾād*, 13.

23 Al-Subkī informs the reader that he had initially intended to give the treatise the much more aggressive title, *Shann al-Ghāra ʿalā man Ankara Safar al-Ziyāra* (*A Predatory Attack on He Who Rejects Traveling to Visit [the Prophet]*).

follow their capricious whims and vested interests, and who depart from the guidance of rightly guided imams. The considered positions of the great scholars of the past are widely accepted (*maqbūl*), and for good reason, while the opinions of the antagonistic *ʿulamāʾ al-sūʾ* ought to be cast to the side (lit. "behind the back," *wajaba nabdh aqwālahu ẓahriyyan*). The premier example of a scholar of ill repute for Bakhīt is Ibn Taymiyya, a characterization attested by a series of prominent contemporary scholars who considered the Damascene iconoclast an impious innovator, and even a disbeliever.[24]

But because the *ʿulamāʾ al-sūʾ* can be found in all times, not just the fourteenth century, Bakhīt's appropriation of the critique is a transparent attempt to castigate the Reformists of his own time. Muḥammad ʿAbduh's student Qāsim Amīn (d. 1908) is named explicitly,[25] but the more general complaint is that such figures hide behind calls to command the good and forbid evil (*amr bi-l-maʿrūf wa-l-nahy ʿan al-munkar*) in order to censure the ulama and challenge their authority. "This was the practice of Ibn Taymiyya in his time and the practice of all those of his ilk in every era."[26] Central to Bakhīt's critique of Ibn Taymiyya and "those of his ilk" is their flouting of the *ijmāʿ* (consensus) of the scholars. These departures were conceptualized by Bakhīt not as legitimate disagreement (*ikhtilāf*), or as simple departures from a majority opinion, but as ruptures in a settled order determined by scholarly consensus (*ijmāʿ*). The term he uses on more than one occasion to describe the nature of these unorthodoxies is *kharq*, "a tear," thereby representing them as not mere disagreement but a deeper breach bordering on the heretical.[27]

If Bakhīt's preface made his antagonism toward the Reformists explicit, Riḍā's response only confirmed the rivalry. In a review of both volumes, Riḍā sided with Ibn Taymiyya in *al-Wāsiṭa*, depicting him as heroically "defending the reality of *tawḥīd*." More intriguingly, however, he used the opportunity to attack what he termed the *ʿulamāʾ al-taqlīd*, conformist scholars, who, finding their livelihood and prestige threatened by the possibility that Ibn Taymiyya's critiques could be brought to bear on their own positions, decided to go on the offensive to produce this collection of articles. This rebuttal effectively cemented the analogy between their present rivalry and the intrigues of the fourteenth century. What stands out most starkly in this exchange is the partisanship, the taking of sides in a live controversy

24 Bakhīt al-Muṭīʿī, *Taṭhīr al-Fuʾād*, 7–9, 11.
25 Bakhīt al-Muṭīʿī, *Taṭhīr al-Fuʾād*, 5–6.
26 Bakhīt al-Muṭīʿī, *Taṭhīr al-Fuʾād*, 17.
27 Bakhīt al-Muṭīʿī, *Taṭhīr al-Fuʾād*, 9, 11.

conducted via the proxy of history. Riḍā and Bakhīt agree that Ibn Taymiyya is an important point of historical reference for this present-day controversy, though they position themselves on either side of the debate. On the one hand, Bakhīt warns of the mortal danger to faith and society posed by transgressing widely accepted doctrinal positions and crossing the scholarly authorities, past and present, that uphold them. On the other, Riḍā finds this attitude to be little more than a recipe for intellectual stagnation and blind conformity to the past, driven not by a sincere attachment to the principles of Islam, but the worldly benefits that accrue from the culture of saints, shrines, and superstitions.

In his important work on Jadidist Muslim reform in Central Asia, Adeeb Khalid has pointed out that "the struggle between the Jadids and their opponents was over the possession and redistribution of what Pierre Bourdieu has called 'cultural capital.' The Jadids sought to redefine the culture their society should value. . . . Their opponents met the challenge by valorizing the cultural values that guaranteed their status and prestige."[28] In early twentieth-century Egypt, too, the controversies between Reformists and their opponents are best understood as contestations over cultural capital that both conditioned, and were conditioned by, their respective intellectual projects. The aforementioned skirmish between Riḍā and Bakhīt took the form of a conflict over the legacy of Ibn Taymiyya, but it stood in rather transparently for a broader battle that pitted a Reformist reimagination of a purified Islam against a settled older order and its custodians.

In the next section, however, we will see that one important way Bakhīt participated in this struggle over cultural capital was by asserting the *social* capital available to him through his membership in the Ḥanafī school and other transregional scholarly networks.

The Social *Madhhab* and Networks of Belonging

In a throwaway comment in *Taṭhīr al-Fuʾād*, Bakhīt had criticized "some journals" for including decontextualized quotations from medieval authorities in a manner that distorted their import.[29] This seemingly passing comment was in fact an allusion to a larger divide between Reformists and their

[28] Adeeb Khalid, *The Politics of Muslim Cultural Reform: Jadidism in Central Asia* (Berkeley: University of California Press, 1988), 5–6.
[29] Bakhīt al-Muṭīʿī, *Taṭhīr al-Fuʾād*, 16.

opponents in this period. The pervasive use of journals was a crucial component of the Reformist presence in Egypt, and Bakhīt's offhanded reference, therefore, was a way of distinguishing his own intellectual activity in this early stage from that of the Reformist movement. While he was often left seeking out the help of contacts and acquaintances to help him publish his *risālas* (monographic treatises) and *ḥāshiyas* (commentaries on earlier texts), genres of writing that were much more familiar to the Islamic tradition, Reformists had editorial control over their own journals.[30] Jakob Skovgaard-Petersen has referred to this phenomenon as the "Salafī press."[31] For example, ʿAbduh, after having gained experience working as the editor of the official organ of the Egyptian government *al-Waqāʾiʿ al-Miṣriyya*, collaborated with his teacher al-Afghānī to establish the magazine *al-ʿUrwa al-Wuthqā* in 1884. Most noteworthy, however, was the indefatigable output of Rashīd Riḍā in *al-Manār*, whose frequent publication cycle and global readership were key to his efforts to make his ideas widely accessible.[32] This was, there is no doubt, a concerted effort by Reformists to utilize the latest technologies to spread their politics and conception of reform.[33] Skovgaard-Petersen notes that Riḍā conceived of the press as "the link between those who govern and their subjects, demonstrating for each party its rights and duties with respect to the other party."[34] To the extent that the ulama often saw their own social position as go-betweens speaking to both the rulers and the populace, it was quite obvious that the press as exploited by Riḍā posed a direct challenge to the scholarly elite. Further, the discourse carried out in journals functioned as an alternative forum of intellectual debate and dissemination, and therefore a threat to the ulama's long-standing dominance

30 Al-Ghumārī, *al-Baḥr al-ʿAmīq*, 1:202–3. Aḥmad b. Ṣiddīq published Bakhīt's treatise on the permissibility of photography with his own money (al-Ghumārī, *al-Baḥr al-ʿAmīq*, 1:201–2) and directed him to Maṭbaʿat al-Saʿāda when he was looking for a publisher for *Tawfīq al-Raḥmān* (al-Ghumārī, *al-Baḥr al-ʿAmīq*, 1:203). I discuss the former text briefly in chapter 4, and the latter more extensively in chapter 3. For the phenomenon of private publishing, see Kathryn A. Schwartz, "The Political Economy of Private Printing in Cairo as Told from a Commissioning Deal Turned Sour, 1871," *International Journal of Middle East Studies* 49, no. 1 (February 2017): 25–45.

31 Skovgaard-Petersen, *Defining Islam for the Egyptian State*, 69–71.

32 Umar Ryad, "A Printed Muslim 'Lighthouse' in Cairo: *al-Manār*'s Early Years, Religious Aspiration and Reception (1898–1903)," *Arabica* 56, no. 1 (2009): 27–60. Ami Ayalon discusses *al-Manār* as part of a larger discussion on "pious printing" in Ami Ayalon, *The Arabic Print Revolution: Cultural Production and Mass Readership* (Cambridge, UK: Cambridge University Press, 2016), 90.

33 By contrast, the official journal of the Azhar, *Nūr al-Islām*, later renamed *Majallat al-Azhar*, did not publish its first issue until 1930. For an early study of this journal, see Wilfred Cantwell Smith, "The Azhar Journal: Survey and Critique" (PhD diss., Princeton University, 1948).. See also Wilfred Cantwell Smith, *Islam in Modern History* (Princeton, NJ: Princeton University Press, 1957), 122*ff.*.

34 Skovgaard-Petersen, *Defining Islam for the Egyptian State*, 70.

over epistemic and moral authority. The contrast between Bakhīt's dismissal of "some journals" and Riḍā's enthusiasm for print journalism speaks eloquently to the shifting tides of fortune in this period, capturing well what Dyala Hamzah has noticed as the shift from *ʿilm* to *ṣiḥāfa*, from Islamic scholarship to journalism, as the dominant medium of intellectual work.[35]

In this section, we examine one particularly acrimonious debate between Bakhīt and Riḍā to demonstrate once more the bitter partisanship and territorialism that resulted from some ulama's sense that their authority was being encroached upon as a result of the Reformists' active participation in this new public sphere. Bakhīt, unaccustomed to the competition and resentful that those outside elite Azharī circles were being given a hearing at all, is again found responding defensively to Riḍā's provocations. What emerges from a reading of this episode, though, is not the straight-forward claim that the authority and standing of the ulama was simply usurped by the Reformist camp, but rather the conclusion that it was reconfigured along different lines, transregional in scale, demonstrating the shifting contours of authority construction in this period.

***

Brinkley Messick has often been a sophisticated commentator on the nature of Islamic law in modern contexts. In one of his articles, Messick has followed the circulation of a fatwa issued in 1905 by a Haḍramī mufti based out of Singapore in order to track the roots of a shift in conceptions of Islamic law he identifies more firmly with the period of "media muftis" we are living in today.[36] The mufti's response to a question from Aden about the permissibility of insuring cargo transported by ship was noticed by Riḍā, who published it in *al-Manār* along with his own thoughts.[37] The content of the mufti's response, its being picked up by Riḍā, and Riḍā's own commentary all signal, according to Messick, important developments in the unfolding of shariʿa in the modern world, developments which became increasingly central and entrenched as the century unfolded.

[35] Dyala Hamzah, "From *ʿilm* to *Ṣiḥāfa* or the Politics of the Public Interest (*Maṣlaḥa*): Muḥammad Rashīd Riḍā and His Journal *al-Manār* (1898–1935)," in *The Making of the Arab Intellectual: Empire, Public Sphere and the Colonial Coordinates of Selfhood*, ed. Dyala Hamzah (London: Routledge, 2013), 90–127.

[36] Brinkley Messick, "Madhhabs and Modernities," in *The Islamic School of Law: Evolution, Devolution, and Progress*, ed. P. Bearman, R. Peters, and F. Vogel (Cambridge, MA: Harvard University Press, 2005), 159–74.

[37] For a history of the development of the insurance industry, and the positions of prominent muftis on the practice, see Skovgaard-Petersen, *Defining Islam for the Egyptian State*, 335–73.

The Singaporean mufti, ʿAlawī b. Aḥmad al-Saqqāf (d. 1916), was a follower of the Shāfiʿī school of law but saw fit to refer to the Ḥanafī authority Ibn ʿĀbidīn, because the issue "is among the occurrences of the latest period and I do not see anyone among our leading Shāfiʿī jurists who had addressed it in their books in what I have read."[38] Noting that Aden would meet the criteria of *dār al-ḥarb* ("the abode of war") in the Ḥanafī school, al-Saqqāf quotes Ibn ʿĀbidīn as permitting outside the jurisdiction of *dār al-islām* ("the abode of Islam") what would otherwise be considered defective transactions.[39] Because Aden cannot be classified as a *dār al-ḥarb* under the criteria of his own school, however, the mufti goes on to offer that in his opinion, this should be seen not as a case falling under the traditionally recognized rubric of *ḍamān* (i.e., the *fiqh* chapter on guarantees and securities) but rather under the category of a simple sale, which, importantly, turns upon the presence of consent.

Riḍā, for his part, takes up this last point, amplifying it into a virtual governing principle of commercial law. Because the particulars of contracts are not matters of religion by whose observance (or omission) one draws closer to God, they are merely value-neutral ways through which people have agreed to regulate their transactions. As such, "they do not deprive people of the freedom of transactional disposition of their wealth, according to what they see as beneficial to them in its preservation or its growth, [always] with an obligation to [observe] the limits of God . . . such as the forbidding of deceit and deception and trickery and usurpation and suchlike."[40]

For Messick, this fatwa and its reception by Riḍā can be seen as harbingers of the modern democratization of authority that is increasingly evident in the present day. The Singaporean mufti, for example, deems fit to draw upon the resources of a school other than his own to provide a convincing response to the question. More radically, Riḍā engages in a "post-school synthesizing and reformist legal discourse."[41] "Taken together," Messick concludes, "the compound fatwas on commercial insurance prefigure the modern trend toward the dissolution of the conventional authorities of madhhabs as the standard discursive schools."[42] On this reading, Riḍā's approach to law not only

[38] Messick, "Madhhabs and Modernities," 165.

[39] Premodern jurists had regularly divided the world into these two domains, allowing for an accommodation of differential rulings due to context and circumstance.

[40] Messick, "Madhhabs and Modernities," 168.

[41] Messick, "Madhhabs and Modernities," 172.

[42] Messick, "Madhhabs and Modernities," 171. For a more detailed discussion of the *madhhabs*, see the next chapter.

operated outside the constraints of the conventional *madhhabs*; it augured a shift in which the *madhhabs* came to be eclipsed by a post-*madhhab* legal reasoning.

While this is not of course entirely off the mark, I want to pursue this claim, arguing that the shifts in religious authority of this period must not always be seen simply as precursors of phenomena we recognize today. Rather, authority was restructured and reconfigured in much more complex and entangled ways; "traditional" authority, that is, did not simply dissolve but realigned itself in networks constitutive of what might be called "the social *madhhab*." This label seeks to capture my claim that "traditionalist" scholars drew upon their networks to mobilize in identifiable ways to address the impending threat of Modernist ascendancy, though in so doing, found themselves on an altogether new, or *modern*, intellectual terrain. As I argue in the following chapter, the "social *madhhab*" was a distinctly modern phenomenon in terms of its newly emergent interpretive commitments and notions of epistemic authority. As such, it ended up participating in the conceptual logic of the Modernist critique. However, it continued to draw upon a common training, vocabulary, and self-identification with long-standing juristic institutions like the older, interpretive *madhhab*. The "social *madhhab*" was also a transregional network, drawing together disparate figures united by their commitment to working within older discursive genres and institutions, even as they transformed them radically. As we will see later, even as the hermeneutic authority of the *madhhab* weakened and dissolved, its character as an association of living scholars, just-deceased authorities, and agreed-upon masters continued to exert a social influence in the form of "old world" demands for certain types of deference, or even simple engagement.

To trace the contours of this shift, let us now turn to the polemic which followed Bakhīt's own fatwa on insurance. Strikingly, the question posed to him is almost precisely the same as the one sent to the Singaporean mufti al-Saqqāf: namely, the permissibility of purchasing insurance on freight entrusted to a European company. This similarity provoked Riḍā to imply that Bakhīt had in fact fabricated his questioner (*mustaftī*). Be that as it may, Bakhīt's response hews close to the Ḥanafī position referenced in al-Saqqāf: such a transaction is permitted in *dār al-ḥarb*. However, we are less interested in this particular conclusion than we are in the discussion that follows.

Since Bakhīt's fatwa was issued merely a year after Riḍā had printed al-Saqqāf's, it is not surprising that the *al-Manār* editor would see fit to respond to what he saw as the problems in Bakhīt's responsum. What is more intriguing, however, is that the issues he takes up are not direct critiques of the substance of Bakhīt's response, but rather inaccuracies, often tangential, he finds in the latter's treatment of the issue. Equally noteworthy is the subsequent back and forth in which the two draw upon a wide array of sources revealing their own commitments and underpinnings in a much more textured way than we are apt to conclude if we focus solely on their respective legal doctrines.

Riḍā's choice of topics in his initial salvo can be easily explained—though, I think only in part—by the mutual animosity held by the two parties. So, for example, Riḍā begins by pointing out that Bakhīt mistakenly places his questioner in a number of disparate locations. Though corrected in subsequent editions after Bakhīt claimed it was a printing error,[43] Bakhīt's original text had said that he had "received a letter from some ulama resident in Anatolia in Eastern Rumelia in the province of Salonica." Ever quick to point out scholarly errors, Riḍā responded by commenting sarcastically on Bakhīt's lack of conversance with simple geography, a familiarity without which "*ijtihād* cannot be achieved today":

> Would that the gentleman (*al-ustādh*) had notified one of his children still studying in school of his discovery before its publication. Perhaps [the child] would have warned him that the invention of a questioner resident in Anatolia, which is actually a number of provinces in Asia; and in Eastern Rumelia, which is among the provinces of Bulgaria in Europe; and in Salonica, in Macedonia, is easily rebutted by anyone who knows that the residence of a person in different provinces in different continents is impossible.[44]

[43] Muḥammad Bakhīt al-Muṭīʿī, "Izāḥat al-Wahm wa-l-Ishtibāh ʿan Risālatay al-Fūnūghrāf wa-l-Sūkūrtāh," in *Thalātha Rasāʾil* (Cairo: Jamʿiyyat al-Azhar al-ʿIlmiyya, 1932), 27. The 1932 edition I consulted refers simply to the "Ottoman province of Salonica." Muḥammad Bakhīt al-Muṭīʿī, "Fī Aḥkām al-Sūkūrtāh," in *Thalātha Rasāʾil* (Cairo: Jamʿiyyat al-Azhar al-ʿIlmiyya, 1932), 11.

[44] Muḥammad Rashīd Riḍā, "Risālatān fī Qirāʾat al-Fūnughrāf wa-l-Sukūrtah," *al-Manār* 9, no. 2 (1906): 153. Interestingly, Bakhīt seems to have taken this criticism to heart, for his personal library contains a number of textbooks on geography that date to after this year. For more on Reformists' criticism of Azharis' lack of familiarity with geography, see Muḥammad ʿAbduh, *al-Islām wa-l-Naṣrāniyya*, ed. Muḥammad Rashīd Riḍā (Cairo: Maṭbaʿat Majallat al-Manār, 1323H), 114–15, 117*ff*. See also *al-Manār* 3 (April 1, 1900): 79–84, in which a student reports on a shaykh's opposition to including modern subjects, among them geography, in the Azhar curriculum (likely a glimpse into the debate ʿAbduh mentions in his article).

Not to be outdone, Bakhīt insults Riḍā throughout the dialogue, addressing him only as *al-muʿtariḍ al-ʿanīd*, the obstinate objector "whose love for criticism blinds and deafens."[45] He also comments derisively on Riḍā's attempt to insert himself into scholarly matters, suggesting that he is simply "misrepresenting himself to the people as a player on the field [of scholarship] (*min fursān hādhā al-maydān*),"[46] a strategic insult surely intended to stress Riḍā's being a non-Azharī, and therefore unqualified to take part in such scholarly discussions. In the same dismissive vein, after rebutting one of Riḍā's points elsewhere, Bakhīt concludes the discussion with a parting shot: "Let him review the books of the *madhhab* if he is capable, or otherwise remain silent and conceal his ignorance."[47] In addition to all this, accusations and innuendo of both scholarly and personal impropriety abound, from Riḍā's (subsequently retracted) claim that Bakhīt sent an embarrassing letter to the editor of a journal under a pseudonym, to his lengthy attempt at taking the high road by pointing out Bakhīt's poor etiquette.[48]

All this is to affirm that personal animosity, despite both parties' denials, cannot be dismissed as part of the ensuing polemic. The partisanship we saw in the last section is clearly on display here, too. This does not, however, tell the whole story about the shifts in authority at play. Indeed, it is not hard to see Riḍā's attempt to castigate Bakhīt's lack of familiarity with "modern subjects" or Bakhīt's attempts to cast Riḍā as an unwelcome novice, as efforts to articulate their respective scholarly identities, thereby staking out intellectual ground and demarcating boundaries in light of the shifting balance of power.

To see this second aspect of the debate at work more clearly, we must turn our attention to the other, more substantive and much more technical, critiques Riḍā offers in his initial response. His second of the three objections centers on Bakhīt's use of a weak tradition (hadith) to argue that a land that is *dār al-islām* does not cease being one simply because of the emergence of a disbelieving or tyrannical ruler; rather, according to Bakhīt, a nonbeliever (*kāfir*) can in fact become the sultan of a principality like Egypt without the jurisdiction losing its claim to being part of *dār al-islām*. After getting in a dig that Bakhīt misquotes the narration from the hadith collection of Ibn Māja,

45 Bakhīt al-Muṭīʿī, "Izāḥat al-Wahm," 29.
46 Bakhīt al-Muṭīʿī, "Izāḥat al-Wahm," 45.
47 Bakhīt al-Muṭīʿī, "Izāḥat al-Wahm," 39.
48 A whole section of Riḍā's response is titled "The Manners (*Adab*) of Shaykh Bakhīt in His Response."

Riḍā offers that the hadith is considered by leading authorities to be either a rejected narration or an outright fabrication.[49] He then goes on to object vociferously to the substance of Bakhīt's conclusion, on substantive grounds as well as on the methodological principle that it is invalid to use unreliable hadiths such as this one as a conclusive proof (*ḥujja*).[50]

In Bakhīt's subsequent response, we are permitted our first glimpse into the make-up of the network that constitutes the "social *madhhab*." Responding to Riḍā's accusation that he misquoted and made improper use of the hadith, Bakhīt attempts to display his mastery of the sources, enumerating the various versions of the narration and the books containing them, and clarifying that the narration he offered was not in fact a misquotation but was taken from his older contemporary Shihāb al-Dīn al-Marjānī's (d. 1889) treatise *al-Barq al-Wamīḍ*.[51]

In response to Riḍā's objection to using unreliable hadiths, Bakhīt disputes the categorization in this specific case, running through each of the narrators, before going on to suggest that even if he were to accept Riḍā's characterization of some of the narrators,

> weakness of narrators does not disqualify the hadith from being a *ḥujja* (conclusive proof) unless it is opposed by something stronger, which is then given precedence. But there is no such opposition to this hadith; rather, there exists in the Book [the Qur'an], correct sunna, and ijmāʿ that which testifies to the validity of its meaning and supports it.[52]

Elsewhere, he strengthens the claim, arguing that the deficiencies of one of the narrators

> does not imply that the text is fabricated. If it had been a forgery, these notable masters of the sunna would not have narrated [this hadith], all the while remaining quiet about it and not explaining the matter.[53]

[49] It was al-Bukhārī who believed it was *munkar* ("rejected"), while Wakīʿ deemed it *mawḍūʿ* ("fabricated"), both because of the presence of certain narrators in the chain of transmission. Muḥammad Rashīd Riḍā, "Bāb al-Murāsala wa-l-Munāẓara," *al-Manār* 9, no. 9 (1906): 694.
[50] Muḥammad Rashīd Riḍā, "Bāb al-Murāsala wa-l-Munāẓara," 697.
[51] Bakhīt al-Muṭīʿī, "Izāḥat al-Wahm," 29.
[52] Bakhīt al-Muṭīʿī, "Izāḥat al-Wahm," 33.
[53] Bakhīt al-Muṭīʿī, "Izāḥat Al-Wahm," 34.

This procedural commitment to the use of hadith is an important difference when compared to Riḍā's more precise textual approach, centered on narrator criticism. This distinction in its general contours is one that has been previously recognized by those who have studied Reformist figures.[54] But what is even more telling here is Bakhīt's characterization of Riḍā's initial critique, in which he astutely picks up on the fact that Riḍā is simply reproducing, in abbreviated form, a verbatim quote from the *Nayl al-Awṭār* of the famous Yemeni Reformist Muḥammad al-Shawkānī (d. 1834)[55]—although, Bakhīt says, al-Shawkānī never himself claims the hadith to be inauthentic or fabricated the way Riḍā "has the audacity to do."[56] Noting al-Shawkānī's general tone of disapproval, however, Bakhīt deftly defers to another authority, Aḥmad al-Maqarrī al-Maghribī (d. 1632), who speaks approvingly of the disputed narrator, ʿAbd al-Mālik b. al-Ḥabīb. In so doing, he marks out in clear terms that al-Shawkānī, the maverick Reformist, is not an authoritative reference as far as he is concerned.

What we have here is the beginnings of a sketching out of the networks of influence and alliances that form the contours of a "social *madhhab*"—and, indeed, those of its most present opponent, Reformism. This explains, for example, Bakhīt's allying Riḍā with al-Shawkānī, even though he has nothing negative to say about the latter. It also gives us an insight into Bakhīt's own alliances, especially with one of his most oft-quoted writers, al-Marjānī. Importantly, Riḍā, in his response, makes an effort to dismiss the importance of al-Marjānī's work to the issue at hand, only further entrenching the alliance. "*Al-Barq al-Wamīḍ*," he writes, "is not one of the books of hadith on which one may rely. So, his using it as a *ḥujja* has no value."[57]

What, we may ask, are the material circumstances through which Bakhīt is connected to the Tatar al-Marjānī? This is where Messick's claim about the dissolution of the *madhhabs* as interpretive schools fails to account for their

[54] On the willingness of the majority of premodern scholars to accept "inauthentic" hadiths as arguments, and the Modernists' opposition to this, see Jonathan A. C. Brown, "Even If It's Not True It's True: Using Unreliable Hadiths in Sunni Islam," *Islamic Law and Society* 18, no. 1 (2011): 1–52. Note that chapter 4 will show how Bakhīt himself shifts from a procedural to a "scientistic" mode of thinking in *fiqh* matters, indicating the profound way in which he internalized major Reformist commitments in a different domain.

[55] Riḍā had studied parts of this text early on as a student at the hands of ʿAbd al-Ghanī al-Rāfiʿī. Riḍā, *al-Manār wa-l-Azhar*, 142. For another example of Riḍā's selective appropriation of al-Shawkānī, see Ahmad Dallal, "Appropriating the Past: Twentieth-Century Reconstruction of Pre-Modern Islamic Thought," *Islamic Law and Society* 7, no. 3 (2000): 325–58.

[56] Bakhīt al-Muṭīʿī, "Izāḥat al-Wahm," 30. Here, too, Bakhīt cannot resist going toe to toe with Riḍā, noting that the latter has in fact "omitted parts of the hadith."

[57] Riḍā, "Bāb al-Murāsala wa-l-Munāẓara," 692.

continued relevance, though that relevance survives in a radically different mode. Bakhīt and al-Marjānī are connected, of course, by their Ḥanafism, still an important form of social capital, and the rule that older contemporary, and just-deceased, scholars are important points of reference for understanding the *madhhab* as it stands at any given point. As Brannon Wheeler argues,

> The individual Ḥanafī scholar does not inherit the authority of the revelation by claiming to know how to interpret the Qurʾān. Rather, the authority of a given scholar's definition of practice is predicated on demonstrating the claim that this definition of practice is a continuation of earlier generations' definition of practice, originating with the prophet's definition of practice.[58]

Indeed, in the dialogue we have just looked at, one can detect the ethos of the old interpretive *madhhab* and its social protocols at play even as the strict hermeneutic principle at stake was being compromised by Modernist incursions in this same period.[59] Here, then, we see the *madhhab* acting not as an interpretive entity—of course, its famous historical manifestation—but as a site of sociality, binding together two different scholars in different locations.

For the moment, I want to continue to pursue this idea of the "social *madhhab*" as we can decipher it from this one episode. To return to what I have called the procedural tack of Bakhīt, consider that he invokes the hadith scholar ʿAbd al-Ḥayy al-Kattānī al-Fāsī (d. 1962) to argue for the permissibility of using *munkar* (rejected) hadiths in making *fiqh* arguments.[60] Rebutting the claim of the famous hadith master Ibn Ḥibbān that *munkar* hadiths are not in fact admissible, al-Kattānī labels this an opinion "issued without due investigation."[61] Bakhīt continues relying on al-Kattānī to dispute the claims of hadith authorities as prominent as Ibn Ḥajar, Ibn ʿAbd al-Barr, and al-Bayhaqī so that he can thereby deny the transitivity of the weakness of this hadith's *isnād* (chain of transmission) to its *matn* (text). This is because, as al-Kattānī says in his *al-Raḥma al-Mursala*,

[58] Brannon M. Wheeler, *Applying the Canon in Islam: The Authorization and Maintenance of Interpretive Reasoning in Ḥanafī Scholarship* (Albany: State University of New York Press, 1996), 15.

[59] See the next chapter for a detailed discussion of this compromising.

[60] On al-Kattānī, see Garrett A. Davidson, *Carrying on the Tradition: A Social and Intellectual History of Hadith Transmission across a Thousand Years* (Boston: Brill, 2020), 276–303.

[61] Bakhīt al-Muṭīʿī, "Izāḥat al-Wahm," 34.

> the many [different] paths [of the chain of transmission] preclude this hadith from being extremely weak (*wāhī* and *shadīd al-ḍuʿf*). For when weakness undergoes even the slightest vitalization, it attains some strength. And it is well-known that two weak [narrations] reach the level of strength, such that the *ḥāfiẓ* ʿAbd al-Raʾūf al-Munāwī says . . . "None deny [the validity] of deeming the weak hadith strong (*taqwīya*) by virtue of its many paths and the proliferation of its sources except he who is ignorant of the craft of hadith (al-*ṣināʿa al-ḥadīthiyya*) or the obstinate partisan."[62]

What we find once again is that Bakhīt is insistent on making use of the expertise of contemporary scholars. This is in contrast to Riḍā, who is much more concerned about the technicalities of *isnād* and narrator criticism as settled by earlier authorities. Indeed, whereas much of the narrative of Islamic Reformism has sought to portray Reformists as interested in claiming increased authority for contemporary figures, here we find the opposite. It is the supposed "traditionalist" who makes much of the expertise of his contemporary. But this is not surprising, for it is in keeping with what we have identified as the ethos of the traditional *madhhab* structure. Indeed, Riḍā makes it a point to mention that Bakhīt depends strongly on some of the *mutaʾakhkhirīn* of the *muḥaddithīn* (the "moderns" among the hadith scholars), even going so far as to mock Bakhīt's reliance on al-Kattānī:

> And do you know, dear reader, who is this *ḥāfiẓ* ʿAbd al-Ḥayy al-Kattānī al-Fāsī from whose knowledge of hadith Shaykh Bakhīt quotes, and based on whose opinion he attempts to make his argument (*iḥtajja bihi*)? He is Shaykh al-Kattānī al-Maghribī who passed through Cairo last year. *Al-Raḥma al-Mursala* is his book in which he tries to claim that the hadith about the *basmala* is sound (*ḥasan*) . . . And Shaykh Bakhīt has made him into a *ḥāfiẓ* [an honorific title given to the senior-most hadith scholars] so that he may use him to argue his points. And there is no honor for him in [doing] that, for the one he deems one of the *ḥuffāẓ* [plural of *ḥāfiẓ*] does not even know the sciences of hadith.[63]

Clearly the animosity shown here by Riḍā to a man he may never have met makes clear that Riḍā, too, understands the contours of the alliances at work

[62] Bakhīt al-Muṭīʿī, "Izāḥat al-Wahm," 35.
[63] Riḍā, "Bāb al-Murāsala wa-l-Munāẓara," 699.

and is seeking to cast doubt on al-Kattānī's credentials as a proxy for his ongoing battle with Bakhīt.

As the relationship between Bakhīt and al-Kattānī, and indeed al-Ghumāri, whom we encountered earlier, indicates, the alliance formed among "traditionalists" of various stripes transcended the conventional dividing lines of the historic Sunni schools. In my own treatment over the next few chapters, however, I focus on Bakhīt's invocation and appropriation of other Ḥanafīs in accordance with the ethos of the "social *madhhab*." The figure whose specter lurks most prominently in the *Irshād Ahl al-Milla* is al-Marjānī. Though he is not officially credited there, his appearance in the earlier debate indicates that he was very much on Bakhīt's mind, and a key influence on his thinking in the *Irshād*. However, Bakhīt also drew on other nineteenth-century Ḥanafīs like the prolific Indian scholar ʿAbd al-Ḥayy al-Laknawī (d. 1887) and the famous Iraqi exegete Shihāb al-Dīn al-Ālūsī (d. 1854). Each of these figures, though they continued to identify as Ḥanafīs, departed on some key points from the prevailing expression of the school. Bakhīt, often remembered as one of the most erudite scholars at the Azhar, expertly brought these departures together into a system that allowed him to speak to the challenges of his time and place. The transregional impact of ʿAbduh's and Riḍā's thought has been noted in recent works as an important feature of twentieth-century Reformism.[64] A key finding of this book is that transregionalism was just as important a feature of how "traditionalists" constituted themselves. The Ḥanafī school, long a global entity with a variety of regional subtraditions, functioned in the hands of Bakhīt as a transregional network of recent authorities, on whom he could draw to address particular deficiencies within the prevailing expression of Ḥanafism, while maintaining his authority by continuing to distinguish himself from Reformists.

[64] Amal N. Ghazal, *Islamic Reform and Arab Nationalism: Expanding the Crescent from the Mediterranean to the Indian Ocean (1880s–1930s)* (London: Routledge, 2010), 44, 94–95; Orit Bashkin, "The Iraqi Afghanis and ʿAbduhs: Debate over Reform among Shiʿite and Sunni ʿUlamaʾ in Interwar Iraq," in *Guardians of Faith in Modern Times: ʿUlamaʾ in the Middle East*, ed. Meir Hatina (Leiden: Brill, 2008), 141–70; R. Michael Feener, *Muslim Legal Thought in Modern Indonesia* (Cambridge, UK: Cambridge University Press, 2007); Roman Loimeier, *Islamic Reform in Twentieth-Century Africa* (Edinburgh: Edinburgh University Press, 2018), 75; Zvi Ben-Dor Benite, "Taking ʿAbduh to China: Chinese-Egyptian Intellectual Contact in the Early Twentieth Century," in *Global Muslims in the Age of Steam and Print*, ed. James L. Gelvin and Nile Green (Berkeley: University of California Press, 2014), 249–67. Riḍā's encounter with Deobandi "traditionalism" is discussed in Muhammad Qasim Zaman, *Modern Islamic Thought in a Radical Age: Religious Authority and Internal Criticism* (Cambridge, UK: Cambridge University Press, 2012), 76–86.

Conclusion

In a curious comment, al-Ghumārī observes that, during his stay in Egypt, many students at the Azhar expressed to him that they believed Bakhīt to be over one hundred years old. This is highly unlikely, but it may well reveal something about how Bakhīt was perceived at a time of rapid and drastic change: outdated and belonging to a bygone age. Al-Ghumārī also writes that he considered Bakhīt "a wonder of his time, rather, a scholar of the top rank [like] the ancient imams of the fourth and fifth centuries."[65] Intended as a mark of his accomplishment, the compliment nonetheless strikes a particular note at a time in which Riḍā and Shākir took pride in their association with attempts to introduce the "new sciences" into school curricula.[66]

This perception, though clearly exaggerated, was not altogether without merit. Bakhīt did in fact belong to a culture of scholarship and scholarly authority that he felt was being rivaled and indeed surpassed by a new intellectual and social regime. As we have seen in this chapter, this state of affairs resulted in an atmosphere of partisanship and territorialism that heavily conditioned his thinking. In supporting his arguments, Bakhīt revived key historical episodes to make sense of this state of affairs. He also drew on the resources of a facet of the Ḥanafī *madhhab* to embed himself within a network of belonging. It is precisely this network of belonging that afforded him an opportunity to both preserve his authoritative bona fides and innovate, sometimes rather radically, by reference to senior members of the *madhhab* itself.

[65] Al-Ghumārī, *al-Baḥr al-ʿAmīq*, 1:196.
[66] Riḍā, *al-Manār wa-l-Azhar*, 139, 141; Shākir, *Min Aʿlām al-ʿAṣr*, 14.

2

Authority, *Ijtihād*, and Temporality

Somewhere in Cairo in the waning days of the twentieth century, a *shaykh* met a *shābb*. The *shaykh* was a preacher and venerable teacher at the Azhar, having been reared in its circles of classical Islamic learning. The young man, however, belonged to a new generation that had been trained in both the modern and religious sciences. Through his earnest diligence, he had become a man of wealth and prestige, markers of status that impressed the *shaykh*, signaling to him that his conversation partner was a worthy interlocutor. Immediately upon encountering the young man that day, however, the *shaykh* noticed in him signs of worry and a deep sadness, as if he had been afflicted by some great distress. This was perplexing because the *shaykh* knew the *shābb* to be a man not just of means but also of good health and pious character. Evidently, the two were already well acquainted, but the *shaykh*'s inquiry into the young man's state that day would lead to a dozen more meetings, methodical and wide-ranging discussions, in which each explored and elaborated on their respective religious and intellectual views.

Though they were known to one another, the identities of the debating parties are a mystery to us. We owe our knowledge of their extended conversation only to the fact that it appears in issues of Rashīd Riḍā's journal *al-Manār* spanning a roughly year-long period from December 1900 to February 1902.[1] Riḍā chose to anonymize the two men, referring to them instead as the conformist (*muqallid*) and the reformer (*muṣliḥ*). Asked directly by a regular correspondent whether the dialogue was a fictional account or a

[1] The installments in *al-Manār* appeared irregularly as a series in the following issues: *al-Manār* 3, no. 28 (December 7, 1900): 635–43; 3, no. 29 (December 23, 1900): 675–83; 3, no. 30 (January 7, 1901): 715–28; 3, no. 32 (February 6, 1901): 795–804; 4, no. 2 (March 7, 1901): 51–60; 4, no. 5 (May 5, 1901): 161–70; 4, no. 6 (May 18, 1901): 205–17; 4, no. 8 (June 18, 1901): 281–97; 4, no. 10 (July 17, 1901): 361–71; 4, no. 14 (September 29, 1901): 521–29; 4, no. 15 (October 14, 1901): 567–73; 4, no. 18 (November 28, 1901): 692–702; and 4, no. 22 (February 9, 1902): 852–66. They were subsequently gathered together in one volume (with a short preface by the author, also published in the journal) in 1906 as Muḥammad Rashīd Riḍā, *Muḥāwarāt al-Muṣliḥ wa-l-Muqallid wa-l-Waḥda al-Islāmiyya* (Cairo: Maṭbaʿat Majallat al-Manār al-Islāmiyya, 1324H). My references are to the most recent edition of the collection, which contains a short biography by the author's grandson. Muḥammad Rashīd Riḍā, *Muḥāwarāt al-Muṣliḥ wa-l-Muqallid wa-l-Waḥda al-Islāmiyya* (Cairo: Dār al-Nashr, 2008).

Transformations of Tradition. Junaid Quadri, Oxford University Press (2021). © Oxford University Press.
DOI: 10.1093/oso/9780190077044.003.0003

faithful transcription of a real conversation, Riḍā played coy, insisting that it made no difference because the point of publishing the discussion was not to convince people to take sides based on individual personalities, but rather to unpack and examine their respective arguments so that readers could come to know the truth on its merits.[2]

There are, however, good reasons to think the reformer (*muṣliḥ*) was either Riḍā himself or a character in whose mouth Riḍā placed his own views. In addition to the detail with which he "recounts" the dialogue, the clearest indication is that Riḍā explicitly envisioned his life's work as advancing the reform (*iṣlāḥ*) project inaugurated by Jamāl al-Dīn al-Afghānī and Muḥammad ʿAbduh, a congruence in vocabulary too obvious to be a mere coincidence.[3] Secondly, despite the stated objective of a neutral airing and exchange of ideas, it is the *muṣliḥ* who clearly puts forth the most compelling and considered arguments, and the *muqallid* who is on the defensive throughout. For three of the sessions, the conformist is joined by another *muqallid*, a judge from his hometown visiting his old classmate from the Azhar. The nature of the two elders' reservations against their younger colleague's arguments betrays their indebtedness to an older way of thinking, a product of the Azharī curriculum in which they were trained. The *muṣliḥ*'s responses, however, reveal not only a facility with "your Azharī books"[4] reminiscent of Riḍā's own critical mastery of classical texts but also a general suspicion of the scholarly establishment that is a hallmark of his reformism.[5] Too, the description of the reformer as being acquainted with both the religious and modern sciences parallels the way Riḍā would later describe his influential teacher in Tripoli, Ḥusayn al-Jisr, himself an Azhar-trained scholar who had impressed upon Riḍā his deep conviction that "the Islamic *umma* would not advance or be reformed except by combining the religious and

[2] *Al-Manār* 4, no. 11 (August 16, 1901): 429–30. For a more complete justification of why Riḍā chose to preserve the anonymity of some of the writers and others who appear in pages of *al-Manār*, see 4, no. 2 (March 7, 1901): 67–68. It appears that teachers and civil servants were prohibited from writing in journals. Others chose to conceal their names either for the reason given above (i.e., fear that their positions would be dismissed based on their known leanings and orientations) or because journals were not a valued medium of scholarship.

[3] Although Riḍā certainly did position himself in this way, recent scholarship has cast doubt on the straight-forwardness of this stated genealogy. See Mohamed Haddad, "ʿAbduh et ses Lecteurs: Pour une Histoire Critique des 'Lectures' de M. ʿAbduh," *Arabica* 45, no. 1 (1998): 22–49.

[4] *Al-Manār* 4, no. 10 (July 17, 1901): 363.

[5] Riḍā's most direct and sustained critique can be found in Rashīd Riḍā, *al-Manār wa-l-Azhar* (Cairo: Maṭbaʿat al-Manār, 1353H), published late in his life, but it is a regular theme of the journal itself dating as far back as the very first year of its publication. See *al-Manār* 1, no. 42: 822–26. The Gregorian date listed in the issue I looked at seems to be incorrect, but the Hijrī date is Shaʿbān 24, 1316, which corresponds to January 7, 1899.

worldly sciences in the manner of modern Europe."[6] Al-Jisr's stress on the importance of the "modern sciences" (*al-ʿulūm al-ʿaṣriyya*) made a lasting impression on Riḍā, and their absence from the Azharī curriculum was a central part of his critique.[7]

Notable also is the reformer's self-description as a "human," by which he means "a social creature who perceives himself to be a member of the *umma* (the Muslim nation), and is therefore pleased at its good fortune and distressed at its misfortune."[8] This captures in one rather succinct self-description Riḍā's emphasis on pan-Islamic unity (*al-waḥda al-islāmiyya*), an identitarian allegiance he is at pains to contrast with the prevailing Azharī focus on Egypt and the Egyptian state. In an earlier dialogue Riḍā had staged between another "human" and another Azharī *shaykh*, the latter had identified government as the necessary ingredient for rectifying Islam and restoring it to its proper place, with the human responding that when he speaks of reform, the jurisdiction he has in mind is that of the *umma*, not the administrative and political concerns of the state.[9] Toward the end of his life, too, Riḍā lamented both the absence of Azharī names from a list of exceptional scholars that spanned the rest of the Muslim world, and the Egypt-centrism that caused the prominence of those scholars to be all but unknown in Egypt.[10] It is the preoccupation with the *umma* shared by Riḍā and the *muṣliḥ*, in fact, that is given as the reason for the sadness the conformist noticed in the reformer at the outset of their first meeting: "I see that my *umma* is the most wretched and miserable of nations. How, then, can I be happy and content in an *umma* whose situation is one of disappointment and failure, and which is a cautionary example?"[11]

Key to Riḍā's diagnosis of the *umma*'s ills was the position that it had been ravaged by the disease of *taqlīd*, the conformism he had attributed to the *muqallid-shaykh*. *Taqlīd* was often used by Riḍā in a general manner to refer to the uncritical following of customary ways. When interrogated about the

[6] Riḍā, *al-Manār wa-l-Azhar*, 139. For Riḍā's approach to his autobiographical remarks, see Elizabeth Sirriyeh, "Rashid Rida's Autobiography of the Syrian Years, 1865–1897," *Arabic & Middle Eastern Literature* 3, no. 2 (July 1, 2000): 179–94.

[7] On Riḍā's criticism in this period of the Azharī attitude toward the modern sciences, see *al-Manār* 1, no. 42: 822–26. A little more than a year later, there were official measures taken to introduce them into the curriculum, but not without significant internal opposition. See *al-Manār* 3 (April 1, 1900): 79–84.

[8] Riḍā, *Muḥāwarāt*, 16.

[9] *Al-Manār* 1, no. 42: 825.

[10] Riḍā, *al-Manār wa-l-Azhar*, 7.

[11] Riḍā, *Muḥāwarāt*, 16.

appropriateness of anonymizing his discussion, for example, he responded by saying that the only ones who object to the practice are those who are unable to grasp the truth without relying on appeals to authority, and are thereby naturally constrained (*mafṭūr*) to *taqlīd*, having no intellectual discernment (*baṣīra*) of their own.[12] The term's best-known definition, however, was the one used by Islamic jurists for centuries: the acceptance of a legal opinion on the authority of another, without an examination of the latter's proof or argumentation.[13] Western scholarship has long considered the dominance of *taqlīd* to be a defining characteristic of later Islamic legal history. The monopoly of the "regime of *taqlīd*," as it came to be known, has been cast into serious doubt over the past few decades, but it was precisely the apparent hegemony of *taqlīd* that so agitated Riḍā, and that he took as the main target of his critique.[14] The defining institution of this settled period of Islamic law was the *madhhab*, the legal school that regulated and directed legal interpretation in a manner that demanded loyalty to, or at least serious engagement with, the accumulated thought of past authorities and texts.[15] In the Sunni world, four orthodox schools had structured and dominated the practice and teaching of Islamic law for centuries. So it comes as little surprise that for

[12] *Al-Manār* 4, no. 11: 429. More commonly, this looser usage of the term took the plural form, *taqālīd*. See, for example, Riḍā, *Muḥāwarāt*, 15.

[13] "Taqlīd," in *al-Mawsūʿa al-Fiqhiyya* (Kuwait: Wizārat al-Awqāf wa-l-Shuʾūn al-Islāmiyya, 1988), 13:154–68; ʿAlī b. Muḥammad al-Sharīf al-Jurjānī, *al-Taʿrīfāt* (Beirut: Maktabat Lubnān, 1985), 58.

[14] For the conventional account of the postformative transition to a "regime of *taqlīd*" (i.e., "the unquestioning acceptance of the doctrines of the established schools and authorities"), see Joseph Schacht, *An Introduction to Islamic Law* (Oxford: Clarendon Press, 1982), 69–75. This narrative has been challenged most prominently by Wael B. Hallaq, "Was the Gate of Ijtihad Closed?," *International Journal of Middle East Studies* 16, no. 1 (March 1, 1984): 3–41. See also, for alternative readings of the "regime of *taqlīd*," Mohammad Fadel, "The Social Logic of Taqlīd and the Rise of the Mukhtaṣar," *Islamic Law and Society* 3, no. 2 (January 1, 1996): 193–233; Sherman A. Jackson, "Taqlīd, Legal Scaffolding and the Scope of Legal Injunctions in Post-Formative Theory Muṭlaq and ʿĀmm in the Jurisprudence of Shihāb al-Dīn al-Qarāfī," *Islamic Law and Society* 3, no. 2 (January 1, 1996): 165–92; Wael B. Hallaq, *Authority, Continuity, and Change in Islamic Law* (Cambridge, UK: Cambridge University Press, 2001), chap. 4; Ahmed El Shamsy, "Rethinking Taqlīd in the Early Shāfiʿī School," *Journal of the American Oriental Society* 128, no. 1 (January 2008): 1–23; and Ahmed Fekry Ibrahim, "Rethinking the *Taqlīd* Hegemony: An Institutional, *Longue-Durée* Approach," *Journal of the American Oriental Society* 136, no. 4 (2016): 801–16.

[15] Norman Calder, "Al-Nawawī's Typology of Muftīs and Its Significance for a General Theory of Islamic Law," *Islamic Law and Society* 3, no. 2 (January 1, 1996): 137–64; Norman Calder, "The 'Uqūd Rasm Al-Muftī' of Ibn ʿĀbidīn," *Bulletin of the School of Oriental and African Studies, University of London* 63, no. 2 (January 1, 2000): 215–28; Brannon M. Wheeler, *Applying the Canon in Islam: The Authorization and Maintenance of Interpretive Reasoning in Ḥanafī Scholarship* (Albany: State University of New York Press, 1996); Eyyup Said Kaya, "Continuity and Change in Islamic Law: The Concept of Madhhab and the Dimensions of Legal Disagreement in Hanafi Scholarship of the Tenth Century," in *The Islamic School of Law: Evolution, Devolution, and Progress*, ed. Peri J. Bearman, Rudolph Peters, and Frank E. Vogel (Cambridge, MA: Harvard University Press, 2005); Hallaq, *Authority, Continuity, and Change in Islamic Law.*

Riḍā's reformer, frustrated with the state of Muslim thought and power, reform was nothing short of "the abolition (*ibṭāl*) of the *madhhabs*." This is what would "put the Muslims on a single path, as was the case at the origin of Islam."[16]

Riḍā conceived his call to abolish the *madhhabs* as an act of creative destruction. It would indeed dismantle the complex and intricate edifice that had been painstakingly assembled in the commentaries and glosses that virtually defined the legal schools, and therefore the historical shariʿa itself. In its place, however, Riḍā imagined the emergence of a new approach to the law, one that both restored Muslims to the simplicity (*basāṭa*) of the early period of Islam and freed them to provide fresh interpretations suitable for a modern age. The rallying cry of this new approach was the assertion of *ijtihād*, the historical complement to *taqlīd*.[17] Because *ijtihād* implied not trust in a higher authority, but rather referred to "the exertion of effort to arrive at a legal ruling via an encounter with the foundational sources," the points of reference for this new approach were not the texts of the *madhhab*, but the Qur'an, the Sunna, and the example of the "pious predecessors" (*al-salaf al-ṣāliḥ*).[18] It is these sources that embodied the authoritative "origin of Islam" that Riḍā so insistently emphasized throughout his oeuvre as the touchstone for modern Muslim thinking. For Riḍā, the medieval hair-splitting and jargon-laden discourse of the developed schools of law must give way to the clear Arabic of the foundational texts, which incidentally

[16] Riḍā, *Muḥāwarāt*, 19.

[17] Aharon Layish offers a particularly concise and straight-forward account of Modernists' attitude toward *ijtihād* and *taqlīd*: "The keystone of modernism was that the gates of the *ijtihād* should be reopened, i.e., that a free, rationalistic approach to the sources of the religious law—the Qur'ān and the *sunna*—should be enabled in order to adapt it to the requirements of the time. This demand comprised two proposals, a negative one and a positive one. The modernists wished to get rid of the oppressive burden of the *taqlīd*; the selection within this narrow framework did not satisfy them. They also wished to restrict the validity of the *ijmāʿ*, the infallible consensus, by means of which the gates of the *ijtihād* had been closed. . . . The positive proposal consisted in the mechanism of the new *ijtihād*, which in several material respects was different from the traditional one." Aharon Layish, "The Contribution of the Modernists to the Secularization of Islamic Law," *Middle Eastern Studies* 14, no. 3 (October 1, 1978): 264–65.

[18] Riḍā, *Muḥāwarāt*, 15. This is, of course, why the term *salafi* is applied to them. Henri Laoust, "Le Réformisme Orthodoxe des Salafiyyah et les Caractères Généraux de son Orientation Actuelle," *Revue Des Études Islamiques* 6 (1932): 175–224. For a critical reading of the appropriateness of this term, see Henri Lauzière, "The Construction of Salafiyya: Reconsidering Salafism from the Perspective of Conceptual History," *International Journal of Middle East Studies* 42, no. 3 (2010): 369–89. For a spirited back and forth between Lauzière and Frank Griffel, see Frank Griffel, "What Do We Mean By 'Salafi'? Connecting Muḥammad ʿAbduh with Egypt's Nūr Party in Islam's Contemporary Intellectual History," *Die Welt des Islams* 55, no. 2 (June 2015): 186–220; Henri Lauzière, "What We Mean Versus What They Meant by 'Salafi': A Reply to Frank Griffel," *Die Welt des Islams* 56, no. 1 (April 19, 2016): 89–96; Frank Griffel, "What Is the Task of the Intellectual (Contemporary) Historian?—A Response to Henri Lauzière's 'Reply,'" *Die Welt des Islams* 56, no. 2 (June 2016): 249–55.

themselves disparage *taqlīd*.[19] Far from having to rely on specialized texts, all Muslims can easily come to know the beliefs, morality, ethics, necessary (*ḍarūrī*) elements of ritual practice, and central principles of interpersonal conduct (*muʿāmalāt*) required of them through unmediated access to the Qurʾan and Sunna.[20] These are all relatively simple matters, easily accessed, and do not require the intricate interpretive efforts that characterized the intellectual work of medieval ulama.

Grouping their rulings with the overly speculative interventions of medieval philosophers and theologians, and the theosophical and ascetic excesses of medieval Sufism, Riḍā excludes from the essential elements of ritual practice any matter on which there is disagreement among jurists. In the case of the *muʿāmalāt*, he lists only general principles of interpersonal conduct: justice; equal rights; the outlawing of rebellion, aggression, deceit, and treachery; and punishments fixed by the foundational texts (*ḥudūd*).[21] Details on how to implement these rather abstract rules should be left to the judgment of rulers, leaders, and scholars who must consult among themselves to arrive at rulings that are most consonant with the social welfare (*maṣlaḥa*) of the community, especially in light of the exigencies of the time in which they find themselves. Scholars have pointed out that this formulation, in accounting for changing circumstances, both provides room for creative solutions and amounts to a theory of natural law or a case of "religious utilitarianism" which prioritizes the exigencies of the time over even textual considerations in the sunna.[22]

Above all, it is this Modernist emphasis on *ijtihād* that has caused Egypt in the late nineteenth and early twentieth centuries to be a context of extensive and sustained interest to specialists of Islamic studies, concerned about Islam's capacity to "keep up with the times"[23] and intrigued by the Reformist call to loosen the interpretive monopoly held by the class of ulama.[24] Keenly

19 Riḍā, *Muḥāwarāt*, 55–57.

20 Riḍā, *Muḥāwarāt*, 63, 68–69. This parallels al-Ghazālī's *al-Qisṭās al-Mustaqīm*, which Riḍā discusses approvingly in *al-Manār* 4, no. 9 (June 18, 1901): 314.

21 A slightly different listing is given in Muḥammad Rashīd Riḍā, *Al-Khilāfa aw al-Imāma al-ʿUẓmā* (Cairo: Maṭbaʿat al-Manār, 1923). See also Malcolm Kerr, *Islamic Reform: The Political and Legal Theories of Muḥammad ʿAbduh and Rashīd Riḍā* (Berkeley: University of California Press, 1966), 188–89.

22 Kerr, *Islamic Reform: The Political and Legal Theories of Muḥammad ʿAbduh and Rashīd Riḍā*, 201–2; Wael B. Hallaq, *A History of Islamic Legal Theories: An Introduction to Sunnī Uṣūl al-Fiqh* (New York: Cambridge University Press, 1997), 214ff; Felicitas Opwis, "Maṣlaḥa in Contemporary Islamic Legal Theory," *Islamic Law and Society* 12, no. 2 (2005): 182–223.

23 For this language, see Joseph Schacht's EI2 entry on ʿAbduh.

24 A representative but partial list includes the following: Charles Adams, *Islam and Modernism in Egypt: A Study of the Modern Reform Movement Inaugurated by Muḥammad ʿAbduh*

aware of the ways in which Modernist Reformists positioned themselves against partisans of *taqlīd*, Western scholars have often celebrated their efforts at reinvigorating *ijtihād*, even as they have worried about their precarity at the hands of their opponents.[25] While the centrality of the *ijtihād/taqlīd* debate to the rivalry between Reformists and "traditional" ulama has long been recognized, the historiography of the period has struggled to understand this latter group as anything more than idealized foils against which to view Reformists' efforts to displace their monopoly on interpretation.[26] The dominance of this depiction is partly a result of the relative lack of attention paid to the works of ulama themselves, but Indira Falk Gesink has pointed out that it is also due to the impact of the prodigious output of reformers like ʿAbduh and Riḍā, whose views of their avowed opponents have passed unchallenged into "authoritative scholarly tradition" for reasons of accessibility and conceptual alignment and convergence.[27] These scholarly tendencies have served to reaffirm the characterization of ulama as conservative and reactionary, very often as marked by their opposition to *ijtihād*, the legal

(London: Oxford University Press, 1933); H. A. R. Gibb, *Modern Trends in Islam* (Chicago: University of Chicago Press, 1947); Ignác Goldziher, *Die Richtungen der islamischen Koranauslegung* (Leiden: E.J. Brill, 1970); Henri Laoust, "Le Réformisme Orthodoxe Des Salafiyyah et Les Caractères Généraux de Son Orientation Actuelle," *Revue Des Études Islamiques* 6 (1932): 175–224; Jacques Jomier, *Le Commentaire Coranique Du Manâr: Tendances Modernes de l'Exégèse Coranique En Égypte* (Paris: G.-P. Maisonneuve, 1954); Malcolm Kerr, *Islamic Reform: The Political and Legal Theories of Muḥammad ʿAbduh and Rashīd Riḍā* (Berkeley: University of California Press, 1966); Elie Kedourie, *Afghani and ʿAbduh: An Essay on Religious Unbelief and Political Activism in Modern Islam* (New York: Humanities Press, 1966); Nikki R. Keddie, *Sayyid Jamāl ad-Dīn "Al-Afghānī": A Political Biography* (Berkeley: University of California Press, 1972); H. Gibb, *Whither Islam?: A Survey of Modern Movements in the Moslem World* (London: V. Gollancz, 1932); Fazlur Rahman, "Internal Religious Developments in the Present Century Islam," *Cahiers d'histoire Mondiale/Journal of World History* 2 (1955): 862–79; Hisham Sharabi, *Arab Intellectuals and the West: The Formative Years, 1875–1914* (Baltimore: Johns Hopkins Press, 1970); Albert Hourani, *Arabic Thought in the Liberal Age, 1798–1939* (London: Oxford University Press, 1970).

[25] For a clear example of these two sentiments, see Schacht's entry on ʿAbduh, *EI2*, 419. "Deeply convinced of the superiority of true Islam, unaffected by the vicissitudes of time, Muḥammad ʿAbduh wished to get rid of the abuses which falsified the Muslim religion and made it out of keeping with the times, and to adapt Islam to every real advance by going back to its true principles. He was thus brought to attack the *madhāhib* and *taḳlīd*, to demand the restoration of *ijtihād* and a new *idjmā*ʿ in keeping with modern conditions, based on the Kur'ān and the true *sunna*, for the establishment of which he laid down strict criteria; he was also brought to reject the hairsplitting of the *fuḳahā*', the worship of saints and all *bidʿa*, and to the endeavour to create a more ethical and deeper religion instead of a mechanical formalism" and "The advanced ideas put forward by Muḥammad ʿAbduh provoked the most vigorous hostility in orthodox and conservative circles, which manifested itself not only in serious refutations but also in attacks and intrigues against him, as we see from a whole literature of lampoons."

[26] An important exception to this is Indira Falk Gesink, *Islamic Reform and Conservatism: Al-Azhar and the Evolution of Modern Sunnī Islam* (London: Tauris Academic Studies, 2010).

[27] Gesink, "Beyond Modernisms: Opposition and Negotiation in the Azhar Reform Debate in Egypt, 1870–1911" (PhD diss., Washington University in St. Louis, 2000), 38.

instrument usually invoked by scholarship as a barometer of jurists' willingness to accept change within the shariʿa.

In contrast, this chapter makes the argument that the Reformist emphasis on *ijtihād* found its way into the discourse of their "traditionalist" opponents in Egypt. Taking Bakhīt as an example of this turn, I examine the appendix (*khātima*) to his *Irshād Ahl al-Milla ilā Ithbāt al-Ahilla* to explore its reconceptualization of juristic authority structures, the arguments it advances for the legitimacy of that reconceptualization, and the background epistemological commitments that underpin those arguments. The catalyst for Bakhīt's arguments was the competition between him and reformists in Egypt that we have already seen to have structured his mature career. There is little doubt that Bakhīt's interest in valorizing *ijtihād* was largely motivated by the need to keep up with the ascendancy of Reformist discourse and to regain a foothold on an intellectual ground quickly shifting under him. Yet, in making his case, he was careful not to draw on the sweeping language of the Reformists, but rather on key trends within modern Ḥanafism. In contrast to Riḍā, then, who expressly advocated abolishing the *madhhabs*, it is the Ḥanafī school itself that remained the primary point of reference for Bakhīt. Adopting this tack allowed Bakhīt to assert his authority vis-à-vis that of the Reformists in a manner that emphasized both his distance from them and his belonging to an authoritative and widely acknowledged tradition of interpretation that continued to resonate within an Egypt where it remained the official legal school.[28] This was a savvy strategic move that allowed him to buttress his own standing by capitalizing on both the growing clamor from proponents of *ijtihād* and the enduring affective and institutional bonds among Ḥanafīs. In doing so, Bakhīt not only added his voice to the increasing acceptance of *ijtihād* but also effectively entrenched that acceptance by couching it within the familiar language and venerable authority of Ḥanafism. This, however, was not an intellectual move that came without any deeper intellectual effects. On the contrary, I argue in this chapter that Bakhīt's mode of argumentation reveals his adoption of an entirely new temporality, a historical consciousness that upended the traditional manner of understanding the nature of the *madhhab*'s authority.

Our primary approach will be a careful—and at times, quite technical—study of the textual record, and in particular the argumentative moves

[28] Rudolph Peters, "Muḥammad al-ʿAbbāsī al-Mahdī (d. 1897), Grand Muftī of Egypt, and His 'al-Fatāwā al-Mahdiyya,'" *Islamic Law and Society* 1, no. 1 (January 1, 1994): 66–82.

adopted by the late nineteenth- and early twentieth-century writers—both Reformists and "traditionalists"—with whom we are concerned. These intellectual shifts, however, cannot be understood independent of the social background which at once grounded, enabled, and gave meaning to these contributions. Indeed, the ascendancy of print culture and the creation of new publics mentioned in the last chapter were prime motivators in Bakhīt's affirmation of *ijtihād* and the emergence among the ulama of a historical consciousness toward the prevailing Ḥanafī tradition with which Bakhīt and his associates identified.

The Prevailing Tradition: The Egyptian Context

Bakhīt's rethinking of *ijtihād* finds its immediate roots in the 1906 debate with Riḍā we examined in the last chapter. Bakhīt's introductory encomium to his fatwa on insurance, which had sparked the heated debate, had made use of the word *istinbāṭ*, a term that was often used as a synonym for *ijtihād* in the pointed sense of deriving rulings directly from the foundational proof-texts.[29] The introduction praised God for "granting to those of His servants whom He wills [the capacity for] deducing (*istinbāṭ*) rulings from correct sources. He did not restrict it [*istinbāṭ*] to one era over another; rather, He made it perpetual, enduring as long as the moon does."[30]

This phrasing struck Riḍā, accustomed to critiquing Azharī traditionalists for their opposition to *ijtihād* and their blind adherence to *taqlīd*, as an audacious claim for such a high-ranking member of the ulama. Seizing on the opportunity to drive home the central point of the Reformist project, Riḍā drew attention to Bakhīt's choice of wording:

> We were delighted that the shaykh called his opinion an *istinbāṭ* . . . for this confirms that *ijtihād* is permissible in our day, in opposition to what is said in the books of his *madhhab* about the closing of the gate [of *ijtihād*], and the extinction of those endowed with [the capacity to undertake] it.[31]

[29] For Riḍā's use of *istinbāṭ* in this manner in the discussions between the reformer and the conformist, see *Muḥāwarāt*, 71.
[30] Muḥammad Bakhīt al-Muṭīʿī, "Fī Aḥkām al-Sūkūrtāh," in *Thalātha Rasāʾil* (Cairo: Jamʿiyyat al-Azhar al-ʿIlmiyya, 1932), 11.
[31] Muḥammad Rashīd Riḍā, "Risālatān fī Qirāʾat al-Fūnūghrāf wa-l-Sukūrtah," *Al-Manār* 9, no. 2 (1906): 154.The closing of the gate of *ijtihād* was a central theme of western scholarship on Islamic law. See Schacht, *An Introduction to Islamic Law*, 70–71. For an influential critique of this trope, see Hallaq, "Was the Gate of Ijtihad Closed?," March 1, 1984.

In response, however, Bakhīt held his ground, insisting that no ulama have ever claimed what Riḍā attributes to them.

> And we say in response that nowhere in all the world has even one of the *madhhab*ic ulama in general, and especially not any of the ulama of the four [Sunni] *madhhab*s,[32] claimed that the gate of *ijtihād* was closed or that those endowed with [the ability to undertake it] died out. Whoever consults the works of *uṣūl* (legal theory) or *furū*ʿ (substantive law), especially those of the Ḥanafī school . . . will find them definitively contradicting what this objector says. This is a claim which can only issue from his lack of understanding of their words.[33]

This is a remarkable claim for an opponent of the Reformists, no less for its decided tone than for its content.[34] The reader of the debate is left with the clear sense that the straightforward way in which Bakhīt states this opinion has caught Riḍā off guard, for despite leading his initial critique with this comment, he does not broach it again in any of the later installments of the debate. The audacity of Bakhīt's position is all the more revealing, however, when we place his strong affirmation of *ijtihād* in the context of the severe critiques launched by previous generations of traditionalist scholars against the disruptive consequences of questioning the prevailing authority structures.

Consider, for example, the case of Muḥammad ʿIllīsh (d. 1882), one of Bakhīt's teachers and the head of the Mālikī school in Egypt.[35] ʿIllīsh was remembered by Riḍā as one of ʿAbduh's most hostile opponents.[36] The two

[32] The Arabic is *ʿulamāʾ al-madhhab ʿalā wajh al-ʿumūm khuṣūṣan ʿulamāʾ al-madhāhib al-arbaʿa.*

[33] Muḥammad Bakhīt al-Muṭīʿī, "Izāḥat al-Wahm wa-l-Ishtibāh ʿan Risālatay al-Fūnūghrāf wa-l-Sūkūrtāh," in *Thalātha Rasāʾil* (Cairo: Jamʿiyyat al-Azhar al-ʿIlmiyya, 1932), 50–51.

[34] In his later writings, Bakhīt tempers this language, himself citing figures who argued that the gate of *ijtihād* had closed.

[35] For a detailed examination of ʿIllīsh's life and works, see Gilbert Delanoue, *Moralistes et Politiques Musulmans Dans l'Égypte Du XIXe Siècle (1798–1882)* (Paris: Institut français d'archéologie orientale du Caire, 1982), I:129–67; Gesink, *Islamic Reform and Conservatism*, 89–93. His name is vocalized in the sources in a variety of ways. Vikør suggests that ʿIllaysh is most appropriate since it is the "rendering given by the family itself," but Gesink has located a testimony from ʿIllīsh himself stating that "his name is spelled with a kasra on the ʿain and the lam." Knut Vikør, *Sufi and Scholar on the Desert Edge: Muḥammad b. ʿAlī al-Sanūsī and His Brotherhood* (Evanston, IL: Northwestern University Press, 1995), 250n23. Gesink, *Islamic Reform and Conservatism*, 253n1.

[36] The rivalry between the two was a heated but peculiar one, with ʿAbduh accusing ʿIllīsh of everything from sabotaging his career aspirations to plotting to poison rival scholars. See Gesink, *Islamic Reform and Conservatism*, 93–96; and Reinhard Schulze, *Islamischer Internationalismus Im 20. Jahrhundert: Untersuchungen Zur Geschichte Der Islamischen Weltliga* (Leiden: Brill, 1990), 26n36.

had a rivalry which dated to the enterprising young ʿAbduh's days as a student at the Azhar. It is one famous incident involving the two that Riḍā remembered as the turning point after which some of the scholarly establishment—Riḍā refers to them as the *jāmidīn*, or "the ossified" conservatives—focused their critical attention more intently on the ideas of ʿAbduh and his teacher al-Afghānī.[37] ʿIllīsh had come to know of informal circles of learning led by ʿAbduh at the neighboring Muḥammad Bey Abū al-Dhahab mosque. There, just outside the walls of the august seat of ancient learning, a growing number of students from the Azhar had taken to studying books outside of the standard curriculum in a pedagogical format that stressed conversation and discussion over didactic lectures. ʿIllīsh sent one of his sons and another student to the study circle on a reconnaissance mission, and they reported back that participants were covering the advanced theology text, *Sharḥ al-ʿAqāʾid al-Nasafiyya*, and that ʿAbduh had preferred the Muʿtazilī school of theology to orthodox Ashʿarism. Disturbed by this news, ʿIllīsh sent for ʿAbduh, who paid him a visit while the elder scholar was teaching at the mosque of al-Ḥusayn, revered for housing a shrine believed to be the burial place of the severed head of the Prophet Muḥammad's grandson. Upon ʿAbduh's arrival, ʿIllish interrogated him about both his qualifications and his reported heterodoxy. In response, ʿAbduh stood his ground. He defiantly offered to be tested to prove his mastery of the text and carefully avoided the question of his Muʿtazilism, offering instead that he disavowed *taqlīd* of all theological schools and relied only on foundational evidences to arrive at his conclusions: "If I have abandoned *taqlīd* of the Ashʿarī, why then would I commit to *taqlīd* of the Muʿtazilī. I have, therefore, abandoned *taqlīd* of all, and adhere only to the evidence (*ākhidh bi-l-dalīl*)."[38] The students present at ʿIllīsh's class, unable to tolerate what they took to be the young ʿAbduh's impertinence toward their teacher, surrounded him and stripped him of his turban, sending him home bareheaded and humiliated. Rumors thereafter abounded that ʿIllīsh had prohibited ʿAbduh from leading classes, and even that he had beat him. In his telling of the episode, however, Riḍā concluded that neither of these claims was true, and that ʿAbduh continued teaching

[37] *Al-Manār* 8, no. 10 (July 19, 1905): 390–92; *Tārīkh al-Ustādh al-Imām*, 1:133–35. See also Gesink, *Islamic Reform and Conservatism*, 93–96. Adams, *Islam and Modernism in Egypt*, 42–43.

[38] In his telling of the story, Riḍā intimates, without saying outright, that ʿIllīsh's reporters were mistaken, and that ʿIllīsh was prone to "believing everything he heard." *Tārīkh*, 1:133. ʿAbduh too suggests that the reporters were unqualified to distinguish between the two schools. *Tārīkh*, 1:134.

at the Muḥammad Bey Abū al-Dhahab mosque, only now with a stick at his side in case ʿIllīsh ever came by with a staff of his own.

Later, when it came time for ʿAbduh to take the final oral exam for his degree, he suspected that ʿIllīsh had conspired with a number of other examiners to fail him. Upon witnessing the superior quality of his responses, however, the examination turned into a debate, before deteriorating into a partisan display of dissension and stubbornness. When it came time to settle on a grade, the famous Ḥanafī mufti al-ʿAbbāsī al-Mahdī, impressed by ʿAbduh's performance and evidently perturbed by ʿIllīsh's stubbornness, swore an oath that the examinee's responses merited better than even the highest grade available. In the face of the other examiners' obstinance, one of the other examiner-*shaykhs*, likely al-Rāfiʿī, arrived at a compromise by granting him a second-class pass.[39]

As is evident from their earliest run-in, a central element of what irked ʿIllīsh about ʿAbduh was his radical abandonment of the *taqlīd* of Azharite orthodoxy. In that case, it was the "blind following" of ancient theological schools that was at issue, but ʿIllīsh's most explicit and sustained defense of *taqlīd* stems from an earlier episode. The first half of the twentieth century had already witnessed the emergence of a family of Sufi orders who were strident critics of *taqlīd* and proponents of *ijtihād*. The progenitor of this trend, Aḥmad b. Idrīs (d. 1837), was a reformer hailing from a town near Fes who was concerned with both curbing Sufi excesses and in restoring the supremacy of foundational texts over the opinions of scholars.[40] Upon his death in Mecca, Aḥmad b. Idrīs's community splintered into a number of separate orders, the Mirghāniyya and the Sanūsiyya being the two best known. In his important work on Sufi orders, J. Spencer Trimingham notes that these "offshoots were independent *ṭarīqas*, making only cursory acknowledgement of their debt to Aḥmad ibn Idrīs, and consequently followed different lines in their teaching and exercises."[41] The leaders of both orders, however, held strongly to their *shaykh*'s emphasis on *ijtihād*. As a result of this position, each provoked strong responses from the Egyptian scholarly establishment. In 1817 or 1818, Ḥasan al-ʿAṭṭār, who would become the rector of the

[39] *Al-Manār* 8, no. 10: 392–93. Gesink, *Islamic Reform and Conservatism*, 95. Adams, *Islam and Modernism in Egypt*, 43.

[40] J. Spencer Trimingham, *The Sufi Orders in Islam* (Oxford: Clarendon Press, 1971), 114–16.For Aḥmad's opinions on the latter count, see the translation of his *Risālat al-Radd ʿalā Ahl al-Raʾy* in Bernd Radtke et al., *The Exoteric Ahmad Ibn Idris: A Sufi's Critique of the Madhahib and the Wahhabis: Four Arabic Texts with Translation and Commentary* (Leiden: Brill, 1999).

[41] Trimingham, *The Sufi Orders in Islam*, 116.

Azhar toward the end of his life, fielded a request for a fatwa from a resident of Sinnar in the Sudan, asking about an unnamed man who had assembled a group of devotees around him, claiming that anyone "who tread[s] the path, even if he is a [*sic*] uncivilized beduin, is a *mujtahid*."[42] The iconoclast being referred to was the founder of the Mirghāniyya, Muḥammad 'Uthmān al-Mirghānī, who had visited Sinnar upon being sent by Aḥmad b. Idrīs to establish a group of followers in Nilotic Sudan in 1816.[43] Al-'Aṭṭār responded firmly that the only proper course of action in these days was "*taqlīd* pure and simple, and rigorous adherence to the doctrine we have received from our predecessors and learned from our masters. . . . What is an obligation, for the community in our times, is to undertake *taqlīd* of one of the four *madhhabs*."[44]

The Azharite establishment was confronted by similar questions some twenty-five to thirty years later, this time in reference to the Sanūsiyya. In his compilation of fatwas, the staunch Mālikī 'Illīsh devotes considerable space to the movement headquartered in nearby Cyrenaica, having known al-Sanūsī from the latter's visit to Egypt in the mid-1820s. In addition to his own fatwa, he recruits the authority of his teacher, Muṣṭafā al-Būlāqī, who had issued a corroborating responsum earlier. The central methodological complaint lodged by al-Sanūsī (and for that matter Aḥmad b. Idrīs and al-Mirghānī) was captured in his succinct formulation: "I say to you, 'God says' and 'His messenger says'; and you say, 'Mālik or Ibn al-Qāsim or al-Khalīl says.'"[45] In other words, al-Sanūsī faulted the ulama for their excessive reliance on the central figures of the *madhhab* to the exclusion of the Qur'an

[42] Vikør, *Sufi and Scholar on the Desert Edge*, 244. On 'Aṭṭār, see Delanoue, *Moralistes et Politiques Musulmans Dans l'Égypte Du XIXe Siècle (1798–1882)*, II:344–57; Peter Gran, *Islamic Roots of Capitalism: Egypt, 1760–1840* (Austin: University of Texas Press, 1979).

[43] Vikør, *Sufi and Scholar on the Desert Edge*, 243. Gran and De Jong think the man referred to by the *mustaftī* is al-Sanūsī. Delanoue and Vikør's attribution to al-Mirghānī seems to be most compelling. On the Mirghāniyya, see Trimingham, *The Sufi Orders in Islam*, 116–18; Octave Depont and Xavier Coppolani, *Les Confréries Religieuses Musulmanes* (Alger: Jourdan, 1897), 542–44.

[44] Translated from Delanoue, *Moralistes et Politiques Musulmans Dans l'Égypte Du XIXe Siècle (1798–1882)*, II:350–51.

[45] Muḥammad 'Illīsh, *Fatḥ al-'Alī al-Mālik* (Cairo: Maṭba'at Muṣṭafā al-Bābī al-Ḥalabī, 1958), 89. For a similar sentiment from Aḥmad b. Idrīs, see Radtke et al., *The Exoteric Ahmad Ibn Idris*. For al-Mirghānī, see Vikør, *Sufi and Scholar on the Desert Edge*, 244. The text from al-Sanūsī that is most often relied upon by scholars is *Īqāẓ al-Wasnān fī al-'Amal bi-l-Ḥadīth wa-l-Qur'ān*, which can be found in Muḥammad ibn 'Alī al-Sanūsī, *al-Majmū'a al-Mukhtāra min Mu'allafāt Muḥammad ibn 'Alī al-Sanūsī* (Manchester, 1990). A version of this text can be found in manuscript form at the Egyptian National Library (*Dār al-Kutub*) under the name *Al-Tuḥfa al-Munīfa* under the call number *'ilm al-kalām*, 892.

and sunna.[46] In response, al-Būlāqī and ʿIllīsh were in agreement with al-ʿAṭṭār that *taqlīd* of one of the four schools is mandatory. For al-Būlāqī,

> commanding the people to follow the Book and the Sunna is truthful language used in the service of falsehood (*kalimat ḥaqq urīdu bihā bāṭil*). For, what is meant by it is the abandoning of the long-followed *madhhab*s and taking rulings directly from the Book and the Sunna, without any mediation. This is misguidance, and commanding it is the clearest evidence of ignorance.[47]

Similarly, for ʿIllīsh,

> It is not permissible for the layman (*al-ʿāmmī*) to abandon *taqlīd* of the four *madhhab*s and take rulings directly from the Qurʾan and hadith, for [the latter] has many conditions, explained in the *uṣūl*, which are not found in the great majority of ulama, especially at the end of time when Islam will revert to seeming strange just as it began.[48]

In contrast to Bakhīt, then, ʿIllīsh is much more pessimistic that *ijtihād*—in the sense of direct recourse to the foundational texts—is a possibility at this late stage of Islamic history. Al-Būlāqī is even more definitive: "It is known to everyone that the rank of *ijtihād* has come to an end (*qad inqaṭaʿat*) ages ago, and that there is no one in these times that has attained the rank of *ijtihād*. Whoever imagines otherwise, his soul laughs at him, and Satan mocks him."[49]

The unanimity with which Azharite scholars spoke on this question in the first half of the nineteenth century helps us both understand the extent of Bakhīt's departure and explain Riḍā's surprise that such a prominent member of the ulama should affirm *ijtihād* so confidently and unequivocally. To fully appreciate how radical this shift was, however, we must take a step back to consider not only individual Azharīs' stated positions on the question of

[46] Importantly, what is meant by sunna by reformers is the textual hadith record. Hadith, as we shall see later, comes to take on an increased importance in these discourses. ʿIllīsh, however, contests this definition of sunna, relying on the Mālikī notion of ʿamal, as well as a statement from a forerunner of the Ḥanafī school, al-Nakhaʿī. ʿIllīsh, *Fatḥ al-ʿAlī al-Mālik*, 90.

[47] ʿIllīsh, *Fatḥ al-ʿAlī al-Mālik*, 109. Al-Būlāqī's full fatwa is translated in Nicola Ziadeh, *Sanūsīyah: A Study of a Revivalist Movement in Islam* (Leiden: E.J. Brill, 1958), 40–44.

[48] ʿIllīsh, *Fatḥ al-ʿAlī al-Mālik*, 89–90. A translation of ʿIllīsh's fatwa can be found in Depont and Coppolani, *Les Confréries Religieuses Musulmanes*, 546–52. The last clause is a reference to a hadith.

[49] ʿIllīsh, *Fatḥ al-ʿAlī al-Mālik*, 110.

ijtihād and *taqlīd*, but the very conception of the *madhhab* and its history that underlay those determinations. For ʿIllīsh, this is captured vividly in a key passage of his fatwa in which he quotes at length from the influential sixteenth-century jurist and Sufi, ʿAbd al-Wahhāb al-Shaʿrānī (d. 1565).[50] In the chapter cited by ʿIllīsh, al-Shaʿrānī draws heavily on his own teachers, notably the illiterate mystic ʿAlī al-Khawwāṣ (d. 1532–3) and the famed Shāfiʿī chief qadi Zakariyyā al-Anṣārī (d. 1520), thereby forming a distinctly Egyptian genealogy to ʿIllīsh's understanding of the shariʿa and its historical unfolding, an understanding that stressed the organic compatibility of Sufism and *fiqh*.[51]

The chapter quoted by ʿIllīsh is intended by al-Shaʿrānī as a valorization of the *mujtahid* imams against some Sufis who doubted the jurists' ability to rule in accordance with hidden spiritual realities. In response, al-Shaʿrānī says he often heard al-Khawwāṣ maintaining that the imams of the madhhabs were "heirs (*wārithīn*) to the Prophet" in both esoteric and exoteric domains (*fī ʿilm al-aḥwāl wa-ʿilm al-aqwāl*).[52] Later, he turns to al-Anṣārī for help in explaining the crucial role played by the *mujtahids* in extracting or discovering (*istinbāṭ*) legal judgments embedded in the Qurʾan and Sunna. "I heard our *shaykh*, the *Shaykh al-Islām* Zakariyyā, may God the Exalted have mercy on him, saying, 'If it were not for the Messenger of God, peace be upon him, and the *mujtahid*s elucidating (*bayān*) what was concisely embedded (*mujmal*) in the Book and the Sunna, none of us would have been capable of doing so.'"[53] This, in turn, paves the way for a fuller statement of the history of Islamic law. Against those content to rely on the plain meaning (*ṣarīḥ*) of the Qurʾan and sunna, al-Shaʿrānī bases himself

[50] On al-Shaʿrānī, see Michael Winter, *Society and Religion in Early Ottoman Egypt: Studies in the Writings of ʿAbd al-Wahhāb al-Shaʿrānī* (New Brunswick, NJ: Transaction Books, 1982).

[51] On al-Khawwāṣ, see the articles by Geoffrey and Sabra in Richard McGregor, Adam Sabra, and Mireille Loubet, eds., *The Development of Sufism in Mamluk Egypt/La Développement Du Soufisme En Egypte à l'époque Mamelouke* (Cairo: Institut Français d'Archéologie Orientale, 2006). On al-Anṣārī, see Matthew B. Ingalls, "Subtle Innovation Within Networks of Convention: The Life, Thought, and Intellectual Legacy of Zakariyyā al-Anṣārī (d. 926/1520)" (PhD diss., Yale University, 2011). The chapter ʿIllīsh draws from can be found in al-Shaʿrānī, *al-Mīzān* (Cairo: Maṭbaʿat al-Kastaliyya, 1279H), 1: 37–40, but he includes multiple interpolations from elsewhere in the text. Al-Shaʿrānī was important for some reformists too. See Samuela Pagani, "The Meaning of the *Ikhtilāf al-Madhāhib* in ʿAbd al-Wahhāb al-Shaʿrānī's *al-Mīzān al-Kubrā*," *Islamic Law and Society* 11, no. 2 (2004): 178n4. Riḍā himself was more ambivalent, directing a questioner who asked about al-Shaʿrānī's *Kashf al-Ghumma* to al-Shawkānī's *Nayl al-Awṭār* instead, on the grounds that the former contained some hadiths that were not entirely authentic (*ṣaḥīḥ* or *ḥasan*). See *al-Manār* 6, no. 6 (June 12, 1903): 236.

[52] ʿIllīsh, *Fatḥ al-ʿAlī al-Mālik*, 94.

[53] ʿIllīsh, *Fatḥ al-ʿAlī al-Mālik*, 95.

on the Qur'anic verse, "We have not omitted anything from the Book,"[54] to argue that the shariʿa consists of a gradual unraveling of latent meanings that links together generations of Muslim jurists. The role of the Prophet on this account is to elucidate what is *mujmal* in the Qur'an, "for if he had not clarified for us the manner (*kayfiyya*) of ritual purity, prayer, pilgrimage, etc., none of the imams would have been able to extract (*istikhrāj*) that from the Qur'an."[55] He then extends this model down throughout the ages:

> Just as the lawgiver [the Prophet Muhammad] elucidated for us through his example (*sunna*) what is *mujmal* in the Qur'an, the *mujtahid* imams clarified for us what was *mujmal* in the hadiths of the shariʿa. If it were not for their elucidation, the shariʿa would have remained in its *mujmal* (concise) form. And so can it be said of the people of every period (*dawr*) with respect to the period that preceded them, until the Day of Judgment. For *ijmāl* (concision) obtains in the language of the imams until the Day of Judgment. If not for that, books would not have been commented upon, and glosses (*ḥawāshī*) would not have been written on commentaries (*shurūḥ*).[56]

This is an understanding of *fiqh* that fits squarely within the etymological sense of "tradition" as something "handed down" or "transmitted" from one generation to the next.[57] Gilbert Delanoue argues that what is significant about ʿIllīsh's thought is that the agents of this transmission are men, rather than books.[58] The passage quoted, however, gives us reason to reconsider this characterization. Not only do books feature prominently in the unfolding of this tradition, the central consideration seems to be the interpretation of inherited language. This instead evokes Gadamer's twin observations that "the essence of tradition is to exist in the medium of language,"[59] and, given the necessity of tradition to understanding, that understanding is inherently and irreducibly an act of linguistic interpretation. "All understanding

[54] Al-Anʿām 6:38.
[55] ʿIllīsh, *Fatḥ al-ʿAlī al-Mālik*, 97.
[56] ʿIllīsh, *Fatḥ al-ʿAlī al-Mālik*, 97.
[57] Edward Shils, *Tradition* (Chicago: University of Chicago Press, 2006), 12–13; Josef Pieper, *Tradition: Concept and Claim*, trans. E. Christian Kopff (South Bend, IN: St. Augustine's Press, 2010), 9–14; Theodor W. Adorno, "On Tradition," *Telos* 94 (December 21, 1992): 75.
[58] Delanoue, *Moralistes et Politiques Musulmans Dans l'Égypte Du XIXe Siècle (1798–1882)*, I:154–55.
[59] Hans-Georg Gadamer, *Truth and Method*, trans. Joel Weinsheimer and Donald G. Marshall (New York: Continuum, 2006), 391.

is interpretation, and all interpretation takes place in the medium of a language that allows the object to come into words and yet is at the same time the interpreter's own language."[60] The notion of understanding here as a "coming into words" captures well ʿIllīsh's acceptance of the idea that later generations' shariʿa determinations come into being through an encounter with texts, or to be more specific, an articulation by later jurists of meanings latent in texts (both oral and written). Because this linguistic transmission is channeled through the masters and writings of individual *madhhabs*, ʿIllīsh provides us with a *traditional* view of *fiqh* in which jurists' encounters with Islamic law are always mediated by the past as represented in the texts of the *madhhab*, dependent on pathways forged by predecessors and writings considered authoritative.

Embedded in this conception of the *madhhab* as mediator is a commitment to both diversity and hierarchy, vividly illustrated in al-Shaʿrānī's chapter through the telling metaphor of water. A central term in al-Shaʿrānī's work is *ʿayn al-sharīʿa*. The word *ʿayn* used in this compound is multivocal, but the various meanings it yields in this context reinforce one another: the shariʿa itself, the shariʿa as it really is, and importantly, the fount of the shariʿa in the sense of both source and spring. Elsewhere, al-Shaʿrānī uses the term *yanbūʿ al-sharīʿa*, referring more unambiguously to a water source to cement the metaphor.[61] This spring, according to Zakariyyā al-Anṣārī, is in reality a vast ocean: "no matter which side of it you draw from, it is one."[62] This image is meant to underscore the legitimacy of the various opinions of the *mujtahid* imams, each of whom draws from the single divine source, though they experience that singular truth from different sides. Aron Zysow has termed this pluralistic approach "infallibilism" and noted that it was epitomized in the formula "every *mujtahid* is correct (*kull mujtahid muṣīb*)," a phrase that is adduced explicitly by al-Shaʿrānī as he paints a picture of an afterlife in which all the ulama will be found standing alongside the Prophet himself, confirming the ultimate conformity of their views with his.[63] On the Day of Judgment,

60 Gadamer, *Truth and Method*, 390.

61 Al-Shaʿrānī, *Mīzān*, vol. 1, 2. Samuela Pagani also notes that the variation *ʿayn al-sharīʿa al-ūlā*, commonly used by al-Shaʿrānī, is a reference to the central mesh ("first hole") of the fishing net, widely recognizable in Egypt. Pagani, "The Meaning of the *Ikhtilāf al-Madhāhib* in ʿAbd al-Wahhāb al-Shaʿrānī's *al-Mīzān al-Kubrā*," 195n85.

62 ʿIllīsh, *Fatḥ al-ʿAlī al-Mālik*, 96.

63 Aron Zysow, *The Economy of Certainty: An Introduction to the Typology of Islamic Legal Theory* (Atlanta, GA: Lockwood Press, 2013), 259–78, especially 262. Ahmed Fekry Ibrahim shows that a commitment to the multiplicity of truth (*taʿaddud al-ḥaqq*) is a hallmark feature of al-Shaʿrānī's

> how happy will be the one to whom God the Exalted discloses the original fount of the shariʿa—as He has disclosed to us—and he finds that every *mujtahid* is correct. . . . And how regretful will be the one who said that only one was correct, and the rest were mistaken.[64]

The fortunate Muslim who believes in the ultimate righteousness of all of the *mujtahids* thereby makes himself eligible for their intercession on his behalf before God. He will ultimately find himself standing before the original fount of the shariʿa and drawing water (*ightirāf*) from it beside the man he took as his imam. "Just as you followed him on your path despite your being veiled from the fount you now behold, so shall you follow him in drawing from the spring he draws from."[65]

This vision of a blissful hereafter embraces the diversity of the *mujtahid* imams, but it also instates a clear hierarchy.[66] The latter-day Muslim jurist is always a follower of his imam, even when he is experiencing the ultimate reality of the shariʿa in the afterlife—a reality concealed to him in his worldly life, but revealed to his imam.[67] Their relationship is anything but balanced: he drinks from water presided over (*ashrafa ʿalā*) by his imam, and his imam intercedes on his behalf before God. This imagery, usually reserved in Islamic eschatology for the Prophet, who will intercede for his followers and preside over the paradisiacal river of Kawthar on the Day of Judgment, clearly places later generations in a position of dependency upon their predecessors.

In contrast, scholars of pro-*ijtihād* movements have often pointed out that the antipathy of these groupings toward *taqlīd* was animated, at least in

legal thought. Ahmed Fekry Ibrahim, "Al-Shaʿrānī's Response to Legal Purism: A Theory of Legal Pluralism," *Islamic Law & Society* 20, no. 1/2 (February 2013): 126–35.

64 ʿIllīsh, *Fatḥ al-ʿAlī al-Mālik*, 97.

65 ʿIllīsh, *Fatḥ al-ʿAlī al-Mālik*, 97.

66 These twin themes are also captured in a second metaphor employed by al-Shaʿrānī, borrowed once more from ʿAlī al-Khawwāṣ. "There exists no opinion of the ulama that is not supported by one of the fundamental sources [*aṣl min al-uṣūl*] of the sharīʿa . . . Among their opinions are those which are close to [the *ʿayn al-sharīʿa*] and those which are even closer; those that are far from it, and those that are even farther. But the source of all of them is the sharīʿa, because they are taken from the rays of its light. For us, there is never any substantive ruling that is not derived from a source, but the further a scholar gets from the *ʿayn al-sharīʿa*, the weaker the light of his opinions relative to the original light of the *ʿayn al-sharīʿa al-ūlā*." ʿIllīsh, *Fatḥ al-ʿAlī al-Mālik*, 96.

67 Al-Shaʿrānī leaves open the possibility that "an enlightened mystic" may apprehend the *ʿayn al-sharīʿa* directly, but doing so would mean "swimming upstream against the flow of history, passing through the fifteen epochs (*adwār*) of the preceding generations of scholars." Pagani, "The Meaning of the *Ikhtilāf al-Madhāhib* in ʿAbd al-Wahhāb al-Shaʿrānī's *al-Mīzān al-Kubrā*," 196; al-Shaʿrānī, *Mīzān*, vol. 1, 23.

part, by their desire for unity and equality.[68] *Taqlīd* within the framework of *madhhabs*, it was thought, both divided the *umma* into rival schools of thought despite the clear and unifying message of the Qur'an and sunna, and assumed the superiority of the schools' eponyms and early authorities over later adherents, thereby corroding the default Islamic commitment to the equality of all believers. Though these various movements were far from identical, and the extent of their commitment to unity and equality stand on a spectrum, they agree on emphasizing these ideals over free-flowing diversity (usually expressed pejoratively as disunity) and hierarchy in the form of generational decline.

ʿIllīsh's fatwa, then, emerges as more than a simple defense of *taqlīd*; it is the articulation of a traditional vision of the shariʿa: an unfolding throughout history which both embraces diversity to accommodate the teeming multiplicity of humankind and places jurists in a chain that links them to generations past and present. As it is the temporal question that is of primary concern to us in this chapter, it bears noting that as remarkable as the fatwa is for its self-conscious elaboration, the picture of the *madhhab* it depicts is by no means specific to the Egyptian milieu that gave rise to ʿIllīsh, al-Shaʿrānī, al-Khawwāṣ, and al-Anṣārī. In his important study, Brannon Wheeler has noted that authority in the Ḥanafī school functioned through the demand that jurists "read 'backward' through the scholarship of previous generations":[69]

> The individual Ḥanafī scholar does not inherit the authority of the revelation by claiming to know how to interpret the Qur'ān. Rather, the authority of a given scholar's definition of practice is predicated on demonstrating the claim that this definition of practice is a continuation of earlier generations' definition of practice, originating with the prophet's definition of practice.[70]

[68] Ziadeh, *Sanūsīyah: A Study of a Revivalist Movement in Islam*, 87; John Voll, "The Sudanese Mahdi: Frontier Fundamentalist," *International Journal of Middle East Studies* 10, no. 2 (1979): 149–50; Rudolph Peters, "Idjtihād and Taqlīd in 18th and 19th Century Islam," *Die Welt des Islams*, New Series, 20, no. 3/4 (January 1, 1980): 131–32.

[69] Wheeler, *Applying the Canon in Islam*, 14. Eyyup Said Kaya formulates the matter slightly differently and suggests the existence of three subtraditions within Ḥanafism, but he similarly concludes that part of what makes the *madhhab* a *madhhab* is "intra-madhhabic reasoning": "a reasoning that operates in a particular juristic tradition, one that builds on what has been accomplished in a certain juristic past." Kaya, "Continuity and Change in Islamic Law: The Concept of Madhhab and the Dimensions of Legal Disagreement in Hanafi Scholarship of the Tenth Century," 39.

[70] Wheeler, *Applying the Canon in Islam*, 15.

In this traditional outlook, "no operative distinction is made separating the 'original text' and 'later interpretation' or between canon and application. The contents of the canon are not limited to . . . the text of the Qurʾān, but include subsequent interpretations."[71] This resonates well with al-Shaʿrānī's depiction of the *ʿayn al-sharīʿa* as a seed already containing all future iterations of the law simply waiting to blossom with the passing of time.[72]

The Ḥanafī case treated by Wheeler is an important one for our purposes, because it is through the language and apparatus of the Ḥanafī school that an innovative reformulation of authority and its relationship to history is offered by a group of jurists in the late nineteenth and early twentieth centuries that includes Bakhīt. In the next section, I set the stage for our consideration of that reformulation by examining in more detail Ḥanafism's traditional self-conception of its authority structure, best encapsulated in what Ḥanafīs called the *ṭabaqāt* (ranks) of the school, and what Western scholarship has often referred to as a "juristic typology."

Tradition as Typology: The Ḥanafī Context

Wael Hallaq defines a juristic typology as "a form of discourse that reduces the community of legal specialists into manageable, formal categories, taking into consideration the entire historical and synchronic range of that community's juristic activities and functions." "One of the fundamental characteristics of a typology," according to Hallaq, "is the elaboration of a structure of authority in which all the elements making up the typology are linked to each other, hierarchically or otherwise, by relationships of one type or another."[73]

As such, the purpose of the typology is to clearly delineate the relative standing of the various jurists of the school, and therefore the juristic functions to which they are entitled.[74] In the case of the Ḥanafī school, the

[71] Wheeler, *Applying the Canon in Islam*, 15.

[72] Al-Shaʿrānī himself uses the example of a tree to explain this unfolding, with the *ʿayn al-sharīʿa* being the water source from which branches and fruits of the tree proliferate (*fa-nẓur ilā . . . al-furūʿ wa-l-aghṣān wa-l-thimār tajiduhā kullahā mutafarrʿa min ʿayn al-sharīʿa*). al-Shaʿrānī, *Mīzān*, vol. 1, 42.

[73] Hallaq, *Authority, Continuity, and Change in Islamic Law*, 1.

[74] For a short introduction to the genre of *ṭabaqāt* writing, see Guy Burak, *The Second Formation of Islamic Law: The Hanafi School in the Early Modern Ottoman Empire* (New York: Cambridge University Press, 2015), 68–71; Cl. Gilliot, "Ṭabaḳāt," in *Encyclopaedia of Islam 2*, ed. P. J. Bearman et al. (Leiden: Brill, 2000), 7–10.

typology that had prevailed as the dominant expression of the school for roughly three and a half centuries before encountering direct criticism was the one devised by the Ottoman *Shaykh al-Islām* Ibn Kamāl Pāshā (or Kemalpaşazade) (d. 1533).[75] Writing at approximately the same time as al-Shaʿrānī, Ibn Kamāl did so not from the provincial center in Cairo, but rather the imperial capital in Istanbul and as a towering member of the imperial learned classes of the Ottoman realm. The ascendant authority of Ottoman Ḥanafism helps explain why his typology was widely reproduced in standard works of Ḥanafī jurisprudence and prosopography after him. By the end of the century, it had been included by the prominent Ḥanafī scholar Mullā ʿAlī al-Qārī (ʿAlī b. Sulṭān al-Qārī, d. 1606) in his supplement (*dhayl*) to al-Qurashī's famous eighth-century prosopographical work *al-Jawāhir al-Muḍīʾa*.[76] In the nineteenth century, Ibn ʿĀbidīn (d. 1836) included it in the last authoritative compendium of Ḥanafī law, *Ḥāshiyat Radd al-Muḥtār*, as well as in a commentary on his own didactic poem *ʿUqūd Rasm al-Muftī*.[77]

Under Ibn Kamāl's typology, there are seven levels of membership in the school.[78] The topmost rank is occupied exclusively by the entirely independent eponyms of the four surviving Sunni schools—in the Ḥanafī case, Abū Ḥanīfa (d. 150/767). These scholars were the absolute *mujtahids* of the shariʿa (*mujtahidīn fī al-sharʿ*) who set the principles of their methodology and derived (*istinbāṭ*) rulings from them through recourse to the fundamental sources. This is the default sense of *ijtihād* deployed by reformists like Riḍā. The second highest rank is reserved for his immediate companions, prominent among them his two master students Abū Yūsuf (d. 182/798–9) and Muḥammad b. Ḥasan al-Shaybānī (d. 189/804). The members of this

[75] Ibn ʿĀbidīn alludes to comments related to the categorization, and therefore perhaps the categorization itself, being found in "some of [Ibn Kamāl's] treatises (*rasāʾil*). A manuscript version of the categorization is at Harvard library online (https://iiif.lib.harvard.edu/manifests/view/drs:10324232$338i), but a number of later authors have reported it with only slight variations; see below.

[76] *Al-Jawāhir al-Muḍīʾa* (Hyderabad: Maṭbaʿat Majlis Dāʾirat al-Maʿārif al-Niẓāmiyya, n.d.), 2:558. Interestingly, it is omitted from al-Qārī's own prosopographical work, *al-Athmār al-Janiyya*, whose introduction is virtually identical to the *dhayl*, except for the latter's inclusion of a few pages of *fawāʾid* at the end (one of which is the *fāʾida ʿajiba* that lists Ibn Kamāl's *ṭabaqāt*).

[77] Muḥammad Amīn ibn ʿUmar Ibn ʿĀbidīn, *Ḥāshiyat Radd al-Muḥtār*, 8 vols. (Riyadh: Dār ʿĀlam al-Kutub, 2003), 1:179–81, and Muḥammad Amīn Ibn ʿĀbidīn, "Sharḥ al-Manẓūma al-Musammāt bi-ʿUqūd Rasm al-Muftī," in *Majmūʿat Rasāʾil Ibn ʿĀbidīn*, 2 vols. (Āstāna, 1325H), 1:11–12. For a translation and discussion of the poem on which the latter is a commentary, see Calder, "The ʿUqūd Rasm al-Muftī' of Ibn ʿĀbidīn." For similar discussions of the Shāfiʿī ranks, see Hallaq, *Authority, Continuity, and Change in Islamic Law*, 7–14; Calder, "Al-Nawawī's Typology of Muftīs and Its Significance for a General Theory of Islamic Law."

[78] For an in-depth explanation and discussion of these ranks, see Hallaq, *Authority, Continuity, and Change in Islamic Law*, 14–17.

group are considered *mujtahid*s within the madhhab (*mujtahidīn fī al-madhhab*), meaning that they are capable of practicing *ijtihād* within the methodological parameters set by their master. Though they may "oppose their teacher in certain rulings, they adhere to (*yuqallidūn*) his methodological principles," a feature that distinguishes them from members of other *madhhab*s. The third rank is inhabited by those capable only of exercising *ijtihād* on cases unaddressed by the master (*mujtahidīn fī al-masāʾil*), again in strict accordance with the latter's methodology. Because their competencies are restricted to new cases, their rulings do not conflict with those of the eponym. Ibn Kamāl names here seven jurists spanning the third/ninth to the sixth/twelfth centuries: al-Khaṣṣāf, al-Ṭaḥāwī, al-Karkhī, al-Ḥalwānī, al-Sarakhsī, al-Bazdawī, and Qāḍīkhān. These three top ranks round out those jurists technically capable of some version of *ijtihād* (*mujtahid*s), the rest being practitioners of *taqlīd* (*muqallid*s) of varying degrees. Those in rank four are the men of *takhrīj*. Though unqualified to perform *ijtihād*, they still possess a mastery of both the school's principles and the sources, and so are able to resolve juridical ambiguities within the school. For example, they may pronounce on the correct interpretation of language that lends itself to multivocality due to its brevity or succinctness, or weigh in authoritatively on an ambiguous ruling that could give rise to multiple readings. The exemplary figure in this ranking is a certain al-Rāzī, whose identity as it turns out was itself the subject of some ambiguity. Rank five jurists are capable of giving preponderance (*tarjīḥ*) to one among a set of conflicting rulings adopted by their predecessors on grounds of a stronger textual proof, a stricter inference from analogy, or public interest. The representative figures Ibn Kamāl has in mind for this grouping are al-Qudūrī and al-Marghīnānī. The jurists in rank six, represented by the latter-day authors of the "reliable compendia" (*aṣḥāb al-mutūn al-muʿtabara min al-mutaʾakhkhirīn*) *al-Kanz*, *al-Mukhtār*, *al-Wiqāya*, and *Majmaʿ al-Baḥrayn*, are allowed only to distinguish between sound and weak opinions. Their charge is to ensure that weak narrations and rejected opinions are not transmitted in their texts. The seventh rank jurists are left with the negative definition that they are unable even to distinguish between "the right and the left" or "the skinny and the fat."[79] Rather, they simply collate their predecessors' work "like the one who gathers firewood at night (*ḥāṭib layl*). So woe be to the one who performs *taqlīd* of them."

[79] Ibn ʿĀbidīn, *Ḥāshiyat Radd al-Muḥtār*, 1:179–81.

As with the depiction of the shariʿa given by al-Shaʿrānī and ʿIllīsh, Ibn Kamāl's schematic account of the *madhhab* is structured as a narrative of historical decline in juristic authority. It is a history in which the summit of intellectual acuity, hermeneutic competency, and juristic potency resides at the origin, with the passing of generations representing a graded diminishment of those qualities. Later jurists on this scheme are charged with working at the margins to "fill out" a system whose foundations were put in place by the eponym and his immediate students. Certainly by the middle of the nineteenth century, the scope of juristic authority within the Ḥanafī self-conception had been severely narrowed, if not extinguished altogether, for centuries. Only years earlier, the illustrious Ibn ʿĀbidīn, the dominant figure of post-eighteenth-century Ḥanafism, left no doubt about the heavily reduced competencies he understood himself to possess relative to his predecessors when he relegated himself to seventh-level status.[80] In his commentary on *al-Durr al-Mukhtār* of ʿAlāʾ al-Dīn al-Ḥaṣkafī (d. 1088/1677), Ibn ʿĀbidīn affirms and reinforces the self-aware humility of al-Ḥaṣkafī that was characteristic of the Ḥanafism of centuries past. Al-Ḥaṣkafī, himself relying on language from at least the fifteenth century, had already held in the seventeenth-century base-text that "With regards to us, our duty is to follow what has been preferred and verified [by earlier jurists] as if they issued fatwas during their lives." In his gloss of this statement in the early nineteenth century, then, Ibn ʿĀbidīn clarifies that by "us" what is meant is "those of the seventh rank (*ahl al-ṭabaqa al-sābiʿa*)" whose task is to "follow [the earlier jurists] as if they were alive, and we were simply issuing fatwas according to their conclusions, for we are not capable of opposing them."[81]

This phrasing evokes the themes of incapacity and dependency on earlier jurists that are reminiscent of the quote from al-Anṣārī (via al-Shaʿrānī and ʿIllīsh) in the last section. The ethos to which Bakhīt ought to have been heir, then, embodied both in the self-conception of the Ḥanafī school to which he belonged and the circles of Egyptian Azharism in which he was reared, was one that saw successive generations of jurists taking up their place at the

[80] Muḥammad Amīn ibn ʿĀbidīn is perhaps the most prominent authority of latter-day Ḥanafism, having died in 1252/1836. For a short biographical entry, see Khayr al-Dīn Ziriklī, *Al-Aʿlām*, vol. 6 (Beirut: Dār al-ʿIlm li-l-Malāyīn, 2002), 42.

[81] Ibn ʿĀbidīn, *Ḥāshiyat Radd al-Muḥtār*, 1:180–81. Ibn ʿĀbidīn points out that al-Ḥaṣkafī's wording can already be found in *al-Taṣḥīḥ wa-l-Tarjīḥ* of Qāsim ibn Quṭlūbughā (d. 879/1474). On the author and the text, see Talal Al-Azem, *Rule-Formulation and Binding Precedent in the Madhhab-Law Tradition: Ibn Qutlubugha's Commentary on the Compendium of Quduri*, Islamicate Intellectual History (Leiden: Brill, 2016).

end of a long regression of juristic authority in order to work within a school of thought whose principles and major tenets had already been formulated, articulating its details and working at its margins to account for situational differences. Whether this understanding was an accurate historical representation of the trajectory of juristic thought or a meaningful reconstruction of the sorts of powers exercised by both earlier and later jurists is not a question that can be settled by reference to the texts I have looked at in these two sections. The secondary scholarship of recent decades gives us ample reason to suspect that these particular constructions both underestimate the extent of the creativity that could be exercised by later jurists and overestimate the chasm between them and earlier authorities. My concern, however, is not the question, by now largely settled, of whether later Islamic law was creative, but rather how latter-day jurists *themselves* understood, and portrayed, their place within the *madhhab*-tradition they inhabited, and how they envisioned their relationship to the authority of the *madhhab* as constituted by their predecessors. As the contributions of ʿIllīsh, al-Shaʿrānī, al-Anṣārī, Ibn Kamāl, al-Ḥaṣkafī, and Ibn ʿĀbidīn show, jurists' stated stance toward the past was one of allegiance and dependency, even as they were engaging in audaciously creative argumentation to forge new juristic options for their communities. Indeed, it was by claiming allegiance to a venerable past that they could be granted the legitimacy to engage in the sorts of innovative and sophisticated reasoning that was conducted within the *madhhab* but was no less creative and path-breaking for being "intra-*madhhab*ic."

We will see in the remainder of this chapter, however, that Bakhīt's approach to the question of juristic authority, and the underlying temporality that it assumed, represented a marked departure from the prevailing Ḥanafī tradition. Indeed, it echoed much more clearly the self-confidence and independence found in Riḍā. I lay out the nature of this transformation in the next section, before placing it within a larger context and tracing its implications.

Reformulating *Ijtihād*ic Authority within Ḥanafism

In the last chapter, we saw Bakhīt, in his attempt to salvage the ulama's authority, engaging in a new mode of authority construction that rested on the creation of a scholarly network, itself reliant on the echoes of a social ethos inherited from the long-standing hermeneutic practices of the *madhhab*. I will argue in this section, however, that for the very same reason—that is, the overwhelming desire to reverse what he takes to be the erosion of the ulama's influence in the face of Reformist incursions—the underlying interpretive commitment, and conception of historical time, on which the *madhhab* rested was subjected to a radical transformation. By the time Bakhīt was writing the *Irshād Ahl al-Milla ilā Ithbāt al-Ahilla* in 1910, the balance of power had shifted far enough that a straight-forward assertion of the traditional typology of Ibn Kamāl—in particular, its insistence that the latter-day jurist's encounter with the law had to be heavily mediated by layers of accumulated interpretation—was no longer tenable. It was clear that the Modernist project, in no small part thanks to the "Salafī press," was making substantial gains in the attempt to marginalize the ulama as outdated and unable to cope with the demands of the period. It is in an attempt, then, to both enhance his own authority and demonstrate his relevance in a changing world that Bakhīt chose to adopt a recasting of the Ḥanafī school.

In a pointed characterization, Norman Calder has succinctly spelled out the inseparability of legal reasoning and the institution of the *madhhab* in premodern Islam, an attitude we have previously labeled the *madhhab* tradition:

> [T]he dominant traditions were contained and expressed within the successful juristic schools: the Ḥanafī, the Shāfiʿī, the Mālikī and the Ḥanbalī. Neither the Scripture nor common sense had (direct) authority. The interpretations of established figures stood firmly between the present and the sources. Tradition counted; and knowledge and learning (of tradition) . . . Only the learned jurist could speak authoritatively, and not by virtue of his access to the sources, but by virtue of his control of tradition.[82]

As a trained and committed Ḥanafī within this tradition, it is clear that Bakhīt could not bypass the *madhhab* altogether except at the expense of the source of his own authority. Indeed, to do so would be to undercut dramatically the precise criteria by which he can distinguish himself from the Reformists he opposed—mastery over the accumulated intellectual heritage of the *madhhab* and the prestige accrued from studying with, and acknowledging the authority of, its recognized masters. Despite this, in his appendix (*khātima*) to the *Irshād*, Bakhīt lays bare the extent to which he had internalized the ideals of the Modernist critique.

[82] Calder, "The ʿUqūd Rasm al-Muftī' of Ibn ʿĀbidīn," 216–17.

Bakhīt's discussion in the appendix is loosely framed around the question of what to do when the settled position of the *madhhab* conflicts with a Prophetic hadith. Only a decade earlier, in a retrospective on the first year of *al-Manār*, Riḍā had noted that his unqualified emphasis on the foundational texts over the developed opinions of later jurists had been the central substantive issue on which he had been faulted by his Azharī opponents.[83] In 1910, however, echoing Riḍā's methodological insistence, Bakhīt is adamant that "it is never permissible to grant priority to the opinion of a mere mortal (*qawl min aqwāl al-rijāl*), no matter his station, over an authentic hadith."[84] Flying in the face of not only prevailing Azharī sentiment but also Ḥanafī tradition,[85] this forthright statement already constituted a significant concession to the Reformist critique. The deeper resonance of Bakhīt's arguments with Riḍā's project, however, is revealed through a key centerpiece of the appendix: the juristic typology he suggests as a replacement for Ibn Kamāl's seven-fold categorization. It is through his discussion of this juristic typology and the reasons he advances for favoring it that Bakhīt most effectively decenters the emphasis on later scholars that Riḍā had earlier pointed to as the cause of Azharī decline after the tenth/sixteenth century.[86]

In a recent work, Guy Burak has shown that Ibn Kamāl's delineation of the *ṭabaqāt* sparked a spate of works in the genre by members of the Ottoman establishment seeking to consolidate the place of the imperial learned hierarchy in the Ḥanafī school. Ibn Kamāl figured as a key bridge figure in works subsequent to him, and so his position as the official *Shaykh al-Islām* was not a tangential detail, but rather a key element in a particular process of canonization.[87] If this was part of a phenomenon Burak calls a "second formation" of Islamic law, the reformulation of the *ṭabaqāt* in which Bakhīt participated some four centuries later may well be considered an undoing of the canon, an "unforming" or indeed a "re-formation" of Ḥanafī juristic authority. This was a re-formation carried out not in the spirit of Riḍā's desire to abolish

[83] *Al-Manār* 1, no. 49: 954–55.

[84] Muḥammad Bakhīt al-Muṭīʿī, *Irshād Ahl al-Milla ilā Ithbāt al-Ahilla*, ed. Ḥasan Aḥmad Isbir (Beirut: Dār Ibn Ḥazm, 2000), 205.

[85] As an example of the manner in which the Ḥanafī establishment had grappled with this tension to preserve the authority of the Imam's opinion, see Ibn ʿĀbidīn, *Radd al-Muḥtār*, vol. 1, 167.

[86] *Al-Manār wa-l-Azhar*, 7. Bakhīt gestures to his desire to downplay the importance of later writings elsewhere in the appendix as well. *Irshād*, 242, 247, but also 241. Ibn Kamāl and the official Ottoman order are implicated in these critiques as well. Many of the texts he expressly criticizes for being "tainted by the opinions of latter-day scholars" (241, 242) are cited as authoritative exemplars of Ibn Kamāl's lower ranks and figured prominently in the Ottoman curricula. The fatawa of Qaḍīkhān is also a recurring target of critique in Bakhīt.

[87] Burak, *The Second Formation of Islamic Law*, 66–100.

the *madhhabs* altogether, but rather to recast them in a manner that better accorded with the intellectual assumptions and currents that struck as most compelling at the time. As we will see in the next section, however, the shift in these intellectual assumptions was dramatic, and not simply cosmetic—the reformulated *ṭabaqāt* signified through their new temporality the *de-traditionalization* of the tradition.[88]

Before doing so, however, we must examine carefully the nature of Bakhīt's intervention. Though the rivalry with Reformists was the proximate context for Bakhīt's decision to set aside Ibn Kamāl's typology, his most direct discursive influence was found within the works of maverick Ḥanafī scholars in the late nineteenth century. A perusal of Bakhīt's personal library turned up copies of two key texts on which he relied heavily, the Tatar Shihāb al-Din al-Marjānī's *Nāẓūrat al-Ḥaqq* and the Indian ʿAbd al-Ḥayy al-Laknawī's *al-Nāfiʿ al-Kabīr*, a commentary on al-Shaybānī's *al-Jāmiʿ al-Ṣaghīr*.[89] Both of these figures, motivated by their own social circumstances and regional intellectual traditions, had earlier made arguments that sought to reconceptualize the role of *ijtihād*. Here once again we see the network and ethos of the "social *madhhab*" at work, even as the very orthodoxy of the *madhhab* is being challenged. Rather than be seen as submitting to trends in Egypt agitating for the reactivation of *ijtihād*, we find Bakhīt looking abroad to other Ḥanafīs, his associates in the *madhhab*, in order to derive the very same conclusions. This move allowed him to maintain his distance from the Reformist currents inside of Egypt, while still exploiting the protocols of the *madhhab* (designed to encourage a continuity) to draw on his immediate Ḥanafī predecessors in a manner that radically transforms the *madhhab* itself.

Bakhīt's appendix in the *Irshād Ahl al-Milla ilā Ithbāt al-Ahilla*, where he directs his critique at Ibn Kamāl and the prevailing temporal structure of Ḥanafism, was almost entirely a verbatim replication of excerpts from al-Marjānī's *Nāẓurat al-Ḥaqq*. At key points, however, he contributes additions intended to strengthen and clarify al-Marjānī's arguments, and intensify

[88] Burak shows how Ḥanafīs in the Arab provinces either offered alternate genealogies, stressing Mamluk contributions to later Ḥanafism, or sought ways to more seamlessly integrate the provinces into the Ottoman-centric reading. Burak, *The Second Formation of Islamic Law*, 101–21. The case of Ibn ʿĀbidīn, however, reveals the enduring influence and centrality of the Ottoman-centric reading of the *ṭabaqāt* into the Tanzimat period.

[89] Indeed, the copy of al-Marjānī's work bears stamps indicating Bakhīt's ownership. For details on al-Marjānī, see Ahmet Kanlidere, "Reform within Islam: The Tajdid (Reform) Movement among the Kazan Tatars (1850–1917): Conciliation or Conflict?" (PhD diss., Columbia University, 1995), 58–73. For more about al-Laknawī, see Qāḍī Mujīb al-Raḥmān, "Al-Shaykh ʿAbd al-Ḥayy al-Laknawī" (PhD diss., Al-Azhar University, Faculty of Shariʿa, 1964).

insights drawn from al-Laknawī. It is these interpolations that make explicit the new conception of historical time at play in Bakhīt's thought, a conception found only in attenuated form in his two predecessors. Given that the appendix is almost entirely lifted from al-Marjānī, it is tempting to view Bakhīt's contribution here as derivative, if not outright plagiarism. The scholarly instinct to focus on determining provenance and evaluating originality, however, distracts us from what is most interesting about this discursive move. The appropriation of language from another author would not necessarily be seen as a serious offence, especially in a writing culture like that of *fiqh* in which argumentation more often than not consisted of the strategic juxtaposition and selective citation of earlier authorities. What is more interesting historically is to think about how and for what reasons these arguments are marshaled by different actors and the work they do in different contexts. Ahmad Dallal has pointed out the mistake in assuming the homogeneity of reformists from very different local contexts, and with very different intellectual projects, on the basis of a convergence in the ideals they espoused.[90] A similar argument can be made with respect to "traditionalists." What stands out quite clearly in the case of Bakhīt is that he was able to draw on his vast learning of the *madhhab* to naturalize transformative Reformist ideals within the language of Ḥanafism, while remaining an ardent opponent of Reformists themselves. This stands in contrast to al-Marjānī and al-Laknawī, who were participating instead in local intellectual trends that constituted dissident forms of Ḥanafism. Al-Marjānī's views on the reassertion of *ijtihād* drew important inspiration from his teacher Abū Naṣr al-Qūrṣāwī.[91] Al-Qūrṣāwī's thoughts on the topic were in turn driven by his desire to rejuvenate Islamic legal authority by wresting it from an encroaching imperial Russian state which had turned Islamic religious institutions into moribund shells of their previous vital selves. Against an earlier Soviet historiography, Nathan Spannaus has, in an important recent book, sought to dissociate

[90] Ahmad Dallal, "The Origins and Objectives of Islamic Revivalist Thought, 1750–1850," *Journal of the American Oriental Society* 113, no. 3 (1993): 341–59.

[91] Abū Naṣr al-Qūrṣāwī, *Nastavlenie Līudeĭ Na Put' Istiny: Al-Irshād li-l-ʿIbād* (Kazan: Tatarskoe knizhnoe izd-vo, 2005); Nathan Spannaus, "The Ur-Text of Jadidism: Abū Naṣr Qūrṣāwī's Irshād and the Historiography of Muslim Modernism in Russia," *Journal of the Economic and Social History of the Orient* 59, no. 1–2 (2016): 93–125; Nathan Spannaus, *Preserving Islamic Tradition: Abū Naṣr Qūrṣāwī and the Beginnings of Modern Reformism* (New York: Oxford University Press, 2019), 293. Spannaus does, however, draw a distinction between the two, arguing that al-Marjānī was "more grounded within *madhhab* structures." On al-Marjānī's approach to *ijtihād* from the perspective of ritual law, see also Dinara Mardanova, "Debates around Ibādah between Shihab Ad-Din Mardjani and His Opponents," *Islamology* 7, no. 1 (2017): 180–93. I am grateful to Zukhra Kasimova for translating this article from the original Russian so I could consult it.

the intellectual project of al-Qūrṣāwī from the Jadidist reform movement, arguing instead that it should be considered a particularist strain of Ḥanafism responding to tsarist power.[92] Al-Marjānī's advocacy for *ijtihād* similarly fails to correspond to Soviet readings that align him unproblematically with Jadidism, but although no straight line can be drawn from his ideas to those of Jadidists, al-Marjānī is nonetheless linked to the movement "through his support for educational reform and personal ties to reformers and early Jadids."[93] In contrast, we have seen that Bakhīt's antipathy toward the Reform movement persisted throughout his life. Al-Laknawī's thoughts, on the other hand, belonged to a strain of thought attributed to the independent-minded luminary of South Asia, Shāh Walī Allāh (d. 1773), and included also Baḥr al-'Ulūm al-Laknawī (d. 1810).[94] Like 'Abd al-Ḥayy al-Laknawī, who was renowned for his prowess in hadith scholarship, Shāh Walī Allāh's thought was markedly hadith-centric. As a result, in general, he felt less bound to Ḥanafism than other Ḥanafīs and often made recourse to other schools as well.[95] This helps explain the central place given by al-Laknawī to the Shāfi'ī Ibn Ḥajar al-Makkī (and, by extension, Ibn al-Ṣalāh) in his discussion. Bakhīt's contribution, therefore, is the mainstreaming and intensification of this dissident trend within Ḥanafism—using the opening provided by the etiquette of the "social *madhhab*" to lodge it within the heart of the Ḥanafī-Azharī establishment and assimilate it to a set of intellectual commitments that had come to be normalized, and assumed, within Egyptian society. Unlike most champions of *ijtihād*, Bakhīt's aim is not the disruption of the prevailing social-intellectual order, but rather its preservation.

In his appendix, Bakhīt follows al-Marjānī in discarding the typology of "Aḥmad b. Sulaymān al-Rūmī, known as Ibn Kamāl Pāshā, one of the celebrated ulama of the Ottoman state."[96] The inclusion of Ibn Kamāl's full name

[92] Spannaus, *Preserving Islamic Tradition*, 136–43, 288–98.

[93] Spannaus, *Preserving Islamic Tradition*, 293.

[94] 'Abd al-Ḥayy al-Laknawī, *al-Nāfi' al-Kabīr li-man Yuṭāli' al-Jāmi' al-Ṣaghīr* (Karachi: Idārat al-Qur'ān, 1990), 13–17. Baḥr al-'Ulūm would also be influential for modernist interpreters like Cheragh Ali. See Muhammad Qasim Zaman, *Modern Islamic Thought in a Radical Age: Religious Authority and Internal Criticism* (Cambridge, UK: Cambridge University Press, 2012), 88n43.

[95] For Shāh Walī Allāh's views on *ijtihād*, see Marcia Hermansen's translations of *al-Inṣāf fī Bayān Sabab al-Ikhtilāf* and *'Iqd al-Jīd fī Aḥkām al-Ijtihād wa-l-Taqlīd* in *Shāh Walī Allāh's Treatises on Islamic Law* (Louisville, KY: Fons Vitae, 2010). See also Muhammad Daüd Rahbar, "Shāh Walī Ullāh and Ijtihād," *The Muslim World* 45, no. 4 (October 1, 1955): 346–58. On the importance of Shāh Walī Allāh to the South Asian context, see, for example, Zaman, *Modern Islamic Thought in a Radical Age*, 78–80.

[96] Bakhīt al-Muṭī'ī, *Irshād Ahl al-Milla ilā Ithbāt al-Ahilla*, 248; Shihāb al-Dīn al-Marjānī, *Nāẓūrat al-Ḥaqq fī Farḍiyyat al-'Ishā' wa in lam Yaghib al-Shafaq* (Amman: Dār al-Fatḥ, 2012), 190.

(and certainly his affiliation with the state) is significant. Burak has pointed out that references to the "Rūmī way" came to be used by some Ḥanafīs from the Arab provinces as a coded shorthand to comment on the specificity of official Ottoman Ḥanafism.[97] The invocation of it here by Bakhīt and al-Marjānī, then, functions as a way of parochializing Ibn Kamāl's influential categorization, signaling its belonging to a particular strand of Ḥanafism, and leaving open the possibility of alternatives. Despite its widespread influence, they go on to criticize it with some vigor. In Bakhīt's telling:

> Al-Tamīmī[98] mentioned [Ibn Kamāl's typology] in his *Ṭabaqāt* verbatim, and then said, "It is a very good categorization (*taqsīm ḥasan jiddan*)," even though it is quite far from being sound (*baʿīd jiddan ʿan al-ṣiḥḥa*), let alone good. It is pure arbitrariness (*taḥakkum maḥḍ*). [Al-Tamīmī] has no precedent in this claim, even though some who imitated him followed him without any supporting evidence.[99]

In place of the old typology, Bakhīt and al-Marjānī substitute a relatively simple categorization of three ranks.[100] For them, *mujtahids* are of two types. The first is the absolute *mujtahid*, the *mujtahid muṭlaq*, who "possesses complete mastery over law, is farsighted, and is able to derive rulings independently." The capacities of this jurist correspond precisely to the first rank of Ibn Kamāl's categorization, but by their insistent inclusion of not only the eponyms but also Abū Ḥanīfa's students Abū Yūsuf, Muḥammad, and Zufar, we can safely infer that Bakhīt and al-Marjānī are collapsing the top two ranks of the old typology into this new category.[101] Bakhīt criticizes the Ottoman jurist on this point, asking, "How is it that Ibn Kamāl Pāshā counted the imam Aḥmad b. Ḥanbal among the [absolute] *mujtahid*s, and not Abū Yūsuf, Muḥammad or Zufar? The meaning of their being Ḥanafīs is not that they are *muqallid*s of Abū Ḥanīfa, but rather that they helped in propagating and

[97] This was evidently an allusion that was shared by South Asian writers who disagreed with Ibn Kamāl, as al-Laknawī, too, calls him al-Rūmī. *Al-Nāfiʿ al-Kabīr*, 9. In contrast, Ibn ʿĀbidīn, the establishment scholar in Burak's telling, tellingly does not use this ascription.

[98] For a discussion of Taqī al-Dīn al-Tamīmī's *al-Ṭabaqāt al-Saniyya fī Tarājim al-Ḥanafiyya*, see Burak, *The Second Formation of Islamic Law*, 111–18.

[99] Bakhīt al-Muṭīʿī, *Irshād Ahl al-Milla ilā Ithbāt al-Ahilla*, 249; al-Marjānī, *Nāẓūrat al-Ḥaqq*, 191–92.

[100] Bakhīt al-Muṭīʿī, *Irshād Ahl al-Milla ilā Ithbāt al-Ahilla*, 247–48; al-Marjānī, *Nāẓūrat al-Ḥaqq*, 189; cf. al-Laknawī, *al-Nāfiʿ al-Kabīr*, 14.

[101] For an insightful discussion of Ibn Kamāl's conflation between juristic capacities (*waẓāʾif*) and juristic figures (*ashkhāṣ*), see Muḥammad Taqī al-ʿUthmānī, *Uṣūl al-Iftāʾ wa-Ādābuhu* (Karachi: Maktabat Maʿārif al-Qurʾān, 2011), 101–5.

transmitting his doctrine, that they studied with him, and did not distinguish their *madhhabs* from his."[102]

The second type of *mujtahid* is what they term "the *mujtahid* within the *madhhab* of a specific imam," an expert jurist possessing insight and discernment, though it becomes clear he has in mind something like what corresponds to the third rank in Ibn Kamāl's scheme, not the second; for although this type of *mujtahid* "takes the texts of the imam as *uṣūl* (principles) and derives from them the *furūʿ*," he is "in reality a *mujtahid* in some issues (*masāʾil*), not in all of them." Thus, we are left with one last rank which Bakhīt and al-Marjānī use as a catch-all category of non-*mujtahid*s in which to gather everyone else (ranks 4–7 on Ibn Kamāl's scheme), admitting that it encompasses groups (*ṭawāʾif*) whose members are of different levels in knowledge (*yatafāwatūna fī al-ʿilm*), between trustworthy and weak in narration (*bayna thiqa wa-ḍaʿīf fī al-riwāya*), and between expert and incapable in law (*bayna kāmil wa-qāṣir fī al-fiqh wa-l-dirāya*).

If, as Wael Hallaq has observed, the articulation of the juristic typology is in fact an exercise in "self-representation,"[103] we may well ask how exactly Bakhīt is attempting to represent or cast himself here. In another one of his articles, Hallaq comments that the historical augmentation in the number of the ranks of the jurists from three to five to finally Ibn Kamāl's seven in the tenth/sixteenth century was a result of the

> ever-growing conviction that fewer and fewer scholars could perform ijtihad and that most jurists were mere muqallids. . . . This conviction had chiefly contributed to the augmentation of the new ranks of muqallids that in theory did not exist before, while maintaining at the same time the old ranks of mujtahids without a change. . . . This classification was promoted by later taqlid advocates who espoused the view that mujtahids had become extinct.[104]

Taking these observations together, Bakhīt's move cannot but strike the reader as a strategic one which allows him to emphasize his own status—and that of his contemporaries—within the school, thereby expanding the range

[102] Bakhīt al-Muṭīʿī, *Irshād Ahl Al-Milla Ilā Ithbāt al-Ahilla*, 250; compare to al-Marjānī, *Nāẓūrat al-Ḥaqq*, 192–98; al-Laknawī, *al-Nāfiʿ al-Kabīr*, 11–12.

[103] Hallaq, *Authority, Continuity, and Change in Islamic Law*, 1.

[104] Wael B. Hallaq, "Was the Gate of Ijtihad Closed?," *International Journal of Middle East Studies* 16, no. 1 (March 1, 1984): 29–30.

of interpretive functions to which they are entitled, all the while reasserting himself over and against his Reformist opponents who lack the credibility afforded by the *madhhab* itself. Although Bakhīt is not explicit about where he places himself in this new scheme, it is clear that his newfound proximity to the highest ranks under the condensed typology amounts, at bottom, to the accruing of immense interpretive authority in and of itself. This is especially striking when compared to Ibn ʿĀbidīn's permitting himself access to only the lowly seventh level, which licensed him to do little more than gather together his predecessors' opinions and prohibited him from diverging from their conclusions.

New Temporalities and Historical Consciousness

Even more striking than Bakhīt's self-positioning, though, is his insistence that *ijtihād* remains a viable possibility at this late stage of the *madhhab*'s history. Addressing a hypothetical interlocutor who offers that "some have suggested that the era of *ijtihād* has passed, and those capable of it have been absent for ages, and [so] the argument of the *muqallid* is simply the statement of the *mujtahid*,"[105] he responds, in line with the Modernist emphasis on relying on the Qurʾan and sunna, by having the matter turn on fidelity to the foundational sources:

> All indications clearly point to the necessity of abiding by the Book, the sunna, consensus (*ijmāʿ*) and analogical deduction (*qiyās*). This is a general principle which compels us to arrive at judgments without privileging some person over another person, or some era over another era. . . . As such, more than one scholar has pointed out that *ijtihād* is a perpetual obligation, and a right available until the end of time (*ilā qiyām al-sāʿa*).[106]

What emerges from a reading of Bakhīt's following of al-Marjānī and al-Laknawī is his strong desire to level the playing field on which he and his Ḥanafī predecessors play. As such, he is at pains to point out that no era must be privileged over any other. We have seen that the prevailing way of structuring the typology was by chronology: the earliest Ḥanafīs dominating the

105 Bakhīt al-Muṭīʿī, *Irshād Ahl al-Milla ilā Ithbāt al-Ahilla*, 218.
106 Bakhīt al-Muṭīʿī, *Irshād Ahl al-Milla ilā Ithbāt al-Ahilla*, 219.

functions of *ijtihād*, and later jurists being assigned to successively lower ranks. This configuration seemed an entirely natural arrangement to Ḥanafīs from at least as early as Ibn Kamāl to as late as Ibn ʿĀbidīn, who accepted the characterization of the *madhhab* as a holistic unity with the most capable jurist-scholars at its origin and a gradual decline in capacities until they were extinguished altogether. This strikes Bakhīt, however, as nonsensical. The *madhhab* is to him no longer the mediating institution through whose history all hermeneutics necessarily proceeds, and which must be confronted and grappled with in its totality and according to long-developed procedures guiding the sifting and evaluating of accrued opinions. It is now a social institution carrying the prestige of a revered past, but one interpretive resource among many (albeit an important one) which facilitates his direct encounter with the foundational texts.

To contextualize this move, a comparison with Riḍā is appropriate here. If, as we have argued earlier, the conception of the *madhhab*'s history, enshrined for centuries in the works of post-sixteenth-century jurists starting with al-Shaʿrānī and Ibn Kamāl, was one of a decline, this stood in stark contrast to the historical progressivism advocated by Riḍā. In a telling passage in the debate between the conformist and the reformer, Riḍā speaks through the reformer to advance a familiar argument in the service of an unfamiliar end. Responding to the conformist's praise for the four Sunni *mujtahid*-imams ("I believe, as does anyone who knows Islam, that were it not for the imams, the religion would have been entirely lost, and that upon the neck of every Muslim until the Day of Judgment is their favor and benevolence"[107]), Riḍā argues that while he has no quarrel with praising the imams, Islam was better before the time of the *mujtahid*-imams than it was during their generation, and it was better during their generation than in the periods that followed. What seems initially to be the germs of an argument for historical decline, however, turns out to be anything but. The reason Riḍā gives for his comparative judgment is that fewer people performed *taqlīd* of the *mujtahid*-imams during their lives (and, of course, none did before their lives), while later generations veritably accorded them the status of Prophets. Indeed, says Riḍā, they implicitly regarded the *mujtahid*-imams as greater than Prophets because they placed greater value on the words of the former than those of the latter:

[107] Riḍā, *Muḥāwarāt*, 52.

> Some of them even dare to apply the principle of the Popes to Islam: [They claim] it is not permissible for one to take his religion from the Book because he does not understand it. Only the men of religion (*rijāl al-dīn*) understand it, so he must adhere to whatever they say, even if it contradicts the Qurʾan. And it is impermissible to adhere to what the Qurʾan says if it contradicts what they say. Rather, it is impermissible for him to occupy himself with understanding the rulings of his religion altogether. Similarly, some of our jurists have said: It is impermissible for one to say, "this is permissible" or "this is impermissible" because God said so, or because the Prophet said so, but [they may pronounce on a matter's permissibility] on the basis that a given jurist said so.[108]

We have already seen that the complaint that prominent jurists were preferred over the foundational texts was a common refrain among proponents of *ijtihād* like al-Sanūsī, Aḥmad b. Idrīs, and al-Mirghānī, but here Riḍā puts it to a specific purpose: to displace the sacred history, centered on the generation of the *mujtahid*-Imams, that functioned as the cornerstone of the *madhhab*ic approach.[109] In its stead, Riḍā bases himself on the epistemological egalitarianism that was also a hallmark of pro-*ijtihād* groupings to offer a progressivist take on the history of knowledge and the knowledgeable:

> There is no *ḥaqīqī* science whose subject matter (*masāʾil*) is above the comprehension of the masses, and possessed only by some individuals at a given time while the rest of humanity is incapable of [understanding] it. When a science is found in a nation (*umma*) it develops and is perfected gradually. And the practice of God in this matter (*sunnat Allāh taʿālā fī dhālika*) is that he who comes later (*al-mutaʾakhkhir*) is more advanced than the one who precedes him (*al-mutaqaddim*), for the beginning of the end proceeds from the end of the beginning (*bidāyat al-ākhir min nihāyat al-awwal*).[110]

For Riḍā, the history of knowledge, including and especially juristic knowledge, is a story of accumulation and progress.[111] In this

[108] Riḍā, *Muḥāwarāt*, 52.

[109] For the central importance of Abū Ḥanīfa to the Ḥanafī school, see Behnam Sadeghi, *The Logic of Law Making in Islam: Women and Prayer in the Legal Tradition* (New York: Cambridge University Press, 2013), 128–34.

[110] Riḍā, *Muḥāwarāt*, 53–54.

[111] For his explicit inclusion of "religious knowledge"—by which is clearly meant law, as we can see through his invocation of *ijtihād* and *taqlīd*—in this category, see Riḍā, *Muḥāwarāt*, 54.

developmental-civilizational narrative, the healthy nation builds upon the contributions of its predecessors to surpass them. Though those predecessors may well have been giants, later participants stand on their proverbial shoulders to see farther. Modern Muslims' relatively late presence in the world signals not a deficiency but an advantage—contra ʿIllīsh and Ibn Kamāl, they possess greater, not lesser, intellectual capabilities and opportunities than their predecessors. This is an optimistic telling, one which is aimed at encouraging Muslims to see themselves not as bound by the past, but as empowered by their capacity to build upon it.

Key to this conception is Riḍā's keen sense of his unique historical moment, the idea that Muslims are at the threshold of a modern world. This historical consciousness formed a consistent theme of Riḍā's thought from the very first issue of *al-Manār*, in whose opening pages (*fātiḥa*) he enjoined the slumbering Easterner to awake and "look to this new world. The ground (*arḍ*) has been replaced by another, and man has entered into a new age."[112] The very project of *al-Manār* may be understood as an exhortation to Muslims to harness the potential of their intellectual capabilities, unencumbered by the commitments of the old world, to exploit this new opportunity, this key moment of rupture from the past. Science and technology, for Riḍā, are central to this process. It is through the expertise that has shrunk the earth through modern communications and transportation, and enabled a newfound familiarity with the heavens through astronomical instrumentation, that the "awakened" Western man has subjected the world to his will. This is a model of civilizational success, and it is the model on which all intellectual work must proceed—the confronting of new situations with an open mind, looking to the unexperienced future rather than to the familiar past.

Reinhart Koselleck has commented how a philosophy of progress was a central ingredient of a historical consciousness, a conception of time as *dynamic*, distinctive from what preceded it: "Progress opened up a future that transcended the hitherto predictable, natural space of time and experience, and thence—propelled by its own dynamic—provoked new, transnatural, long-term prognoses."[113] A key characteristic of the future on this conception, according to Koselleck, is its unknown quality: " 'Unknown' because . . . accelerated time, i.e., our history, abbreviated the space of experiences, robbed

[112] *Al-Manār* 1, no, 1: 9.

[113] Reinhart Koselleck, *Futures Past: On the Semantics of Historical Time*, trans. Keith Tribe, reprint edition (Cambridge, MA: The MIT Press, 1990), 22.

them of their constancy and continually brought into play new, unknown factors, so that even the actuality or complexity of these unknown quantities could not be ascertained."

Koselleck sees this historical consciousness as the marker of modernity, the conception that "first detached [it] from its past."[114] Before this, experience took place on a "static temporal structure." Even in the most dynamic version of this earlier temporality (what he calls "static mobility"), "the past can be experienced only insofar as it contains an element of what is to come (and vice versa)."[115] The past, present, and future are all experienced within the bounds of a common historical plane. This latter conception recalls the schematic characterizations we have seen earlier, and which prevailed in the sixteenth to nineteenth centuries. On those *ahistorical* readings, all future iterations of the law were always already contained in its earlier formulation. This is best illustrated by al-Shaʿrānī's explanation of the work of later legal authorities as simply clarifying and articulating what is implicit in earlier authorities on the metaphor of a seed blossoming over time, or a river with tributaries emanating from a single source. As Wheeler has helpfully characterized, there was "no operative distinction . . . made separating the 'original text' and 'later interpretation' or between canon and application. The contents of the canon are not limited to . . . the text of the Qurʾān, but include subsequent interpretations."[116]

Readers familiar with the scholarship on Islamic law over the past few decades may well raise an objection here. Much of this work has sought to show how jurists adapted legal doctrine to accommodate new circumstances and social conditions, a finding that seems to run counter to the depiction of al-Shaʿrānī.[117] This is not a conclusion I wish to challenge. Rather, my emphasis is on how jurists belonging to the *madhhab*-tradition themselves conceived of that tradition and their role in it when they self-consciously reflected on these questions and articulated their understanding of them. In Ibn ʿĀbidīn's famous treatise *Nashr al-ʿArf fī Bināʾ Baʿḍ al-Aḥkām ʿalā al-ʿUrf*, often referred to for its potential for legal change, reconsiderations of rulings are largely restricted to cases that are thought of as exceptional circumstances: variant customary practices (*ʿurf, ʿāda*),

[114] Koselleck, *Futures Past*, 21.
[115] Koselleck, *Futures Past*, 22.
[116] Wheeler, *Applying the Canon in Islam*, 15.
[117] For just two examples, see Baber Johansen, *Contingency in a Sacred Law: Legal and Ethical Norms in the Muslim Fiqh*, Studies in Islamic Law and Society (Leiden: Brill, 1998) and Sadeghi, *The Logic of Law Making in Islam*.

the degeneration and corruption of time (*fasād ahl al-zamān*), and exigent necessity (*ḍarūra*).[118] The difference between these circumstances and a "normal" state of affairs is conceived of as not a difference in kind, but rather as predictable and manageable aspects of the complexity of life. The rulings that result, therefore, are not thought to be qualitatively different from the default norms that characterize the *ẓāhir al-riwāya*, the most authoritative level of doctrine among Ḥanafīs, attributed to the *mujtahid*-imam; rather, the former are encompassable within the larger governing logic of the *madhhab*. Ibn ʿĀbidīn's telling conceptualization of the way these exceptional rulings relate to the norm proceeds not by asserting their difference but rather by confirming their sameness: If the *mujtahid*-imam had been alive he would have ruled in accordance with the later scholars' determinations, precisely because the latter's rulings fall under the governing principles (*qawāʿid*) of the *madhhab*. What come across as departures are in fact an exercise in "*preserving* the orderliness of the world (*baqāʾ al-ʿālam ʿalā atamm niẓām*)."[119] The experience of the mujtahid, therefore, occupies the same historical plane as that of the later scholars who put forth the exceptional norms.

Elsewhere, Ibn ʿĀbidīn makes the case even more strongly. *Fiqh*, when properly understood, does not admit of augmentation (*ziyāda*) because it is exhaustive and self-contained. This is because, he says, quoting his older Egyptian contemporary, Aḥmad b. Muḥammad al-Ṭaḥṭāwī (d. 1231/1816), *fiqh* has attained such a level of sophistication, intricacy, comprehensiveness, and settledness (*naḍj wa iḥtirāq*) that "all possible occurrences in creation (*ḥawādith al-khalāʾiq*) in their numerous situational contexts and varieties have been distinctly and definitively addressed in writing, either directly or through implication. The jurists even addressed matters that did not occur at all, or occurred only rarely. That which they have not explicitly written about is rare. In fact, it may be that they *have* written about it, but an observer is simply unable to locate where, or to properly understand the text's implied or express meanings."[120]

118 Muhammad Amin Ibn ʿĀbidīn, "Nashr al-ʿArf fī Bināʾ Baʿḍ al-Aḥkām ʿalā al-ʿUrf," in *Majmūʿat Rasāʾil Ibn ʿĀbidīn*, vol. 2 (Damascus: al-Maktaba al-Hashimiyya, 1907), 125. This text is discussed at length in Wael B. Hallaq, "A Prelude to Ottoman Reform: Ibn ʿAbidin on Custom and Legal Change," in *Histories of the Modern Middle East: New Directions* (Boulder, CO: Lynne Rienner, 2002) and Samy Ayoub, *Law, Empire, and the Sultan* (New York: Oxford University Press, 2020), 103–13.

119 Ibn ʿĀbidīn, "Nashr al-ʿArf," 125, emphasis added.

120 Ibn ʿĀbidīn, *Radd al-Muḥtār*, vol. 1, 140–41; al-Ṭaḥṭāwī, *Hashiyat al-Ṭaḥṭāwī ʿala al-Durr al-Mukhtār*, vol. 1, 275.

It is against the backdrop of this early nineteenth-century belief in the predictability of history, and confidence in the mature Ḥanafī tradition's ability to encompass that history, that Bakhīt is writing. Though his response is framed in conciliatory terms, the contrast between his sense of history and Ibn ʿĀbidīn's is striking. Adopting a posture that recalls his contemporary opponent Riḍā rather than his Ḥanafī forebears, Bakhīt clearly sees himself as inhabiting a world characterized not by past prefigurements, but constant change and unprecedented novelty demanding perpetual engagement. It is not a coincidence, after all, that his extended meditation on *ijtihād* forms part of a work devoted to grappling with the legal status of the telegraph. It is precisely the context of explosive technological advancement in which he is living, and the acceleration in life it represented, that motivated Bakhīt's adoption of the reformulated juristic typology and his insistence on the ongoing necessity of *ijtihād*.

Unlikely to find resources for this historical consciousness within his own juristic tradition, Bakhīt reaches outside it to make his case. *Ijtihād* must remain a viable possibility because, as the heresiologist Muḥammad b. ʿAbd al-Karīm al-Shahrastānī remarked, "texts are finite, but events are infinite."[121] In order to make the former speak to the latter, they must be made to do so via the efforts of a *mujtahid*. The modern world in which Bakhīt now lives presents itself as an inexhaustible series of previously unencountered occurrences, themselves the result of "newly originating persons (*ashkhāṣ*), circumstances (*aḥwāl*) and eras (*azmān*)."[122] The word he uses here is *tajaddud*, whose primary signification is "to be cut off" in the manner that the udder of an animal is "cut off" when it goes dry.[123] These new occurrences, then, are the result of the ordinary course of events no longer flowing in the present. His age is experienced as an historical interruption, an emptying of the substance of the past from the present. Unlike Ibn ʿĀbidīn, Bakhīt makes no claim about what Abū Ḥanīfa would have done, because this age of technology is not reducible to previous experience the way even his most immediate forebears thought their eras to have been. Following Koselleck, it is this particular historical consciousness of Bakhīt that marks him off as a subject of modernity.

***

[121] Bakhīt, *Irshād*, 219–23; al-Shahrastānī, *al-Milal wa-l-Niḥal*, 210.
[122] Bakhīt, *Irshād*, 223.
[123] Lane's *Lexicon*, *al-Qāmūs al-Muḥīṭ*.

I have noted earlier that Bakhīt leaned heavily on al-Marjānī's text in *Nāẓūrat al-Ḥaqq* in his appendix. It is all the more notable, then, that this last discussion is entirely an interpolation of his own, inserted amid al-Marjānī's original comments. Al-Marjānī was himself a writer of history, and a certain historical sensibility is discernible also in al-Laknawī, especially inasmuch as he inherited it from Shāh Walī Allāh. But, outside of pointing out the inner incoherence of Ibn Kamāl Pāshā's scheme, it is not until Bakhīt that we find a clearly articulated basis for the need for a reformulated typology. Responding to the circumstances in which he finds himself, Bakhīt intensifies and repositions lines of thought found among his maverick Ḥanafī elders to not only affirm his own continued relevance within a contested Egyptian space but also to bring *fiqh* in line with his understanding of the world, reconceptualizing it as a modern enterprise in an era of *tajaddud*.

In another addition to al-Marjānī that reveals his commitment to a historical consciousness, Bakhīt notes that the problem with the older typology, and the regime of interpretation that it represented, is that it confused chronology for merit, unjustifiably granting precedence to earlier scholars. In Bakhīt's opinion, the new classification is superior for

> the people of one era are not privileged over another era; rather, the central factor in [setting forth] ranks is the description of qualities, not priority in time (*al-taqaddum fī al-zamān*). For, how many have there been early in time, but they have been *muqallid*s, understanding nothing of the evidences. And how many have there been later in time, but they have reached the status of *ijtihād* as is clearly known.[124]

By Bakhīt's reckoning, intellectual accomplishment, logical consistency, and juristic merit have replaced chronology as the primary consideration in ranking jurists. The jurists are, according to Bakhīt, like a "seamless circle. One does not know where its sides are. And the grace of God is expansive, bound neither by time nor place, nor restricted to some people at the expense of others."[125] Contemporary Ḥanafī jurists, then, need no longer feel bound by the historic decisions of the past simply because earlier scholars have been stipulated to be more authoritative than themselves.

124 Bakhīt al-Muṭīʿī, *Irshād Ahl al-Milla ilā Ithbāt al-Ahilla*, 248.
125 Bakhīt al-Muṭīʿī, *Irshād Ahl al-Milla ilā Ithbāt al-Ahilla*, 258.

It is useful to recall here Riḍā's allusion to "the principle of the Popes" to castigate the illegitimacy of his ulama opponents. If what is most distinctive about Bakhīt's account is that it carries embedded within it a historical consciousness, it is precisely this historical consciousness that Hans-Georg Gadamer, another of Heidegger's students, linked explicitly to the Reformation.[126] Reliant on what he calls "the scriptural principle of the Reformation [that] . . . we do not need tradition to achieve the proper understanding of Scripture,"[127] the central claim of a historical consciousness is its capacity to take up a historical orientation, to have a "historical viewpoint on everything. It sees this as its culminating achievement. Hence it is concerned to develop the 'historical sense' in order to transcend the prejudices of one's own time."[128]

Yoav Di-Capua has convincingly documented the Egyptian emergence of "the modern idea of history": "a form of thought and a habit of mind that arrived in Egypt in the late nineteenth century, bringing with them specific institutions and modes of reasoning."[129] As he explains, at the turn of the twentieth century, this historicism took a particular view on the structure of time: "the present is no longer an extension, an expansion, or simply a repetition of the past. Rather, it is the future's point of beginning 'as an open, un-built site never visited before but a place reachable and constructible.' "[130] For Di-Capua, this new historicism was a central plank of Egyptian modernity.[131] Indeed, he argues that historicism so came to dominate Egyptian intellectual life in this period that it could be said to be the "single grand concept" held in common by the remarkable range of ideologies, movements, and currents circulating at the time.[132] It is thus unsurprising that Bakhīt, as a man firmly embedded within the intellectual currents and intrigues of this period, should consider this new mode of thinking about the past so natural and obvious.

[126] Gadamer, *Truth and Method*, 175–76. This does not correspond precisely to, and is not to be confused with, Gadamer's *wirkungsgeschichtliches Bewusstsein*, which has been translated into English as "historically effected consciousness." The historical consciousness I speak of is a constituent feature of *wirkungsgeschichtliches Bewusstsein*, but for the latter, Gadamer has something much more particular in mind, namely a historical consciousness which remains open to its encounter with tradition and the other. See Gadamer, *Truth and Method*, xv.

[127] Gadamer, *Truth and Method*, 176.

[128] Gadamer, *Truth and Method*, 225.

[129] Yoav Di-Capua, *Gatekeepers of the Arab Past: Historians and History Writing in Twentieth-Century Egypt* (Berkeley: University of California Press, 2009), 11.

[130] Di-Capua, *Gatekeepers of the Arab Past*, 61.

[131] Di-Capua, *Gatekeepers of the Arab Past*, 3.

[132] Di-Capua, *Gatekeepers of the Arab Past*, 28.

Notably, Bakhīt's historicist stance as applied to law stands in sharp contrast to what we have seen earlier in Ibn ʿĀbidīn and his predecessors. His commitment to "equalizing" the jurists of all eras, by deeming them equally entitled to engage in *ijtihād*, ceteris paribus, also differs from the recent findings of Brannon Wheeler and Eyyup Said Kaya with respect to the premodern Ḥanafī madhhab, which they characterize precisely as an authoritative corporate juristic history whose cumulative corpus acts as the primary point of contact for later jurists' encounters with legal matters.[133] As such, Bakhīt constitutes, to my mind, a significant shift from "tradition" which, though it may consider itself to possess internal structuring principles that render it amenable to change, remains loyal to an overarching model and temporality exemplified by Ḥanafism's premodern history.

For Calder, Wheeler and Kaya, the later jurist, when he is sufficiently qualified, considers himself a part of a holistic entity: the duty to take account of, contend with, and subject oneself to the claims of the juristic tradition that is the *madhhab* is precisely what it means to be part of that *madhhab*.[134] The shift from this understanding to one that identifies the prevailing typology not as a discursive representation of a holistic entity but rather as a misplaced exercise in chronological placement is one which has naturalized a historical consciousness. Gadamer might say that the historicism that we find in Bakhīt which considers intermediate layers of tradition not as part and parcel of how he ought to understand a given issue and argue about the law, but rather contingent and particular opinions which can be put aside or drawn upon eclectically but exercising no ultimate authority over him, is constituent of a modern approach to knowing.[135] As one commentator of Gadamer explains, "When an historical text is read as 'merely historical,' the present has already been dogmatized and placed outside of the question."[136] This is ironic, for it

133 Wheeler, *Applying the Canon in Islam*; Kaya, "Continuity and Change in Islamic Law: The Concept of Madhhab and the Dimensions of Legal Disagreement in Hanafi Scholarship of the Tenth Century." See also Calder's more general observation earlier, 83. I should like to point out that this older, Ḥanafī way of understanding the past corresponds to what Di-Capua thinks is being displaced by modern historicism in Egypt. Following Koselleck, Di-Capua identifies premodern history as holding the theological position that "the future could bring nothing fundamentally new" and that "the nature of individuals, society, and humanity in general was destined to remain the same until the arrival of the Day of Judgment." Di-Capua, *Gatekeepers of the Arab Past*, 3.

134 Indeed, this account may square better with Gadamer's *wirkungsgeschichtliches Bewusstsein*, but this line of inquiry awaits future research.

135 Catherine H. Zuckert, "Hermeneutics in Practice: Gadamer on Ancient Philosophy," in *The Cambridge Companion to Gadamer*, ed. Robert J. Dostal (Cambridge, UK: Cambridge University Press, 2002), 205–6.

136 Richard E. Palmer, *Hermeneutics: Interpretation Theory in Schleiermacher, Dilthey, Heidegger, and Gadamer*, Northwestern University Studies in Phenomenology & Existential Philosophy (Evanston, IL: Northwestern University Press, 1969), 193. See also Zuckert, "Insofar as it treats the

is precisely through his tireless efforts to level the scholarly playing field that Bakhīt has made of his modern period an exceptional case.

Conclusion

Central to Asad's formulation of tradition is its unique inner temporal structure—in which the past authoritatively constitutes present practices, and the present is in turn included within other epochs—and that structure's difference from linear time. As this chapter shows, however, we have in Riḍā, and then in Bakhīt, a very different formulation of the relationship between past and present. While it is true that the premodern Ḥanafī tradition did in fact occupy a certain temporality in which futures were always thought to be contained in the origin, we find in Riḍā's historiography of knowledge an argument for a much more progressive notion of time. This is an account of overcoming and surpassing the past, not of maintaining an organic link to it as per Ḥanafī tradition. Riḍā, in fact, affirms linear time, and indeed progressive time, in a manner that makes it difficult to speak of him as participating in a tradition on Asad's formulation.

The concern with historical time, the relationship between past, present, and future, is, of course, a hallmark feature of Heidegger's thought. As we have seen in this chapter, Gadamer and Koselleck, students of Heidegger, have placed an important emphasis on historical consciousness as a distinguishing feature of a modern conception of time. While Bakhīt does not participate overtly in Riḍā's progressivism, the instinct to historicize the past that is a feature of a linear, teleological temporality (historicize, because only then can it be overcome) is articulated quite clearly in his understanding of the *madhhab*'s history. This, in turn, forces us to consider the temporality that underlies his formulation—one in which he is keenly aware of the fundamental difference of his time to those of his predecessors—as a departure from the premodern Ḥanafī tradition as expressed by the likes of Ibn Kamāl and Ibn ʿĀbidīn.

past as simply the past, as the product of a set of circumstances and expressing an understanding of the world that cannot possibly be duplicated in the present, an exclusively historical or scholarly reading of a past text precludes that text from challenging the truth of our current conceptions, including the historical insight itself." Zuckert, "Hermeneutics in Practice: Gadamer on Ancient Philosophy," 206.

3

Colonialism, Translation, and Seduction

In July 1919, a certain Sayyid Ḥasan Muḥammad forwarded a request for a fatwa to the Mufti of Egypt, Muḥammad Bakhīt. We are uncertain who precisely Sayyid Ḥasan Muḥammad was, but his was not a simple request for individual guidance on everyday affairs. Instead, the questioner was asking about a major world phenomenon of the day, though his one-sided language gave away rather transparently his own view on recent developments. "What is your judgment concerning the 'Way' of the Bolsheviks which is spreading and doing harm everywhere these days?"[1] As if to remove any doubt, Muḥammad went on to define what he thought Bolshevism consisted of, providing a laundry list of evils ranging from anarchy and atheism to the denial of property rights and the dissolution of the family through practices like the holding of women and children in common.

In his response, translated and preserved in a remarkable file in the archive of the Foreign Office, Bakhīt began in a manner that may seem curious to modern historians but fit with his general practice of speaking to modern developments through the language of Islamic learning and history. He traced the beginnings of this "Way" to ancient Persia and the beliefs of Zoroaster and Mazdak, who "taught communism of property and of persons and put it in their mind that this, although it might not be from religion, was at least honorable in the doing."[2] The arrival of Islam "swept this false Way aside";[3] the Prophet Muḥammad came to set things aright and institute an upright morality. After citing Qurʾanic verses affirming God's prerogative to distribute wealth according to His own purposes, Bakhīt quotes the Prophet's

[1] FO 141/779/1, 18. This translation is reproduced in Tareq Y. Ismael, *The Communist Movement in Egypt, 1920–1988*, 1st ed. (Syracuse, NY: Syracuse University Press, 1990), 163–67. The translator is identified in a different document as Upson of the Nile Mission Press. FO 141/779/1, 4. The original Arabic is located in the Dār al-Iftāʾ archives, DIM register 17/#152, and is published in a selection of Bakhīt's fatwas.

[2] This was a common understanding of Zoroastrianism within the Islamic tradition. See Patricia Crone, "Zoroastrian Communism," *Comparative Studies in Society and History* 36, no. 3 (1994): 448–49. Crone discusses the appropriateness of comparing Zoroastrian practices to modern-day communism at 455–56.

[3] FO 141/779/1, 19.

Transformations of Tradition. Junaid Quadri, Oxford University Press (2021). © Oxford University Press.
DOI: 10.1093/oso/9780190077044.003.0004

final sermon which includes provisions on the inviolability of life and property, the evils of usury and bloodshed, and exhortations to respect familial duties and boundaries. In conclusion, he writes,

> It is known from all this that the "Way" of the Bolsheviks is one which destroys all Divine laws especially the doctrines of Islam, because it recommends what God hath considered illegal in His Book. It legalizes blood shedding, allows trespass upon the property of others, treachery, lies, and rape, causing anarchy to spread among the people in their properties, their women, children, and inheritance until they become at last worse than beasts. God hath verily and plainly forbidden all these things, and such people are but infidels whose "Way" demolishes human society, destroys the order of the world, leads to denying religion, threatens the whole world with horrible distress and bitter troubles, and instigates the lower classes against all system founded upon reason, morals and virtue.[4]

When British officials first saw Bakhīt's response, they took it to be a boon to their imperial ambitions. "The Mufti of Cairo has published a remarkable Fetwa calling on all Mohammedans to oppose Bolshevism," reads a note sent to the Foreign Office.[5] Plans were quickly made to print hundreds of copies and distribute them across the Muslim world "for propaganda purposes."[6] The Brits were particularly interested in spreading the fatwa among Muslims in Russia, India, and Afghanistan, and arrangements were made to forward copies to the Residencies at Aden and Ramleh, the Civil Commissioner at Baghdad, the High Commissioner in Istanbul, and the Governor General of Sudan, in addition to the Viceroy of India.[7]

Their high hopes for propagating the fatwa would, however, come to naught. In early fall, the Indian Viceroy began the process of having the fatwa translated into various local vernaculars, but he quickly reversed this decision due to advice that the reference to Zoroastrians, "a rich and influential community in the Bombay presidency," would be seen as offensive. In the interim, the fatwa did appear in a local newspaper, but the British government decided to maintain their distance from it.[8] Soon afterward, the Political

[4] FO 141/779/1, 29. I've amended the translation slightly in three places.
[5] FO 141/779/1, 12.
[6] FO 141/779/1, 3.
[7] FO 141/779/1, 3, 13.
[8] FO 141/779/1, 93.

Office in Baghdad decided not to circulate the fatwa in Mesopotamia on similar grounds, but also because it was issued by a Sunni authority and would therefore be ineffective in much of that region.[9]

The fatwa received even more opposition within Egypt. Throughout the second half of August, a number of journals published critical reviews of the fatwa, including some that advanced Islamic grounds for Bolshevik sympathies.[10] The general consensus of these pieces was that Bakhīt had misrepresented Bolshevism, and was ill equipped to properly understand it.[11] The strength of this response was noted by British officials. A confidential missive in the archives bemoans

> the somewhat reckless and unrestrained campaign carried on by the Press in favour of Bolshevism and Syndicalism. . . . The Fetwa of Sheikh Bekheit caused, as you know, a storm of criticism, and practically all the articles that are written in the Native Press at present seem to be endeavouring to persuade the man in the street that true Bolshevism, if adopted in this country, would be the saving of Egypt.[12]

That Bakhīt's fatwa had had the opposite of the desired effect, serving instead to rally common Egyptians around Bolshevik ideals, was confirmed also by Rashīd Riḍā in an encounter he had with a British informant. Their conversation was memorialized in a confidential intelligence report, in which Riḍā takes the opportunity to revive his ongoing rivalry with Bakhīt once more, referring to him as a "senile old man" who wrote his fatwa in a "weak style" and based on "weaker historical sources." "Nobody ever knew in Egypt, so much about real Bolchevism before the publication of the Fetwa, and the newspapers never wrote so much about Bolchevism, before the publication. . . . Everybody here believes that Bolchevism is good to make the English go out of Egypt."[13] Riḍā also believed that the question was in fact a

[9] FO 141/779/1, 91.

[10] FO 141/779/1, 34, 46–47, 50–53.

[11] An Italian subject in Cairo named Pizzuto, who was an agitator on behalf of Bolshevism, "laugh[ed] at the naiveté of the Egyptian Moufti who has proved to be absolutely ignorant of the A.B.C. of Bolshevism. 'The terms of the Fetwa, said Pizzuto, are so stupid that they constitute an easy ground for the defence of Bolshevism, not only in Egypt, but even in India and Afghanistan, for whom it was intended.'" FO 141/779/1, 44.

[12] FO 141/779/1, 57.

[13] FO 141/779/1, 39–40. Riḍā's own views on the Bolshevik revolution are harder to pin down. For a rather stand-offish public response, see "al-Ishtirākiyya wa-l-Bulshafiyya wa-l-Dīn," in *al-Manār*, reprinted in Muḥammad Rashīd Riḍā, *Maqālāt al-Shaykh Rashīd Riḍā al-Siyāsiyya*, ed. Yūsuf Ībish and Yūsuf Q. Khūrī, vol. 3 (Beirut: Dār Ibn ʿArabī, 1994), 1136–41. In his conversation

contrived one through the ruse of an invented questioner, because no serious Muslim could be in doubt as to the Islamic view on the beliefs and behaviors the questioner attributed to Bolshevism. As a result, "everybody now believes that the Moufti was even forced to publish this Fetwa, and forced only by the British authorities." There is nothing in the reports of the Foreign Office that suggests that British officials had anything to do with instigating the fatwa.[14] But the general suspicion that Bakhīt was too cozy with the British is one that recurs.

The sources themselves give a mixed view of Bakhīt's attitude toward the British. As discussed in the Introduction, he was a prominent participant in the 1919 revolution, chairing the committee that resolved to initiate a national strike and attending meetings of the Liberal-Constitutionalist Party. On December 20, 1919, amid the Egyptian boycott of the Milner Commission, deputed to Egypt to decide what to do about the nationalist demands for independence, Milner paid a visit to Bakhīt in the latter's home in the Cairo suburb of Zaytun. In his private diary of conversations with Egyptians, Milner seemed relatively unimpressed, characterizing Bakhīt's comments during their meeting as "the usual Nationalist repertory."[15] However, the reaction in much of the Egyptian press seems to have been positive, and Saʿd Zaghlūl wrote Bakhīt a letter expressing his "great delight (*ibtihāj ʿaẓīm*) at your responses to Lord Milner."[16] The account of this meeting corresponds to the way his run-ins with British officials are presented in sympathetic sources, namely in the form of anecdotes in which he bests British representatives and spies in verbal jousting.[17]

with the British informant, he opines that "every verse in the Coran can be interpreted in favour of Bolchevism," before suggesting that if the British really wish to stem the rise of Bolshevism, they should emphasize its denial of "the principle of Proprietorship" given the "four million proprietors of Egypt" who would feel their interests threatened. FO 141/779/1, 39–40. In another intelligence report, Riḍā tells a British agent named "Yusef" that he had been approached by propagandists who sought his support to spread Bolshevism in Syria and Palestine. Riḍā declined their advances but refused to name the propagandists, saying only that all were Europeans, save "one notable Egyptian." FO 141/779/1, 67.

14 There is a note in the Foreign Office file that suggested that, after the fact, "it has been hinted to us that the Grand Mufti would be flattered by receiving the thanks of the Commander-in-Chief through a Staff Officer at G.H.Q." FO 141/779/1, 4.

15 FO 848/5, 25–26.

16 Muḥammad al-Dasūqī, *Muḥammad Bakhīt al-Muṭīʿī: Shaykh al-Islām wa-l-Muftī al-ʿĀlamī* (Damascus: Dār al-Qalam, 2011), 63–64.

17 For an example in which he makes a joke at the expense of spies who frequent his lessons at al-Azhar to ask him sensitive political questions, see Aḥmad ibn al-Ṣiddīq al-Ghumārī, *al-Baḥr al-ʿAmīq fī Marwiyyāt Ibn al-Ṣiddīq*, vol. 1 (Cairo: Dār al-Kutubī, 2007), 197.

However, the reputation that he was compromised by closeness to the British continued to dog him. Critics like Riḍā had some reason to think the way they did. Already in 1908, Bakhīt was involved in British attempts at reforming the shariʿa courts. His "especial duty," according to a confidential report in the archives, "was to help in convincing the religious party that the proposed regulations were in accordance with the religious law or that, at least, there was no sufficient reason for raising objections on that ground."[18] Al-Ghumārī records that some described Bakhīt as harboring tendencies toward the British, while others accused him of outright treason. Some students at the Azhar, at once awed by his learning and repelled by his opportunistic politics, went so far as to tell al-Ghumārī that Bakhīt was "the most knowledgeable person on earth, but also an infidel."[19]

The most damning evidence of his coziness with the British, however, was always the Bolshevism fatwa. Among the onslaught of critiques made of Bakhīt in the aftermath of his fatwa on Bolshevism was a circular under the heading, "O Egyptians! Embrace Bolshevism: Bolshevism, Islam and Shaykh Bakhīt." Numbered Circular 73 and issued by an unknown "emergency committee (*al-lajna al-mustaʿjala*)," the lengthy critique rehearsed several familiar complaints: that Bakhīt spoke without knowledge, that he had rendered a service to the English in issuing his fatwa, and that the very terms of the question were dubious.[20] It also went on to explain what Bolshevism really was, conceptualizing it as a movement of justice and liberty sent by God to the world to restore Islam to its origin of unswerving justice. One of the effects of this restoration, it held in a caustic rejoinder to Bakhīt, would be that "a *mudhabdhab* mufti like you" would no longer exist. The word used here is a telling one. The colonial translation found in the British archives translates *mudhabdhab* as "hypocrite." And indeed its occurrence in the Qurʾan is in reference to the Hypocrites (*munāfiqūn*) of Medina. But the term itself captures a specific feature of this group. The Qurʾanic invocation of *mudhabdhab* is clarifying.

> Those who wait upon you and, if a victory comes to you from God, say, 'Were we not with you?' but if the unbelievers get a share, they say, 'Did we not gain the mastery over you, and did we not defend you from the

[18] FO 141/553/375, 4; Jakob Skovgaard-Petersen, *Defining Islam for the Egyptian State: Muftis and Fatwas of the Dār al-Iftā* (Leiden: Brill, 1997), 134.

[19] Al-Ghumārī, *al-Baḥr al-ʿAmīq fī Marwiyyāt Ibn al-Ṣiddīq*, 1:200.

[20] Both the circular and an English translation can be found in FO 141/779/1, 98–109.

> believers?' God will judge between you on the Resurrection Day, and God will not grant the unbelievers any way over the believers. The hypocrites seek to trick God, but God is tricking them. When they stand up to pray they stand up lazily, showing off to the people and not remembering God save a little; wavering (*mudhabdhabīn*) all the time—[belonging] not to these, not to those.[21]

The figure of the *mudhabdhab* is not simply a hypocrite whose outward behavior fails to match his inner convictions; he is more specifically someone whose opportunism and lack of commitment deprive him of fully belonging to either side. It is the partiality and ambivalence inherent in this characterization that is crucial to understanding Bakhīt's relationship to European colonialism. He was not, as zealous Azharī students would have it, an infidel cravenly beholden to British power. And a simplistic charge of opportunism, while not irrelevant for someone who navigated the changing intellectual and political terrain of modern Egypt, does not do full justice to his complex personality. It does not explain, for example, why he was associated with European tastes in his private life. His admiring student, al-Ghumārī, who had travelled from Morocco to study at the feet of the famous Shaykh Bakhīt, marveled at the foreign influence on the way his home was kept and his children dressed. On the first count, Bakhīt is noted as keeping dogs—indeed, "large European dogs"—inside the home, and for putting marble busts on display in room corners, practices that were more in step with European expectations of civility and taste than Egyptian-Islamic ones. More consequential, perhaps, was that his children were known for dressing in European fashions, and that his daughters and granddaughters appeared in public unveiled (*sāfirāt*) and wearing European hats (*al-baranīṭ*). These observations speak less to careerist opportunism than to the deep penetration of European manners and behaviors as marks of distinction in the lives of ambitious and prominent classes in Egypt, whatever their politics.[22]

But rather than focus on the largely unproductive and ultimately irresolvable questions of whether or not he was "actually" a British agent or how thoroughly Europeanized he was, it is much more interesting to think through the relationship of Bakhīt's *ideas* to colonial power. I show in this chapter how writings of his that posit a harmony between modern science and

[21] *Al-Nisā'* 4: 141–43. The translation is from A. J. Arberry's *The Koran Interpreted*, with one slight amendment in square brackets for clarity.
[22] Al-Ghumārī, *al-Baḥr al-'Amīq fī Marwiyyāt Ibn al-Ṣiddīq*, 1:201.

Islamic learning fit rather neatly into the architecture of colonial discourse. That the "emergency committee" circular should label him a *mudhabdhab* was not an accident; instead, the term evokes the very nature of his intervention. Notably, the circular's framing of Bakhīt's fatwa is not as an embrace, heart and soul, of British designs but rather as a deception that has taken him in. The first sentence is "They have deceived you, O Bakhit!" This characterization resists reducing the mufti to a mere stooge, but neither does it gainsay his complicity in colonial discourse. What the translation of *mudhabdhab* as mere hypocrisy misses is that it is precisely Bakhīt's *ambivalence* that the Arabic captures, not an undercover allegiance to British power despite a Muslim facade. Homi Bhabha famously reminds us that this ambivalence, and the partiality that it engenders, are constituent features of colonial mimicry. For colonial discourse is always premised on a disavowal. The native mimic is "almost the same, but not quite,"[23] because it remains essential to colonialism that it continue to assert difference, even as it strives to create a native subject in its image.

In Egypt, this mode of cultural imperialism was negotiated through what Shaden Tageldin has called translational seduction. Drawing on Baudrillard's notion of seduction as "a power that exercises itself through the subtle manipulation of illusion"[24]—recall the emergency committee's "They have deceived you, O Bakhīt!"—Tageldin brilliantly shows that in Egypt, "cultural imperialism might be better understood as a politics that lures the colonized to seek power *through* empire rather than against it."[25] This is accomplished through the register of translation, in particular a translation in which Europeans present themselves in a language of Arab-Islamic authenticity that seduces the colonized Egyptian into imagining a sort of equivalency between the two parties. In this chapter, then, I examine Bakhīt's translation of modern science into his Arab-Islamic milieu. After providing a brief history of the relationship between science and religion within the Muslim world as it is depicted in the secondary literature, I zero in on modern Egypt to track the emergence of a new intellectual culture which valorized science, often to the exclusion of traditional modes of knowing. One of the demands of this new intellectual culture was to harmonize Islamic commitment with the

[23] Homi Bhabha, "Of Mimicry and Man: The Ambivalence of Colonial Discourse," *October* 28 (1984): 126.

[24] Shaden M. Tageldin, *Disarming Words: Empire and the Seductions of Translation in Egypt* (Berkeley: University of California Press, 2011), 11.

[25] Tageldin, *Disarming Words*, 10, emphasis in original.

"new science." This is best represented in a new genre of writing that made use of scriptural commentary to advance justifications for modern science. I examine Bakhīt's contributions to this genre, in particular his account of the historical development of astronomy, to suggest that this narrative is a translation of the demands of modern science into the idioms of Arabic and Islam that corresponds to Bhabha's theorization of mimicry and exemplifies the seduction Tageldin has detected in modern Egypt.

A Brief History of Islamic Philosophy and Science

Like the concept of *ijtihād* discussed in the last chapter, Muslim attitudes toward scientific inquiry have long been taken by Western scholarship as a critical measure of Islam's intellectual vitality and openness. The received view for much of the twentieth century offered an unhappy assessment of Muslim society on this count. On this reading, Islamicate civilization was thought to be essentially religious, and therefore inhospitable to a culture of science. Proponents of this view held that because Muslim scientists and philosophers drew from the intellectual traditions of Greek antiquity, their contributions were foreign and therefore irredeemably heretical in the judgment of their orthodox opponents, and derivative and unoriginal by the standards of a backward-looking assessment of the history of philosophy. An especially harsh evaluation was offered by the German scholar T. J. de Boer, for whom Muslim philosophy

> has always continued to be an Eclecticism which depended on their stock of works translated from the Greek. The course of its history has been a process of assimilation rather than of generation. It has not distinguished itself, either by propounding new problems or by any peculiarity in its endeavours to solve the old ones. It has therefore no important advances in thought to register.[26]

A slightly more positive assessment by the famed Orientalist G. E. von Grunebaum some sixty years later admits the possibility that Muslims may

[26] T. J. de Boer, *The History of Philosophy in Islam* (New York: Dover Publications, 1967), 29. This is a reprint of a 1903 translation from the original German: T. J. de Boer, *Geschichte Der Philosophie Im Islam* (Stuttgart: F. Frommanns Verlag [E. Hauff], 1901).

have made some important contributions to the natural sciences, but nonetheless concludes that

> those sciences (and their technological application) had no root in the fundamental needs and aspirations of their civilization. Those accomplishments of Islamic mathematical and medical science which continue to compel our admiration were developed in areas and in periods where the élites were willing to go beyond and possibly against the basic strains of orthodox thought and feeling. For the sciences never did shed the suspicion of bordering on the impious which, to the strict, would be nearidentical [*sic*] with the religiously uncalled-for. This is why the pursuit of the natural sciences as that of philosophy tended to become located in relatively small and esoteric circles and why but few of their representatives would escape an occasional uneasiness with regard to the moral implications of their endeavors, a mood which not infrequently did result in some kind of an apology for their work. It is not so much the constant struggle which their representatives found themselves involved in against the apprehensive skepticism of the orthodox which in the end smothered the progress of their work; rather it was the fact which became more and more obvious that their researches had nothing to give to their community which this community could accept as an essential enrichment of their lives.[27]

Science was therefore a marginal and derivative endeavor in the Muslim world on this reading, concerned exclusively with the "reception, preservation and transmission"[28] of the Greek heritage, a fortuitous historical episode inasmuch as it later allowed European civilization to once more take up its rightful inheritance upon emerging from the Dark Ages into the Renaissance. Indeed, because it was a foreign interloper in a society defined by religion, science and the broader philosophical tradition suffered its demise at about

[27] G. E. von Grunebaum, "Muslim World View and Muslim Science," *Dialectica* 17, no. 4 (1963): 356–57.

[28] A. I. Sabra, "The Appropriation and Subsequent Naturalization of Greek Science in Medieval Islam: A Preliminary Statement," *History of Science* 25 (1987): 225. This is Sabra's characterization of the prevailing historiography. For his own part, he expresses misgivings about this language: "'Reception' might connote a passive receiving of something being pressed upon the receiver, and this might reinforce the image of Islamic civilization as a receptacle or repository of Greek learning. This, however, was not quite what happened; the transmission of ancient science to Islam would be better characterized as an act of appropriation performed by the so-called receiver. . . . 'Reception' is, at best, a pale description of [their] enormously creative act." Sabra, "The Appropriation and Subsequent Naturalization of Greek Science in Medieval Islam," 225–26.

this time, coming into conflict with the settled orthodoxy laid out by Abū Ḥāmid al-Ghazālī.[29] Indeed, this is assumed by von Grunebaum in the very next sentence when he speaks matter-of-factly about the near death of science in the Muslim world: "When in the later Middle ages scientific endeavor in certain fields very nearly died down."

These features of what George Saliba has called the "classical narrative"[30] of the scientific enterprise in Islam have been the subject of severe criticism over the last thirty years. An underlying assumption of this narrative, as we have seen, is a division within Islamic society between a religious orthodoxy which maintained dominance, and circles of philosophical and scientific learning which were always in the minority and on the defensive. For the early period, even revisionist scholars have tended to agree that such a division existed, though they have doubted the assumption that hostility was the de facto attitude of the former toward the latter. Dimitri Gutas, for example, has said that Arabic philosophy "was not a fringe activity frowned upon by a so-called 'orthodoxy,'" but rather a "vigorous and largely autonomous intellectual movement."[31] Similarly, David A. King has pointed out that the "folk astronomy" preferred by jurists for ritual matters constituted a parallel tradition that existed alongside the more sophisticated mathematical astronomy of Muslim scientists "with few records of serious discord between the two groups."[32] A. I. Sabra, however, has suggested that this early dichotomy—which was always more complex and variegated than is usually portrayed—dissolved as scientific activity came to be gradually assimilated and eventually naturalized within Muslim society in what has come to be known as the postclassical period. In this stage of development,

[29] Al-Ghazālī's name is invariably mentioned in this context, the story being that his anathematization of Greek philosophy in the *Tahāfut al-Falāsifa* (*Incoherence of the Philosophers*) gained such traction in a culture in which scientific research already verged on the impious that philosophy "ceased to exist after the death blow allegedly dealt to it by al-Ghazālī." Dimitri Gutas, "The Study of Arabic Philosophy in the Twentieth Century: An Essay on the Historiography of Arabic Philosophy," *British Journal of Middle Eastern Studies* 29, no. 1 (May 1, 2002): 5. Gutas disagrees with this assessment: "Arabic philosophy did not die after al-Ghazālī," 6. Much recent scholarship has agreed with him and has spoken instead of a postclassical tradition of philosophy and science in the Muslim world.

[30] George Saliba, *Islamic Science and the Making of the European Renaissance*, Transformations (Cambridge, MA: MIT Press, 2007), 1–25.

[31] Gutas, "The Study of Arabic Philosophy in the Twentieth Century," 6.

[32] David A. King, "Science in the Service of Religion: The Case of Islam," in *Astronomy in the Service of Islam* (Aldershot, UK: Variorum, 1993), 261.

> The carriers of scientific and medical knowledge and techniques now largely consisted of men who were not only Muslim by birth and faith, but who were imbued with Muslim learning and tradition, and whose conceptual framework had been produced in the process of forging a consciously Muslim outlook. No longer was the scientific scholar committed to the presuppositions of the earlier philosophers.[33]

In Sabra's estimation, this led to a formalization of certain roles for scientists in the world of Islam. This was the period

> in which *falsafa*, the type of thought and discourse found in the writings of philosophers like Fārābī and Avicenna, began to be practised in the context of *kalām*; and in which the philosopher-physician (represented by Rāzī) was replaced by the jurist-physician (represented by Ibn al-Nafīs), the mathematician (*taʿlīmī*) by the *faraḍī*, and the astronomer-astrologer by the *muwaqqit*.[34]

It is against this background that we can understand the postclassical dominance of Islamic astronomy (*ʿilm al-hayʾa*), a field whose very *raison d'être* was the maintenance of a balance between scientific rigor and a sensitivity to the dictates of revelation.[35] In Egypt, at least, this dominance would continue well into the nineteenth century,[36] and only came under challenge with the emergence of the new European science. As we will see, the reception of the "new science" resulted in a reinstitution of the dichotomy between men of religion and men of science that had been dissolved by the postclassical synthesis.

[33] Sabra, "The Appropriation and Subsequent Naturalization of Greek Science in Medieval Islam: A Preliminary Statement," 237.

[34] Sabra, "The Appropriation and Subsequent Naturalization of Greek Science in Medieval Islam: A Preliminary Statement," 236–37. The *faraḍī* is responsible for calculating the shares of inheritance. The *muwaqqit* is the timekeeper for prayers.

[35] For a detailed reading of the emergence and nature of *ʿilm al-hayʾa*, see Saliba, *Islamic Science and the Making of the European Renaissance*. See also Ahmad Dallal, *Islam, Science and the Challenge of History* (New Haven, CT: Yale University Press, 2010).

[36] Pascal Crozet, *Les Sciences Modernes en Égypte: Transfert et Appropriation, 1805–1902* (Paris: Guethner, 2008), 211–15; Daniel A. Stolz, *The Lighthouse and the Observatory: Islam, Science, and Empire in Late Ottoman Egypt* (Cambridge, UK: Cambridge University Press, 2018).

The "New Science" in Modern Egypt: Emergence and Impact

The "new science" took root in Egypt over the long nineteenth century, a period of remarkable intellectual and political upheaval in the country. Taking Bakhīt as an example, the next two sections show that by the end of this period, modern science and its attendant commitments had been thoroughly embedded within the discourses of Egyptian intelligentsia, and that the ulama were no exception to this phenomenon. In making this claim, I do not mean to argue for a unanimity where there was none, but rather to point to the remarkable headway a culture of science made into domains, like Islamic law, that had historically exhibited a remarkable autonomy from the investigations of Muslim scientists.

Much of the ulama's engagement with modern science was motivated by the intellectual tumult of the period. The proliferation of a variety of currents of thought, and the options these made available to people, meant that it was no longer possible for ulama to avoid dealing with these subjects without rendering themselves irrelevant. The destabilizing of Azharī authority over the past century had already presented a serious challenge to the ulama. Though he had come to power in no small part thanks to the support of the Azharī elites, Muḥammad ʿAlī had made a concerted effort to marginalize them by confiscating the tax farms and endowments that had long sustained this scholarly class.[37] So as to further displace the ulama, he went on to create rival educational institutions, whose graduates were thereafter privileged in terms of appointment to jobs as legal and governmental functionaries.[38]

[37] Daniel Crecelius, for example, notes that "The ulama were an indispensable ally to Muhammad Ali in his rise to power, for they secured for him the one important element of authority which force alone could not command, legitimacy. They besieged their former wali in the citadel, wrote to the Sultan praising Muhammad Ali's justness and administrative skills, and organized popular defense forces to defend their capital against Mamluks, Ottomans, Bedouins, and a British expeditionary force which reentered Egypt in 1807." Daniel Crecelius, "Nonideological Responses of the Egyptian Ulama to Modernization," in *Scholars, Saints, and Sufis: Muslim Religious Institutions in the Middle East Since 1500* (Berkeley: University of California Press, 1972), 177. In response, however, Muḥammad ʿAli embarked on a policy of "financial starvation," moving "against the wealth of the entire religious establishment. He abolished the system of iltizam [tax farms], thereby taking from the higher ulama an important source of personal wealth, and seized the revenues of the lucrative and extensive awqaf khairiya [charitable endowments] of the religious community, giving in its place a fixed stipend that was sufficient only to keep the largest mosques and schools from falling into total ruin." Ibid., 181–82.

[38] See, for example, Livingston, who describes this state of affairs as follows: "Another motive driving their endeavor to legitimize innovation . . . was the threat posed by the state to religion and the religious institution, whose monopoly on education had been unquestioned until the founding of Muhammad ʿAli's new schools in the early part of the century. . . . During the brief tenure of the French in Egypt, Bonaparte, Kléber, and Menou had in fact enhanced the prestige of the

The earliest manifestations of this phenomenon are the delegations sent by Muḥammad ʿAlī to France to study Western learning. The most famous personality associated with these delegations was Rifāʿa al-Ṭahṭāwī, who spent five years in Paris from 1826 to 1831.[39] Later, in the second half of the nineteenth century, institutions came to be established for professional training, including a law school (1866), the Dar al-ʿUlūm for teachers (1868), and the School for Qadis (1908), producing a cadre of potential employees for the "knowledge professions" who were now independent of the Azhar, the educational institution which had until then held a monopoly in the country. At the turn of the century, one starts to witness the increasing role of al-Jāmiʿa al-Miṣriyya (founded 1908; later renamed King Fuʾād I University; now Cairo University), where European lecturers were often invited to address the student body.[40] To this we may add the influx of scientific ideas from organs like *al-Muqtaṭaf*, now newly transplanted to Cairo, and the ascendancy of the Reform movement associated with the Afghānī-ʿAbduh-Riḍā trajectory. The outcome of all this was an Egyptian intellectual scene in major flux, with a number of conflicting theoretical currents with their own agendas, commitments, and assumptions all vying for recognition and influence in Egyptian society and politics. Within this scene, science came to occupy a central role.

In an important article, Marwa Elshakry has insightfully pointed out the manner in which the conception of the "new science" as a modern and Western institution came to formation in late Ottoman and colonial-era Egypt.[41] Whereas early interactions with European science "did not so much replace older disciplines or traditions of knowledge as redefine them"[42]—a process she refers to as "conceptual syncreticism"—the early twentieth

shaykhs in their inept attempt to use them as a front of religious legitimacy. The modernizing state of Muhammad ʿAli and his successors was making irrelevant the religious institution that the French had pretended to make a ruling partner." John W. Livingston, "Western Science and Educational Reform in the Thought of Shaykh Rifaʿa al-Tahtawi," *International Journal of Middle East Studies* 28, no. 4 (November 1, 1996): 543–44.

[39] See Albert Hourani, *Arabic Thought in the Liberal Age, 1798–1939* (London: Oxford University Press, 1970), 69–83.

[40] For details on the history of Cairo University and its entwining with modern Egyptian society, see Donald Malcolm Reid, *Cairo University and the Making of Modern Egypt* (Cambridge, UK: Cambridge University Press, 2002). On the significant role of Orientalists in the early days of the institution, see Donald Malcolm Reid, "Cairo University and the Orientalists," *International Journal of Middle East Studies* 19, no. 1 (February 1, 1987): 51–75.

[41] Marwa Elshakry, "When Science Became Western: Historiographical Reflections," *Isis* 101, no. 1 (March 1, 2010): 98–109.

[42] Elshakry, "When Science Became Western: Historiographical Reflections," 99.

century witnessed the "coming into being of modern science"—universalist in its scope, "Western in its inception and signaling through its own new history a radical break with knowledge traditions of the past."[43] The hallmark of this conception of science was that of an "undivided truth . . . contrasted sharply against truth claims that divided men."[44] Representative of this way of thinking, in Elshakry's reading, was George Sarton, an important proponent of the emergent discipline of the history of science, who once remarked that "One should never speak of religious truth . . . only scientific truth exists."[45]

Elshakry goes on to point out that this doctrinaire emphasis on modern science to the exclusion of other ways of knowing rested uneasily with some Egyptian scholars who then took up a "search for an indigenous cosmological or natural philosophical tradition to supplement—or, indeed, to reinforce—the modern sciences."[46] This found expression in what came to be known as *tafsīr ʿilmī* ("scientific exegesis"), a new genre of Qurʾanic commentary concerned with providing scriptural evidence in support of the findings of modern science.[47] The desire to locate a conformity between Islam and science took a variety of forms, such as attempts in India to construct a new theology (*ʿilm-i kalām-i jadīd*), and glowing histories from Young Ottoman quarters of Muslim contributions to science and learning in places like medieval Andalusia.[48] In Egypt, much of this energy seems to have been spent on *tafsīr ʿilmī* writing, with important names such as Muḥammad ʿAbduh, Farīd Wajdī, Ṭanṭāwī al-Jawharī, and Tawfīq Ṣidqī (in Rashīd Riḍā's famous *al-Manār* journal) penning the most prominent contributions. Yet the earliest such work known to us has been shown by Daniel Stolz to have an interesting pedigree that situates nineteenth-century Egyptian writers of the genre squarely within the apparatus of the Egyptian state but also in their late Ottoman context and indeed in the broader Muslim world. The 1876 *Treatise on Comparing Some Texts of Astronomy with What Appears in Shariʿa Texts* (Ar. *Risāla fī Muqāranat Baʿḍ Nuṣūṣ al-Hayʾa bi-l-Wārid fī al-Nuṣūṣ al-Sharʿiyya*) was written by ʿAbd Allāh Fikrī, an educational reformer in the

[43] Elshakry, "When Science Became Western: Historiographical Reflections," 104–5.
[44] Elshakry, "When Science Became Western: Historiographical Reflections," 104–5.
[45] Quoted in Elshakry, "When Science Became Western: Historiographical Reflections," 105.
[46] Elshakry, "When Science Became Western: Historiographical Reflections," 106.
[47] Elshakry, "The Exegesis of Science in Twentieth-Century Arabic Interpretations of the Qurʾān," in *Nature and Scripture in the Abrahamic Religions: 1700*–Present (Leiden: Brill, 2008); Elshakry, *Reading Darwin in Arabic, 1860–1950* (Chicago: University of Chicago Press, 2014), 177–80.
[48] M. Alper Yalçınkaya, *Learned Patriots: Debating Science, State, and Society in the Nineteenth-Century Ottoman Empire* (Chicago: The University of Chicago Press, 2015), 110–13.

Department of Education.[49] Its publication in journals sympathetic to the Khedive's reform projects, *Wādī al-Nīl* and *Rawḍat al-Madāris*, leads Stolz to conclude that "By publishing Fikri's work . . . the viceregal state was using the power of its presses to double down on its defense of 'new' science against criticism."[50] At the same time, however, in writing his short book, Fikrī was heavily influenced by a Turkish work called *Efkâr ül-Ceberût*, which in turn was an expanded translation and commentary on an Arabic-language introduction to *al-hay'a al-jadīda* ("the new astronomy"). That Arabic-language introduction, *Asrār al-Malakūt*, was written by an Azeri prince, Abbaskulu Ağa Bakülü Kudsi, "who had traveled extensively through Eastern Europe and the Caucusus while in Russian service." Thus, Stolz writes,

> by the time, "new astronomy" reached Fikrī's readers, it had moved from the Russian imperial schools in which Kudsi was educated, through the Russian-Qajar frontier, to Istanbul, and finally to Cairo and Beirut, while passing linguistically from Russian to Arabic (possibly via Persian), from Arabic to Turkish, and finally back into Arabic.[51]

For our purposes, what is most intellectually noteworthy about Fikrī's work is its reinstitution of the dichotomy between men of science and men of religion that prevailed in early Islam, though it drew this distinction along different lines and in response to different stakes.

The book is largely structured around a dialogue between an astronomer (*ṣāḥib al-hay'a*) and a *faqīh* (literally "a jurist," though Stolz rightly points out that the word is here used as a looser signifier pointing instead to simply a religious scholar), in which the latter cites verses from the Qur'an he takes to be challenges to modern astronomy, and the former responds by reinterpreting them in ways that indicate agreement between the two. The distance that emerges between the two protagonists through their mode of argumentation reveals that "those who studied the stars and those who studied the scripture were newly remote from each other."[52] This reconfiguration was another example of the important cultural shifts of the nineteenth century, but the newfound distinction was not the drawing of a line

[49] ʿAbd Allāh Fikrī, *Risāla fī Muqāranat Baʿḍ Nuṣūṣ al-Hay'a bi-l-Wārid fī al-Nuṣūṣ al-Sharʿiyya* (Cairo: Maṭbaʿat al-Madāris, 1876).
[50] Stolz, *The Lighthouse and the Observatory*, 182.
[51] Stolz, *The Lighthouse and the Observatory*, 180.
[52] Stolz, *The Lighthouse and the Observatory*, 188.

between two coequal segments of society. Rather, the astronomer came to occupy a privileged position in Egyptian learned society, a position that reflected science's increasing cultural dominance and astronomers' ascendant cultural authority in the country.[53] Fikrī's stance, that scripture ought to be construed such that it accorded with modern science, came to be an irresistible norm that defined not only the genre he inaugurated but intellectual life more generally.

The "New Science" in Modern Egypt: Commentary and History

Bakhīt, too, was a participant in this trend of writing. His thinking about science was in line with, and indebted to, the basic premise of *tafsīr ʿilmī* writing. In two explicit engagements with modern science, both published in 1923, he is at pains to show that Islam is in no way opposed to investigating the nature of the world; indeed, he argues that not only is science compatible with scripture, the Qurʾan encourages scientific inquiry and itself points to the "reality of all things."[54] The first such contribution is a lecture he delivered framed as a response—albeit some forty years later—to a famous exchange between Ernest Renan and Jamāl al-Dīn al-Afghānī on the relationship between Islam and science. Bakhīt's remarks were quickly published in an expanded version under the revealing title, *Drawing the Attention of Human Minds to Cosmological and Civilizational Knowledge in the Verses of the Qurʾan* (Ar. *Tanbīh al-ʿUqūl al-Insāniyya li-mā fī Āyāt al-Qurʾān min al-ʿUlūm al-Kawniyya wa-l-ʿUmrāniyya*).

The 1883 debate between Renan and al-Afghānī has come to be well known for the stridency of Renan's provocation and the remarkable timidity and acquiescence of the usually fiery al-Afghānī. The major thrust of Renan's argument can be encapsulated in this excerpt:

> Every person, however slightly he may be acquainted with the affairs of our times, sees clearly the actual inferiority of Mohammedan countries,

[53] Stolz, *The Lighthouse and the Observatory*, 188–89. The linkage between the emergence of science and social capital has also been studied elsewhere in the Middle East. See Cyrus Schayegh, *Who Is Knowledgeable Is Strong: Science, Class, and the Formation of Modern Iranian Society, 1900–1950* (Berkeley: Univerity of California Press, 2009); Yalçınkaya, *Learned Patriots*.

[54] Muḥammad Bakhīt al-Muṭīʿī, *Tanbīh al-ʿUqūl al-Insāniyya li-mā fī Āyāt al-Qurʾān min al-ʿUlūm al-Kawniyya wa-l-ʿUmrāniyya* (Maṭbaʿat al-Saʿāda, 1923), 7.

> the decadence of states governed by Islam, and the intellectual nullity of the races that hold, from that religion alone, their culture and education. All those who have been in the East, or in Africa, are struck by the way in which the mind of a true believer is fatally limited, by the species of iron circle that surrounds his head, rendering it absolutely closed to knowledge, incapable of either learning anything, or of being open to any new idea. . . . [T]he Mussulman has the most profound disdain for instruction, for science, for everything that constitutes the European spirit.[55]

In response, while al-Afghānī recoils at some of the explicit racism found in Renan's article, he advances what Nikki R. Keddie has called an "evolutionary" argument,[56] which effectively admits the superiority of European civilization as a result of its having had six centuries longer to "[free] itself from the tutelage of religion."[57] In line with this historiographical progressivism, al-Afghānī is hopeful that "Muhammadan society will succeed someday in breaking its bonds and marching resolutely in the path of civilization after the manner of Western society, for which the Christian faith, despite its rigors and intolerance, was not at all an invincible obstacle,"[58] but he goes on to agree with Renan's categorical assessment of the corrosive effects of Islam, before extending it to all religion:

[55] Ernest Renan, "Islamism and Science," in *The Poetry of the Celtic Races, and Other Essays*, trans. William G. Hutchison (London: W. Scott, 1896), 85. Originally published in French as Ernest Renan, "L'Islamisme et la Science," *Journal des Débats Politiques et Littéraires*, March 30, 1883. A recent, perhaps more accessible, edition of the original French along with the subsequent exchange with al-Afghānī may be found in Ernest Renan, *L'Islam et la Science: Avec la Réponse d'Afghâni* (Montpellier: Archange minotaure, 2003). The editor interestingly explains the change in title in the first footnote, "Pour éviter une confusion fâcheuse et restituer le sens voulu par Renan, nous avons modifié l'intitulé original *L'islamisme et la science*; à cette époque l'*islamisme* (forgé sur le meme schema que *christianisme*) n'a pas la connotation que nous lui attribuons aujourd'hui." For a general overview of the life of Renan, see the biographical work David C. J. Lee, *Ernest Renan: In the Shadow of Faith* (London: Duckworth, 1996).

[56] Nikki R. Keddie, *An Islamic Response to Imperialism: Political and Religious Writings of Sayyid Jamāl ad-Dīn "al-Afghānī"* (Berkeley: University of California Press, 1968), 86. For a slightly different reading of this debate by Keddie herself, see Nikki R. Keddie, "Islamic Philosophy and Islamic Modernism: The Case of Sayyid Jamāl ad-Dīn al-Afghānī," *Iran* 6 (January 1, 1968): 53–56, where she views her protagonist's often inconsistent writings as a manifestation of the old philosophical strategy of speaking to different audiences in different voices. It is in such arguments addressed to an elite European audience that Keddie locates al-Afghānī's personal beliefs, while appeals to orthodox sentiment as in his "Refutation of the Materialists" and other popular works were aimed at harnessing "Islamic sentiment in an anti-imperialist political struggle."

[57] Keddie, *An Islamic Response to Imperialism*, 183.

[58] Keddie, *An Islamic Response to Imperialism*, 183.

> It is permissible, however, to ask oneself why Arab civilization, after having thrown such a live light on the world, suddenly became extinguished; why this torch has not been relit since; and why the Arab world still remains buried in profound darkness. Here the responsibility of the Muslim religion appears complete. It is clear that wherever it became established, this religion tried to stifle the sciences and it was marvellously served in its designs by despotism. . . . Religions, by whatever names they are called, all resemble each other. No agreement and no reconciliation are possible between these religions and philosophy. Religion imposes on man its faith and its belief, whereas philosophy frees him of it totally or in part.[59]

That Bakhīt would choose to revive this debate to offer his own remarks forty years later is an indication of its continued relevance; however, he took it as an opportunity to intervene in the specific controversies of his period, and he did so within the *tafsīr ʿilmī* stream of writing which had only just begun to emerge at the time of the original debate.

Ostensibly, Bakhīt's lecture was a response to another given by an Azharī scholar, published a month prior in the journal *al-Siyāsa* (March 21, 1923), in which the Renan-Afghānī exchange made an appearance and was thus brought to Bakhīt's attention. However, issues of science, and especially astronomy, had been recurrent themes of the European-Egyptian encounter all throughout this time, and they could not have escaped Bakhīt's attention. As an example, we may point to the influence of the Italian scholar Carlo Nallino, who lectured at Cairo University from 1909 to 1912. If Aḥmad Amīn is any indication, Nallino's presence and works had made quite the impression on Egyptian intelligentsia. Amīn remembers Nallino's *Tārīkh al-Falak ʿinda al-ʿArab* (*History of Astronomy among the Arabs*) as among the very best books he had read, because he "learned from it how the leading orientalists did their research, and how they persisted in their investigations, how they actually lived in the subject of their specialization, and how they proceeded carefully and deliberately from the simple to the complex in their research. It would scarcely be an exaggeration to say that I learned the methodology of research from this book."[60]

In response to this growing trend in Egyptian society, Bakhīt resurrected the Renan-Afghānī exchange in the *Tanbīh* to offer a robust defense of Islam

[59] Keddie, *An Islamic Response to Imperialism*, 187.
[60] Quoted in Donald Malcolm Reid, "Cairo University and the Orientalists," 51.

by providing examples of verses that he took to elucidate scientific facts, thereby aligning his work with the *tafsīr ʿilmī* genre that scholarship has primarily identified with modernist figures. After casting doubt on both Renan's standing as a philosopher,[61] and the authenticity of the positions attributed to al-Afghānī,[62] he clearly sets out his purpose in the text:

> Here I mention some simple and clear Qurʾanic verses which include something of the sciences of the world. There are many Qurʾanic verses pertaining to cosmological sciences—the heavens, earth, the atmosphere—and many more concerning laws, and even more treating metaphysics. I have restricted myself here to a small portion as a sample to guide readers to what is in the Qurʾan, to direct them to contemplating its verses, and to know that the Qurʾan freed minds from the chains of *taqlīd* and liberated them from its constraints. It is not acceptable for responsible adults [*mukallafīn*] to be anything but *mujtahid*s in terms of their beliefs, which are to be understood via reason.[63]

An even more striking example of Bakhīt's participation in the genre is his other 1923 book, *Success from The Merciful in Finding Conformity Between what the Astronomers Say and what comes to us in Sound Traditions and*

[61] "Whoever deems [Renan] a philosopher has done a great injustice, for he knows nothing of philosophy. Philosophy is wisdom, and wisdom is beneficial knowledge. . . . The philosopher is a lover of knowledge, and a practitioner of it . . . Had Renan been a philosopher, among his personal characteristics would have been knowledge of the truth of the Qurʾan and its essence, and what is included within it in terms of science and philosophy. He would also have been aware of the extent of the influence of religions in ordering nations and preventing chaos. Every nation without a religion is without order. Every person without a religion is without accountability, and there is no good in anyone who is without accountability." Bakhīt al-Muṭīʿī, *Tanbīh al-ʿUqūl*, 3.

[62] "I believe that our teacher the Sayyid Jamāl ad-Dīn al-Afghānī is innocent of [what is attributed to him]. How can it be otherwise when these are words that accept the insults of Renan towards Islam and the Muslims. Our teacher al-Jamāl traces his lineage back to the man who brought us this religion, his grandfather Muḥammad, peace be upon him. So, he is best placed to defend this religion. We had been close associates from when he first set foot in Egypt until he departed. We learned much from him in the fields of science and philosophy. Never throughout this lengthy period, in which we met often, did we see him profess that which Renan professed, or say anything that even smelled of defaming Islam or the Muslims. Rather, what we knew of him and also what the Shaykh Muḥammad ʿAbduh knew of him was that he was truly a philosopher and a faithful adherent of the religion of Islam, defending it with all the power he was given, knowledge, outstanding rhetoric, and strong proofs." Bakhīt al-Muṭīʿī, *Tanbīh al-ʿUqūl*, 3–4. This passage supports Keddie's claim that those in the Muslim world were ill disposed to believing that al-Afghānī would do anything but rebuke Renan and defend Islam's friendliness to science, although it does cast into doubt her supposition that they did not read al-Afghānī's response. "In the Muslim world the discussion between Afghānī and Renan has been distorted by those who have not read Afghānī's response to Renan and assume that since Renan had called Islam hostile to science, Afghānī must have said that Islam was friendly to the scientific spirit." Keddie, *An Islamic Response to Imperialism*, 85.

[63] Bakhīt al-Muṭīʿī, *Tanbīh al-ʿUqūl*, 4.

Qur'anic verses (Ar. *Tawfīq al-Raḥmān li-l-Tawfīq bayna mā Qālahu ʿUlamā' al-Hay'a wa-bayna mā jā'a fī al-Aḥādīth al-Ṣaḥīḥa wa-Āyāt al-Qur'ān*). If the *Tanbīh* only alluded to the de facto separation of the domains of science and religion that Stolz shows to have been (re-)initiated by Fikrī, *Tawfīq* leaves little doubt that this was how Bakhīt conceived the relationship between the two. The title itself echoes Fikrī's in setting up astronomy and religious learning as separate fields to be compared (Fikrī) or brought into conformity (Bakhīt). But Bakhīt leaves no doubt in his introduction, where he sets out the book's agenda of convincing the dubious that scripture aligns with the findings of astronomy:

> Many of the ulama have come to be in doubt regarding what has come [to us] from the field of astronomy, both ancient and modern. . . . They have taken to thinking that this conflicts with what has come [to us] from our religion and the magnanimous shariʿa, and that Qur'anic verses and sound Prophetic traditions pertaining to these matters contradict what the scholars of astronomy have settled upon. So, I want to write a book, small in size, but—God willing—great in benefit, abundant in knowledge, and accessible to students.[64]

In this text, Bakhīt is at his most explicit in stipulating that the shariʿa and the Qur'an accord with the most current scientific thinking. Perhaps even more telling, though, is that this acceptance of modern science is accompanied by an equally modern reading of the history of science. In her article, Elshakry assigns the delineation of a conscious historical narrative a central role in establishing the unique character of modern science as a break from premodern knowledge traditions. In the case of the early, heavily syncretic, encounters of the early nineteenth century, "the forging of new meanings did not necessarily imply a complete break with older ones. . . . new categories and disciplines of knowledge were often simply understood in terms and indeed as extensions of longer-standing traditions of knowledge *and* belief."[65] The way Darwin was read in that period, for example, was by reference to "older, medieval discussions of transformism [which] both helped pave the way for the new evolutionary sciences and shaped the very way in which

[64] Muḥammad Bakhīt al-Muṭīʿī, *Kitāb Tawfīq al-Raḥmān li-l-Tawfīq bayna mā Qālahu ʿUlamā' al-Hay'a wa-bayna mā Jā'a fī al-Aḥādīth al-Ṣaḥīḥa wa-Āyāt al-Qur'ān* (Cairo: Maṭbaʿat al-Saʿāda, 1341H), 2.

[65] Elshakry, "When Science Became Western," 104.

they were understood."[66] While "the new [was] explained in reference to the old, . . . *no particular history of science was implied*."[67] Eventually, however, this syncretic approach "gave way to the construction of a new linear history of science" which, when combined with the idea of the Scientific Revolution, "marked the coming into being of modern science . . . signaling *through its own new history* a radical break with knowledge traditions of the past."[68]

In the Arabic-speaking world, this new history was introduced through the production of textbooks for consumption among the literate educated and schoolchildren. Particularly influential were two primers on astronomy, published within a year of one another in Beirut in the 1870s. Through the efforts of American missionaries, Beirut had by that time become an important site for the dissemination of religious and scientific texts. The missionaries had first set up a printing press there in 1834, facilitating what continues to be an influential translation of the Bible into Arabic by Cornelius Van Dyck.[69] Importantly, it was also the site of the Syrian Protestant College (later to become the American University of Beirut), founded in 1866.[70] By 1876, the College had established *al-Muqtaṭaf*, "the first scientific and technological journal of the type in the Syro-Lebanese region,"[71] under the coeditorship of Yaʿqūb Ṣarrūf and Fāris Nimr, two "native tutors,"[72] who were in turn supervised by Van Dyck, also Professor of Astronomy at the College.[73]

66 Elshakry, "When Science Became Western," 104.

67 Elshakry, "When Science Became Western," 104, emphases mine.

68 Elshakry, "When Science Became Western," 104–5, emphases mine.

69 Van Dyck is an important figure in this story as we shall see below. For a lengthy biographical note bordering on the hagiographic, see Lutfi M. Sa'di, George Sarton, and W. T. Van Dyck, "Al-Hakîm Cornelius Van Alen Van Dyck (1818–1895)," *Isis* 27, no. 1 (May 1, 1937): 20–45. See also Jurjī Zaydān, *Tarājim Mashāhīr al-Sharq fī al-Qarn al-Tāsiʿ ʿAshar*, vol. 2 (Cairo: Maṭbaʿat al-Hilāl, 1922), 40–48.

70 For the early history of the College, see A. L. Tibawi, "The Genesis and Early History of the Syrian Protestant College: Part I," *Middle East Journal* 21, no. 1 (January 1, 1967): 1–15; A. L. Tibawi, "The Genesis and Early History of the Syrian Protestant College: Part II," *Middle East Journal* 21, no. 2 (April 1, 1967): 199–212.

71 Olivier Meïer, *Al-Muqtataf et le Débat sur le Darwinisme: Beyrouth, 1876–1885* (Le Caire: CEDEJ, 1996).

72 For the language of "native tutors" and an important revision to preceding accounts of the history of the journal, specifically the controversy raised by a speech on Darwinism by the young American professor Edwin Lewis which led to the coeditors', and the journal's, eventual exile to Cairo, see Nadia Farag, "The Lewis Affair and the Fortunes of al-Muqtataf," *Middle Eastern Studies* 8, no. 1 (January 1, 1972): 73–83. A more detailed version of this story can be found in Meïer, *Al-Muqtataf et le Débat sur le Darwinisme*. For a rather disappointing piece which nonetheless provides some further information on both the journal and its coeditors, see L. M. Kenny, "East Versus West in al-Muqtaṭaf, 1875–1900: Image and Self-Image," in *Essays on Islamic Civilization: Presented to Niyazi Berkes*, ed. Donald P. Little (Leiden: Brill, 1976), 140–54.

73 The convergence of religious proselytism and the promotion of modern science among Beirut missionaries is treated ably by Elshakry in another article: "Far from viewing science as engaged in

The two Beiruti works on astronomy that exerted great influence in the Arabic-speaking world, either through their circulation among local intellectuals or their insertion into school curricula, were those of Van Dyck himself and Eliza Ephrat, on the latter of whom there seems to be little available information beyond her position as head teacher at the Syrian Missionary School for Girls, a division of the College run by the missionaries' wives.[74] The titles of both works may be translated into English as "The Principles of Astronomy": *Uṣūl ʿIlm al-Hayʾa* (Van Dyck) and *Mabādiʾ ʿIlm al-Hayʾa* (Ephrat).[75]

What is noteworthy about these texts is that each leads off with a history of the field in which the modern advancements of Copernicus, Kepler, Tycho Brahe, and Galileo are given pride of place, remembered as revolutionary contributions, and contrasted starkly with the work of their predecessors writing within the Ptolemaic paradigm. The discarding of Ptolemy's geocentric universe for Copernican heliocentrism and Galileo's invention of the telescope are the central features of this story. Ephrat, for example, writes, "Then, in the mid-sixteenth century, when the teachings of Ptolemy were celebrated in all the schools of Europe, Copernicus, a Prussian, rose to revive the teachings of Pythagoras, which is the true doctrine (*al-taʿlīm al-ḥaqīqī*) relied upon today."[76] Van Dyck offers a more detailed account in the lead passage of his section on history which reads similarly:

> Astronomy is one of the oldest disciplines, treated from ancient times by the Assyrians, Chaldeans, Phoenicians, Egyptians, Indians, and Chinese. Pythagoras, a Greek, was a teacher of this science in the school of Croton,

constant 'warfare' with theology, many missionaries in Beirut regarded the natural and allied sciences as integral to their broader spiritual commitments and theological vision, and saw in them a means to promote the path to salvation and to advance the reformation of minds and daily habits." Marwa Elshakry, "The Gospel of Science and American Evangelism in Late Ottoman Beirut," *Past & Present* 196, no. 1 (August 1, 2007): 177–78. For an account of American missionaries in Beirut more generally, see Ussama Makdisi, *Artillery of Heaven: American Missionaries and the Failed Conversion of the Middle East* (Ithaca, NY: Cornell University Press, 2009). For the specific experience of Evangelical missionaries in Egypt, see Heather J. Sharkey, *American Evangelicals in Egypt: Missionary Encounters in an Age of Empire* (Princeton, NJ: Princeton University Press, 2008). A more general treatment can be found in Mehmet Ali Doğan and Heather J. Sharkey, eds., *American Missionaries and the Middle East: Foundational Encounters* (Salt Lake City: University of Utah Press, 2011).

[74] The entry in the catalogue of the al-Azhar library, as well as the title page of the work itself, mentions that Ephrat's work was prepared specifically for the instruction of students (*ḍammathā li-tilmīdhāt wa-talāmīdh al-madāris* and *min ajl istiʿmāl al-madāris*).

[75] Cornelius Van Dyck, *Uṣūl ʿIlm al-Hayʾa* (Beirut, 1874); Eliza Ephrat, *Mabādiʾ ʿIlm al-Hayʾa* (Beirut, 1875).

[76] Ephrat, *Mabādiʾ ʿIlm al-Hayʾa*, 6.

> Italy, five hundred years before Christ. However, his teachings were given no consideration for two thousand years until Galileo and Copernicus revived them in the fifteenth and sixteenth centuries [*sic*]. . . . Ptolemy, in roughly 140 BC, wrote a book in this field called the *Almagest*, which was relied upon till the fifteenth and sixteenth centuries [*sic*], when Copernicus arose from Prussia in the year 1530, and Tycho Brahe in Denmark in 1582, and Kepler in Germany in 1654, and Galileo in Italy in 1649. They demonstrated the falsity of the old views, and placed this science on truthful and strong foundations [*ʿalā asās ḥaqīqī matīn*]. Galileo was the first to use the telescope, and through it, discovered many realities unknown until then.[77]

That the retelling of this account is seen by both authors as an essential element of, and prerequisite to, learning the principles of astronomy is a telling indication of the centrality of the historical narrative to the modern scientific enterprise.

This story of a complete break is familiar to Western historiographies of science, in which Galileo figures as the culmination of a heroic tradition standing against the oppressive power of the Church to defend science and reason. The literature is replete with such portrayals, but we may point here to its staying power by citing the relatively recent comments of Peter Machamer that "Not only was [Galileo] the hero of the Scientific Revolution, but after his troubles with the Catholic Church he became the hero of science."[78] As further evidence of the enormity and uniqueness of his accomplishments, Machamer writes that Galileo created the very constituency that would recognize scientific work as valuable, and thus "created the place of science in our intellectual life."[79]

It is perhaps less obvious that a version of the same story should be adopted by someone like Bakhīt, a non-European and a renowned member of the ulama. And yet the sort of scientism that I want to argue comes to

[77] Van Dyck, *Uṣūl ʿIlm al-Hayʾa*, 1.

[78] Peter Machamer, "Introduction," in *The Cambridge Companion to Galileo*, ed. Peter Machamer (Cambridge, UK: Cambridge University Press, 1998), 1. See also Steven Weinberg, *To Explain the World: The Discovery of Modern Science* (New York: Harper, 2015), 145–88.

[79] Machamer, "Introduction," 1. Later, Machamer addresses arguments that seek to deconstruct the very idea of a Scientific Revolution, such as the influential and pioneering articulation by Steven Shapin, *The Scientific Revolution* (Chicago: University of Chicago Press, 1996). Writes Machamer, "I am well aware that some historians and some philosophers would challenge the claim that there really was a scientific revolution. Whatever might hang on the interpretation of the word 'revolution' is unimportant to my theme. What cannot be in doubt is that between, say somewhat arbitrarily, the dates of 1534 and 1687, many things had radically changed and the world was, and was further becoming, a wildly different kind of place." Machamer, "Introduction," 3.

encompass Bakhīt's thinking does not simply consist of a set of propositions that demand assent; rather, it is a worldview that comes laden with a host of commitments and assumptions, prominent among them a self-conception of its own history as a linear progression toward truth. And thus it should not be so surprising that Bakhīt's prima facie recognition of the findings of modern astronomy in *Tawfīq* was accompanied by a remarkably similar history. Rather, it is a testament to how deeply scientism came to be entrenched that he felt this to be an accurate rendering of the historical record.

Importantly, the history Bakhīt presents in *Tawfīq* relies heavily on the account given by our two Beiruti authors. Indeed, he copies large segments from Van Dyck verbatim, though with some significant emendations and additions lifted from Fikrī's *Muqārana*.[80] (Bakhīt, in fact, owned a copy of Van Dyck's *Uṣūl ʿIlm al-Hayʾa*, which I located in his personal library, now housed as a collection at the al-Azhar library. The copy bears Bakhīt's ownership stamp and a marginal note on the title page attesting to the fact that it belonged to him.[81])

For Bakhīt, the central contours of the linear narrative of history that paves the way for the portrayal of Galileo-as-savior are uncontroversial, with the important exception that that history, though still teleological, is not seen as quite as revolutionary as Van Dyck's historiography posits. Rather, when one expands one's horizons and looks in the right places, it appears as much more of a continuity.[82] Although Bakhīt is at pains to assert the

[80] Fikrī, *Risāla fī Muqāranat Baʿḍ Nuṣūṣ al-Hayʾa bi-l-Wārid fī al-Nuṣūṣ al-Sharʿiyya*, 18–19. Borrowing the language of other authors is not typically considered a blameworthy intellectual practice, but to mitigate charges of plagiarism that may be leveled against him by modern readers, I hasten to point out that Bakhīt makes it clear that his purpose in this work was to "gather together (*ajmaʿu*) what outstanding researchers have written," perhaps suggesting in advance that original research (and evidently even language) will not necessarily be forthcoming. Bakhīt al-Muṭīʿī, *Tawfīq al-Raḥmān*, 2.

[81] In addition, he owned at least two other texts on natural philosophy authored by teachers linked to the American Protestant institutions in Beirut: Asʿad b. Ilyās al-Shudūdī, *al-Durūs al-Badīʿa fī ʿIlm al-Ṭabīʿa* (1873); and Alman (?) Jackson, *al-Durūs al-Awwaliyya fī al-Falsafa al-Ṭabīʿiyya* (1881).

[82] To see that the unwavering commitment to progress and linearity is a marked departure from the prevailing tradition, it is instructive to compare Bakhīt to the famous reform-minded intellectual of the nineteenth century, Rifāʿa al-Ṭahṭāwī. The assessment of Youssef M. Choueiri, though it raises its own set of problems, is helpful in this regard. "Ṭahṭāwī's particular brand of historical consciousness is further illustrated by his treatment of new sciences and technological advances. They are initially perceived as mere 'external things' or, in other words, superficial developments, that may be easily imported. . . . Brushing aside centuries of backwardness and changes, all that Egyptians had to do now, since a centralized political authority had been re-established, was to resume their former inventive activities unhindered. Science in this way has no philosophy or history. Progress remains to a large extent an alien concept in Ṭahṭāwī's repeated appeals and endeavours aimed at resurrecting the body and soul of his ancient fatherland. Scientific discoveries do not follow any logical sequence, nor do they arise as a result of new experimental methods and verifiable data and

truthfulness of the "new science,"[83] he is adamantly opposed to affirming the component of the account that has it emerging in Europe virtually ex nihilo after a two-millennium dormancy. Rather, the unacknowledged "afterlife" of the Pythagorean school mentioned by all four authors, which asserted that the earth revolved around the sun, can be located according to Bakhīt within Muslim texts, specifically works of *kalām* (and not *falsafa*). While he acknowledges the dominance of the Ptolemaic paradigm[84] and the Church's dogmatic insistence on the same,[85] Bakhīt wants to maintain that the Pythagorean school continued to occupy the status of a viable, if minority, tradition in the Islamic world.

To give the reader a full sense of both his debt to, and departures from, Van Dyck, as well as the larger arc of his historical reading and his congeniality to modern science, I translate the bulk of Bakhīt's account here:

> Know that the standing of this science is that it is one of the oldest disciplines, treated from ancient times by the Assyrians, Chaldeans, Phoenicians, Egyptians, Indians, Chinese, the Arabs, both pre-Islamic and Islamic [*jāhiliyyatan wa islāman*], and others from the past and present. Pythagoras was a teacher of this science in the school of Croton in Italy five hundred years before Christ, upon him and upon our Prophet be the choicest blessing and peace. . . . Then, the Alexandrian school was founded by the Ptolemaic kings . . . and the most celebrated of its teachers were the philosopher Hipparchus, circa 150 BC and Ptolemy, circa 140 BC. [Ptolemy] wrote a book in this field which he called the *Almagest*. In it, he held the position that the earth was stationary, and that the sun revolved around it. He based his school on this, and his principles and teachings spread

facts." Youssef M. Choueiri, *Modern Arab Historiography: Historical Discourse and the Nation-State* (London: RoutledgeCurzon, 2003), 29.

83 Echoing Van Dyck, he writes that this group of modern astronomers "all reverted to the position of Pythagoras . . . and placed this science on a truthful/real (*ḥaqīqī*) foundation." Bakhīt al-Muṭīʿī, *Tawfīq al-Raḥmān*, 4.

84 "Ptolemy . . . wrote a book in this science that he called the *Almagest*. In it, he maintained the position that the Earth was stationary, and that the sun revolved around it. He based his school on this, and his principles and teachings spread far and wide among the people, becoming celebrated because of Rome's conquest over many parts of the world. . . . The first way, the one which Pythagoras was on, was abandoned until the fifteenth and sixteenth [*sic*] centuries when a man called Copernicus, who had mastered the mathematical sciences and occupied himself with astronomy and observation and philosophy, arose from Prussia." Bakhīt al-Muṭīʿī, *Tawfīq al-Raḥmān*, 4.

85 "The Roman church judged [Copernicus] to be a deviant and a heretic, and prohibited the circulation and reading of his book. If they had been able to burn Copernicus himself, they would have done so." Bakhīt al-Muṭīʿī, *Tawfīq al-Raḥmān*, 4.

far and wide among the people, becoming celebrated because of Rome's conquest over many parts of the world. Then, al-Fārābī from among the philosophers of Islam translated [this doctrine] into his Arabic writings at the beginning of the fourth century AH. Abū ʿAlī Ibn Sīnā and others then followed him, and the position became famous among the scholars of Islam. They relied upon it, and some of them believed it and inserted it into their writings, basing themselves upon it in many of their discussions and teachings. There were some who accepted it at face value, while others examined and verified it, churning it to extract the cream from it, and distinguishing what was correct in it from what was corrupt. Many exegetes and others even interpreted Qurʾanic verses pertaining to the skies and the earth in line with this doctrine. The first way (*ṭarīqa*), the one Pythagoras was on, was therefore abandoned until the fifteenth and sixteenth [*sic*] centuries when a man called Copernicus, who had mastered the mathematical sciences and occupied himself with astronomy and observation and philosophy, arose from Prussia. This was in 1530. Then, [there were] Tycho Brahe in Denmark in 1582, Kepler in Germany in 1654 and Galileo in Italy in 1649. They all reverted to the position of Pythagoras, which was based on the motion of the earth. They determined that the sun is the center of the universe and that the earth and the other heavenly bodies revolve around it. . . . They supported this position by applying to it the rules of mathematics and [thereby] invalidating the opinions of Ptolemy, placing this science on a truthful/real (*ḥaqīqī*) foundation.[86] The most famous of these was Copernicus in his book, *On the Revolutions of Heavenly Spheres*. The Roman church judged him to be a deviant and a heretic, and prohibited the circulation and reading of his book. If they had been able to burn Copernicus himself, they would have done so. Despite this, his book became famous, and his doctrine widespread. [The doctrine] was attributed to him, and called "the astronomy of Copernicus." As for Galileo, he was the first to use the telescope in the field of astronomy, and through it, discovered many realities unknown until then. Then, at the outset of the tenth century, Isaac Newton discovered the universal law of gravitation, to which all heavenly bodies are subject. Laplace, the Frenchman, then clarified and further established these laws. There then arose in different times and places in Europe groups other than those we have mentioned

[86] In order to highlight the representational nature of the new science, I have intentionally preserved (even if awkwardly) the bivalence of the Arabic *ḥaqīqī*: at once truthful *and* real.

who treated this science in accordance with this approach (*ṭarīqa*) until it became well-known throughout Europe. *It was known among them as the "new astronomy," even though it is, in reality, old. This is why both approaches are transmitted widely and abundantly in the Islamic books, both before and after Copernicus.* Among those who mentioned these two ways is ʿAḍud al-Dīn b. ʿAbd al-Raḥmān b. Aḥmad [al-Ījī], who died in 756 AH . . . From this, it is known that the school [which upheld] the movement of the earth and its revolution in the manner maintained by the astronomers today was known as a counter approach [to the dominant, Ptolemaic, one] before 756 AH, when [al-Ījī][87] died, and before its fame and diffusion in the European lands. . . . [It is also known from this] that this school, though it is referred to today as a new path in astronomy, is in reality an ancient way. *It is simply that it was abandoned and ignored for a long time, so when awareness of it was revived, and it came to be relied upon once again, becoming the standard reading and invalidating the position of the stationariness of the earth, it was called a new approach. Many people thought it was a newly invented way, but the matter is not so.*[88]

On Bakhīt's reading, then, Muslims and Arabs are integral to the story of astronomy throughout. This is signaled from the very first line. Where Van Dyck had omitted any mention of Arabs in his otherwise expansive listing of contributors to ancient astronomy, Bakhīt expressly includes them as part of that history.[89] But Bakhīt also makes specific reference to a history of Muslim contributions to fill in a nearly two-thousand-year gap in Van Dyck's genealogy between Pythagoras and Ptolemy, on the one hand, and Copernicus and Galileo, on the other. Islamic texts, Bakhīt asserts, continuously recognized both schools of astronomy, the geocentric and the heliocentric. Al-Fārābī and Ibn Sīnā, representing the philosophers, the most direct inheritors of Greek antiquity, upheld the Ptolemaic paradigm, while support for Pythagoras could be found in the *kalām* writings of al-Ījī and his commentator al-Jurjānī.

[87] Bakhīt actually refers to him as "the author of *al-Mawāqif*," which I have replaced by his *nisba* for clarity's sake.

[88] Bakhīt al-Muṭīʿī, *Tawfīq al-Raḥmān*, 3–5, emphases mine.

[89] This position would be later taken up by his student Aḥmad al-Ghumārī to indicate that the Arabs were in no way an illiterate nation, as the literal meanings of some traditions indicate, but rather that they were without a scripture, and as such "illiterate" in comparison to Jews, Christians, and Magians. Aḥmad al-Ghumārī, *Tawjīh al-Anẓār li-Tawḥīd al-Muslimīn fī al-Ṣawm wa-l-Ifṭār* (Amman: Dār al-Nafāʾis & Dār al-Bayāriq, 1999), 67–68.

This cannot but strike the reader as a significant move, because what Bakhīt is effectively doing is legitimating the "new science" by finding precedents for it in Islamic writings. My observation of this discursive strategy is less a comment on the historical accuracy of Bakhīt's claims[90] than it is a note on both his impulse to indigenize the new science and, relatedly, the manner in which this attempt at legitimatization, through the invocation of a particular history, served to neuter criticisms of the modern scientific enterprise as inauthentic to a Muslim milieu. Just as we saw in the last chapter that the sudden emergence and dominance of the printing press on the Egyptian intellectual scene, and the attendant creation of new reading publics, drove the Egyptian ulama to conceive of authority in different ways, the social prestige and political weight attached to the propagation of modern science[91] left them in no position to do much but accept it—and, indeed, effectively entrench that acceptance further by grounding it within authoritative Islamic texts.

That this was the course of events in intellectual circles is borne out when we compare Bakhīt to the premier reform figure of the nineteenth century. Rifāʿa al-Ṭahṭāwī had been recommended by Muḥammad ʿAli to head the first delegation of students sent to Paris to be exposed to French learning. In the face of prevailing antipathy, or indifference, to the Western science brought by Napoleon, al-Ṭahṭāwī was "the first to argue the case of science. . . . As the prize student of what turned out to be the most famous student mission of many over a quarter-century, he returned from Paris versed in physics, geometry, astronomy and political science."[92] Nor was he simply a passive learner. Al-Ṭahṭāwī speaks of having translated twelve books during this time, and—importantly for our purposes—authored a small treatise on astronomy, the *Kanz al-Mukhtār fī Kashf al-Arāḍī wa-l-Biḥār.*[93] Although he seems in this work to have expressed positive

[90] However, I hasten to point out that his comments fit well with the findings of Jamil Ragep in Ragep, "Copernicus and His Islamic Predecessors: Some Historical Remarks," *History of Science* 45, no. 1 (2007): 65–81.

[91] That the Egyptian state in the nineteenth century put its considerable weight behind the scientific project can be gleaned not only from what we've said earlier but also from J. Heyworth-Dunne's (chagrined) observation that "In vain does one seek a book worth reading which was written during the Muḥammad ʿAlī period, one only finds scientific translations from works written by Europeans." J. Heyworth-Dunne, "Rifāʿah Badawī Rāfiʿ aṭ-Ṭahṭāwī: The Egyptian Revivalist," *Bulletin of the School of Oriental Studies, University of London* 9, no. 4 (1939): 964. On the relationship between science and social capital in other locales in the Middle East, see Schayegh, *Who Is Knowledgeable Is Strong* and Yalçınkaya, *Learned Patriots*.

[92] John W. Livingston, "Western Science and Educational Reform in the Thought of Shaykh Rifaʿa al-Tahtawi," 544.

[93] Livingston, "Western Science and Educational Reform in the Thought of Shaykh Rifaʿa al-Tahtawi," 548.

sentiments for the Copernican system and Newtonian physics, by the end of his life, "when he pondered heliocentricity, Cartesian rationalism, and the mathematical relationships expressing a system of natural law that governed the physical structure of the universe, his enthusiasm for Western science chilled to skepticism. The very heart of science was rejected."[94] Indeed, in his final writing on the topic in the *Anwār Tawfīq al-Jalīl*, al-Ṭahṭāwī concludes emphatically, "It is incumbent upon the Sunni community to believe in the moving sun and to follow the God-ordained system followed by our ancestors."[95] This leads John W. Livingston to conclude, not without justification, that whatever enthusiasm al-Ṭahṭāwī displayed for science was instrumental, and not a principled commitment.[96] When placed within the context of such views from the man who was the nation builder Muḥammad ʿAli's delegate to the French academy and widely hailed as a seminal revivalist, Bakhīt's views a mere fifty years later are all the more striking for the manner in which he wholeheartedly accepts—and indeed justifies—the truths of modern science.

Cultural Imperialism as Seduction and Translation

That Bakhīt does accept and justify the truths of modern science, though, is the result of a particular relationship between the European colonizer and the Egyptian colonized. In *Disarming Words*, Shaden Tageldin insightfully plumbs the history of European-Egyptian encounter to suggest a particular way of understanding how the uneven ideational relationship between the two—what we might call cultural imperialism—proceeds: through the power of seduction. Ever since Napoleon claimed to local ulama that the French came to them as sincere Muslims no different than previous rulers, the mode by which the colonized Egyptian related to the cultural output of Europe was through the seduction of recognition—recognition of the colonizer, that is, as an aspirational version of oneself.

[94] Livingston, "Western Science and Educational Reform in the Thought of Shaykh Rifaʿa al-Tahtawi," 554.

[95] He also expresses the conviction that the French themselves will eventually revert to the Ptolemaic system given enough time. Livingston, "Western Science and Educational Reform in the Thought of Shaykh Rifaʿa al-Tahtawi," 558–59.

[96] "Science was to be pursued for what it could produce; it was not a valid field of metaphysical speculation." Livingston, "Western Science and Educational Reform in the Thought of Shaykh Rifaʿa al-Tahtawi," 554.

"Napoleon arrives," Tageldin writes, "under the banner of equivalence, not difference."[97] Orientalists like Sylvestre de Sacy seduced the Egyptian *literati* through their virtuoso use of the Arabic language and their masterful deployment of classical Islamic references.

This is perhaps best exemplified by an episode in Ḥasan al-ʿAṭṭār's *Maqāmāt al-Faransīs*, an imaginative representation of the French-Egyptian encounter, in which the fictional Egyptian protagonist encounters a European youth who speaks perfect Arabic and evinces familiarity with central Islamic texts.[98] The Egyptian protagonist is "sent reeling" toward this remarkable Frenchman and is entirely taken in by him when he goes on to quote a line from the famous devotional poem, *al-Burda*. Reversing Homi Bhabha, Tageldin uses this passage to position the European colonizer, and not the native subject, as the mimic. It is by participating in, indeed identifying with, the high Arab-Islamic culture of Egypt that cultural imperialism proceeded in Egypt, as much in al-ʿAṭṭār as for Napoleon. As in Bhabha, however, this act of mimicry contains within itself a slippage. The French youth informs al-ʿAṭṭār's fictional Egyptian that he not only knows the *Burda*, but had translated it into French. For Tageldin, this is a reassertion of the primacy of French in the relationship, a reminder of the relationship of dominance that underlies this intellectual encounter. This marking of difference goes hand in hand with the claim to identity. The European youth evinces mastery of Arabic only to thereafter domesticate it, laying bare the uneven field of power on which the encounter proceeds.

Egyptian intellectuals' response to this two-sided presence was curious. They objected to the military, economic, and political domination to which their lands were being subjected but tended to imagine European culture through the lens of "love," in part because it was presented to them in terms that were indigenous to their own cultural formations.

> As Egyptian intellectuals came to see their colonizers and themselves as translatable—or exchangeable—terms, they could in turn "love" those colonizers enough to translate French or English idioms and ideas. In so doing, they negotiated a complex and often conflicted surrender to the

[97] Tageldin, *Disarming Words*, 33.
[98] Tageldin, *Disarming Words*, 79–80.

> ideology of European supremacy and to the imperatives of European colonialism.[99]

Importantly, this dynamic, a mode of politics Tageldin labels translational seduction, was attractive to Egyptians not only because it was presented in venerable terms but also because it flashed the illusory possibility of cultural superiority. By positing European and Arab-Islamic learning as translatable equals, the former could validate the latter. "As a translational form of cultural imperialism, Orientalism appeared to affirm Egypt's Pharaonic and Arab-Islamic pasts as unbroken, still vital—uncolonized."[100]

The trappings of this mindset, I argue, are on full display in the carefully constructed history of astronomical knowledge Bakhīt has given us. Unlike Napoleon or al-ʿAṭṭār's Orientalist youth, Van Dyck's straight-forward triumphalist account of the Scientific Revolution, though it is written in Arabic, makes no effort to couch itself in the idioms and ideas of the Arab-Islamic world. It is, in fact, Bakhīt who does this work. The seduction of the "new science" is, as we have seen earlier, a fait accompli; scientism had become a domain of intellectual prestige that required assent. Bakhīt's engagement with modern science, then, is a translation into an idiom that affirms Arab-Islamic pasts as equivalent with Western ones, seamlessly insertable into Van Dyck's Eurocentric account. Galileo and Copernicus do not emerge, as if out of a void, as iconoclastic exemplars of modernity but are already anticipated in their heliocentrism by the Muslim theologian al-Ījī (d. 1355), himself part of a line of thought initiated in Greek antiquity by Pythagoras. Astronomy was to Bakhīt a shared pursuit that did not recognize the distinction between East and West advanced by diffusionist accounts of the Scientific Revolution, in which the new science is portrayed as a departure particular to early modern Europe that could then be exported to the world.

Embedded in this characterization, however, is also an assertion of difference—the "almost the same, but not quite" of Bhabha's mimicry. Even as he engages in integration, Bakhīt claims a sovereign Arab-Islamic tradition that is independent of the new science, preceding its central proposition by centuries, and that should therefore be taken as a civilizational competitor. What Bakhīt offers is an account that valorizes the Arab-Islamic past just as it valorizes the new science. He emerges then as a producer of colonial discourse, not because he was politically servile to the British or Europeanized in manner and

[99] Tageldin, *Disarming Words*, 10.
[100] Tageldin, *Disarming Words*, 8.

taste, but rather because he engages in a mimicry which positions him as a coauthor of a European-origin universal. Native coauthors, as Tageldin explains, "are invited to imagine themselves, their languages, and their cultures in relations of kinship to the world dominant, to an Other whose power already marks it as *unlike*."[101] This quote captures the ambivalence I attribute to Bakhīt, and that Bhabha deems essential to colonial mimicry. Bakhīt participates, then, in a colonial discourse in which he emerges as a *better* defender of modern science because its commitments have always belonged to his Arab-Islamic past.

Conclusion

Tageldin suggests we understand the seduction of cultural imperialism in terms of an interpellation.[102] The colonizer addresses himself to the colonized as a recognizable version of himself. The interpellation is not an address of the sort of "Hey, you there!" but the counterintuitive "Hey, *I* there!" The colonized, in turn, responds in a way that links an admired past to a potential future, via an amnesiac and disempowered present: "That once *was* me but is *not* (now) me; yet that *could be* me *again*. Therefore, that *must* be me!" It is through this sort of an interaction that the colonized assimilates to the colonizer through a constructed equivalence that preserves the former's assumed superiority.

Bakhīt's participation in *tafsīr ʿilmī* was simply part of a larger trend in the period in which Islamic scripture was called upon to do the work of naturalizing the modern scientific enterprise. Through his participation in this genre, he is constructing precisely this equivalence, one which makes Islam available for assimilation to the value of scientism. Tageldin's interpellation-as-seduction, however, is most prominently on display in the version of history Bakhīt supplies for the Scientific Revolution. By tracing a narrative that insists on the presence of both the Ptolemaic and Pythagorean schools, Bakhīt permits the assertion of a sovereign Arab-Islamic past that simply needs reactivation to conform to the demands of the scientistic present, while implicitly admitting the present relationship of uneven exchange that defines the interaction. If the structure of colonial discourse is, as Bhabha would have it, to be understood in terms of a mimicry that is "almost the same, but not quite," Bakhīt's account of the development of astronomy positions him as an author—or better, coauthor—of colonial discourse.

[101] Tageldin, *Disarming Words*, 137.
[102] Tageldin, *Disarming Words*, 64–65.

4
Science, Perception, and Objectivity

In November 1906, the *Shaykh al-Azhar*, ʿAbd al-Raḥmān al-Shirbīnī, sent a concerned letter to the Ministry of the Interior requesting action be taken to regulate a new technology that was "proliferating widely among the people, even though it is an instrument of diversionary entertainment (*lahw*) that the Lawgiver has prohibited."[1] The technology that was distressing al-Shirbīnī was the phonograph, but he was evidently not writing the Minister to educate him on its legal status. Instead, he was asking him to exercise his power to halt the sale of phonographic recordings of Qurʾanic recitations. Thanks to this technological advancement, only recently made available to the people of Cairo, greater numbers of people were able to listen to the Qurʾan being recited. Though this increased exposure might have conceivably been seen by the pre-eminent religious figure in the land as a welcome development, the ease of access by a wide public instead raised the concern for al-Shirbīnī that the sacred scripture was being subject to treatment that fell short of the sanctity and reverence it was due. Such records were being handled just like others that played unlawful music and otherwise objectionable language, and were being played in disreputable centers of idle amusement (*malāhī*) and public places where proper etiquette was not observed. This, in al-Shirbīnī's opinion, constituted a desecration (*intihāk*) of the Word of God.

Throughout the Muslim world, the encounter with the phonograph at the turn of the twentieth century gave rise to a number of anxieties, of which the fear of defiling the Qurʾan was but one particularly charged example.[2] On September 17, 1899, the Syrian scholar Ḥusayn al-Jisr published a fatwa in his journal *Ṭarābulus* responding to a question posed by Sayyid ʿUthmān b. ʿAbd Allāh b. ʿAqīl al-ʿAlawī from Batavia, a renowned scholar in his own

[1] ʿAbbās Ḥilmī II Papers at Durham University, HIL 52/135 and 52/129.

[2] Leor Halevi notes a similar rationale given by a scholar in Singapore, and connotations of idle amusement and play that were associated with the phonograph figured also in a disagreement on the issue between *jadids* and *qadims* in Kazan. Leor Halevi, *Modern Things on Trial: Islam's Global and Material Reformation in the Age of Rida* (New York: Columbia University Press, 2019), 138–50.

Transformations of Tradition. Junaid Quadri, Oxford University Press (2021). © Oxford University Press.
DOI: 10.1093/oso/9780190077044.003.0005

right. Evidently, the phonograph had been a matter of some debate in the East Indies as well, and Sayyid ʿUthmān called on al-Jisr to state his opinion on the controversies in the former's homeland. Because the position al-Jisr adopted echoed Sayyid ʿUthmān's own conclusions, the Batavian shaykh proceeded to republish it in a lithograph alongside his own opinion on the matter.[3]

Al-Jisr is well known as the teacher of Rashīd Riḍā, who had studied as a young man at the short-lived school al-Jisr founded in Tripoli. The Madrasa al-Waṭaniyya pointedly included not only the shariʿa sciences in its curriculum but also logic, mathematics, natural philosophy, and French.[4] In his own work, al-Jisr is remembered for his attempts at reconciling the disciplines of religious learning with modern science "in accordance with the way of modern Europe,"[5] an approach most prominently on display in his most famous treatise, *al-Risāla al-Ḥamīdiyya*. Despite this general intellectual orientation, al-Jisr was markedly conservative in his approach to the phonograph question. In his response, he consciously positions himself vis-à-vis the juristic tradition. Making the point that scholars do not permit departing from the *taqlīd* of previous authorities, he nonetheless broaches the possibility that sometimes one is confronted by situations that were not encountered in earlier times. Here, argues al-Jisr, one must think carefully to arrive at a solution that calms the heart of a believer, even if it does not produce a definitive solution. His own fatwa sets out to do precisely that, tackling the issue with a variety of desiderata in mind: propriety, necessity, precision, and realism. Al-Jisr begins by focusing on the sanctity of the Qurʾan and the impropriety inherent in the process of recording it, a process in which the etiquette of recitation is unlikely to be respected. Even if great efforts are made to do so, this would count as an exception, not the default norm. As such, reciting for the purpose of recording is deemed by him impermissible. Anticipating that some may draw an analogy with printed copies, and counter that such impropriety is also found in the process of printing, al-Jisr

[3] *Ṭulūʿ Badr al-ʿIlm al-Murtafaʿ wa-Ẓuhūr Najm al-Ṣidq al-Muntafaʿ ʿalā Ṣiḥḥat Jawāb Ḥukm al-Ṣawt al-Mukhtaraʿ* (Batavia, 1899). For a rendering of the argument, see C. Snouck Hurgronje, *Islam und Phonograph* (Batavia, 1900). The portion of Snouck's essay that treats Sayyid ʿUthmān's own fatwa has been translated in "Islam and the Phonograph," *The Muslim World* 5, no. 2 (April 1, 1915): 159–65. A summary can also be found in Nico J. G. Kaptein, *Islam, Colonialism and the Modern Age in the Netherlands East Indies: A Biography of Sayyid ʿUthman (1822–1914)* (Leiden: Brill, 2014), 195–97. See also Ali Altaf Mian, "Troubling Technology: The Deobandī Debate on the Loudspeaker and Ritual Prayer," *Islamic Law and Society* 24, no. 4 (October 3, 2017): 357–59.

[4] Muḥammad Rashīd Riḍā, *al-Manār wa-l-Azhar* (Cairo: Maṭbaʿat al-Manār, 1353H), 139.

[5] Riḍā, *al-Manār wa-l-Azhar*, 139.

turns to a utilitarian argument. Basing himself on the maxim that "necessities permit what is otherwise forbidden," al-Jisr argues that such concerns may be set aside in the latter case because print allows for much wider access to the sacred text than phonographic recordings. From the perspective of pronunciation, al-Jisr is skeptical that the phonograph will be capable of rendering the subtle differences between letters of the Arabic alphabet that sound similar, running perilously close to the possibility that this would distort the text itself. Once again heading off a comparison with print, he offers that printed errors are much easier to correct than phonographic ones. Finally, al-Jisr treats the question of listening to recitations made through the phonograph. Although he avoids definitively claiming that it is prohibited, he doubts that it may be plausibly considered permissible and dismisses outright that it could be at all meritorious (*mandūb*). What he is more certain about, however, is the ontological status of the recitation itself. These are for al-Jisr mere "echoes," not a real recitation. To illustrate this point, he offers that when a listener hears through the phonograph one of the verses that typically require a prostration when heard or recited, he is not obliged to prostrate. After surveying the discussions of both scholars in 1900, the famous Dutch Orientalist C. Snouck Hurgronje concluded that "the consensus . . . is therefore not favorable to the phonograph, and it can be expected that most ulama will agree with Sayyid ʿUthmān and Sayyid Ḥusayn al-Jisr."[6]

In early 1906, however, some six years after al-Jisr's fatwa and just before the *Shaykh al-Azhar* was petitioning the Interior Minister, Bakhīt published a treatise on the phonograph that belied Snouck's prediction. *Al-Muqtaṭaf*, the journal that was at the vanguard of introducing modern science and technology to Arabic-speaking audiences, thought it fit to publish a review of the text which they recapitulated in an approving manner.[7]

> The scholar and researcher, His Virtue, Shaykh Muḥammad Bakhīt al-Muṭīʿī al-Ḥanafī has written two concise treatises (*risālatayn wajīzatayn*) on the rulings of the phonograph and the rulings of insurance.[8] He explains in the first [treatise] that if the language of the Qurʾan (*kalām al-Qurʾān*) is recorded onto a phonographic record, just as other speech is recorded

[6] Snouck Hurgronje, *Islam und Phonograph*, 197.

[7] Indeed, they simply lift a paragraph found toward the end of Bakhīt's *risāla*, providing further substantiation for my observation in the last chapter that the borrowing of language was not considered a serious academic offence.

[8] For the latter, see chapter 1.

> on it, and [the record] is then rotated; if Qur'anic words are then emitted from it, respecting conditions [of propriety] and without deficiencies; if the intent of the one who recorded the sounds of these words on the record is [to facilitate] hearing them for the sake of experiencing their sublimity and engaging in contemplation, there is no doubt that it is permissible and that [such] listening is worship. But if the letters of these words are deficient, and they are not emitted [in a way that] fulfills [the conditions of propriety], or if the intention behind the recording of these sounds or listening to them is idle amusement, or if it is [played] in a place where it is not appropriate for the Qur'an to be recited or listened to, there is no doubt that this is prohibited and impermissible.[9]

On these counts, the difference between Bakhīt and al-Jisr is less one of substance than it is of degree. Bakhīt leaves greater room for the possibility that both the recording and listening of phonographic sounds can be done in a respectful and precise way, while al-Jisr admits that possibility but thinks of it as an exception that does not justify overriding the rule. This reflects a broader attitude of *technological optimism* that defined Bakhīt's approach to the various new technologies that appeared on the Egyptian market, and began to feature in Egyptian consciousness, during his lifetime. Though he was often faulted by Riḍā for having an inferior knowledge of modern matters, Bakhīt was remembered by at least one of his students, Ahmad b. Ṣiddīq al-Ghumārī, as a voracious reader of books by foreigners (*kutub al-ifranj*), modern writings (*kutub al-ʿaṣriyyīn*), and scientific journals (*jarāʾid*).[10] Despite his acknowledged mastery of the classical religious sciences, al-Ghumārī claimed that "when he spoke on astronomy and the foreign modern sciences, someone hearing him would think it impossible that he could also similarly excel in other fields."[11] It is perhaps precisely because of the taint of stodginess and obsolescence that followed him, that Bakhīt both focused his attention on the questions to which these new technologies gave rise and exhibited a relative openness toward them.

This openness to the new, however, was often justified by reference to age-old discussions and debates. As eager as *al-Muqtaṭaf* may have been to find

[9] *Al-Muqtaṭaf* 31, no. 4 (April 1906): 353. Muḥammad Bakhīt al-Muṭīʿī, "Fī Aḥkām Qirāʾat al-Fūnūghrāf," in *Thalātha Rasāʾil* (Cairo: Jamʿiyyat al-Azhar al-ʿIlmiyya, 1932), 9–10.

[10] Aḥmad ibn al-Ṣiddīq al-Ghumārī, *al-Baḥr al-ʿAmīq fī Marwiyyāt Ibn al-Ṣiddīq*, vol. 1 (Cairo: Dār al-Kutubī, 2007), 200.

[11] Al-Ghumārī, *al-Baḥr al-ʿAmīq fī Marwiyyāt Ibn al-Ṣiddīq*, 1:196.

religious warrant for the phonograph in Bakhīt's treatise, the journal ignored the bulk of his argumentation: an attempt to situate the new device within the world of Islamic thought by reference to a lengthy excursus on the nature of language and especially of God's Speech that was long an area of concern and controversy for Muslim theologians. As Bakhīt explains, language can be both internal (*nafsī*) and articulated (*lafẓī*). These two differ in existence (*wujūd*), but they are the same in reality (*ḥaqīqa*), in their nature (*ṭabī'a*), and in their essence (*māhiyya*). "The essence is one, the existence is plural."[12] Therefore the terms "Qur'an," "God's Speech" and "His Book" all refer to both the internal words formed by God in His Knowledge from pre-eternity, as well as the articulated words that appeared in the world in accordance with what was always in His Knowledge, and were revealed to the Prophet Muḥammad in connection with particular incidents.[13] The uttered speech shares in that reality without regard for the worldly source from which it is uttered and heard. It is the Word of God before anyone articulates it and before anyone hears it. Indeed, God may will for His Messengers to hear it without mediation at all, as most Sunnīs believe to be the case with Moses in the sacred valley of Ṭuwā. The Mu'tazilīs and Central Asian (Ḥanafī) Sunnīs, however, believe that what Moses heard was a voice created by God in a tree so that it could be heard by the Prophet from there. Based on this second opinion, Bakhīt concludes that there is no conceptual objection to the idea that articulated speech can be produced by nonhumans. "The criteria for its being considered articulated speech (*lafẓ*) is the existence of sounds (*ṣawt*) and letters (*ḥurūf*), no matter the form (*wajh*) in which they are found. And its being the Word of God is [similarly] independent of its being produced by the articulations of humans."[14] So, Bakhīt concludes,

> that which is heard from the box [of the phonograph] are real words and articulations, not echoes of the words of a speaker like that which is heard in the mountains and other places. For, an echo is the "reflection" of an auditory event that is heard a second time, like the reflection of rays of sight by which we see an image in the mirror. Therefore, if the articulations heard are of the Qur'an, they are the Qur'an in reality and truly the Speech of God

[12] Bakhīt, "Fī Aḥkām Qirā'at al-Fūnūghrāf," 3.
[13] Bakhīt, "Fī Aḥkām Qirā'at al-Fūnūghrāf," 7.
[14] Bakhīt, "Fī Aḥkām Qirā'at al-Fūnūghrāf," 7–8.

(*fa-hiya qur'ān ḥaqīqatan wa-kalām Allāh*), just like what Moses heard—whether unmediated or through the medium of the tree.[15]

This argumentation is a prime example of the *scientific realism* that, alongside his technological optimism, informed Bakhīt's approach to new technologies. The phonograph emerges on his reading as simply an inert medium which does not affect the objective reality of the speech it conveys.[16] Elsewhere, in an influential work on photography, which is widely referenced as the first sustained defense of the technique and helped settle the debate on the issue at the Azhar, Bakhīt argues similarly, holding that the well-known prohibition against image-making found in numerous hadiths did not apply to the camera on the grounds that the latter simply "captures" the creation of God and does not itself create.[17] As we will see later, this sort of realism is an integral component of a model of knowledge that I, following others, call *representationalist*.

This chapter considers the question of how precisely to proclaim the beginning of Ramadan in this technological age. While innumerable scholars before Bakhīt had addressed a constellation of issues surrounding the determination of new months, and had done so at great length, Bakhīt was writing in a world in which both the telegraph and the telescope had become normalized features of Egyptian society and the ascendant prestige of science provided a much more hospitable environment for relying on astronomical computations. Just as we observed the substantial effects of the printing press on ulama discourse in chapters 1 and 2, the introduction of the telegraph in the late nineteenth century and the 1903 establishment of a new observatory in Helwan to succeed one in ʿAbbasiyya both had a major impact in heightening the presence of technological innovation in the everyday lives of Egyptians, and therefore pushed ulama like Bakhīt to reconsider conventional understandings.[18] We have already had occasion to discuss telegraphy, and we will return to it in the next chapter. As for the telescope, the Helwan Observatory was presented a 30-inch reflector telescope designed by

[15] Bakhīt, "Fī Aḥkām Qirā'at al-Fūnūghrāf," 9.

[16] For Riḍā's critique of Bakhīt's conceptualization of the phonograph, see *al-Manār* 9: 438–40.

[17] *Al-Jawāb al-Shāfī fī Ibāḥat al-Taṣwīr al-Fūtūghrāfī* (Cairo: al-Maṭbaʿa al-Khayriyya, n.d.). Aḥmad al-Ghumārī, who financed the publication of the work records the debate at the Azhar in *al-Baḥr al-ʿAmīq fī Marwiyyāt Ibn al-Ṣiddīq*, 1:201–2.

[18] On Helwan and the observatory situated there, see Daniel Stolz, *The Lighthouse and the Observatory: Islam, Science, and Empire in Late Ottoman Egypt* (Cambridge, UK: Cambridge University Press, 2018), 10, 212–214, 238–41.

amateur English astronomer John Reynolds in 1907. This became "the first large telescope to study objects lying well into the southern skies."[19]

As we will see in the next section, this changed context would have an impact not only on the answers Bakhīt offered to the relevant legal questions but also on the very way he conceived of the social-technological world in which those questions resided, and because of which they were newly in need of reconsideration. Building upon my findings in chapter 3, I argue that Bakhīt's assent to the cultural prestige of science was accompanied by a scientistic view of the world that scholars have long identified with the emergence of modernity. Embedded, that is, within his broad embrace of science and technology was an ontology of objectivity and a representationalist epistemology. In what follows, I excavate these commitments through an examination of another section of the *Irshād*, ostensibly a narrow legal work which nonetheless reveals—as it did in chapter 2—a much more thoroughgoing underlying epistemological commitment.

Fiqh and Astronomy: The Prevailing Tradition

The introduction of the new science into an intellectual world has never been a case of simply importing a discrete and inert set of beliefs in a manner that leaves others unperturbed; or, as Bakhīt might have it, innocently reverting to a forgotten paradigm without any intellectual consequences or side effects. Rather, modern science and technology is, as Heidegger puts it, an essential component of the modern world picture, and its attendant assumptions, commitments, and entailments.[20]

Charles Taylor has referred to the view of knowledge within this world picture, arguably its definitive characteristic, as representationalism: the notion that "knowledge is to be seen as correct [inner] representation of an independent [external] reality."[21] A prominent feature of this representationalism,

[19] Stolz, *The Lighthouse and the Observatory*; David Block and Ken Freeman, *Shrouds of the Night: Masks of the Milky Way and the Awesome New View of Galaxies* (New York: Springer, 2008), 187.

[20] See Heidegger, "The Age of the World Picture." In particular, we may point to his comment that "One of the essential phenomena of modernity is its science. Of equal importance is machine technology." Ibid., 66.

[21] Charles Taylor, *Philosophical Arguments* (Cambridge, MA: Harvard University Press, 1995), 3. See also Hubert L. Dreyfus, "Taylor's (Anti-) Epistemology," in *Charles Taylor*, ed. Ruth Abbey, Contemporary Philosophy in Focus (Cambridge, UK: Cambridge University Press, 2004). The following citation from Dreyfus's personal communications with Taylor restates the point: "To sum it up in a pithy formula, we might say that we (mis)understand knowledge as 'mediational'. In its

according to Taylor, is its congeniality to the mechanistic science of the Copernicus-Galileo-Newton tradition. Viewing the world as mechanistic, subject to a set of predictable natural laws, renders previous ways of knowing—Taylor discusses Aristotelian epistemology, describing it as a "participational" enterprise in which things were known when the mind partook in the very being of the object of its knowing—implausible, if not altogether obsolete. Representationalism, then, emerges as an attractive alternative theory in a world no longer informed by a metaphysics of Platonic forms or Aristotelian universals. It becomes much easier to describe how we know in mechanistic terms: a detached subject observing an extramental reality behaving in accordance with the laws of nature. On such a view, knowledge is representational, it consists of a "passive reception of impressions from the external world . . . [and thus] hangs on a certain relation holding between what is 'out there' and certain inner states that this external reality causes in us."[22] Although he stops short of saying that representationalism is *entailed* by the new science and its mechanistic worldview, the connections are far too compelling for Taylor to not draw the connection that the two fit together naturally within the auspices of a unified intellectual outlook.

The remainder of this chapter examines how precisely this shift to a scientistic representationalism manifests itself in Bakhīt's writing. To do so, I turn to the *Irshād* and track how certain legal changes are reflective of a commitment to representationalism which does not appear in the prevailing Ḥanafī tradition.

Law, in fact, was historically quite resistant to the findings of science, contenting itself to work within its own procedures of knowability and action.[23] Despite the long history of *ʿilm al-hayʾa* in the Islamic world, we will see that the *fuqahāʾ* more often than not felt justified to put aside the findings of astronomy in favor of their own internal, genre-specific, epistemological

original form, this emerged in the idea that we grasp external reality through internal representations. Descartes in one of his letters, declared himself 'assuré que je ne puis avoir aucune connaissance de ce qui est hors de moi, que par l'entremise des idées que j'ai eu en moi'. When states of mind correctly and reliably represent what is out there, there is knowledge." Dreyfus, "Taylor's (Anti-) Epistemology," 53. For a slightly restated statement, see Hubert Dreyfus and Charles Taylor, *Retrieving Realism* (Cambridge, MA: Harvard University Press, 2015), 2.

22 Taylor, *Philosophical Arguments*, 3–4.

23 Ahmad Dallal has recently suggested that science and "religion" might be profitably thought of as independent disciplines, with their own particular rationalities and standards. Importantly, what he means by "religion" in his discussion tends to focus on theology (*kalām*) and not law (*fiqh*). Ahmad S. Dallal, *Islam, Science, and the Challenge of History* (New Haven, CT: Yale University Press, 2010), chapter 3.

methods and norms. That Bakhīt is no longer able to maintain this customary disciplinary separation signals a qualitatively different relationship between science and law than the one that prevailed in the premodern period.

In what follows, I look at one particular case study (*mas'ala*) previously addressed repeatedly and at length by Ḥanafī scholars but now newly in need of revisiting thanks to this changed relationship. In this case, I argue, Bakhīt's argumentation is marked by a shift from the prevailing tradition's focus on procedural integrity, as mandated by the *fiqh* tradition, to epistemological criteria, that is a confidence in, and reliance on, the certainty engendered by science and technology with respect to the process of knowing the outside world.

***

The *mas'ala* under consideration in this section has to do with whether the calculations of astronomers may be relied upon to announce the beginning or end of Ramadan.[24] The dominant position was that astronomical calculations were inadmissible in arriving at declarations of the new month. In the very early, formative period of Islam, there were a handful of intriguing opinions from prominent figures favoring calculations but these were few, and in any case quickly eclipsed and deemed anomalous by the settled *madhhab* traditions.[25] So, while it is not the case that the acceptance of astronomy to declare the beginning of a new month was entirely unheard of within the vast corpus of arguments and counterarguments that comprises *fiqh*, these individual opinions came, very early on, to be subsumed by the processes of sifting and evaluation which was so characteristic of the famous *madhhab*s in their mature forms.[26]

[24] Months in the *hijrī* calendar may be either twenty-nine or thirty days, a determination that, historically, could only be made on the eve of the thirtieth. On these traditional standards, which eschew the specification of a lunar calendar in advance, if the new moon (*hilāl*) is sighted that evening, the month is only twenty-nine days long, and the next day is deemed to be the first of the new month. If not, the month is considered to be thirty days long.

[25] After discussing the various nuances among the pro-calculation camp, Aḥmad al-Ghumārī writes that "the common element among them is that calculations are given consideration, and the *ḥukm* (legal ruling) is not restricted to naked-eye sighting, for the latter is not authoritative in and of itself. Rather, it is sought because it furnishes evidence of the new moon. So, if this is established by definitive calculations, it is obligatory to act upon it due to the attainment of what is desired, just as in the case of a sighting. This is the position of Muṭarrif bin ʿAbd Allāh bin al-Shikhkhīr from among the elders of the Followers (Tābiʿūn); and Ibn Surayj who claims it from a text of the Imam al-Shāfiʿī; and Muḥammad bin Muqātil al-Rāzī, the student of Muḥammad bin al-Ḥasan, the companion of Abū Ḥanīfa." Al-Ghumārī, *Tawjīh al-Anẓār li-Tawḥīd al-Muslimīn fī al-Ṣawm wa-l-Ifṭār*, 43. This is based on a similar listing in Ibn Rushd's *Bidāyat al-Mujtahid*.

[26] A possible exception to this statement is the Shāfiʿī school. Al-Ghumārī says that "many of the Shāfiʿīs preferred [astronomical calculations]. It is a famous opinion in their school, such that it

Among these early opinions, the one that needed to be reckoned with in the case of the Ḥanafīs is that of Muḥammad bin Muqātil al-Rāzī, of whom it was said that he would consult the astronomers and rely on their calculations if a large number of them agreed upon it.[27] This was already subject to a strong rebuttal as early as al-Sarakhsī, who died in the late fifth century AH:

> Some of them say that the opinions of those who calculate ought to be resorted to in cases of doubt. But this is far [from the truth]. For the Prophet, peace be upon him, said, "He who visits a soothsayer or astronomer[28] and believes in what he says has disbelieved in what was revealed to Muḥammad."[29]

This latter view, which insisted that astronomical calculations are of no consequence, came to be the dominant *madhhab* opinion within the Ḥanafī school. As the famed Ibn ʿĀbidīn would write less than a hundred years before Bakhīt,

> The texts of the primary works (*mutūn*) of our Ḥanafī scholars agree on the position that Ramadan is established either by sighting the crescent (*hilāl*) or by completing the 30 days of Shaʿbān. And it is well-known that

became renowned as the position of the school itself." Al-Ghumārī, *Tawjīh al-Anẓār li-Tawḥīd al-Muslimīn fī al-Ṣawm wa-l-Ifṭār*, 43. However, he himself later quotes al-Nawawī as saying a majority disagreed with Ibn Surayj's opinion. Al-Ghumārī, *Tawjīh al-Anẓār li-Tawḥīd al-Muslimīn fī al-Ṣawm wa-l-Ifṭār*, 45. Taqī al-Dīn al-Subkī is a later Shāfiʿī who also favored calculations; in this, he served as important inspiration for both Bakhīt (as we will see) and Aḥmad Shākir. See Ebrahim Moosa, "Shaykh Aḥmad Shākir and the Adoption of a Scientifically-Based Lunar Calendar," *Islamic Law and Society* 5, no. 1 (January 1, 1998): 57–89. But al-Subkī himself acknowledged that he was going against the majority in doing so: "The great majority (*al-jumhūr*) of our associates has maintained that [astronomical calculations] are not to be relied on at all, neither for signifying obligation nor permissibility; neither with respect to oneself nor another." Taqī al-Dīn al-Subkī, "al-ʿAlam al-Manshūr fī Ithbāt al-Shuhūr," in *Arbaʿa Rasāʾil fī Hilāl Khayr al-Shuhūr* (Beirut: Dār Ibn Ḥazm, 2000), 21. Al-Subkī's position was subsequently roundly rejected after him by the likes of al-Ramlī and a group of later scholars. See Muḥammad Amīn Ibn ʿĀbidīn, "Tanbīh al-Ghāfil wa-l-Wasnān ʿalā Aḥkām Hilāl Ramaḍān," in *Arbaʿa Rasāʾil fī Hilāl Khayr al-Shuhūr* (Beirut: Dār Ibn Ḥazm, 2000), 101–3.

27 From Ibn Nujaym's *al-Ashbāh wa-l-Naẓāʾir*, quoted in Ibn ʿĀbidīn, "Tanbīh al-Ghāfil wa-l-Wasnān," 96. See also the numerous Shāfiʿīs quoted by al-Laknawī in ʿAbd al-Ḥayy al-Laknawī, "al-Qawl al-Manshūr fī Hilāl Khayr al-Shuhūr," in *Arbaʿa Rasāʾil fī Hilāl Khayr al-Shuhūr* (Beirut: Dār Ibn Ḥazm, 2000), 150–53. These include, among others, Mullā ʿAlī al-Qārī and Ibn Ḥajar al-Makkī.

28 The word is *munajjim* in the text of Ibn ʿĀbidīn's quotation of Ibn Nujaym. However, the word used in the edition of the *Mabsūṭ* I consulted is *ʿarrāf* (fortune teller or diviner). This is a conflation which tells us quite a bit about the negative way that astronomical calculations were viewed in this period—namely as inextricably linked to astrology. In any case, it is clear from the context that what is being argued against is calculations.

29 Shams al-Dīn al-Sarakhsī, *al-Mabsūṭ*, vol. 3 (Beirut: Dār al-Maʿrifa, n.d.), 78.

> the purport of the reliable works [of the school] is that it is not established by other than these two. This is why . . . the writer of *al-Nahr* explained in his commentary on *al-Kanz* that "the upshot of these words . . . is that the beginning of the Ramadan fast is not established except by one of these two. So, the statement of the astronomers that [the moon] was in the sky on such and such a night is not authoritative, even though they may be morally upright (*ʿadūl*), as is stated in *al-Īḍāḥ*. Majd al-Aʾimma [al-Tarjamānī] has said, "The companions of Abū Ḥanīfa have all agreed on this, excepting a very few (*illā al-nādir*) and al-Shāfiʿī."[30]

He then goes on to list a long and impressive line of scholars who have upheld this position. These include al-Sarakhsī; Shams al-Aʾimma al-Ḥalwānī; Majd al-Aʾimma al-Tarjamānī; Ibn Wahbān; al-Ḥaṣkafī in *al-Durr al-Mukhtār*; Ibn Nujaym in *al-Baḥr al-Rāʾiq*; the author of *Miʿrāj al-Dirāya*, a commentary on al-Marghīnānī's *Hidāya*; and ʿĀlim b. al-ʿAlāʾ al-Andarītī in the *Tātārkhāniyya*.

This position is justified by Ibn ʿĀbidīn on procedural grounds. Rather than rely on the hadith cited by al-Sarakhsī, whose generality and absoluteness he thought to be untenable given that calculations were indeed used to determine the celestial phenomena that signaled the times of prayer, Ibn ʿĀbidīn prefers a set of hadiths which allows him to draw a sharp distinction between *ʿilm* (knowledge) and sighting (*ruʾya*), and then prefer the latter to the former.

> It is preferable to justify this by reference to hadiths indicating that sighting (*ruʾya*) is to be relied upon, not knowledge (*ʿilm*). For he, peace be upon him, said, "Fast upon sighting it, and break your fast upon sighting it." And he said, "If [the sky] is obscured over you, complete the count [of thirty days]." He did not say, "Ask those who calculate." Instead, he said, "We are an unlettered nation; we neither write nor calculate."[31]

Since the hadith makes clear that the Muslims should "fast upon sighting it, and break the fast upon sighting it," mere knowledge of the birth of the new moon is insufficient to effect a religious duty. Rather, what is of consequence is that the procedure outlined in Prophetic traditions is followed diligently.

[30] Ibn ʿĀbidīn, "Tanbīh al-Ghāfil wa-l-Wasnān," 96.
[31] Ibn ʿĀbidīn, "Tanbīh al-Ghāfil wa-l-Wasnān," 98.

Against those who gave priority to the "conclusive (*qaṭʿī*)" conclusions of astronomy over the merely "probabilistic (*ẓannī*)" testimonies of sightings,[32] Ibn ʿĀbidīn cites approvingly the opinion of Shihāb al-Dīn al-Ramlī that "witnessing (i.e., *shahāda*) has been granted the status of certainty by the Lawgiver."[33]

This is a position, needless to say, that does not put much trust in science. If he was at all aware of modern science, Ibn ʿĀbidīn was certainly unimpressed by its pretensions to discover an unknown conceptual reality in a manner characterized by both objectivity and certitude.

> Just as what is known through measuring, weighing or counting a pile of things is not knowledge of the unseen, neither is what is known through geomancy. For all of these are merely probabilistic, and even preponderant probabilities are not tantamount to knowledge of the unseen. The expert astronomers are agreed that [calculations] are simply preponderant possibilities. [In the case of] these lofty bodies, the one who calculates is in need of surveying their size, a knowledge of their paths, and of the direction of their rays. But all of these are known only approximately (*bi-ṭarīq al-taqrīb*) and not in reality (*lā ʿalā al-ḥaqīqa*). As such, some of [the astronomers] are wrong, and others are correct.[34]

The "certain" procedure of the tradition thus takes precedence over an astronomy that is merely approximate, but most importantly without any assent in the sacred texts. Indeed, Ibn ʿĀbidīn is not shy to say so explicitly, choosing to conclude this discussion with a summary that hammers the point home:

> Thus it is known that, in the matter of establishing the months, there is to be no reliance on what is stated by the scholars of astronomy and calculation, due to the inadmissibility of this consideration in the eyes of the Law—which renders the necessity of fasting [at the beginning of Ramadan]

[32] According to Shihāb al-Dīn al-Ramlī, among these is al-Subkī, whom he quotes as saying, "Even if you witness a clear proof of a moon-sighting on the eve of the thirtieth of a night, if the astronomer maintains that it was impossible to see it that night, we act on the opinion of the astronomer. This is because astronomical calculations are conclusive, and *shahāda* (observation or testimony of an observation) is probabilistic." See al-Laknawī, "al-Qawl al-Manshūr," 150–51; and Ibn ʿĀbidīn, "Tanbīh al-Ghāfil wa-l-Wasnān," 102.

[33] Ibn ʿĀbidīn, "Tanbīh al-Ghāfil wa-l-Wasnān," 102.

[34] Ibn ʿĀbidīn, "Tanbīh al-Ghāfil wa-l-Wasnān," 98.

> and breaking the fast [at its end] dependent on the sighting itself, not on astronomical principles. As such, it is clear that [those who took the opposing view, in part on astronomical grounds, did so] with no legal justification, but rather in accordance with mere rational probability, in defiance of the foundational texts (*nuṣūṣ*) of the Law which have long been regarded as reliable by the *mujtahid* imams and their trustworthy followers.[35]

Ibn ʿĀbidīn's discussion of this issue took the form of a full-length *risāla* in response to a specific incident which provoked controversy between Ḥanafīs and Shāfiʿīs in Damascus in the year 1240/1825. However, inasmuch as it can be gleaned from often less sustained treatments dispersed throughout the corpus of traditional compendiums (*kutub al-furūʿ*), his treatment accurately captures the Ḥanafī tradition's overwhelming suspicion of the authority of astronomy in the domain of *fiqh*.[36]

Bakhīt's Scientistic Representationalism and Its Influences

No more than a century later, however, this historically dominant position would prove untenable in an Egypt undergoing significant technological developments, and Bakhīt would take a diametrically opposed position to his Ḥanafī predecessor. Bakhīt's argument consists of a remarkable series of reinterpretations, selective citations, elevation of minority opinions, and generalizations of exceptions, revealing a mind with such a remarkable command of the Ḥanafī tradition (and indeed *fiqh*, more broadly) that he is able to mold it to fit the intuitions and imperatives of an entirely new context.

[35] Ibn ʿĀbidīn, "Tanbīh al-Ghāfil wa-l-Wasnān," 104.

[36] As evidence, we may point to both Bakhīt and al-Subkī admitting this to be the dominant position, and thus conceiving their own interventions as departures from the tradition. "The great majority (*al-jumhūr*) of our associates have maintained that [astronomical calculations] are not to be relied on at all, neither for signifying obligation nor permissibility; neither with respect to oneself nor another." Al-Subkī, "al-ʿAlam al-Manshūr," 21. As for Bakhīt, he notes at the beginning of his chapter that the Ḥanafīs took to acting upon the hadiths, which were explicit about the manner of beginning and breaking the fast of Ramadan. "The Messenger of God, peace be upon him, did not relate in the hadith any express instruction to take into account the calculations of timekeepers in [determining] the obligation to fast or break the fast. And most jurists [*akthar al-fuqahāʾ*], whether early or late, did not turn to the scholars of timekeeping [*ʿulamāʾ al-mīqāt*] and their reliance on calculation in [determining] the beginning of the months of Ramadan and Shawwāl. This is because the Lawgiver made both fasting and breaking the fast dependent on sighting through [the Prophet's] saying 'Fast upon sighting it; and break your fast upon sighting it.' And by 'sighting' what is *prima facie* understood is an actual naked-eye sighting." Muḥammad Bakhīt al-Muṭīʿī, *Irshād Ahl al-Milla ilā Ithbāt al-Ahilla*, ed. Ḥasan Aḥmad Isbir (Beirut: Dār Ibn Ḥazm, 2000), 174.

His primary sources in this section of the *Irshād* ("the ninth discussion") are treatises written by the eighth/fourteenth-century Shāfiʿī Taqī al-Dīn al-Subkī,[37] and the thirteenth/nineteenth-century Tatar Ḥanafī jurist, Shihāb al-Dīn al-Marjānī. Relying heavily on these works, Bakhīt made ingenious use of what amounted to outlying or exceptional legal opinions within them to advance a radical argument that established the primacy of science in considerations of the law, and he did so by reference to a representationalist theory of knowledge. No doubt aware of how revolutionary his intervention was, Bakhīt felt it necessary to append al-Subkī's *risāla* to the end of the first edition of his book,[38] thereby recruiting the prestige and cultural capital of an acknowledged and revered Egyptian master to lend legitimacy to his own thesis.

Al-Subkī's *al-ʿAlam al-Manshūr fī Ithbāt al-Shuhūr*[39] was written to address what he took to be a recurring problem in Damascus: testimonies that claimed the crescent had been spotted when it was astronomically impossible to see it. Al-Subkī held that such testimonies ought to be disregarded. As part of its general concern with astronomical calculations, however, the treatise also took up the question with which we are concerned in this section. For al-Subkī, the hadith's characterization of the Muslim *umma* as illiterate is neither a denigration nor a proscription against writing and calculating.[40] Rather, it is an honor that accrues to the early Muslim community by virtue of its connecting them to their unlettered Prophet. It is furthermore a mercy from God in that it provides a simple and accessible mechanism for following the commandments of the shariʿa and does not oblige a largely illiterate community to undertake the expert task of calculation. None of this invalidates the accuracy of the astronomer's determination of the beginning of a lunar month; it simply insists that the legal determination (*ḥukm sharʿī*) of the same must be considered independent from the conclusions of astronomy.

One of the specific legal questions that occupies al-Subkī, however, is what is to be done in the exceptional case that the new moon could have been

[37] For a Ḥanafī biography of al-Subkī, see ʿAbd al-Ḥayy al-Laknawī, *al-Fawāʾid al-Bahiyya fī Tarājim al-Ḥanafiyya* (Cairo: Maṭbaʿat al-Saʿāda, 1324H), 44–45.

[38] This edition is Muḥammad Bakhīt al-Muṭīʿī, *Kitāb Irshād Ahl al-Milla ilā Ithbāt al-Ahilla* (Miṣr: Maṭbaʿat al-Kurdistān al-ʿIlmiyya, 1329H).

[39] Ebrahim Moosa vocalizes this title as *al-ʿIlm al-Manshūr*, but both the editor of the new edition of the work, as well as the editor of *Arbaʿa Rasāʾil fī Hilāl Khayr al-Shuhūr* (from which I cite), have it as *al-ʿAlam al-Manshūr*.

[40] See Ibn ʿĀbidīn's usage of this earlier. Al-Subkī's position is set out in al-Subkī, "al-ʿAlam al-Manshūr," 17–25.

sighted (according to the assessment of astronomical calculations) had it not been for an overcast sky obscuring the view. It is clear that, in the opinion of Ibn ʿĀbidīn and indeed the great majority (*al-jumhūr*) of scholars, this scientific data is inadmissible in informing us of the beginning of the month. However, al-Subkī chooses to endorse a position he attributes to the early judge and jurist Ibn Surayj: namely, that *it is permissible for the expert astronomer who himself comes to this conclusion* to fast, or break the fast, based on his personal calculations.[41]

While one could conceivably argue for the permissibility of calculations for determining the months based on an analogy to prayer timings whose cosmological indicators were indeed calculated (and uncontroversially so), al-Subkī chooses not to follow this tack. Instead, he maintains the distinction between prayer and fasting, saying that in the case of proclaiming the months, what is asked for is not the existence (*wujūd*) of the new moon "in reality" (*fī nafs al-amr*), but a *sighting* of it. "So, we follow in each case (*fī kulli bāb*) the [evidential standards] the shariʿa has set out for it."[42] However, what if we have (1) confidence in the birth of the new moon (i.e., the separation of the moon from the sun); and (2) clear (*jalī*) astronomical evidence of its visibility; but (3) the sole reason that it was obscured from view in our preponderant estimation (*ghalabat al-ẓann*) was an overcast sky? In this very limited case, al-Subkī responds, "the permissibility of fasting has been strengthened. The position that holds that it is not permissible in this circumstance is far-fetched, though [saying it is an] obligation is odder still."[43] Al-Subkī reiterates the strict conditions he has spelled out earlier, and then comments that this sort of knowledge is available to none but the expert (*māhir*).[44]

This is a heavily hedged and cautious response. Indeed, even in the carefully specified case he sets forth, al-Subkī refers to his position as "my choice" among a spectrum of opinions of varied strength. Although he, like Ibn ʿĀbidīn, locates the locus of obligation in the individual observer, al-Subkī places greater faith in astronomers' ability to get at a judgment suitable for being acted upon. Whereas scientific calculations are inadmissible for Ibn ʿĀbidin because they are mere approximations, al-Subkī has greater

[41] Abū Isḥāq al-Shīrāzī claims in *al-Muhadhdhab* that Ibn Surayj's position was that it was not permissible, but obligatory, for the astronomer to act on his knowledge. Al-Subkī, "al-ʿAlam al-Manshūr," 21.
[42] Al-Subkī, "al-ʿAlam al-Manshūr," 22.
[43] Al-Subkī, "al-ʿAlam al-Manshūr," 22.
[44] Al-Subkī, "al-ʿAlam al-Manshūr," 22.

confidence in the capacity of science to arrive at a reliable determination of both the birth of the new moon and people's capacity to spot it in clear skies.

When compared to the prevailing tradition, this concession to science is a significant development, but it is a markedly conservative one.[45] As if to underscore the point, al-Subkī is quick to point out that priority must always be given to empirical considerations because they are the clearest form of evidence (*al-amr al-maḥsus alladhī huwa min ajlā al-umūr*). Interestingly, this is derived from the hadith in which the Prophet gestured repeatedly with two open hands, saying "A month is like this and this and this. A month is like this and this and this." On the third repetition of the first set, he folded his thumb in to indicate a count of twenty-nine. In the second set, he extended all ten figures each time, indicating a final count of thirty. This is interpreted by al-Subkī as an instruction to give precedence to material and bodily considerations, like sighting by the naked eye. In instances where evidence of this sort is forthcoming, one must put aside calculation.

It is precisely the conservatism that characterizes al-Subkī's response that is missing in Bakhīt. Although he quotes heavily from *al-ʿAlam al-Manshūr*, and his decision to append the half-a-millennium-old treatise to his own clearly marks his desire to align his intervention with al-Subkī's, Bakhīt's appropriation of the Shāfiʿī authority represents at bottom a marked departure from the heavily empirical, observation-centric focus of the *fiqh* tradition. Bakhīt is at home in the language of the tradition and seems at first to hew rather closely to al-Subkī's position, envisioning his own comments as merely "supporting remarks."[46] However, in the course of these remarks, he begins to speak in unmistakably general terms, abstracting the argument away from the case-specific circumstances set out by his predecessor, thereby effectively expanding its scope and turning a limited defense of calculations into a thoroughgoing scientism. This is accomplished rather gradually throughout his discussion, but, by the end, the reader is left with no doubt that Bakhīt is at least as intellectually indebted to the epistemology and ontology of the new science as he is to the precedents of his fellow *fuqahā*ʾ.

[45] My assessment here corresponds to that of Aḥmad Shākir, who says of those few jurists who, like al-Subkī, were well versed in the astronomical sciences: "[W]hen they did take recourse to astronomy, they did so with great trepidation." Moosa, "Shaykh Aḥmad Shākir and the Adoption of a Scientifically-Based Lunar Calendar," 73. It is also a position that was known by the later tradition as a personal choice, an anomaly, even an aberrant opinion.

[46] He more than once leads into his own observations with "And that which supports (*yuʿayyidu*) this is . . ."

Bakhīt's innovation is to establish the bindingness of scientific knowledge by valorizing the epistemological status of *ʿilm* and downplaying the necessity of an actual sighting. Recall that in Ibn ʿĀbidīn's formulation, sighting (*ruʾya*) was counterposed to *ʿilm* (knowledge, and in particular, astronomical knowledge), with the express goal of subordinating the latter to the former. In a direct reversal of this position, Bakhīt is explicit that, for him, the legal cause (*al-sabab*) for the proclamation of a new month is *ʿilm*. This is based on his novel reading of the word *shahida* (to witness) in the Qurʾanic verse, "Whosoever amongst you witnesses the month, let him fast" (2:185). "Witnessing" here, according to Bakhīt—and he is careful to divert attention away from the verbal noun generally used in this context, *shahāda*, usually taken to mean either an observation of the new moon, or a testimony thereof, to the related *shuhūd*—could mean either being present in the month and not forsaking it (*ḥuḍūr fīhi wa-ʿadam al-safar*), or alternatively having knowledge of its existence (*ʿilm bi-wujūdihi*). It is clear to him that what is meant here is the latter, and as such whoever is aware, or made aware, of the *wujūd* of the month is to fast. The *wujūd* (existence) of the month is, for Bakhīt, signaled by the *wujūd* of its new moon, which may in turn be attested to by the usual ways of gaining knowledge—a sighting, or information of the sighting of a trustworthy person, or the ruling of a judge—but equally an astronomical calculation.

> The "witnessing" (*shuhūd*) of a month may mean either being present in it and not forsaking it, or having knowledge of its existence. It is clear that it is this second which is meant by the verse. . . . It is thus [equally] clear from the verse that any of you who knows of the existence of the month in question—i.e., the month of Ramadan—is obligated to fast. And legally, the existence of the month is—as the hadith demands—through the existence (*wujūd*) of the new moon after sunset in a manner that it may be seen by an observer. So, whoever knows of the existence of the new moon after sunset through any means that furnish preponderant knowledge must fast—regardless of [whether this means] an actual sighting, or a report of a sighting from a trustworthy person, or knowledge of the ruling of a qadi, or an astronomical calculation which indicates [the new moon's] existence and the possibility of seeing it without difficulty in the absence of any impediments (*lawlā al-mānīʿ*). What is demanded by "seeing" [in the hadith] is stated by al-Qushayrī: "If calculations indicate that the new moon has risen from the horizon in a manner that it may be seen (*ʿalā wajh yurā*) in the absence

of an impediment—such as an overcast sky—this entails the obligation [to fast] due to the existence of the legal cause (*al-sabab al-sharʿī*). An actual sighting is not required to effect the obligation [to fast]."[47]

This phraseology is striking, because it appears to authorize an abstraction away from the particulars of al-Subkī's formulation. No longer does Bakhīt speak of the specific case of an overcast sky obstructing our view, except as an illustrative example. Rather, the language is purposely general: other impediments are envisioned, and the heavily conditioned demands of al-Subkī gradually begin to give way to the simple demand for an astronomical assertion that the new moon *may* be seen in the absence of such impediments. Whether such impediments actually do present themselves seems to be an afterthought, if that.

The differential emphases of Bakhīt and al-Subkī are underscored in the next passage in which Bakhīt goes on to reinterpret the connection between fasting and sighting (*ruʾya*) made so clear by numerous hadiths. He does this by exploiting a line of argument only broached by al-Subkī. Contemplating the hadith, "Do not fast until you see the crescent, and do not cease fasting until you see the crescent," al-Subkī had suggested in a rather academic tone that, if taken literally, the hadith yields four legal rulings: the impermissibility of fasting before the Ramadan crescent is spotted, the impermissibility of ceasing fasting before the Shawwāl crescent is spotted, the obligation of fasting after the Ramadan crescent is spotted, and the obligation to cease fasting after the Shawwāl crescent is spotted. This focus on the legal categories of impermissiblity (*ḥurma*) and obligation (*wujūb*), al-Subkī points out, leaves out the realm of the legally permissible (*jawāz*). Perhaps, permissibility can be reinserted into the equation, he offers, if we distinguish between two possible understandings of "sighting" (*ruʾya*): (1) an actual sighting and (2) mere visibility, the crescent's "appearance such that it may be seen." Here, al-Subkī's use of the passive, paralleling the language in the earlier quote (*bi ḥaythu yurā*), appears to countenance the use of calculations, and importantly does so outside of the limited case in which he has sanctioned them for the personal use of the expert astronomer. But, crucially, he prefers not to follow this opening, instead leaving it as an open question, and suggesting that the matter hinges on whether one adopts a literal (*lafẓ)* or conceptual (*maʿnā*) approach to the text. For his part, Bakhīt seizes on this

[47] Bakhīt, *Irshād*, 182–83.

opportunity, to declare: "There is no doubt that what is of consideration here is the concept."

Missing from Bakhīt's interpretation is the caution found in al-Subkī's—his decisiveness in settling the question in favor of a departure from the letter of the text permits a bold and unorthodox generalization from al-Subkī's insistence that calculations must only be resorted to by an expert when the exceptional circumstance of an overcast evening obtains. Bakhīt legitimates this departure (though he is careful not to let on that it is a departure) by making reference to an obscure opinion attributed to one al-Qushayrī, on whose identity we have no firm information.[48] Al-Qushayrī drew upon what he claimed to be a widely held opinion that a prisoner held in an underground jail who concludes, based upon simple counting or his own judgment (*ijtihād*), that a given day falls in Ramadan is obliged to fast on that day. By analogy, then, if astronomical computation indicates that a new moon has "risen from the horizon" and is visible, but it may not be seen because of some impediment, the obligation to fast still holds, even though there may have been no actual sighting. This was not considered a compelling argument by Badr al-Dīn al-ʿAynī, from whom Bakhīt takes it. Al-ʿAynī merely mentions it in a comprehensive listing of opinions but goes on to restate the dominant view that in cases of overcast nights, one should simply "complete" the thirty days of the month due to the nonsighting. This is partly due to a number of hadiths that corroborate this position explicitly, but must also be, at least partly, because of the difference in the sources of knowledge of the prisoner and the nonprisoner—the former "knows" it's Ramadan by counting or by a subjective estimation, both widely considered acceptable substitutes for a sighting; the latter "knows" by an astronomical calculation. Al-Qushayrī's language can also be found in the work of the Shāfiʿī Ibn Daqīq al-ʿĪd, but this opinion was explicitly rebutted in the later Shāfiʿī school by Ibn Ḥajar al-ʿAsqalānī.[49] This history of debate seems not to matter for Bakhīt. Resurrecting an anomalous position of an obscure Ḥanafī jurist provides him just enough room to expand the scope of al-Subkī's carefully delimited response and thereby legitimate his positioning of scientific calculation as a full-fledged option for determining the months. Indeed, in his

[48] Z. A. Shah suggests it is the famous Sufi, ʿAbd al-Karīm b. Hawzān al-Qushayrī, and that he followed the Shāfiʿī Ibn Daqīq al- ʿĪd.

[49] Taqī al-Dīn Ibn Daqīq al-ʿĪd, *Iḥkām al-Aḥkām*, ed. Ahmad Shakir (Beirut: ʿĀlam al-Kutub, 1987), vol. 2, p. 8; Ibn Ḥajar al-ʿAsqalānī, *Talkhīṣ al-Ḥabīr* (Mecca: Mu'assasat al-Qurṭuba, 1995), vol. 2, p. 360.

view, it seems to be the most reliable option due to the precision and expertise of the astronomers: "Have you not seen that the astronomer, if he relies on his calculations to say that an eclipse will occur at such and such a time on such and such a day, it always (*qaṭʿan*) occurs without fail (*wa lā yatakhallaf*)."[50]

Absent, also, in Bakhīt is the primary emphasis on encouraging attempted sightings for the empirical evidence they furnish. Indeed, in marked contrast to al-Subkī for whom it was calculations that were prone to mistakes,[51] Bakhīt is at pains to point out the many false positives that occur "in this age":

> We have seen many [instances] of people—otherwise dependable both in terms of their reason and their religion—making mistakes when it comes to sighting the new moon. And we have heard that some ignoramuses intend piety by testifying [that they have seen it]. They believe they have earned the reward of those who fast by claiming this. And we have heard of some fools who [seek to] establish their moral uprightness (*ʿadāla*) and propagate their integrity [in the eyes of the court, by having their testimonies accepted].[52]

In the face of this lack of confidence in individual sightings by the naked eye, simply the knowledge, arrived at through calculations, that the new moon may be spotted, all things being equal, is sufficient. One is left feeling, after reading this strong defense of prospective calculations and the simultaneous downplaying of the prevailing tradition's empiricism, that even if no sightings are attempted, nothing has been violated. The opposition is now between those who advocate for an actual sighting and those who are content with a decontextualized "indication from calculations that a sighting is possible in the absence of any impediments."[53] This latter constitutes *ʿilm*, the crucial criteria for proclaiming a new month on Bakhīt's reading.

[50] Bakhīt, *Irshād*, 182.

[51] Al-Subkī agrees with those opposed to calculation that, as opposed to [prayer] timings, "mistakes proliferate (*yakthuru al-ghalat*)" in the case of sighting the new moon. Al-Subkī, "al-ʿAlam al-Manshūr," 22, 56.

[52] Bakhīt, *Irshād*, 199. For his part, Bakhīt is aware that this is a change in emphasis from the prevailing tradition. After concluding that it is improper to accept a report which may be a lie (or mistake) or a testimony of a sighting when none is possible, he notes, "We have not encountered this issue spelled out, so we studied it, concluding that such a testimony or observation must not be accepted. The jurists were only silent about this because it occurred so infrequently (*li annahā nādirat al-wuqūʿ*). But now that it occurs in our age, we are in need of addressing it. The *fiqh* is an ocean without a shore." Ibid.

[53] Bakhīt, *Irshād*, 183.

Though this move toward abstraction and generality is unmistakable, Bakhīt does not let on except obliquely. Indeed, he does not acknowledge any daylight between his position and al-Subkī's, preferring to leave the impression that they are one and the same,[54] and using this opening as a springboard for a more revealing, and radical, discussion.

Whether the substantive conclusions of the two jurists differ is less interesting than interrogating the underlying worldview that motivates Bakhīt to take up al-Subkī's individual opinion so strongly in the face of the bias against calculations that dominates the tradition. Bakhīt holds that the position he advocates is the best one because "reality (*al-wāqiʿ*) agrees with [it]." What is this new reality? I contend that it is the dominance of a new ontology that places greater stress on the objective structure of the world over the phenomenal experience of it, and an epistemology that thinks of knowledge in terms Taylor would call representational. Itself occasioned by the sudden technological developments in Egypt and the acceptance of the heliocentric model, this new reality is a natural ally to Bakhīt's esteem for science as unimpeachable and yielding knowledge of an irrefutable sort that it should now be seen as a competitor to the traditional standards of *fiqh*.

That he has internalized this worldview becomes evident in his telling choice to draw from the nineteenth-century Tatar Ḥanafī Shihāb al-Dīn al-Marjānī in the rest of his discussion in the chapter. So as to justify his vindication of science, Bakhīt proceeds to embark on an excursus in which he treats the question of what we are to make of lands at extreme latitudes in which the sun does not rise, or alternatively does not set, for months at a time. How should they observe Ramadan? In resorting to this boundary case, Bakhīt is drawing upon a strategy employed by his senior colleague al-Marjānī, who had written a treatise in which he maintained the obligation to pray the night prayer (*al-ʿishāʾ*) in places like his native Volga-Ural region where, at certain times of the year, the evening twilight would not dissipate and give way to complete nightfall.[55] For al-Marjānī, those who suggested that the night prayer might be waived in such locales were making a grave mistake, for they were misunderstanding that prayers were bound not to the astronomical events mentioned in texts—in the case of the night prayer, the disappearance

[54] In turn, these are then assimilated, rather imprecisely, to the opinions of "a camp of scholars, among whom are Ibn Surayj, Muṭarrif, Ibn Qutayba, Ibn Muqātil al-Rāzī . . . and some prominent Followers (Tābiʿūn)." Bakhīt, *Irshād*, 183–84.

[55] Shihāb al-Dīn al-Marjānī, *Naẓurat al-Ḥaqq fī Farḍiyyat al-ʿIshāʾ wa in lam Yaghib al-Shafaq* (Amman: Dār al-Fatḥ, 2012).

of evening twilight—but rather to the passing of time. But time is an objective measure for al-Marjānī, linked not to worldly happenings but rather, as the ancient philosophers would have it, to the motion of the outermost sphere in the heavens. As such, its reality is independent of the traditional worldly indicators that are taken to signify the onset of prayer timings. These latter are mere "signs (*aʿlām*) informing (*muʿarrifāt*) us of the passing of time (*muḍīyy al-azmān*)," and so the obligation of prayer does not fall away simply because these signs happen to be absent.[56] For al-Marjānī, this becomes obvious when we consider the case of extreme latitudes, in which the sun may not rise or set for six months at a time. Of course, this cannot be taken to mean that one must pray only one day's worth of prayers over these six months.[57] Rather, al-Marjānī analogizes time to space, proffering the example of a mail carrier who rents a beast of burden in order to travel a specific distance along a path ordinarily marked by distance markers. Even if the markers are physically removed or the distances etched on them fade away, he would be obliged to pay the animal's owner for the distance traversed.[58] Just as this distance remains stable and unaffected by the absence of markers, so does the underlying realm of time—time still exists even when its indicators do not. It is thus time which emerges as the real measure of when prayers are to be observed. As such, Muslims in these extreme latitudes must pray all five prayers, and they must perform the night prayer in cities like Kazan even if the twilight never completely disappears.

Certainly, al-Marjānī's reasoning will be perfectly intuitive to most readers. But it was not necessarily so to the juristic tradition itself which, even when it upheld the obligation of the night prayer like al-Marjānī did, did so in terms that did not rely on this ontology.[59]

As it turned out, though, this was a welcome framing for Bakhīt's purposes, and indeed a natural one to adopt in a rapidly changing Egypt. Timothy Mitchell has spoken at length of the emergence in colonial Egypt of

[56] Al-Marjānī, *Nāẓūrat al-Ḥaqq fī Farḍiyyat al-ʿIshāʾ wa in lam Yaghib al-Shafaq*, 319.

[57] Al-Marjānī, *Nāẓūrat al-Ḥaqq fī Farḍiyyat al-ʿIshāʾ wa in lam Yaghib al-Shafaq*, 335–36.

[58] Al-Marjānī, *Nāẓūrat al-Ḥaqq fī Farḍiyyat al-ʿIshāʾ wa in lam Yaghib al-Shafaq*, 320–21.

[59] For examples of previous scholars' positions on the issue, see al-Marjānī, *Nāẓūrat al-Ḥaqq fī Farḍiyyat al-ʿIshāʾ wa in lam Yaghib al-Shafaq*, 337–40; and for the practice of the Muslims of the Volga-Ural region, 390–91. Indeed, al-Marjānī explicitly aligns himself with the philosophical tradition precisely so he can draw on its definition of time to put forth this ontology, offering a severe criticism of its major competitor, "orthodox" Muslim theology (*ʿilm al-kalām*). See his defense of philosophy on p. 336, "The shariʿa does not refute philosophy; nor does philosophy deny the shariʿa, for they are twins from the mother of truth." He dedicates a whole chapter entitled "The Falsification of *Kalām*," 85–93.

an ontology of objectivity, drawing primarily on the phenomenon of the exhibition as a symbol of this new reality.

> The person was now thought of as something set apart from a physical world, like the visitor to an exhibition or the worker attending a machine, as the one who observes and controls it. . . . Separated in this way from a physical world and from his own physical body, the true nature of the human person, like that of the observer at the exhibition, was to learn to be industrious, self-disciplined and closely attentive.
>
> In the middle of the nineteenth century, a new term came into vogue for characterising this combination of detachment and close attentiveness—the word "objective." . . . The word denoted the modern sense of detachment, both physical and conceptual, of the self from an object-world—the detachment epitomised, as I have been suggesting, in the visitor to an exhibition . . .
>
> [T]his "objective" isolation of the observer from an object-world, in terms of which personhood was understood, corresponded to a distinction that was now made between the material world of exhibits or representations and the meaning or plan that they represented . . . [O]utlines, guides, tables and plans mediated between the visitor and the exhibit, by supplementing what was displayed with a structure and meaning. The seemingly separate text or plan, one might say, was what confirmed the separation of the person from the things themselves on exhibit, and of the things on exhibit from the meaning or external reality they represented.[60]

For Mitchell, a central feature of the age in which such a conception of the world comes to prominence is its colonialism—"the age of the exhibition was necessarily the colonial age," for the reality the exhibition sought to represent was "the world itself."[61] This manner of ordering and understanding the world accompanied Europeans on their travels as the lens through which they strove to understand, and indeed order, colonies like Egypt. This approach was not without its frustrations, because as Mitchell demonstrates, mid-nineteenth-century European visitors like Flaubert and Nerval first encountered Egypt as a "bewildering chaos" in which one found oneself immersed, and therefore unable to take up the detached viewpoint

[60] Timothy Mitchell, *Colonising Egypt* (Berkeley: University of California Press, 1991), 19–20.
[61] Mitchell, *Colonising Egypt*, 13.

demanded of an objective observer.[62] This experience, however, did not stymie the steady production of an important European intellectual corpus in the forms of maps, ethnographic writings, photographs, paintings, and exhibitions, cultural production that later visitors took with them as structuring and governing representations of the "reality" they witnessed on the ground in Egypt.

Mitchell understands this approach to knowledge to be a property of the European imaginary forged in the crucible of Europe's exercise of colonial power over non-Europeans. However, that Bakhīt's reasoning in support of relying on astronomical calculations was itself articulated in similar terms suggests that the colonial experience was not only the originary ground of a new European metaphysics and epistemology but also a transformative moment in the thinking of colonial Muslim subjects. This argument extends the findings of the last chapter, which already reveal Bakhīt's engagement with modern science to be structured as a mode of colonial discourse that sees his own Arab-Islamic reference points as reflecting European universals. Recall that the carefully constructed history of astronomy offered by Bakhīt in a *tafsīr ʿilmī* work, in which he recasts Cornelius Van Dyck's recapitulation of the standard Eurocentric narrative of the Scientific Revolution to embed it within an Arab-Islamic world, presents itself in accordance with Shaden Tageldin's argument that, in the encounter between colonizers and Egyptian intellectuals, the mode by which the colonized Egyptian related to the cultural output of Europe was through the seduction of recognition—recognition of the colonizer, that is, as an aspirational version of oneself.

It is unsurprising, then, to find the European ontology of objectivity sitting comfortably in Bakhīt's mind alongside what we have already seen to be his wholehearted acceptance of modern science, and his positive assessment of technological development. Indeed, this commitment to objectivity would lay the groundwork for his further commitment to a representationalist view of knowledge. Borrowing al-Marjānī's example of Muslims in extreme latitudes, Bakhīt asks ironically,

> Is it possible for the people of these lands to fast by actually sighting the moon after sunset? Or is it possible for someone to say they are not obligated to fast if Ramadan corresponds to one of the months in which the sun either appears [continuously] or is hidden [continuously], even though

[62] Mitchell, *Colonising Egypt*, 21–22, 27–30.

> the moon conjuncts with the sun once every month and then separates from it? *When it separates, it is the first of the lunar month. And this does not differ in any corner of the Earth. . . . The lunar months are confirmed realities (mutaḥaqqiqa) in all areas, just as is the lunar year.*[63]

This is a rather clear articulation of the ontology of objectivity that Mitchell observed as having made deep inroads into Egyptian society: namely, the detachment of the observer from the world of objects. The focus for Bakhīt is now on the conjunction and separation of the moon, a universal judgment determined by science, and not on its sighting or even visibility. This further abstraction—on top of his earlier generalization of al-Subkī's position—is justified by drawing an analogy to the case sketched out by al-Marjānī. This, too, is a controversial interpretive choice because al-Subkī, Ibn ʿĀbidīn, and al-Marjānī were all adamant that the difference between the respective evidential standards of the two rituals (prayer, on the one hand, and Ramadan declarations, on the other) was to be maintained. That he should be interested in collapsing this distinction is unsurprising given that he has now made of knowledge (*ʿilm*) the new evidential standard for the latter.[64] As such, Bakhīt proceeds with the analogy, citing the Qurʾanic verse 2:189 in support of his move from prayer to fasting: "[The verse's] meaning—and God knows best—is that the crescents and other similar signs are the times (*mawāqīt*) for *ḥajj* and similar rituals. . . . But nothing is negated through the signs' absence, for they are merely informing signs."[65] As such, Bakhīt goes on to conclude that:

> All of [the preceding] is proof that the Lawgiver did not demand prayer upon the setting of the sun, nor fasting upon the sighting of the *hilāl* of Ramadan, nor other events that he made signs for the times of worship, except with an eye to the [needs of the] majority. . . . Neither did the Lawgiver prohibit relying on other signs which also indicate these timings, such as telescopes (*ālāt al-raṣd*), or calculations or astronomical hours.[66]

This objectivity is, on Bakhīt's variation of al-Marjānī's reading, linked to the heliocentricity of the world under the new science. Whereas al-Marjānī

[63] Bakhīt, *Irshād*, 184–85.
[64] The collapsing of the distinction between determining prayers and determining Ramadan was anticipated by Riḍā in 1904. *Al-Manār* 7: 699–701; Stolz, 266–67.
[65] Bakhīt, *Irshād*, 187.
[66] Bakhīt, *Irshād*, 189–90.

had previously defined time as "the measure of the motion of the outermost sphere," Bakhīt notes that the likes of Abū Zayd al-Dabbūsī had conditioned this definition on the perception of the observer (*bi-ḥasb mā yabdū li-l-nāẓir*). But now convinced of heliocentricity, Bakhīt objects to this phenomenological approach, saying it is "closer to the truth [to say] that both the daily and yearly orbits are linked to the earth and its revolution around the sun, as was the position of the ancient philosophers and is the position of astronomers today."[67]

As this argument illustrates, Bakhīt's contribution to this ontology is to integrate it within a larger scientistic worldview, one which embraces the new heliocentric world and the technological era it inaugurates. Key to his conception of the problem is that "ritual worship revolves around the daily, monthly and yearly orbits"[68] which "do not differ in any corner of the earth."[69] It bears noting that al-Marjānī's scheme does not do this. In comparison to Bakhīt, al-Marjānī's embrace of science is notably limited. For one, al-Marjānī, like his predecessors, explicitly refused the use of calculations to declare the month of Ramadan; he is adamant that "the Lawgiver made [the proclamation of Ramadan] conditional on a sighting," and therefore "the Lawgiver simply disregarded them in this case."[70] And, indeed, a reliance on scientific methods does not figure into the solutions he proposes for the case of prayer that most concerns him. While he argues that time is an independent and objective realm, the solutions proposed for the problem of night prayers in northerly latitudes are conventional ones. In locales where the sun sets daily but twilight does not ever entirely disappear before morning, the night prayer was prayed after half the night had transpired (local midnight), or by reference to the nearest regions where twilight did disappear.[71] The reliance on these conventions, needless to say, cannot be compared to Bakhīt's shift in the Ramadan case from the requirement of a physical sighting to an astronomical calculation of mere visibility. In the latter case, no concessions

[67] Bakhīt, *Irshād*, 186.
[68] Bakhīt, *Irshād*, 189.
[69] Bakhīt, *Irshād*, 185.
[70] Al-Marjānī, *Nāẓūrat al-Ḥaqq fī Farḍiyyat al-ʿIshāʾ wa in lạm Yaghib al-Shafaq*, 159. For an explanation of what I call al-Marjānī's constructivism, see Junaid Quadri, "Correspondence, Constructivism, and Representation: Variant Approaches to Astronomical Knowledge in Islamic Legal Texts," *Comparative Studies of South Asia, Africa and the Middle East* 39, no. 3 (December 1, 2019): 519–20.
[71] Al-Marjānī's explanation for this is linked to his denial of time as the *ratio legis* (*sabab*) of prayer, even as he affirms time's objectivity. According to al-Marjānī, the true legal cause that obliges all worship is the continual favor of God upon the worshipper. *Nāẓūrat al-Ḥaqq fī Farḍiyyat al-ʿIshāʾ wa in lam yaghib al-shafaq*, 315–25, 391.

need to be made or conventions drawn up. A wholly scientific system drawn from the orbits of a heliocentric world is sufficient.

What science gives us, for Bakhīt, is the capacity for knowledge, the ability to know reality—namely the objective realm of time—through calculations. The focus of the preceding argumentation had been the defense of astronomical calculations, but as is obvious from his conclusion, Bakhīt envisions other scientific means as well. Later, he elaborates at length as to why telescopes in particular are admissible as sighting aids, with explicit reference to the observatory in Helwan. And it is through this explanation that his commitment to representationalism becomes evident:

> In our view [i.e., the Ḥanafī view], the testimony of one who sights the new moon (*hilāl*) is accepted, even if he spotted it through a telescope (*bi-l-naẓẓāra al-muʿaẓẓima*, lit. magnifying glass) when the new moon was such that it could be seen well only by [means] other than sharp eyesight. *This is because what is seen through [the telescope] is the new moon itself (ʿayn al-hilāl).* [The telescope's] only function is to aid the eyes in seeing faraway or small things, which would not be seen without it. In such a case, there is no objection to he who now looks for the new moon at the Egyptian Observatory, or others, through magnifying telescopes.
>
> As for what our *shaykh*s say about not relying on a sighting through water, or from behind glass, this relates to when what is seen is an image of the new moon, not the new moon itself. Because sighting the new moon through water or from behind glass is only done through reflection. Therefore, what is seen in such a case is not the new moon itself. . . . As for a sighting through a telescope, it is precisely like a sighting with the naked eye, as is known through the usage of reading glasses.[72]

This passage exemplifies a particular mode of argumentation, by building upon the long-standing Ḥanafī emphasis on vision in a telling way: expanding the conventional focus on (naked-eye) sightings to encompass sightings by telescope by arguing that what is seen through the latter is (also) "the thing itself." The outlook Bakhīt expresses here corresponds to what philosopher of technology Don Ihde has called the "instrumental realism" that has

[72] Al-Marjānī, *Nāẓūrat al-Ḥaqq fī Farḍiyyat al-ʿIshāʾ wa in lam Yaghib al-Shafaq*, 204. This is interesting precisely because the Helwan observatory housed a reflector telescope which would seem to align with Bakhīt's description of the problems with certain aids and not others, that is, reflection versus magnification. I thank Daniel Stolz for drawing my attention to this.

characterized the use of the telescope since Galileo—the position that "what could be *seen through* the telescope should be taken as 'real.'"[73]

This realism is a fundamental component of the representationalist epistemology described by Taylor. Knowledge, in this modern episteme, recall, is "the correct representation of an independent reality."[74] That Bakhīt should argue for the telescope by defending the realism of objects seen through it, and equally that he should vouch for the precision of the representation of that reality, is in fact unsurprising. Ihde, for example, notes that:

> Historically one can correlate early optical instrumentation with *early modern epistemology*. Nor is such a correlation simply associational since the optical technologies of this period were often quite explicitly referred to by the early moderns. Other commentators have noticed this as well: Descartes, as one example, quite deliberately used the *camera obscura* (one of the Renaissance's favourite technological toys) not only as part of his theory of optics, but even as a model for the subject. I note here only two features of this use of technologies as models for knowledge: (a) first, continuing the *visualist* trajectories of the Renaissance and Galileo, Descartes made vision the model for much knowledge, but, in contrast to much ancient thought about vision as an active process, made vision "receptive." Here, not unlike his English empiricist friends, vision occurs by means of "stimuli" upon the bodily machine, the retina, which is the back wall of the camera obscura. (b) At the same time, this new "passivity" of vision retains a second order passivity, *representation*, which carries with it the need for *isomorphism* to convey knowledge. "True" knowledge becomes true only when there is an isomorphism between what is "out there" and what is "inside" the subject as camera obscura. The "inside" represents and reproduces the "outside."[75]

This matches almost exactly Taylor's description of how a subject comes to know something on a representationalist understanding: namely, the "passive reception of impressions from the external world. Knowledge then hangs on a certain relation holding between what is 'out there' and certain inner states that this external reality causes in us."[76] Inasmuch as the telescope had

[73] Don Ihde, "The Structure of Technology Knowledge," *International Journal of Technology and Design Education* 7, no. 1–2 (1997): 74.
[74] Taylor, *Philosophical Arguments*, 3.
[75] Ihde, "The Structure of Technology Knowledge," 76.
[76] Taylor, *Philosophical Arguments*, 4.

become an unobjectionable feature of modern Egyptian society—its presence accepted and naturalized, and in some circles even celebrated—it is only to be expected that the conception of knowledge it modeled would accompany it. Bakhīt's identification, then, of what he saw in the telescope with "the new moon itself" is only natural. That he should portray it as such while justifying the use of the telescope is all the more so.

Bakhīt's mode of argumentation, as described earlier, indicates that he has already internalized this way of conceiving what knowledge is. This explains both (1) his insistence on the objectivity and the reality of the object-world he perceives; and (2) his belief that scientific means—whether instrumentation or calculations—give him certain knowledge through a proper representation of that objective reality. Taken together, these constitute representationalism on Taylor's definition.

We saw earlier, however, that Mitchell had included a third element to the structure of reality he thought reigned in Egypt in the colonial period. Having described the modern subject's experience with the material world as corresponding to that of a visitor objectively viewing an exhibition, he conceived that material world in turn as a mere guide representing a larger plan or structure. This, too, Bakhīt seems to have accepted as part of the ontology of the new Egypt: select phenomena (the disappearance of twilight, the crescent moon) observed in Bakhīt's object-world are to be thought of as mere stand-ins for, and indicators to, another realm, namely the fundamental order that is Time (*al-zamān*). As such, a representational knowledge of the existence of the new month of Ramadan—knowledge of existence, recall, being the new evidential standard—consists of knowing (through observation or scientific calculation) of the existence of phenomena, which are themselves indicators to an additional plane of reality called Time.

As we have seen, the acceptance of these elements of the representationalist model are heavily indebted to sudden changes in Egypt's social, political, and intellectual words: in particular, the sudden advance in technology, and the acceptance of the new science and its mechanistic worldview—the latter itself made possible by the widening sphere of intellectual possibilities and institutional diversification. In the final analysis, these significant developments on the ground in Egypt made representationalism not just possible but, it would seem, unavoidable. And as is the case with modern science, its pretension to universalism meant that even fields like *fiqh*, which had been historically resistant to epistemological standards other than its own, would be unable to conceive of knowledge in any other way.[77]

Conclusion

The point has often been made that the invention of the telescope effected a radically new way of understanding not only the world, but the human's place in it. Hannah Arendt, for example, has commented at length not only about the way in which Galileo's telescope was able to deliver the secrets of

[77] As other examples of the universalism of this new worldview, consider that (1) Bakhīt is unable to conceive that the structure of the world could be anything but a universal and objective system. This is precisely why he feels obliged to speak of a realm called Time, applicable to all, and to which the particular astronomical phenomena demanded by the *shar*ʿ are simply indications. This, of course, is what allows him to explain the persistence of ritual obligations in the absence of these phenomena. But the Lawgiver's specification of certain phenomena must be understood within this universalist framework, and so they are explained as being addressed to the majority (*al-ghālib*) of people and circumstances. "Just as the astronomers based their judgments on the majority [of situations], but did not neglect judging the minority; so too the Lawgiver based his rulings for specifying the times for prayer and fasting on the majority [of situations], but likewise did not neglect specifying the ruling for the minority [cases]." Just as the structure of the world as explained by science must be universal, so, too, the law must address its subjects in a universally consistent manner. Therefore, we must admit other means of attaining knowledge of legal obligation to account for those for whom these astronomical phenomena are not available. (2) Jurists like al-Subkī who had previously admitted the possibility of calculations in restricted cases were equally cautious to restrict the scope of these calculations. That is to say, for al-Subkī, in the specific case we discussed, acting upon definitive calculations was permissible, but not obligatory; and it was furthermore only permissible for the expert astronomer who himself performed these calculations (al-Subkī, "al-ʿAlam al-Manshūr," 22). In contrast, Bakhīt makes an impassioned plea for consulting experts and abiding by their findings: "What supports acting in accordance with accurate astronomic calculations is that the jurists resort in each case to the relevant experts. For they adopt the opinions of the linguists in understanding the meanings of the Qurʾan and Hadith, and rely on the opinions of the doctor in cases of abstaining from obligatory fasting, etc. So what stands in the way of us basing the lengths of Shaʿbān, Ramadan, and the other months on calculations, and resorting to knowledgeable experts if the matter is difficult for us. [Especially in light of] their certain premises, and accordance with the above-mentioned verses of the Qurʾan. Have you not seen that the astronomer, if he relies on his calculations to say that an eclipse will occur at such and such a time on such and such a day, it always (*qaṭʿan)* occurs without fail (*wa lā yatakhallaf*). This is especially so if he bases his calculations on sensory considerations, and observes it by virtue of telescopes and the like. Indeed, those (experts) who inform of the presence of the new moon and the possibility of its being sighted may reach the numbers required for *tawātur*, furnishing their report with absolute certainty. Even if they do not, they will be sufficiently many so as to give their report preponderant probability, of the sort approaching certainty, contenting our hearts as to the truth of the report" (Bakhīt al-Muṭīʿī, *Irshād Ahl al-Milla ilā Ithbāt al-Ahilla*, 181–82). That people should consult these experts and act on their pronouncements is alluded to elsewhere: "[The command to undertake calculations] does not mean that everyone is obliged to know the signs which indicate the relevant timing. Rather, it is sufficient that some know this, and that those who do not know come to know from those who do know. The Exalted has said, 'Ask those who know if you know not.' . . . The elite should know the signs through calculation and inform those who don't know" (Ibid., 189).

the universe to human cognition "with the certainty of sense-perception,"[78] but also that it made it possible for a human to occupy an Archimedean point. Arendt writes that with the advent of the telescope,

> the old dichotomy between earth and sky was abolished and a unification of the universe effected, so that from then on nothing occurring in earthly nature was viewed as a mere earthly happening. All events were considered to be subject to a universally valid law in the fullest sense of the word, which means, among other things, valid beyond the reach of human sense experience. . . . All laws of the new astrophysical science are formulated from the Archimedian point.[79]

This was for Arendt a radical epistemological shift. By looking at a particular case study, I have argued that a similarly significant shift occurred in the thought-world of Islamic law as a result of its encounter with modern science. The world came to be understood as objectively ordered, knowledge as representational, and the language of science as a self-evident way of describing reality.

And yet the manner through which this radical shift was realized in Islamic legal circles was not through an overt confrontation, but rather through a series of subtle reinterpretations and hermeneutic decisions. At a moment in which intellectual canons were being undone and intellectual authority was being reconfigured, Bakhīt was able to draw upon a variety of resources to recast Ḥanafī doctrine in a manner that better accorded with the changing intuitions and assumptions of a new world forged by the colonial encounter. The entry of new technologies, the reception of modern scientific ideas, and the prestige both carried in a changing Egypt left Bakhīt with little option but to revisit a long-held position, enshrined in law but seemingly no longer a fit with the larger intellectual context in which he located himself. In arguing for alternative opinions, Bakhīt made ingenious use of the legal tradition, drawing upon scholars like al-Subkī who were acknowledged masters in the Egyptian milieu, as well as just-deceased contemporaries from the broader Muslim world like al-Marjānī, whose primary connection to Bakhīt was through the network of the Ḥanafī *madhhab*, a long-standing nexus of

[78] Arendt, *The Human Condition*, 260. In a footnote, Arendt comments that "Galileo himself stressed this point."
[79] Arendt, *The Human Condition*, 262–63.

connection now strengthened through the increasing ease of intellectual exchange via print and travel that is so characteristic of the modern period. In so doing, however, Bakhīt's argumentation reveals deeper changes in the structure of Muslim thought, shifts that accompanied, and indeed were inseparable from, the irresistible allure of science and technology.

5

Religion, the Secular, and Language

In August 1925, al-Azhar's Council of Senior Scholars (*Hayʾat Kibār al-ʿUlamāʾ*) excommunicated ʿAlī ʿAbd al-Rāziq from the ranks of the ulama. Hailing from a renowned family known for its involvement in both politics and Islamic scholarship, ʿAbd al-Rāziq (1888–1966) had graduated from the Azhar in 1911 with a *shahāda ʿālimiyya* degree that provided him access to a career as a lecturer in affiliated mosque-schools and a judge in the country's shariʿa courts. The Council's unanimous decision, however, stripped him of both his credentials and judicial appointment, and barred him from any future position in Egypt's scholarly officialdom. So as to underscore how intent the Council was on exiling him from the world of religious intelligentsia, ʿAbd al-Rāziq's name was further expunged from the records of the venerable institution at which he had studied many long years.[1] The reason for this dramatic decision was the publication four months earlier of a bombshell book that immediately met with widespread criticism among the scholarly elite. *Islam and the Principles of Governance* (*al-Islām wa-Uṣūl al-Ḥukm*) had advanced a forthright argument for the separation of religion and state in Islam, claiming that the mission of the Prophet Muḥammad was exclusively a spiritual, and therefore not political, one. The famous Egyptian writer Muḥammad ʿImāra has characterized the work as "the first attempt to Islamicize secularism, to claim that Islam is secular."[2]

ʿAbd al-Rāziq has therefore often served as an inspiration to proponents of a Muslim secularism who see him as offering, by reference to Islamic texts, a

[1] The decision was published as *Ḥukm Hayʾat Kibār al-ʿUlamāʾ ʿalā Kitāb al-Islām wa-Uṣūl al-Ḥukm* (al-Maṭbaʿa al-Salafiyya, 1344H). For details of ʿAbd al-Rāziq's arguments and the subsequent debate, see Souad T. Ali, *A Religion, Not a State: Ali ʿAbd Al-Raziq's Islamic Justification of Political Secularism* (Salt Lake City: University of Utah Press, 2009); James Broucek, "The Controversy of Shaykh ʿAli ʿAbd al-Raziq" (PhD diss., The Florida State University, 2012); Hamid Enayat, *Modern Islamic Political Thought: The Response of the Shīʿī and Sunnī Muslims to the Twentieth Century*, new ed. (London: I.B. Tauris, 2005), 62–68.; Charles C. Adams, *Islam and Modernism in Egypt: A Study of the Modern Reform Movement Inaugurated by Muḥammad ʿAbduh* (London: Oxford University Press, 1933), 259–69.; Albert Hourani, *Arabic Thought in the Liberal Age, 1798–1939* (London: Oxford University Press, 1970), 183–92.

[2] Muḥammad ʿImāra, *Maʿrikat al-Islām wa-Uṣūl al-Ḥukm* (Cairo: Dār al-Shurūq, [1989] 1997), 8.

Transformations of Tradition. Junaid Quadri, Oxford University Press (2021). © Oxford University Press.
DOI: 10.1093/oso/9780190077044.003.0006

modern response to a problem created by a medieval political order. On this story, the ferocious opposition to him at the time came from traditionalist quarters for whom secularism was anathema. This opposition took the form not only of the verdict against ʿAbd al-Rāziq but a series of publications rebutting his arguments. Among them was one from Bakhīt: a treatise he titled *Ḥaqīqat al-Islām wa-Uṣūl al-Ḥukm* (a play on words which can be read as either *The Truth of Islam and the Principles of Governance*, or *The Truth about [the Book]* al-Islām wa-Uṣūl al-Ḥukm).[3] In a sweeping indictment, Bakhīt minced no words in making his feelings about ʿAbd al-Rāziq's book known. "Everything that this book holds is negative and a clear denial of what the Muslims have unanimously agreed upon, or of what has been stated explicitly in the Mighty Book or the Prophetic Sunna."[4] Part of the opposition to ʿAbd al-Rāziq's intervention can be explained by its timing, coming as it did in the immediate aftermath of the abolition of the Ottoman caliphate, a demise that was being lamented by the ulama. Indeed, Bakhīt spends much of his own work defending the institution of the Caliphate, which ʿAbd al-Rāziq had taken to be a contingent historical arrangement illegitimately yoked to a timeless divine religion. Yet, as Albert Hourani has noted, the deeper and more fundamental complaint had to do with ʿAbd al-Rāziq's attack on the conventional Muslim understanding of the Prophet's mission, which held that he was at once a messenger of God and a lawgiver who established a political community where that law held.[5]

Given the acrimony of this episode, it is tempting to frame it as one of an opposition between an enlightened modern secularist and the obscurantist guardians of a medieval view of governance. Yet Hourani has quite astutely noted that embedded in Bakhīt's own response is a remarkable naturalization of modern ideals. Bakhīt is clear that he envisions the Caliphate as a democratic institution:

[3] Muḥammad Bakhīt al-Muṭīʿī, *Ḥaqīqat al-Islām wa-Uṣūl al-Ḥukm* (Cairo: al-Maṭbaʿa al-Salafiyya, 1925). In response, the weekly *al-Siyāsa al-Usbūʿiyya*, which had carried ʿAbd al-Rāziq's views on governance, struck back with a front-page "biography" of Bakhīt which emphasized his opportunism (describing him as "covetous for positions") and his intellectual deficiencies and scholarly mistakes. ("Even the Ministry of Justice issued a publication once warning shariʿa court judges from following the fatwas of muftis. The Ministry was referring that day to none other than the disturbing fatwas that Shaykh Bakhīt issues.") "Al-Shaykh Muḥammad Bakhīt," *al-Siyāsa al-Usbuʿiyya*, April 10, 1926. Other critiques by leading Azharī scholars include Muḥammad al-Khiḍr Ḥusayn, *Naqḍ Kitāb al-Islām wa-Uṣūl Al-Ḥukm* (Cairo: al-Maṭbaʿa al-Salafiyya wa-Maktabatuhā, 1344H); and Yūsuf al-Dijwī, *Radd Ḥaḍrat Ṣāḥib al-Faḍīla al-Ustādh al-Kabīr al-Shaykh Yūsuf al-Dijwī ʿalā Kitāb al-Shaykh ʿAlī ʿAbd al-Rāziq al-Islām wa-Uṣūl al-Ḥukm* (Miṣr: Maṭbaʿat al-Samāḥ, n.d.).

[4] Bakhīt al-Muṭīʿī, *Ḥaqīqat al-Islām wa-Uṣūl al-Ḥukm*, 3.

[5] Albert Hourani, *Arabic Thought in the Liberal Age*, 189*ff*.

> The source of the caliph's power is the *umma*, and he derives authority from it. . . . The Islamic government headed by the caliph and universal Imam is a democratic, free, consultative government of which the constitution is God's Book and the Sunna of God's Prophet.[6]

From this citation, Hourani draws the conclusion that,

> In saying this, Bakhit is not simply maintaining that the political institutions of Islam have all the advantages of modern political institutions; he is implying that essentially they are the same. The identification of Islamic with European concepts, put forward by the earlier writers, is now accepted without question; and Bakhit seems unaware that he has opened the door to that very invasion of Islam by the ideas of western rationalism for which he reproaches his opponent.[7]

This is an important observation which finds in Bakhīt's writing a support for democracy that was missing in his traditionalist predecessors. In what follows, I go farther to argue that it was not just a commitment to democracy that Bakhīt adopted. Despite his fierce opposition to ʿAbd al-Rāziq, the very secularizing processes which so exercised the ulama and against which they were unanimously arrayed profoundly structured Bakhīt's thinking in the *Irshād*. Recent theorists of secularity have noted that the historical development of what we call secularism gave rise to a notion of "the secular" that encompassed more than just a formulaic separation of church and state.[8] It also opened up new ways of conceptualizing the world, as for example in the clear differentiation between its "religious" and "secular" domains. I argue in this chapter that it is this dichotomy and its attendant assumptions in a colonial modern context that inform and underlie Bakhīt's reformulation of important Ḥanafī categories and rethinking of long-held positions.

***

In chapters 2 and 4, I sought to detect the appearance of Modernist premises in the work of Bakhīt by closely examining the innovations and

[6] Hourani, *Arabic Thought in the Liberal Age*, 191; Bakhīt al-Muṭīʿī, *Ḥaqīqat al-Islām wa-Uṣūl al-Ḥukm*, 30.

[7] Hourani, *Arabic Thought in the Liberal Age*, 191–92.

[8] For a clear statement, see Charles Taylor's "three secularities" in *A Secular Age* (Cambridge, MA: Belknap Press of Harvard University Press, 2007), 2–3. See also Casanova's discussion later in this chapter.

reformulations to which he subjects entrenched positions within the Ḥanafī school. In the first instance, we saw how his reworking of the hierarchy of jurists within the *madhhab* revealed particular notions of history and authority which valorized the earliest generations, bolstered the standing of contemporary scholars, and downplayed the layers of accrued doctrinal interpretation which had long dominated juristic works. In a similar manner we tracked, in chapter 4, how Bakhīt's strong defense of the conclusions of science depended upon a view of the world, characteristic of colonial Egypt, that had stressed epistemological considerations over long-held procedural ones.

In the present chapter, I show how Bakhīt made use of both of these commitments to recast the Ḥanafī category of the *umūr dīniyya*, or "religious matters," arguing that his understanding of religion in these discussions is indebted to modern processes of secularization, themselves propelled by the encounter with Europe. In the Egyptian case, these modern processes of secularization took a variety of forms. Farhat Ziadeh, for example, has labeled the centralization of legal power that, rooted in the Ottoman period, intensified during the reign of Muḥammad ʿAlī (r. 1805–1848) "the secularization of state and law" on the grounds that the steady expansion of executive power came at the expense of the ulama and their "ideal system of law," the shariʿa.[9] More commonly, scholars have pointed to the European-inspired restructuring of the court system that radically redefined the Egyptian judiciary in the last quarter of the nineteenth century as the key moment in the advent of secularism. In addition to the 1876 introduction of the mixed courts to govern matters involving foreign interests, this period witnessed the institution of the powerful "native" or "national" courts (*maḥākim ahliyya*), the effect of which was to restrict the purview of the previously dominant shariʿa courts to matters of personal status (marriage, divorce, inheritance, etc.), a heavily diminished competence that removed from their jurisdiction civil, commercial, and criminal law.[10] The setting up of an institutional distinction between religious law (as that which is adjudicated in shariʿa courts) and those legal matters that properly belonged to the state suggests secularizing tendencies that correlate with the distinction between private morality and

[9] Farhat Ziadeh, *Lawyers, the Rule of Law and Liberalism in Modern Egypt* (Stanford, CA: Hoover Institution), 3–23.

[10] For this process, see Nathan Brown, *Rule of Law in the Arab World* (New York: Cambridge University Press, 1997); Nathan Brown, "Law and Imperialism: Egypt in Comparative Perspective," *Law and Society Review* 29, no. 1 (1995): 103–26; Ziadeh, *Lawyers*, 24–43.

public law. Talal Asad has argued further that the unwillingness to relegate family law, too, to the national courts should not be seen as a concession made out of fear of offending religious sensitivities, but rather as an element of the ineluctable logic of modern state power, in which the family functions as a site of state management, the locus of an individualistic ethics that is necessary for self-government. The shariʿa thus defined as the law of personal status, and identified with the domain of the family, is not simply a separation, but a secularizing subordination. It amounts to "a secular formula for privatizing 'religion'"[11]—"defining a place in which 'religion' is allowed to make its public appearance through state law."[12]

In a groundbreaking recent work, Khaled Fahmy has taken issue with this characterization, arguing that a better way to understand the developments of the nineteenth century is in terms of bureaucratization, the process by which textuality and written documentation came to gain primacy over orality and spoken presentation. Though Fahmy's primary goal is to dislodge the "narrative of triumphant secularism that is usually used to describe the history of modern Egyptian law,"[13] his conclusion suggests an "unwitting" secularization effected by the abstract functioning of the newly ascendant bureaucracy. The privileging of the disembodied written word over in-person spoken communication downgraded the relevance of communal relationships that had previously been required to effectively manage law. The individual, therefore, was newly disembedded in the eyes of the law from the communal contexts that had hitherto defined his identity. Now that the law could treat people as individuals, and not only, or primarily, as members of communities, identifying markers like freedom, gender, and religion were no longer salient, thereby giving rise to a notion of equality before the law that has been a recurring theme in previous accounts of secularization.

The great contribution of Fahmy's narrative is his restoration of *siyāsa* to its rightful historical place in the administration of Islamic law in Egypt. Whereas Ziadeh equated the shariʿa with the ideal law of the jurists, and pitted it in opposition to the secular encroachments of the state, Fahmy demonstrates through careful examination of the records of *siyāsa* councils that the shariʿa system had always recognized both *fiqh*, the jurists' law, and *siyāsa*, the discretionary powers of the state, as working in tandem.[14] Fahmy

[11] Talal Asad, *Formations of the Secular* (Stanford, CA: Stanford University Press, 2003), 227–28.

[12] Asad, *Formations*, 231.

[13] Khaled Fahmy, *In Quest of Justice* (Oakland: University of California Press, 2018), 92.

[14] Fahmy draws on previous scholarship to show that this arrangement of the relationship between *fiqh* and *siyāsa* can be traced back to the early Islamic empires, the Umayyad and the Abbasid, but

positions *siyāsa* as a complement to *fiqh*, serving the purpose of providing the shariʿa system with a dynamism that could not be guaranteed by strict adherence to *fiqh* doctrine, often impractical and formalist.[15] If one insists on viewing secularization in terms of a separation of law and morality, then "the possibility emerges that law and morality might have already been uncoupled prior to the onslaught of modernity"[16] in the form of the distinction between *fiqh* and *siyāsa*. Secularization, thus understood, emerges on this account not as an instance of Europeanization, but rather as an indigenous configuration of law that predated both the British and Napoleon.

Fahmy's drawing of our attention to the centrality of *siyāsa* and its connection to *fiqh* is no doubt an important contribution to our understanding of the shariʿa system. But in what follows, in keeping with my practice in previous chapters, I focus narrowly on the shifting contours of *fiqh* alone. I turn once more to Bakhīt's *Irshād* to detect a secularizing logic premised on neither the divorcing of morality and law nor the unintended effects of bureaucratization, but rather on a particularly modern understanding of what constitutes religion, the resultant implications of deeming something religious, and how the religious is understood vis-à-vis the secular. This secularization was reflected in and institutionalized through the reorganized court system, but the dividing line between "the secular" and "the religious" on my reading did not run between the national courts and the shariʿa courts, but rather positioned the newly instituted court system itself on one side, as the repository of a secular world, and an abstract and immaterial realm of religion located outside of the courts on the other.

It is only by attending to the subtle conceptual shifts within works of *fiqh* that we are able to see this mode of secularity in action. In deciding to attend to the shifting conceptual grammar of this period, I follow Asad's suggestion that the most fruitful way of coming to understand terms as slippery as "religion" and "secular" is by "attend[ing] more closely to the historical grammar of concepts and not to what we take as signs of an essential phenomenon."[17] This approach has the effect of reinserting

were expressly legitimated by Mamluk-era jurists in the twelfth century. Fahmy, *In Quest of Justice*, 125–26.

[15] Fahmy, *In Quest of Justice*, 124–26. Though note also his references to other scholarship suggesting that *fiqh* too was open to change, 127–28.
[16] Fahmy, *In Quest of Justice*, 279.
[17] Asad, *Formations of the Secular*, 189. See also his insistence in an earlier work on understanding the concept of religion by attending to its location within history and fields of power

the encounter with European thought more centrally into the equation, for it is modern European constructions of religion that find their way into Muslim and Egyptian thinking, and eventually manifest in Bakhīt's reformulation of the *fiqh* category of "religious matters." It would be an immodest overreach to say that any fair reading of Bakhīt yields a thoroughgoing secularism of the sort recognizable from (idealized reconstructions of) the European experience. Nonetheless the shifts in conceptual grammar associated with processes of secularization bear, in important respects, striking similarities to those employed by Bakhīt in his argumentation.

In an influential 1994 work, *Public Religions in the Modern World*, the sociologist of religion José Casanova set out to address the problems posed by the unexpected re-emergence of religion in the 1980s—a phenomenon he calls "deprivatization"—to conventional narratives of the historical secularization process.[18] Casanova claims that the received story of European secularization had come to no longer be tenable due to muddled thinking about the very definition of the term. On his reading, secondary, predictive claims about what would happen in a secular society—namely the privatization of religion such that it no longer plays a role in public discourse, and a precipitous decline in religious belief—were attached to the core of secularization theory. The theory itself, however, could be salvaged when these inessential claims are detached from "the core and central thesis of the theory of secularization":

> [T]he core and the central thesis of the theory of secularization is the conceptualization of the process of societal modernization as a process of functional differentiation and emancipation of the secular spheres—primarily the state, the economy, and science—from the religious sphere and the concomitant differentiation and specialization of religion within its own newly found religious sphere.[19]

instead of as "a transhistorical and transcultural phenomenon." Talal Asad, *Genealogies of Religion: Discipline and Reasons of Power in Christianity and Islam* (Baltimore: Johns Hopkins University Press, 1993), 28.

[18] José Casanova, *Public Religions in the Modern World* (Chicago: University of Chicago Press, 1994).

[19] Casanova, *Public Religions in the Modern World*, 19.

In the aftermath of Asad's critique of his essentialism and value-laden language,[20] Casanova has tended to rely solely on the language of functional differentiation, eschewing talk of emancipation and modernization, but still maintaining the claim that religion came to constitute a distinct sphere of life, differentiated from other spheres.

This revision sits better with Asad's methodological insistence on attending to the "historical grammar of concepts" and their reconfigurations over time because it allows Casanova to examine the development of the mutually constituting binary of religious/secular throughout the process of differentiation. The other limitation of *Public Religions* that Casanova attempted to address in his later writing is the book's parochialism.[21] And so, in a retrospective consideration of his work more than a decade and a half later, Casanova expanded his discussion to offer that "any discussion of secularization as a global process should start with the reflexive observation that one of the most important global trends is the globalization of the category of 'religion' itself and of the binary classification of reality, 'religious/secular,' that it entails."[22] Casanova recognizes that this approach runs the risk of homogenizing disparate experiences, and so he is quick to point out: "It is obvious that when people around the world use the same category of religion, they actually mean very different things. The actual concrete meaning of whatever people denominate as 'religion' can only be elucidated in the context of their particular discursive practices."[23]

It is what precisely "religion" came to mean in the thinking of Bakhīt, or perhaps more precisely how he came to carve out a particularly modern sense of "religion" from within the Ḥanafī legacy, that I trace in this

[20] "I am arguing that 'the secular' should not be thought of as the space in which *real* human life gradually emancipates itself from the controlling power of 'religion' and thus achieves the latter's relocation." Asad, *Formations of the Secular*, 191.

[21] To limit the earlier study in this way seems to have been a conscious decision by Casanova, as he later recalled: "I already acknowledged in the Introduction [of *Public Religions in the Modern World*] that the book was a 'Western-centred study, both in terms of the particular cases chosen for investigation and in terms of the normative perspective guiding the investigation.' The self-limitation of the study to Western Christendom was fully justified in terms of: (1) the genealogical reconstruction of particular historical processes of secularization within Latin Christendom (rather than viewing secularization as a general universal process of human and societal development); (2) the restriction of the study, by and large, to Catholicism and Protestantism as particular forms of religion; and (3) restriction to Western (European and postcolonial) societies. At the time, I pleaded 'limited time, knowledge, and resources, as well as a postmodern enhanced awareness of the dangers of excessive homogenization,' as well, one could add, of the dangers of 'orientalism.'" José Casanova, "Public Religions Revisited," in *Religion: Beyond a Concept*, ed. Hent de Vries (New York: Fordham University Press, 2008), 102.

[22] José Casanova, "The Secular, Secularizations, Secularisms," in *Rethinking Secularism*, ed. Craig J. Calhoun, Mark Juergensmeyer, and Jonathan VanAntwerpen (New York: Oxford University Press, 2011), 62.

[23] Casanova, "The Secular, Secularizations, Secularisms," 62–63.

chapter. To accomplish this, I examine two legal questions found in the Ḥanafī corpus: the criteria for adjudicating the validity of a sighting of the new moon on a night with clear skies, and the method by which reports of sightings should be transmitted from one jurisdiction to another. In each case, premodern authorities had settled on a view that stressed the importance of regulating reports of sightings through set procedures and the oversight of courts. And in each case, Bakhīt challenges the dominant opinion in a manner that emphasizes instead the truth value of reports, doing so by leaning on their categorization as "religious" reports. Bakhīt draws on the recognized category of the *umūr dīniyya* ("religious matters"), whose archetypal example was the report of a sighting of the Ramadan crescent, only to reformulate it in a manner that reads the "religious" in "religious matters" in a decidedly modern way—abstract matters of the mind that must be guaranteed space outside the coercive parameters of the state court system.

Fiqhī Categories: Narrations, Testimonies, and the In-Between

Among the four dominant Sunnī *madhāhib*, it is the Ḥanafī school which seems to have had a notion, though only sketchily articulated, of the category of *umūr dīniyya*, which we might provisionally translate as "religious matters." These were considerations which occupied an interstitial position between two well-defined concepts: the *riwāya* (narration) and the *shahāda* (testimony). In *fiqhī* classification schemes, these latter were considered to be two sorts of "reports" (*akhbār*, sing. *khabar*). The English word "reports" does not adequately capture the category, as the latter subsumes elements of judicial process that are not conveyed by the translation: testimonies, confessions, claims, and legal judgments both binding (the qadi's *ḥukm*) and nonbinding (the mufti's fatwa).[24] So, although the *riwāya* and the *shahāda* were by no means jointly exhaustive of the set of *khabars*, they were often placed in opposition to one another in works of *fiqh* because their validity depended on conditions which were explicitly portrayed as being in contradistinction to one another. The conditions for a valid *shahāda* were:

[24] See, for example, "Khabar," in *al-Mawsūʿa al-Fiqhiyya* (Kuwait: Wizārat al-Awqāf wa-l-Shuʾūn al-Islāmiyya, 1990).

1. *ʿadad* (a "multiplicity" of witnesses—either two or four depending on the type of case),
2. *dhukūra* (that the witnesses be male),
3. *ḥurriyya* (that the witnesses be free and not slaves),
4. *majlis al-qaḍāʾ* (that it be offered in the presence of the qadi, i.e., a courtroom),
5. *taqaddum al-daʿwā* (the specification of an official claim),
6. *lafẓ al-shahāda* (the express language of a testimony), and
7. *ʿadam al-ḥadd fī al-qadhf* (that the witness not have been previously disciplined for slander).

In contrast, none of these are required for a *riwāya*, whose only condition is *ʿadāla* (the moral probity of the witness), which is in turn missing from the list.

Clearly, then, these were if not oppositional, two mutually exclusive categories. But the Ḥanafīs countenanced an intermediate category which both incorporated and excluded characteristics of each—identified by Bakhīt in a rather unwieldy but apt manner as "the report which is neither a *riwāya* nor a *shahāda* but resembles each of them (*shabīh bi-himā*)."[25] This liminal category was the one which pertained to the *umūr dīniyya*, as well as to other reports such as statements from experts, the *qassām* (an officer of the qadi's court entrusted with dividing inheritances), and translators. A reading of the relevant texts leaves little doubt that the *umūr dīniyya* were this category's most prominent exemplars. The sighting of the new moon (*hilāl*) of Ramadan, in turn, was among the most prominent examples of the *umūr dīniyya*.

The question of how precisely to treat issues that fall into this in-between category seems to have been answered in a rather inconclusive manner. Bakhīt himself writes that this was subject to disagreement among the imams: "Some of them deferred to (*rāʿā*) its resemblance to the *riwāya*, so they placed no conditions on it except *ʿadāla*, while others paid heed to its resemblance to the *shahāda*, so they attached it to [the *shahāda*] and applied some of its conditions to it."[26] It seems, though, that in addition to the particular predilections of individual jurists, each member of this in-between set

[25] Muḥammad Bakhīt al-Muṭīʿī, *Irshād Ahl al-Milla ilā Ithbāt al-Ahilla*, ed. Ḥasan Aḥmad Isbir (Beirut: Dār Ibn Ḥazm, 2000), 23.

[26] Bakhīt al-Muṭīʿī, *Irshād Ahl al-Milla ilā Ithbāt al-Ahilla*, 24.

was handled differently, with the conditions applied to it being tailored to the exigencies and specificities of the case in question.

In the case of a report of the Ramadan new moon, and the *umūr dīniyya* more generally, it was clear that the Ḥanafī jurists inclined toward considering it more a *riwāyā* than a *shahāda*. Burhān al-Dīn al-Marghīnānī's renowned sixth/twelfth-century commentary, *al-Hidāya*, for example, takes up the issue in a representative manner.[27] The base-text, *Bidāyat al-Mubtadi'*, upon which al-Marghīnānī wrote his commentary had been explicit that "If there is [any type of] obstruction in the sky, the imam is to accept the testimony (*shahāda*) of one upright person (*al-wāḥid al-ʿadl*) that they sighted the new moon, regardless of whether the person is a man or woman, free or a slave."[28] With this explicit liberality in accepting all sorts of "reporters," the base text had already indicated that the sighting of a new moon bore similarities, and was to be primarily aligned, to a *riwāya*. But al-Marghīnānī makes this association explicit, saying, "This is because this is a religious matter (*amr dīnī*), and so resembles the narration of reports (*ashbaha riwāyat al-akhbār*)."[29] He goes on to specify that this is why we can also exclude the requirement for the formulaic language of testimony (*lafẓ al-shahāda*), thereby dropping another of the requirements of a *shahāda*-report.[30]

This seems to have been the dominant position of the school, and that the *umūr dīniyya* were considered by the Ḥanafīs to be more *riwāya* than *shahāda* is rather indisputable. But, importantly, the *umūr dīniyya* continued to be conceptualized (by their very definition) as *both* part-*shahāda* and part-*riwāya*. The question to be considered by the individual jurist was which of these components of its identity *predominated*. This is why al-Marghīnānī, and indeed all Ḥanafīs, use the language of resemblance and similarity

[27] For a detailed biographical entry on al-Marghīnānī, notable for its extensive treatment, see ʿAbd al-Ḥayy al-Laknawī, *al-Fawāʾid al-Bahiyya fī Tarājim al-Ḥanafiyya* (Cairo: Maṭbaʿat al-Saʿāda, 1324H), 141–44. As for his famous work *al-Hidāya*, it has been translated twice now into English: ʿAlī b. Abū Bakr al-Marghīnānī, *al-Hidāyah: The Guidance: A Translation of Al-Hidāyah Fī Sharḥ Bidāyat Al-Mubtadī, a Classical Manual of Ḥanafī Law*, trans. Imran Ahsan Khan Nyazee (Bristol, England: Amal Press, 2006); and ʿAlī b. Abū Bakr al-Marghīnānī, *The Hedaya, or Guide: A Commentary on the Mussulman Laws*, trans. Charles Hamilton (Lahore: Premier Book House, 1963).

[28] Burhān al-Dīn ʿAli b. Abū Bakr al-Marghīnānī, *al-Hidāya*, vol. 2 (Beirut: Dār al-Fikr, n.d.), 322.

[29] Al-Marghīnānī, *al-Hidāya*, 2:322.

[30] Similarly, Shams al-Aʾimma al-Sarakhsī dropped the condition of two witnesses (*ʿadad*) and insisted on the moral uprightness (*ʿadāla*) of the reporter on the grounds that this was a religious matter: "The more correct position is to stipulate the condition of *ʿadāla* in [the case of sighting the Ramadan new moon] because this is one of the matters of religion (*min umūr al-dīn*). This is why it is sufficient to [rely on] a single reporter. The report of a corrupt person (*khabar al-fāsiq*) in matters of religion (*fī bāb al-dīn*) is unacceptable, on par with narrating traditions (*riwāyat al-ḥadīth*) from the Prophet, peace be upon him."

instead of identity: the *umūr dīniyya resemble (ashbah)* the *riwāyāt*, but they are not *riwāyāt tout court*. The nature of the jurist's interest in locating and specifying which side ought to be emphasized has the potential (as we will see when we discuss Bakhīt's intervention) to obscure the fundamentally dual nature of the *umūr dīniyya*, but the intermediate category envisioned by the Ḥanafīs was intermediate precisely because some of its *shahāda* properties were preserved.

This is why one finds in the very next passage of *al-Hidāya* mention of an opinion of Abū Ḥanīfa in which the *shahāda* component of such reports is reasserted:

> Moral probity (*ʿadāla*) is a condition, because the statement of a corrupt person (*fāsiq*) is unacceptable in religious matters (*fī al-diyānāt*). . . . In the generality of [al-Qudūrī's] response, he included [as having sufficient moral integrity] the one who has been subject to punishment for slander but has repented. This is the dominant position (*ẓāhir al-riwāya*) because this is a religious report (*khabar dīnī*).[31] *Though, it is related from Abū Ḥanīfa, God have mercy upon him, that this is not accepted, because it is also a shahāda in a certain respect (li-annahā shahāda min wajh).*[32]

This position within the school, attributed to the eponym himself, is a rather clear indication that the *umūr dīniyya* were generally considered to have retained certain elements of the characteristics of a *shahāda*, in this case the requirement that the witness not have been previously punished for slander.[33]

As it turns out, why precisely the Ramadan moon sighting continued to be seen as "a *shahāda* in a certain respect" hides only in plain view. All of the texts discuss the manner of establishing the new month by saying it is *the testimony (shahāda)* of a sighting that is to be given consideration. In the quote from the base text of *al-Hidāya* given earlier, the imam is to accept *the shahāda* of any person as long as he or she is judged to be of moral integrity. Similarly in Shams al-Dīn al-Sarakhsī's *al-Mabsūṭ*, the relevant discussion reads:

[31] Such a person is thought to have reinstated their moral probity (*ʿadāla*), and so can participate in conveying *riwāyāt*. However, an express condition of a *shahāda* is that the witness has never been so disciplined. See 174.

[32] Al-Marghīnānī, *al-Hidāya*, 2:322–23.

[33] Though the substance of the position was itself subordinated to the *ẓaḥir al-riwāya*, the assertion that a report of a moon sighting is "a *shahāda* in a certain respect" met with no objections in the commentarial tradition.

> If a man *testifies (shahida)* to a sighting of the new moon of Ramadan, and there is an obstruction in the sky, *his testimony (shahāda)* is to be accepted if he is morally upright (*ʿadl*). We have discussed this issue (*masʾala*) in the chapter on fasting and *istiḥsān*, where it was stipulated that the *witness (al-shāhid)* be morally upright.[34]

Of course, it is clear in light of what we've discussed previously that this cannot be a *shahāda* in the conventional sense of the word, encompassing the full complement of conditions that define a *shahāda* proper. But what is rather evident from a reading of the chapters on how to establish the onset of the month of Ramadan is that this "lesser *shahāda*" is a testimony in the sense of a statement given to the qadi. To take yet another example from *al-Hidāya*, "He who sights the new moon of Ramadan himself should fast, even if the imam does not accept his testimony (*shahāda*)."[35] The word *shahāda* here, then, is to be understood in a looser sense, as informing the qadi of a sighting, with the latter retaining the authority to reject its efficacy with respect to his jurisdiction at large. This is well captured in al-Bābartī's gloss on the *Hidāya*. Explaining Abū Ḥanīfa's opinion, he writes. "It is a *shahāda* in a certain respect . . . in that the obligation to act upon it only obtains after the judgment of the qadi (*baʿda qaḍāʾ al-qāḍī*), and in that it is restricted (*ikhtiṣāṣ*) to the courtroom (*majlis al-qaḍāʾ*)."[36]

The equivocal way in which the term "*shahāda*" is used in the Ḥanafī texts is perhaps what confused a non-Ḥanafī like Taqī al-Dīn al-Subkī when he set out to understand the Ḥanafī position on these matters.[37] Unable to conceive that reports such as the sighting of the new moon occupied a position between testimonies and narrations, partaking in the properties of both,[38] he continued to view the question, in exclusivist terms, as one of *riwāya* versus *shahāda*. As a result, despite a good-faith effort, al-Subkī had trouble understanding how precisely the Ḥanafīs were being consistent.

[34] Shams al-Dīn al-Sarakhsī, *Al-Mabsūṭ*, vol. 3 (Beirut: Dār al-Maʿrifa, n.d.), 139.

[35] Al-Marghīnānī, *al-Hidāya*, 2:320–21.

[36] *Al-ʿInāya ʿalā al-Hidāya*, on the margins of *Fatḥ al-Qadīr* (Cairo: al-Maṭbaʿa al-Kubrā al-Amīriyya, 1315 H), vol. 2, 59.

[37] Cf. the treatment of the Mālikī jurist Ibn al-Shāṭṭ, who is clear that reports of the Ramadan *hilāl* partook in aspects of both *shahādāt* and *riwāyāt*, but did not belong properly to either group. See his commentary, *Idrār al-Shurūq*, on the margins of Aḥmad ibn Idrīs al-Qarāfī, *Al-Furūq, aw Anwār al-Burūq fī Anwāʾ al-Furūq*, al-Ṭabʿa 1 (Beirut: Dār al-Kutub al-ʿIlmiyya, 1998), 1:19–20.

[38] This is, at least in part, due to the fact that the explicit theorization of this intermediate category as its own entity, distinct from, but still partaking in, each of the *riwāya* and *shahāda*, seems to be a later phenomenon.

> The *madhhab* of Abū Ḥanīfa [holds] that if there is obstruction in the sky, [the month] is established by the statement of one person, just as in our *madhhab*. Like our *madhhab*, they differed as to whether this is a *shahāda* or a *riwāya*. The dominant opinion (*al-mashhūr*) among them is that it is a *riwāya*, although Abū Yūsuf and Muḥammad said that [the month] is not established by one person. Among the Ḥanafīs, if the sky is clear, [the month] is not established . . . until a group reports [a sighting]. And the manner of [treating] it is that of the *khabar*,[39] not the manner of the *shahāda*.[40]

Here, al-Subkī recognizes that there were moments in which the Ḥanafīs at least entertained the possibility that a report of a sighting ought to be treated as a *shahāda* in certain respects—the two most famous students of Abū Ḥanīfa, Abū Yusuf and Muḥammad b. Ḥasan al-Shaybānī, demanded more than one testimony in contradistinction to the *riwāya*'s simple requirement of a single reporter—though this position was never strong enough to rival the dominant opinion. Tellingly, however, al-Subkī moves directly from the observation that such reports are to be dealt with as *riwāyāt*, not *shahādāt*, to a discussion on the role of the qadi in all this. For if the Ḥanafīs treat these reports exclusively as *riwāyāt*, as appears to be the case to al-Subkī, is the qadi altogether superfluous? What are we to make of both the tendency to refer to reports of a moon sighting as a *shahāda* and the general practice of conveying the report to a qadi?

The tension between a reported moon sighting's unmistakable physical resemblance to a *shahāda* in the qadi's court, on the one hand, and the theoretical Ḥanafī insistence that it resembled, and was to be dealt with as, a *riwāya*, on the other, seems to have therefore necessitated segueing into an excursus into the qadi's capacity to "establish" the new month:

> What emerges (*alladhī yaẓhar*) from the *madhhab* of Abū Ḥanīfa is that [the new month] is not established by the qadi. This is because the manner of [treating] it is that of the *khabar*, and thus has no connection to the qadi's judgment (*al-qaḍā'*). . . . In some of the Ḥanafī works, there is mention of a procedure (*ṭarīq*) for establishing the month.[41] This does not contradict

[39] What is meant by *khabar* here is Prophetic reports (*ḥadīth*), which are the paradigmatic example of a *riwāya*. See, for example, al-Qarāfī, *al-Furūq*, 1:17. Given their prominence and significance, they were often called by same name as the larger category itself.

[40] Taqī al-Dīn al-Subkī, "al-ʿAlam al-Manshūr fī Ithbāt al-Shuhūr," in *Arbaʿa Rasā'il fī Hilāl Khayr al-Shuhūr* (Beirut: Dār Ibn Ḥazm, 2000), 35–6.

[41] See later in this chapter for an explanation of this procedure, the *ṭarīq mūjib*.

what we have said above; rather it confirms it, because had it been permissible to [have the qadi] establish it, there would not have been a need for an [explicit] procedure.[42] [The qadi] needs, among other things, more [testimonies] due to what befalls [the sighting of] the new moon as a result of doubts, imaginations, its far distance and its small size. It is related on the authority of Anas b. Mālik, may God be pleased with him—and he is who he is[43]—that he set out with a group, among whom was Iyās b. Muʿāwiya. Anas informed [Iyās] that he saw [the *hilāl*]. But no one else had seen it. Iyās was known for his intelligence. He looked at Anas's eye and found in it a white hair from his brow. Iyās removed it with his hand, and then said to [Anas], "Show me the *hilāl*." [Anas] said, "I don't see it."

So, the qadi is to look at the state of the witnesses (*ḥāl al-shuhūd*) after ascertaining their moral integrity (*ʿadāla*), vigilance and alertness (*tayaqquẓ*), and freedom from doubts and accusations; at things which confound sightings, such as the soundness of their senses, the sharpness of their vision, the appropriateness of the horizons and the precise location of the new moon; at the stage of the new moon as it emerges; as well as at what calculations say about the possibility of sighting it or lack thereof. [This is because] a condition of testimony is that [its content] be possible. Given that possibility is a condition for confessions, and the one who confesses is only informing as to himself, and nothing else, what of the *shahāda*, which is a matter of solemnity for the qadi?[44]

In this passage, al-Subkī reads the Ḥanafī position as holding that it is not within the qadi's purview to establish the onset of the month itself, though he does have a role to play in judging the validity of such reports. Al-Subkī, in what amounts to an unconvincing attempt to salvage the consistency of (his understanding of) the Ḥanafī position, addresses the tension between the various demands associated with moon sighting reports by asserting that there is no contradiction (curiously on the grounds that the very existence of a judicial procedure precludes it being a *shahāda*), and by judging the qadi to be charged with the circumscribed tasks of assessing the authenticity of the sighting from a variety of different angles.

42 Presumably, this is because it would follow the standard procedures for a *shahāda*.
43 That is to say, his stature is well known and requires no elaboration or explanation.
44 Al-Subkī, "al-ʿAlam al-Manshūr," 36–37.

Later in the same treatise, however, al-Subkī is less confident in his insistence that there is no contradiction. He notes two cases set out in the Ḥanafī corpus that cast doubt on the unequivocal assertion that the month of Ramadan cannot be subject to the judgment (*ḥukm*) of the qadi:

> In the words of al-Marghīnānī: Some people testified (*shahidū*) to the *hilāl* of Ramadan on the twenty-ninth day [of Ramadan], saying they had in fact spotted it a day before the town started fasting. Their testimony is not to be accepted, because they had been negligent with what was obligatory on them [i.e., testifying to their sighting at the time]. If, however, they came from a distant location, [their testimony] is accepted because this accusation [does not apply].
>
> He mentioned also [the following case]: Two people testified to a qadi, the people of whose town had not seen the *hilāl*, that two other people testified to the qadi of another town [that they had seen it], and that [the second] qadi accepted their testimonies. It is permissible for [the first qadi] to pronounce based on their testimonies. . . .
>
> And in *al-Dhakhīra*, there is an incident in Bukhara [which resembles the first case]. The people began to fast on a Wednesday. On Wednesday, the twenty-ninth day of fasting, two or three men came to the qadi, and said, "We saw the *hilāl* of Ramadan on Monday night, the eve of Tuesday. So, today is the thirtieth." The responses [to this incident] were unanimous that if the sky was overcast when they saw the *hilāl* of Ramadan, the qadi should make Thursday [the next day] the day of Eid, even if they did not see [the new moon] that night. . . .
>
> What we have related from [the Ḥanafīs] in this chapter entails that [reports of a Ramadan *hilāl*] do enter the domain of the qadi's judgment (*dukhūl dhālika taḥt al-ḥukm*). So, it may be that there is a difference among them in respect to this.[45]

It is rather inconsequential for our purposes which of al-Subkī's two readings of Ḥanafism is the correct one. What is relevant is that, on both readings, the qadi clearly seems to have played some important role in regulating the announcement of Ramadan. Indeed, given the way al-Subkī grapples with this issue at length, it would not be unfair to speculate that the qadi's role was significant, if not central.

[45] Al-Subkī, "al-ʿAlam al-Manshūr," 58–59.

The role of the courts, then, was neither marginal nor extraneous, as we will see Bakhīt to have imagined it to be. This is further confirmed by the opinion of Abū Ḥanīfa, as found in the authoritative *Fatḥ al-Qadīr* of the seventh/thirteenth-century Ḥanafī Kamāl al-Dīn Ibn al-Humām.[46] We have already seen that Abū Ḥanīfa was keen to assert the *shahāda* properties of reported sightings of the *hilāl*. In line with this general orientation, Ibn al-Humām records Abū Ḥanīfa as stipulating that such reports be put forth in the form of an official claim (*daʿwā*) in the courts, which, recall, was one of the conditions of a *shahāda*.[47] Ibn al-Humām goes on to elaborate, saying,

> Based on this, what they mentioned—viz. that if one sights the *hilāl* of Ramadan in the countryside (*fī al-rustāq*), where there is no governor or qadi, the people can fast based on his statement if he is reliable (*thiqa*); and in the case of breaking the fast (*fī al-fiṭr*), if two upright people (*ʿadlān*) report that they sighted the *hilāl*, there is no problem with them breaking their fast—is to establish [the months] without any official claim (*bi-lā daʿwā*), and is ruled upon by virtue of necessity (*ḥukm li-l-ḍarūra*).[48]

Taken together, these statements only confirm our earlier intuition that the circulation of reports outside of the system of official qadis was exceptional. Indeed, it was al-Subkī's encountering the position attributed to Abū Ḥanīfa that led him to suggest that, in the end, despite the various reports, Ḥanafīs do likely conceive of the regulation of *hilāl*-reports as *qaḍāʾ* proper: "the stipulation of a legal claim (*ishtirāṭ al-daʿwā*) in the view of Abū Ḥanīfa is an indication that what is meant is the real *qaḍāʾ* (*al-qaḍāʾ al-ḥaqīqī*)."[49]

***

Given our interest in this chapter in tracking the concept of "religion," the preceding section has sought to understand the *umūr dīniyya* by locating their role in the technical discussion in which they feature most prominently. The decision to approach the question of what is meant by the *umūr dīniyya* by tracking the category's actual use was primarily a methodological choice taken up in the Asadian vein. It is also a suitable methodological approach

[46] For biographical information, see al-Laknawī, *al-Fawāʾid al-Bahiyya fī Tarājim al-Ḥanafiyya*, 180–82.
[47] Kamāl al-Dīn Ibn al-Humām, *Fatḥ al-Qadīr*, vol. 2 (Beirut: Dār al-Fikr, n.d.), 325. See also Zayn al-Dīn Ibn Nujaym, *al-Baḥr al-Rāʾiq*, vol. 2 (Beirut: Dār al-Kutub al-ʿIlmiyya, 1997), 465.
[48] Ibn al-Humām, *Fatḥ al-Qadīr*, 2:325.
[49] Al-Subkī, "al-ʿAlam al-Manshūr," 59.

in this instance because simply stated definitions of what is a rather involved concept are not forthcoming, and so its function and content can only be gleaned through a careful survey of the literature itself.[50] This methodological decision comes, however, with an added advantage: the tracking of usage, rather than a reliance on abstract definitions, gives the modern reader traction in resisting the inevitable temptation to naively read references to "religious matters" as isomorphic with the modern category of "religion"; that is to say, that which is opposed to the "secular." Many a student of Islam has reminded us that such a strict bifurcation of the world did not prevail in premodern Islam. To take but one prominent example, in a work remarkable for both its erudition and sheer breadth, Wilfred Cantwell Smith has pointed out that though Islam has always had a rather developed notion of "religion" (pointed at by the term *dīn*) due to its emergence in the Middle Eastern milieu[51]—a conception he calls "remarkable" for its early appearance as compared to Western Christianity[52]—"the differentiation between a secular social sphere and a sphere of religion is not quite shared by the Islamic world."[53] That is to say, there was no sense of a secular realm, as that which sits outside of, and in opposition to, a religious realm. The word *dīn* instead referred to a cohesive system that encompassed both "religion" and "secular sociality" in their worldly manifestations.

While this is an important part of the story, it still does not entirely get at what was meant by *dīn* in the formulation *umūr dīniyya*. Rather, the reports which qualified as belonging to this category were deemed such because they were concerned with ritual observances (*ʿibādāt*), such as fasting in

[50] Consider, for example, that the famous Mālikī al-Qarāfī records that he had a great deal of trouble in trying to pinpoint how precisely to distinguish between the respective essences of *shahādāṭ* and *riwāyāt*, the archetypal case study of which debate he identified as the sighting of the new moon of Ramadan. It is for the very reason of its seeming intractability that he takes it up as the very first discussion in his famous book on *Distinctions (al-Furūq)*: "I begin with the distinction between these two principles because I searched for [the nature of this distinction] for eight years without attaining it." Because al-Qarāfī was after the essence (*māhiyya*) of each category, he was unsatisfied by contemporary scholars' responses to his entreaties for help which approached the question by listing the features that differentiated them: "I asked the *fuḍalā'* about the difference between the two, and about the reality of the essence of each, for each of them is a report (*khabar*). They said, 'The difference between them is that the *shahāda* requires as conditions a multiplicity [of testimonies], and [that the witnesses be] male and freemen; in contradistinction to a *riwāya*, for it is valid through one [witness], male or female, free or slave.' So, I said to them, 'Specifying these conditions is subsidiary to conceptualizing [a *shahāda*], and is simply distinguishing [it] from a *riwāya*. But if we know [the category's] rulings and effects, which are unknown before you know [the category itself], we have circularity.'" Al-Qarāfī, *al-Furūq*, 12–13.

[51] Wilfred Cantwell Smith, *The Meaning and End of Religion: A New Approach to the Religious Traditions of Mankind* (New York: Macmillan, 1962), 92–102.

[52] Smith, *The Meaning and End of Religion*, 76.

[53] Smith, *The Meaning and End of Religion*, 85.

the case of reports of new moon sightings.[54] Hence, for example, al-Subkī's (and later Bakhīt's) interest in determining in the course of the earlier discussion whether the *ʿibādāt*—and so, the *umūr dīniyya* to which they are connected—were subject to the qadi's judgment (*ḥukm*). The most explicit discussion of this can be found in al-Subkī's treatment of a *shahāda* that seemingly relates to the *ḥajj* pilgrimage. Al-Subkī denies this connection, saying it is not to be thought of as pertaining to the essentials of *ḥajj*, because a *shahāda* is by definition something that is subject to the judgment of the qadi, whereas the *ḥajj* belongs to the class of ritual observances (*min bāb al-ʿibādāt*), and so is not subject to *ḥukm*, but instead to (the nonbinding) fatwa.[55]

Further illumination on the meaning of the *umūr dīniyya* can be found by closely following the sorts of discussions that pit them against run-of-the-mill *shahāḍāt*. Consider, for example, the lengthy explanation offered by the Mālikī Ibn al-Shāṭṭ in his commentary on Shihāb al-Dīn al-Qarāfī's *al-Furūq*:

> With regards to [al-Qarāfī's] saying, "[a report of a sighting of the Ramadan *hilāl*] is a *shahāda*": If what he means is that, according to some ulama, its ruling is that of the *shahāda* in stipulating a multiplicity of witnesses, this is true. But if he means that it is a *shahāda* proper (*ḥaqīqatan*), this is not the case. For, it is settled that the word "*shahāda*" in the terminology of the jurists and the legal theorists (*fī ʿurf al-fuqahāʾ wa-l-uṣūlīyyīn*) only properly applies to the report based upon which a judgement is rendered or a judicial decision between litigating parties is given (*yatarattab ʿalayhi al-ḥukm wa faṣl al-qaḍāʾ*). I say: [The position] that is strengthened as a result of investigation is that the issue of the *hilāl* takes the ruling of the *riwāya* in terms of one [witness] being sufficient. But it is neither a *riwāya* nor a *shahāda* properly speaking. Rather, it is another type of report, namely a report of the existence of something that effectuates a shariʿa ruling (*khabar ʿan wujūd sabab min asbāb al-aḥkām al-sharʿiyya*).[56] And it is no secret that

[54] See as a representative example, al-Sarakhsī in *al-Mabsūṭ*: "What is relevant (*al-mutaʿalliq*) to the *hilāl* of Ramadan is [that it] effects a beginning of ritual observance (*al-ʿibāda*), so the report of one [person] is acceptable." Al-Sarakhsī, *al-Mabsūṭ*, 3:139.

[55] Al-Subkī, "al-ʿAlam al-Manshūr," 41–42. Bakhīt is even more explicit about this connection. See, for example, the chapter heading in his treatise: "On whether or not ritual observances are subject to the qadi's ruling (*fī anna al-ʿibāda tadkhūl taḥt al-ḥukm aw lā*)." Bakhīt al-Muṭīʿī, *Irshād Ahl al-Milla ilā Ithbāt al-Ahilla*, 31.

[56] Note that this is a particularly Mālikī description of this third category.

> it is untouched by the possibility of interpersonal adversariality (*ʿadāwa*) of the sort that pertains to worldly (*dunyawī*) adjudication.[57]

It is through this last sentence that Ibn al-Shāṭṭ most explicitly distinguishes the *shahādāt* from what the Ḥanafis call the *umūr dīniyya*. The former are reports which address worldly (*dunyawī*) matters that occur between people, and so raise the possibility of interpersonal conflict.

This sense of the *shahādāt* as pertaining to worldly matters, the parties to which stand to gain from the outcome, is also pointed at in discussions of the sighting of the new moon of Shawwāl, the month after Ramadan. In the tradition that prevails before Bakhīt, this was generally not considered among the *umūr dīniyya*. Indeed, it fell squarely within the class of *shahādāt*. According to al-Kāsānī in *Badāʾiʿ al-Ṣanāʾiʿ*, this is because "it does not demand anything from the witness himself; rather, it is a source of benefit for him in that it waives [the obligation of] fasting for himself."[58] Similarly, al-Sarakhsī says in *al-Mabsūṭ*, "What is most relevant (*al-mutaʿalliq*) in [a report of the sighting of] the new moon of Shawwāl is what it contains by way of material benefit for people, namely a dispensation to break the fast (*al-tarakhkhuṣ bi-l-fiṭr*). Therefore, it is just like a *shahāda*, which pertains to the rights of people (*ʿalā ḥuqūq al-ʿibād*)."[59]

It is precisely because this possible worldly benefit may accrue to a witness (and indeed everyone else) that corroboration is required in the form of a second testimony (*ʿadad*). This is in contrast to a report of the Ramadan *hilāl*, which imposes an obligation (*iḍrār*), not a benefit, on the witness—namely, the ritual obligation to fast.[60]

Classical dictionaries tell us that the opposite of *dunyā* is *al-ākhira*, the other-world or afterlife.[61] We have reason, then, to prefer the interpretation of the *umūr dīniyya* as those matters which are oriented toward the afterlife. This finds attestation in the constellation of terms given by the dictionaries that coalesce around the idea of ritual worship, obedience, and piety (*ʿibāda*,

57 Ibn al-Shāṭṭ, *Idrār al-Shurūq* on the margins of al-Qarāfī, *al-Furūq*, 1:19–20.

58 ʿAlāʾ al-Dīn al-Kāsānī, *Badāʾiʿ al-Ṣanāʾiʿ fī Tartīb al-Sharāʾiʿ*, vol. 2 (Beirut: Dār al-Kutub al-ʿIlmiyya, n.d.), 577.

59 Al-Sarakhsī, *al-Mabsūṭ*, 3:139. See also al-Marghīnānī, al-*Hidāya*, 2:325; and Muḥammad Amīn Ibn ʿĀbidīn, "Tanbīh al-Ghāfil wa-l-Wasnān ʿalā Aḥkām Hilāl Ramaḍān," in *Arbaʿa Rasāʾil fī Hilāl Khayr al-Shuhūr* (Beirut: Dār Ibn Ḥazm, 2000), 77.

60 Al-Kāsānī, *Badāʾiʿ al-Ṣanāʾiʿ fī Tartīb al-Sharāʾiʿ*, 2:577.

61 Muḥammad ibn Yaʿqūb Fīrūzābādī, "Danā," in *al-Qāmūs al-Muḥīṭ* (Miṣr: Maṭbaʿat al-Saʿāda, n.d.).

ṭāʿa, and *waraʿ*).[62] This division between this-worldly concerns and other-worldly ones is distinct from, and ought not to be confused with, the "religious/secular" dichotomy. As Casanova reminds us of premodern Western European Christendom,

> [The] structured division of "this world" into two separate spheres, "the religious" and "the secular," has to be distinguished and kept separate from another division: that between "this world" and "the other world." . . . One may say that, properly speaking, there were not two "worlds" but actually three. Spatially, there was "the other world" (heaven) and "this world" (earth). But "this world" was itself divided into the religious world (the church) and the secular world proper (*saeculum*). . . . We may say, therefore, that premodern Western European Christendom was structured through a double dualist system of classification.[63]

While it is absolutely appropriate to say (as many have) that the second division, between the Church and the *saeculum*, did not have an analog in premodern Islam, this difference ought not to be exaggerated so as to deny the unmistakeable existence of a distinction between the *dunyā* and the *ākhira*.[64] It is the latter with which the *umūr dīniyya* were concerned.

To turn to Asad once more, this way of understanding what is meant by the *umūr dīniyya* respects his concern that the existence of what appear to be similar concepts or arrangements within premodern Islamic law not be mistaken for the modern distinction between the "religious" and the "secular."[65] This modern binary comes with a range of connotations and demands, including "religion" as a private realm outside the ambit of judicial authority in which "conscience"—pre-eminently religious conscience—is given free reign. As we have seen, the story is more complicated than this in the texts we have been considering. Indeed, while the *umūr dīniyya* were matters that were oriented toward the afterlife, and so may be called "religious" in a certain sense of the modern term, their appearance and circulation in the world were

[62] Muḥammad ibn Yaʿqūb Fīrūzābādī, "Dīn," in *al-Qāmūs al-Muḥīṭ* (Miṣr: Maṭbaʿat al-Saʿāda, n.d.). See also Smith, *The Meaning and End of Religion*, 76, 94. Asad would no doubt caution us against taking this to equate, as Smith does, *dīn* with personal religion, that is, faith. See Talal Asad, "Reading a Modern Classic: W. C. Smith's 'The Meaning and End of Religion,'" *History of Religions* 40, no. 3 (February 1, 2001): 205–22.

[63] Casanova, *Public Religions in the Modern World*, 14–15.

[64] This is why it makes good sense that Asad would find that one of the translations of "secular" in Badger's *Lexicon* would be *dunyawī*. Asad, *Formations of the Secular*, 201.

[65] Asad, *Formations of the Secular*, 241–48.

structured in a manner that involved the judicial authorities themselves, regularly and as a matter of course. This is because these authorities, the qadis, were social institutions which played a part in organizing the community's interests and behavior in a manner that exceeds the simple dichotomy between law and religion.

I hasten to point out that I make no claim that the analysis of this chapter necessarily gives us a complete picture of what might have been meant by *dīn* (or cognate terms) when used by Muslim scholars.[66] What this section has done, however, is provide us with a sense for how it was used in premodern *fiqh*, and even more restrictively how it was used in one particular circumstance in works of *fiqh*. Despite these qualifications, I maintain that our examination of this instance reveals much about the way in which modern notions of "religion" and "the secular" would come to impinge on these older understandings and subject them to transformation along certain lines.

Bakhīt on "Religious Matters": Clear Skies and Discrete Witnesses

To examine how precisely this transformation took form, we turn once more to the *Irshād Ahl al-Milla* to consider how Bakhīt, influenced by these modern definitions, came to understand the *umūr dīniyya*. Bakhīt's strategy is to efface the *shahāda* properties of the *umūr dīniyya*, so as to assimilate them entirely to the *riwāyāt*, thus creating a private realm of "religious matters" that exist entirely outside the jurisdiction of the system of qadis and their authority. As we have seen, the *umūr dīniyya* were already seen as leaning heavily toward the *riwāyāt*, though they were thought to retain significant elements of the *shahāda*, most notably the role of the qadi. Bakhīt's contribution is to sever those final ties, effectively eliminating the in-between category altogether.

If, as I show in this chapter, Bakhīt's understanding of "religion" is indebted to the modern transformations associated with new conceptions of the secular, it also bears noting at the outset that the hermeneutic shifts we observed in chapters 2 and 4 feature heavily in his mode of argumentation on

[66] For a preliminary survey of the term in a variety of fields, see Ahmet T. Karamustafa, "Islamic *Dīn* as an Alternative to Western Models of Religion," in *Religion, Theory, Critique: Classic and Contemporary Approaches and Methodologies*, ed. Richard King (New York: Columbia University Press, 2017), 163–71.

this count. The interpretive preference we saw him to have accorded the early generations of Ḥanafī scholars in chapter 2, over and above the substantial and sophisticated tradition that intervenes between that period and his own, manifests itself quite clearly in his mode of argumentation. Bakhīt is quick to justify his positions by reference to the *ẓāhir al-riwāya*, the name given to "the highest level of authoritative doctrine" in the Ḥanafī *madhhab* due to its attribution to Abū Ḥanīfa and his two famous students, Abū Yūsuf and Muḥammad b. Ḥasan al-Shaybānī.[67] Despite the authority these positions wielded in theory, however, they were often reasoned with, particularized, or rationalized such that the going opinion at any given time might stand diametrically opposed to the *ẓāhir al-riwāya*. This trend is not to Bakhīt's liking. At one point, he goes so far as to evidence suspicion of postformative scholars' mastery of the Ḥanafī corpus and questions their attribution of widespread opinions to the early masters, concluding that

> it is necessary for the student of *fiqh* to resort to the books of the early scholars (*kutub al-mutaqaddimīn*) and the reliable books of the later scholars (*al-kutub al-muʿtabara min kutub al-mutaʾakhkhirīn*), and not depend upon the books of the later scholars except after fully enquiring as to the accuracy of their transmission (*ṣiḥḥat al-naql*).[68]

Equally central to Bakhīt's mode of argumentation is his propensity to privilege epistemological understandings of the tradition to settled procedures; recall his insistence in chapter 4 that it was *ʿilm* (knowledge) and not *ruʾya* (sighting) that was the relevant legal cause required to declare a new month. We will see how this impulse to "epistemologize" *fiqh* manifests itself in discussions about religion throughout the remainder of this chapter.

***

The settled position of the Ḥanafī school was that in the case of a clear sky (in contrast to conditions when the sky is overcast or obstructed in some way), *tafarrud* would be deemed insufficient. *Tafarrud* literally means "singularity," though it is appropriate to prefer the term "discreteness" as a translation so as to contrast it to the large-scale transmission the jurists envisioned as its

[67] Wael B. Hallaq, *Authority, Continuity, and Change in Islamic Law* (Cambridge, UK: Cambridge University Press, 2001), 47–48.
[68] Bakhīt al-Muṭīʿī, *Irshād Ahl al-Milla ilā Ithbāt al-Ahilla*, 84.

opposite, as well as to ensure that it is not seen as the opposite of the separate demand for "multiplicity" (*ʿadad*) discussed earlier. Both the single testimony that was ordinarily required in the case of the Ramadan new moon and the two testimonies that were typically demanded to declare the beginning of Shawwāl, and therefore the end of fasting, are considered cases of *tafarrud*. The rationale for the insufficiency of *tafarrud* is that in the case of a clear sky, a large group of people ought to be just as able to spot the new moon as discrete, individual, scattered sighters.[69] As Bakhīt himself summarizes,

> In [the case] of the two new moons, when there is no impediment in the sky, many of the *mutaʾakhkhirīn* have it in their writings that what is required is a report from a large group (*jamʿ ʿaẓīm*). This has been expressed in the *Mukhtaṣar al-Wiqāya*. Al-Quhistānī has said in his commentary on this: "In the *ẓāhir al-riwāya*, the precise number is not specified . . . in the case of breaking the fast (*fiṭr*) and fasting." That is, what is stipulated is a group [large enough] that probability (*ẓann*) accompanies their report, as is mentioned by al-Kirmānī. Certain knowledge that proceeds from *tawātur* (mass-transmission) is not required."[70]

This position of the later scholars is one that Bakhīt would like to dispute because it introduces an evidentiary burden that detracts from the simple standard of *riwāyāt*—namely, the sufficiency of a single discrete testimony.

To accomplish this, Bakhīt bases himself on the opinion of the famous third/ninth-century scholar Abū Jaʿfar al-Ṭaḥāwī.[71] In an opinion that was regularly mentioned in the Ḥanafī corpus, but usually taken to refer to a very particular and exceptional case if not disregarded altogether, al-Ṭaḥāwī had maintained that in both cases, the testimony of a single witness was to be considered sufficient if that witness had seen the *hilāl* outside of the city or from a high altitude. Bakhīt quotes this opinion from the relatively minor text, *al-Fatāwā al-Walwāljiyya*:

[69] As al-Sarakhsī says, if one admits (as one should) the possibility of the witness lying in overcast conditions, this is all the more possible when there are no obstructions whatsoever. Al-Sarakhsī, *al-Mabsūṭ*, 3:64.

[70] Bakhīt al-Muṭīʿī, *Irshād Ahl al-Milla ilā Ithbāt al-Ahilla*, 48.

[71] For biographical details, see al-Laknawī, *al-Fawāʾid al-Bahiyya fī Tarājim al-Ḥanafiyya*, 31–34. Bakhīt says explicitly that the opinion of al-Ṭaḥāwī is "what has helped along [his] proof." Bakhīt al-Muṭīʿī, *Irshād Ahl al-Milla ilā Ithbāt al-Ahilla*, 68.

> If [the witness] comes from outside the city, he is to be accepted if he is morally upright and trustworthy (*ʿadl thiqa*). This is because one can ascertain with certainty things in the desert that one cannot ascertain in cities, due to the number of clouds in [the city]. The same goes for if he is in the city, but at an elevated altitude. [In this respect,] the *hilāl* of *fiṭr* is like the *hilāl* of Ramadan in cases of clear skies.[72]

This position had also been mentioned by al-Sarakhsī in *al-Mabsūṭ*, who wrote that in the case of a single uncorroborated witness,

> the imam must only reject his testimony if the skies are clear and he is from the city. If the skies are overcast, or if [the witness] came from outside the city, or from an elevated altitude, his testimony is to be accepted according to us, contrary to al-Shāfiʿī.[73]

In commenting on this passage, Ibn ʿĀbidīn had understood "according to us" to mean that all three of the pre-eminent Ḥanafī imams (Abū Ḥanīfa, Abū Yūsuf, and Muḥammad b. Ḥasan al-Shaybānī) had agreed on this position, thus strengthening its force. In addition, he goes on, this is further supported by the reasoning supplied by the author of *al-Muḥīṭ*, namely that

> sightings vary as a result of differences in the clarity and cloudiness of the sky; and with changes in altitude. The air of the desert is clearer than that of the city, and the new moon may be spotted from high altitudes where it may not be seen from lower ones. Thus, a single sighting [in such a case] is not opposed to the *ẓāhir* [*al-riwāya*], but in accordance with it.[74]

Because this was recorded in *al-Mabsūṭ*, which "is also one of the books of *ẓāhir al-riwāya*" and because it is also plainly stated in *al-Kāfī*, which is a compilation of the opinions of Muḥammad b. Ḥasan al-Shaybānī, Ibn ʿĀbidīn opined that al-Ṭaḥāwī's position ought to not just be resuscitated but made to join that of the *mutaʾakhkhirūn* at the level of *ẓāhir al-riwāya*. The case of the single witness who sights the moon outside the city or from an elevated location, he says, is to be thought of as an exceptional one, "restricting

[72] Bakhīt al-Muṭīʿī, *Irshād Ahl al-Milla ilā Ithbāt al-Ahilla*, 52.
[73] Al-Sarakhsī, *al-Mabsūṭ*, 3:64.
[74] Muḥammad Amīn Ibn ʿĀbidīn, *Ḥāshiyat Radd al-Muḥtār*, vol. 3 (Riyadh: Dār ʿĀlam al-Kutub, 2003), 357.

the generality (*muqayyida li-l-iṭlāq*)" of the position exclusively favored by postformative writers which stipulated the testimonies of a large group (*jam*ʿ *ʿaẓīm*).[75]

Thus, the single dominant position of the classical Ḥanafī tradition gives way to a dual *ẓāhir al-riwāya* on Ibn ʿĀbidīn's reasoning, with each position taken to refer to different circumstances. This is cited extensively and approvingly by Bakhīt, who then goes on to comment that "what is gathered from these citations is that what is to be relied upon is that found in the books of *ẓāhir al-riwāya*, and there is to be no relying upon [opinions] found in other works that go against it."[76]

In advancing his argument in this way, then, Bakhīt operationalizes his theoretical commitment to early Ḥanafī authorities at the expense of the interpretive preferences of later jurists. Equally worthy of our attention, however, is his second methodological move, namely how his argument serves as an "epistemologization" of the *masʾala* under consideration. Bakhīt not only approves of al-Ṭaḥāwī's (and Ibn ʿĀbidīn's) reading, but extends their very specific conclusion by engaging in a rationalization (*taʿlīl*) that allows him to identify what he takes to be the principle underlying both positions. Abstracting away from their case-based reasoning, Bakhīt concludes that the basis for rejecting a lone testimony had been that "discreteness" (*al-tafarrud*) gives reason to presume error or lies (*maẓinnat al-ghalaṭ aw al-kidhb*)."[77] But al-Ṭaḥāwī's position provides a discursive opening for Bakhīt to opine instead that, if in general terms, "discreteness does not give reason to suspect mistakes or lies, the testimony should be accepted even if it is from just one upright person, according to the *ẓāhir al-riwāya*."[78] With this, the two distinct positions of Ibn ʿĀbidīn, each of which was thought to refer to different circumstances, have been abstracted and conjoined (*tawfīq*) by Bakhīt into a single criteria, itself focussed on the truth value of the content of the report and not the settled procedures of the premodern tradition. Those precisely delineated procedures, bound up as we have seen in the authority of the courts, have given way to an epistemological judgment, whose locus is not juristic procedure but the minds of individuals.

Echoing Ibn ʿĀbidīn, Bakhīt argues that this is in complete accordance with the *ẓāhir al-riwāya*. On the new interpretation in which epistemological

[75] Ibn ʿĀbidīn, *Ḥāshiyat Radd al-Muḥtār*, 3:357.
[76] Bakhīt al-Muṭīʿī, *Irshād Ahl al-Milla ilā Ithbāt al-Ahilla*, 55.
[77] Bakhīt al-Muṭīʿī, *Irshād Ahl al-Milla ilā Ithbāt al-Ahilla*, 54.
[78] Bakhīt al-Muṭīʿī, *Irshād Ahl al-Milla ilā Ithbāt al-Ahilla*, 54.

considerations are foregrounded, and not simply understood through, and subsumed by, the predetermined criteria of what is demanded of a legitimate report, the *ẓāhir al-riwāya* is properly thought to be contravened only upon the acceptance of a singular report that contradicts what is most evident "such that it gives reason to presume error or lies."[79] Many of the *muta'akhkhirīn* have been confused about this, Bakhīt says,

> thinking that *any* acceptance of a singular report is in absolute contravention of the *ẓāhir al-riwāya*, even when its discreteness does not give reason to suspect mistakes or lies. So, they understood what al-Ṭaḥāwī held to be in contravention of [the *ẓāhir al-riwāya*].[80]

Indeed, Bakhīt acknowledges that this was the dominant position before him, but he considers himself to have set matters straight: "All of the later texts (*mutūn*) have taken this position, but I have corrected it. So take this verification (*taḥqīq*), and be thankful to God."[81]

Bakhīt thus envisions himself as having identified the problem with the prevailing position and its demand for a large group of witnesses in the case of clear skies; and instating in its place the simple standard evidentiary condition of all *riwāyāt*: a single report from a morally upright source. Significantly, though, because the condition has now been appropriately abstracted into a general epistemological criterion, he considers it sensible to extend it so that it serves as a universal standard which applies to *all* sightings of Ramadan and Shawwāl new moons, not simply to the particular case of clear skies.

Recall that the *hilāl* of Shawwāl was thought to be a *shahāda* in the dominant premodern tradition on the grounds that it was a source of worldly benefit (*naf*) for the witness in question, and placed no ritual obligation on him. Bakhīt once again disputes his predecessors' categorization, on the basis that he has now shown that the *riwāya* requirement of one reliable witness is sufficient in the specific case of the Shawwāl new moon in clear skies, even though this latter leads to the very same worldly benefit, namely a release from fasting. Similarly, "the claim that it does not impose any obligation on the witness is not granted, for the witness must observe the *fiṭr* and fasting

79 Bakhīt al-Muṭīʿī, *Irshād Ahl al-Milla ilā Ithbāt al-Ahilla*, 57.
80 Bakhīt al-Muṭīʿī, *Irshād Ahl al-Milla ilā Ithbāt al-Ahilla*, 57, emphasis added.
81 Bakhīt al-Muṭīʿī, *Irshād Ahl al-Milla ilā Ithbāt al-Ahilla*, 68.

is prohibited for him."[82] In a remarkable inversion, then, Bakhīt extends the concept of religious obligation to include the celebration of the ʿĪd al-Fiṭr festival, which includes a strict prohibition against fasting. What was considered, rather matter of factly, to have been a worldly benefit before him is now deemed a religious obligation of a particularly modern sort.[83] Thus, he argues, the *hilāl* of Shawwāl is to be considered from among the *umūr dīniyya* and should never be treated as a *shahāda*.[84]

In light of this shift, the testimony of one reliable witness is now an entirely appropriate evidential standard in all cases. As Bakhīt reasons, "the [jurists] are in agreement that the new moon of *fiṭr* in the case of clear skies is like the new moon of fasting in the case of clear skies. All the more so, then, in overcast conditions."[85] Because, in the former case, we have downgraded the demand for a group sighting to a single reliable sighting, it is a fortiori the case that we should be able to downgrade the less stringent demand for a mere two witnesses. With this new universal standard, then, the *umūr dīniyya* have been pushed further, and indeed decisively, toward the category of the *riwāya*.

[82] Bakhīt al-Muṭīʿī, *Irshād Ahl al-Milla ilā Ithbāt al-Ahilla*, 70. Elsewhere, he also includes the obligation to pay the yearly alms-tax *zakāt al-fiṭr* on the day of Eid. This is not to be confused with the well-known *zakāt* of 2.5 percent on one's savings. Bakhīt al-Muṭīʿī, *Irshād Ahl al-Milla ilā Ithbāt al-Ahilla*, 76.

[83] Elsewhere, Bakhīt engages in some remarkable argumentation to prove that the case of breaking one's fast should not be construed as worldly benefit. Recall that it was al-Kāsānī who had made this argument most strongly in *Badāʾiʿ al-Ṣanāʾiʿ* (see 184). Bakhīt responds: "The author of *al-Badāʾiʿ* says there is worldly benefit (*nafʿ*) in it, namely the waiving of [the obligation of] fasting for himself. This is a poor opinion, for the witness does not waive his [obligation to] fast through his testimony. Waiving something entails that it was obligatory in the first place, and that it was then dropped afterward for a reason that necessitates a waiver, such as illness, travel and all of the other excuses due to which the performance of the fast may be skipped, despite the existence of the cause of the obligation, that is, the time [of fasting]. But our present concern is not like this. All the testimony does in this case is impose an end to, and a release from, the period for fasting. With the end of this period, he enters into the time of breaking the fast, and so he is obligated to break the fast." Bakhīt al-Muṭīʿī, *Irshād Ahl al-Milla ilā Ithbāt al-Ahilla*, 74.

[84] This reasoning is extended to include Dhū al-Ḥijja, the month of *ḥajj* and the celebration of ʿĪd al-Aḍḥā, on the basis that it is connected to the prohibition of fasting on the days of the festival (the tenth, eleventh, twelfth, and thirteenth of the month), the entry of the *ḥajj* season, the obligation to slaughter an animal, the ritual glorifications of God on the festival days (*takbīr al-tashrīq*), and "other purely religious rulings." Bakhīt al-Muṭīʿī, *Irshād Ahl al-Milla ilā Ithbāt al-Ahilla*, 76. Premodern support for one of these considerations can be found in the form of a minority opinion (*riwāyat al-nawādir*) attributed to Abū Ḥanīfa that cited the obligation to slaughter as a "right of God" and so a "religious matter." Ibn al-Humām, *Fatḥ al-Qadīr*, 2:325–26; al-Marghīnānī, *al-Hidāya*, 2:325; Ibn Nujaym, *al-Baḥr al-Rāʾiq*, 2:470. The texts that quote it, however, are quick to mention that the dominant premodern position (*ẓāhir al-riwāya*) was that the ʿĪd al-Aḍḥā was, like the ʿĪd al-Fiṭr after Ramadan, a straight-forward *shahāda*. Al-Marghīnānī, *al-Hidāya*, 2:325; Ibn Nujaym, *al-Baḥr al-Rāʾiq*, 2:470. See also Ibn ʿAbidīn, "Tanbīh al-Ghāfil," 77.

[85] Bakhīt al-Muṭīʿī, *Irshād Ahl al-Milla ilā Ithbāt al-Ahilla*, 67.

I say this move is decisive because, for Bakhīt, his proof that all that is required from a testimony is the lack of presumption of error or lying, even if it comes only from a single witness, serves as a catalyst for arguing against the rest of the *shahāda* conditions, and thereby assimilating the in-between category of the *umūr dīniyya* entirely to the *riwāyāt*.

Indeed, Bakhīt laments the premodern scholars' propensity to introduce various of the *shahāda* characteristics to the *umūr dīniyya*, identifying Qāḍīkhān[86] as the culprit who first demanded the formulaic language of an express testimony (*lafẓ al-shahāda*). Others then followed him in this and gradually added more until all of the standard conditions of the *shahāda* had been stipulated by someone or other. These stipulations, according to Bakhīt, are "based on investigations of the *shaykhs* (*abḥāth al-mashā'ikh*)[87] which conflict with clear proof-texts (*al-naṣṣ al-ṣarīḥ*)."[88] What he believes his discussion to have made clear (*ṣarīḥ*) is that reports of the new moons of Ramadan, Shawwāl, and Dhū al-Ḥijja (the month of the *ḥajj*)[89]

> are *dīnī* reports, not from the class of *shahādāt* pertaining to the rights of others.[90] *Since they are dīnī reports, there are no conditions on them other than that which is stipulated for relating Prophetic traditions* (*riwāyat al-aḥādīth*). There is no reason, therefore, that any of the express language of testimony (*lafẓ al-shahāda*), an official claim (*da'wā*), the binding judgment of the qadi (*ḥukm*), the qadi's "court" (*majlis al-qaḍā'*), or the witness's freedom, maleness or lack of prior discipline for slander be conditions. All that is stipulated is the moral probity [of the witness] in reports that do not reach the status of mass-transmission.[91]

86 Ḥasan b. Manṣūr Qāḍīkhān was a sixth/twelfth-century Central Asian Ḥanafī scholar. For biographical details, see al-Laknawī, *al-Fawā'id al-Bahiyya fī Tarājim al-Ḥanafiyya*, 64–65.

87 Elsewhere, he calls them "simply the interpretations and understandings of the scholars (*takhrījāt al-mashā'ikh wa afhāmuhum*)" to similarly distinguish them from the explicit proof-texts (*al-naṣṣ*). Bakhīt al-Muṭī'ī, *Irshād Ahl al-Milla ilā Ithbāt al-Ahilla*, 69.

88 Bakhīt al-Muṭī'ī, *Irshād Ahl al-Milla ilā Ithbāt al-Ahilla*, 73.

89 See note 84.

90 Elsewhere, he expresses his outrage with the latter claim. "More astonishing is the claim that this concerns the rights of others (*min ḥuqūq al-'ibād*), and that there is a sense of obligating another (*ilzām*) like in sales and properties. Let him, then, explain to us: Whose right is this? And who is making the claim? And who is so obliged by this right? And who obligates? Glory be to God. This is a new legislation altogether!" Bakhīt al-Muṭī'ī, *Irshād Ahl al-Milla ilā Ithbāt al-Ahilla*, 70.

91 Bakhīt al-Muṭī'ī, *Irshād Ahl al-Milla ilā Ithbāt al-Ahilla*, 73. Similar sentiments are reported repeatedly throughout the text. See also Bakhīt al-Muṭī'ī, *Irshād Ahl al-Milla ilā Ithbāt al-Ahilla*, 60, 76, 91.

The most important of the *shahāda* characteristics that he wants to disavow is its eligibility for the judgment of the qadi (*dukhūl taḥt al-ḥukm*). "Is it possible," he asks rhetorically,

> that that which admits the report of one [witness alone] can be in any wise said to be a *shahāda*? Or that the *fiṭr* is concerned with the rights of others, and so enters into the qadi's judgment? Or that fasting based on the report of a single upright person, or breaking the fast based on the reports of two, without any enforced ruling (*qaḍā'*) is only out of necessity in the countryside (*li-l-ḍarūra fī al-rustāq*)?"[92]

The answer to all of these questions is a resounding no! "The testimonies of each of the sightings of the three new moons are from the class of religious reports (*al-akhbār al-dīniyya*). Thus, they resemble the *riwāya*, and it is impossible that any of them enter into the qadi's judgment."[93]

With this argumentation, Bakhīt has effectively eliminated the in-between category which had housed the *umūr dīniyya* and has assimilated them entirely to the *riwāyāt*, the paradigmatic example of which are Prophetic *aḥādīth*. Though he still adheres to the time-worn language of resemblance that signified the hybridity of the *umūr dīniyya*, he now effectively posits an identity between them and the *riwāyāt*. The "religious matters" are no longer structured by the dictates and procedures of the qadi's courts but are now subjected to an epistemological standard located in the minds of individuals. As he clearly puts it at the end of his lengthy argument,

> So, what is no longer in doubt is that if a single upright person reports on a sighting of the new moon—whether outside the qadi's presence, or in his presence though the qadi does not thereafter order fasting—fasting is obligatory for the [witness himself], and on everyone he informs or to whom his report is conveyed, as long as the transmitter is reliable in the view of the one receiving the report, and he deems the report to yield a preponderant likelihood.[94]

[92] Bakhīt al-Muṭīʿī, *Irshād Ahl al-Milla ilā Ithbāt al-Ahilla*, 73. Recall the opinion on the *rustāq* had been Ibn al-Humām's, who Bakhīt accuses of having extrapolated (*tawassuʿ*) unjustifiably and in contravention of authoritative textual narrations (*al-manqūl*), despite his high standing (*ʿuluww kaʿbihi*). Bakhīt al-Muṭīʿī, *Irshād Ahl al-Milla ilā Ithbāt al-Ahilla*, 72.

[93] Bakhīt al-Muṭīʿī, *Irshād Ahl al-Milla ilā Ithbāt al-Ahilla*, 76.

[94] Bakhīt al-Muṭīʿī, *Irshād Ahl al-Milla ilā Ithbāt al-Ahilla*, 91.

As this summation makes clear, and as we will see by looking at a different but related *mas'ala* in the next section, Bakhīt is vigilant to ensure that the *umūr dīniyya* are in all situations handled as hadith narrations, and independently of the oversight of qadis.

Bakhīt on "Religious Matters": Transmissions across Horizons

The second issue (*mas'ala*) that exemplifies Bakhīt's reliance on modern connotations of religion in reformulating long-held *fiqh* positions is the one which had motivated him to write the *Irshād Ahl al-Milla* in the first place: determining the legal status of telegraphy. The telegraph had come to proliferate as a communications technology over the course of Bakhīt's lifetime. In a contemporaneous treatise of his own, the Syrian reformer Jamāl al-Dīn al-Qāsimī records that "the judges of Egypt" in the nineteenth century were in the habit of ruling in favor of acting upon telegraph reports, and that Bakhīt's teacher Muḥammad ʿIllīsh was the first to author a fatwa on the matter in 1865, effectively corroborating the general practice of the qadis of his land.[95] In an appendix, al-Qāsimī includes the responsa of a number of other Syrian and Egyptian muftis affirming the validity of telegraph reports, which taken together constituted a sizeable track record.[96] As we have seen in the Introduction, however, Bakhīt's own 1911 fatwa arguing for the acceptability of the telegraph met with some controversy, suggesting that despite these precedents, the place of the relatively novel technology was still unsettled.[97] Rather than offering a concise and straightforward response to the question at hand in the manner of his predecessors, Bakhīt instead composed a detailed treatise which sought to address, comprehensively and convincingly, a number of interrelated issues that clustered around the question

[95] Muḥammad Jamāl al-Dīn al-Qāsimī, *Irshād al-Khalq ilā al-ʿAmal bi-Khabar al-Barq* (Maṭbaʿat al-Muqtabas, 1329 H), 71. A translation of his prefatory methodological comments in *Irshād al-Khalq* can be found in David Dean Commins, "Guiding Mankind to Act on the Basis of Telegraphic Messages," in *Modernist Islam: 1840–1940*, edited by Charles Kurzman (New York: Oxford University Press, 2002), 181–87. For details on al-Qāsimī's argumentation in the treatise, see Vanessa Ogle, *The Global Transformation of Time* (Cambridge, MA: Harvard University Press, 2015), 153–60. On the broader *salafī* reformism of al-Qāsimī within the context of late Ottoman Syria, see David Dean Commins, *Islamic Reform: Politics and Social Change in Late Ottoman Syria* (New York: Oxford University Press, 1990).

[96] Al-Qāsimī, *Irshād al-Khalq*, 81–99.

[97] For examples of opposing positions, see Ogle, *The Global Transformation of Time*, 155–56.

of how to handle reports of crescent sightings in an age of new technologies and modern states.[98] The question at the heart of the Irshād, however, was how telegraphic reports transmitted across distances were to be validated. In other words, what formal requirements were necessary to consider such a report binding on those who receive it? Bakhīt's argumentation on this issue is especially revealing for our purposes, not so much because it demonstrates his endorsement of new technologies—as mentioned, many jurists had already approved the use of the telegraph—but rather because it once again lays bare his conviction that "religious matters" are primarily epistemic, that is, having to do with emergent conceptions of knowledge and not subject to the specific mechanisms of court procedure. As such, they were eligible for circulation outside the oversight of qadis and their systematic court procedures.

Bakhīt's engagement with this issue finds its genesis in a larger debate which had occupied jurists for quite some time: namely, who precisely was bound to follow a reported sighting of the new moon. Some scholars had chosen to differentiate between regions "sharing a horizon" and those that did not, thus making an established sighting of a new moon binding on all those who shared the horizon (*maṭlaʿ*) of the person claiming to have sighted it, and inapplicable to those outside that geographical boundary. The dominant Ḥanafī tradition, however, was opposed to this, arguing that a sighting anywhere applied to all. Ibn ʿĀbidīn, for example, surveyed the various opinions within the *madhhab* before concluding "the relied-upon and preferred (*al-muʿtamad al-rājiḥ*) [opinion] among us is that [difference in horizons] is given no consideration. This is the *ẓāhir al-riwāya*."[99] The classic statement of this position can be found in Ibn al-Humām's *Fatḥ al-Qadīr*:

> If [a sighting of the new moon] is established in a city (*miṣr*), it is binding upon the rest of the people. So, the sighting of the people of the West obliges the people of the East according to the dominant position of the *madhhab*. It is [objected by some] that this changes when there is a difference in horizons, because the legal cause is the month, and its being effected for one people due to a sighting does not entail its being effected for others when there is a difference in horizons. [In this, they say] it becomes akin to when

[98] Al-Qāsimī explains his relationship to Bakhīt's text in terms of a series of coincidences: he was motivated to write about the topic as a result of the exact same circumstance (the controversy over the report from Aswan in 1910) and both scholars independently came to the same conclusions.

[99] Muḥammad Amīn Ibn ʿĀbidīn, "Tanbīh al-Ghāfil wa-l-Wasnān ʿalā Aḥkām Hilāl Ramaḍān," in *Arbaʿa Rasāʾil fī Hilāl Khayr al-Shuhūr* (Beirut: Dār Ibn Ḥazm, 2000), 107.

> the sun reaches the meridian [at one place but not another] or sets on one people and not others: the noontime prayer or the sunset prayer are obligatory for the first group, but not the other one. The reason [for our position] is that the generality of the address in [the Prophet's command], "Fast," is linked to *any* unspecified sighting. . . . The sighting of one people fulfills what is meant by "sighting" [in the hadith]. As such, the general ruling to which it is connected obtains. So, the obligation is universal, as opposed to [the cases of] noontime or sunset.[100]

This is a succinct statement of the stance of the Ḥanafī school, but it needed to contend with the evidence of the (especially Shāfiʿī) opposition, namely the authentic hadith that recounted the story of Kurayb being sent to Syria to visit the governor Muʿāwiya in order take care of some business on behalf of Umm al-Faḍl. While there, he saw the new moon of Ramadan on the eve of a Friday. At the end of the month, he returned to Medina only to find that they had not started observing Ramadan until Saturday, that is a day after the Syrians. Upon being asked about this by the famous Companion ʿAbd Allāh b. ʿAbbās, Kurayb informed him that he and many others had seen the new moon on the Friday eve, and they all, the governor Muʿāwiya included, fasted the next day. ʿAbd Allāh b. ʿAbbās responded that he would continue to abide by his local sighting in Medina a day later and not follow the Syrian sighting. Kurayb asked him, "Does it not suffice for you that Muʿāwiya sighted the new moon and fasted [on Friday]?" ʿAbd Allāh b. ʿAbbās responded, "No, this is what the Prophet, peace be upon him, commanded us."[101]

In an attempt to vindicate the Ḥanafī school, Ibn al-Humām addressed this potential objection head-on. In doing so, he introduced to the debate the question that is bound to follow: how are reports of sightings to be validated? In other words, what are the conditions under which they are considered binding on people receiving the news in another locale? Or simply stated, how are such reports to be scrutinized and authenticated? The answer, as we will see, is that reports are considered valid and binding when they are in line with a strict set of procedural constraints which preserve the authority of local qadis, and the integrity of their standards of evidence.

100 Ibn al-Humām, *Fatḥ al-Qadīr*, 2:313–14, emphasis added.

101 Related in the hadith compilations of Muslim, Abū Dāwūd, al-Tirmidhī, al-Nasāʾī, and Aḥmad b. Ḥanbal. The text of the tradition can also be found in Ibn ʿĀbidīn, "Tanbīh al-Ghāfil wa-l-Wasnān," 106; Ibn al-Humām, *Fatḥ al-Qadīr*, 2:314.

In response to invocations of the hadith of Kurayb, Ibn al-Humām admits its authenticity but contends that

> it does not contain a proof of anything (*lā dalīla fīhi*). If that which transpired according to [the narrator Kurayb's] wording had happened amongst us, neither would we pass a judgment based on it. This is because [Kurayb] did not testify to the testimony of another, nor to the ruling of the *ḥākim* (judge). If it is said, "His reporting that Muʿāwiya fasted implies [the above] because he is the ruler (*al-imām*)," the answer is that he did not present it phrased as a testimony. Even if this [last point] were to be granted, though, he is only one person, and such a testimony does not compel the qadi to rule [in accordance with it]. God the Exalted and Most High knows best. And taking the dominant position (*al-ẓāhir*) of the *madhhab* is more cautious.[102]

The matter is stated in more general terms, abstracted from the specific details contained in the hadith, as follows:

> Those who saw the new moon later are only obliged [to act on the earlier sighting] if [it] is established among them by way of an "appropriately-obligating method" (*ṭarīq mūjib*). This, to the extent that if a group of people testify that the people of such-and-such a city saw the new moon of Ramadan a day before you, and fasted, and today is the thirtieth by their reckoning, if [the people of the town receiving the news] do not sight the new moon of Shawwāl that night, it is not permissible for them to [celebrate] the Feast the next day,[103] nor may they skip the *tarāwīḥ* prayer[104] that night. This is because the group did not testify to a sighting themselves, nor did they testify to the testimony of others. They merely related (*innamā ḥakū*) the sighting of others. Had they instead testified that two people had testified to sighting the new moon that night in the presence of the qadi of the other town, and that the qadi had ruled in favour of their testimony, it would have been permissible for *this* qadi to also rule in favour of their

[102] Ibn al-Humām, *Fatḥ al-Qadīr*, 2:314.

[103] Note that if they would have followed the news of the earlier sighting, the next day would automatically be the celebration of ʿĪd al-Fiṭr (the Feast) because the month would have completed its thirty days. Instead, they are tasked with endeavoring to sight the new moon as they would normally on the eve of the thirtieth of Ramadan. If it is not seen, as in the case specified by Ibn al-Humām, they are to fast another day.

[104] Ritual group prayers performed during the month of Ramadan.

> testimony. This is because the ruling of a qadi is a conclusive proof, and [this group] has testified to it.[105]

The key portion of this passage is the assertion that there are some methods of transmission that compel those who receive the report to act upon it, while others do not hold up to scrutiny and are thus inconsequential in the eyes of the law. The prevailing Ḥanafī tradition, in other words, held that transmissions of reports of new moon sightings were only binding upon the receiving population if they were transmitted by an appropriately obligating method (*ṭarīq mūjib*). But the appropriateness of the method was linked exclusively to the authority and oversight of the courts, and their mechanisms for regulating the world in accordance with precise procedural standards. A *ṭarīq mūjib*, on Ibn al-Humām's reading, therefore, must be a testimony of either (a) others' testimony of a sighting or (b) the ruling of a qadi. These were counterposed to mere retellings, or reports (*ḥikāyāt*, *akhbār*), which carried no weight because they did not travel through the recognized sites of legitimacy. The stipulation of a *ṭarīq mūjib*, therefore, subjects the report to disciplined procedural constraints, and not purely an epistemic judgment of whether or not the report is true.

This was long the dominant position within the Ḥanafī school, but there was a view, within the unwieldy mass of opinions, counteropinions, justifications, and argumentation that characterizes all *madhhab*s, which cut against the grain of this procedural emphasis. Shams al-Aʾimma al-Ḥalwānī had put forth a third possibility for a binding report, and this one seemed to constitute a departure from the institutional orientation of Ibn al-Humām's two. "If a report spreads out in overwhelming numbers (*istafāḍa*) confirming what is [taking place] among those of another town, the ruling of that town obliges [the town receiving the news]."[106]

This seems to open the door ever so slightly to make room for reports outside the judiciary. Subsequently, however, Ibn ʿĀbidīn chose to interpret al-Ḥalwānī's remarks in a manner that assimilated them to one of Ibn al-Humām's cases, and thus also his insistence that all legitimacy flow through the courts.

[105] Ibn al-Humām, *Fatḥ al-Qadīr*, 2:314.
[106] Quoted in Ibn ʿĀbidīn, "Tanbīh al-Ghāfil wa-l-Wasnān," 109. Ibn ʿĀbidīn mentions that the famous al-Shurunbulālī related something similar.

> However, when this *istifāḍa* is at the level of a mass-transmitted report (*al-khabar al-mutawātir*), and it establishes that the people of a given town fasted on such-and-such a day, it must be acted upon. This is because what is meant [here] is a town in which there is a legitimate *ḥākim* (judge), as is customary in the Islamic lands. Since their fast must be based on the ruling of their legitimate *ḥākim*, what is meant by *istifāḍa* is [simply] conveying this ruling. This is stronger than a mere testimony that the people of a given town saw the new moon on such-and-such a day, and fasted on such-and-such a day. Such a testimony does not yield certainty, and so is not accepted. [This latter is opposed to] testifying to a legal ruling or to the testimony of others, because these are testimonies that are acknowledged in the law. Otherwise, it is merely reporting (*ikhbār*).[107]

In line with his impulse to systemize the *madhhab*, Ibn ʿĀbidīn takes it as his task to harmonize the dominant opinions of the school as best he can. Despite his attempt to do so, however, he is equally aware that these two opinions sit rather uneasily together. Though he is explicit that they do not contradict one another, he is quick to suggest a resolution in case this claim remains unconvincing.

> If we concede the existence of a contradiction, we must act on [the position that] is explicitly stated to be correct. The imam al-Ḥalwānī is one of the most esteemed shaykhs of the *madhhab*. And it has been said explicitly that [his position] is the correct one in the school of our associates. I have written in my commentary on *al-Baḥr*: "What is meant by *istifāḍa* is the mass transmission (*tawātur*) of a report from those . . . in one town to another town, not simply an unrestricted *istifāḍa*."[108]

In his quest for a comprehensive examination of the issue, Ibn ʿĀbidīn has broached the possibility of a mode of transmitting reports that resides outside the strictures of in-court testimony. However, his drive toward reconciling the different jurists of the school takes over, leaving him vacillating curiously between the two orientations. He prefers the position which aligns al-Ḥalwānī with Ibn al-Humām's proceduralism, but sensing the tension between the two, and that his attempt at reconciliation has in all likelihood

107 Ibn ʿĀbidīn, "Tanbīh al-Ghāfil wa-l-Wasnān," 109.
108 Ibn ʿĀbidīn, "Tanbīh al-Ghāfil wa-l-Wasnān," 109–10.

been less than satisfactory, he feels methodologically compelled to accept al-Ḥalwānī's position. Even this, though, he does in a heavily constrained way, reading it in a manner that demands the very high bar of *tawātur* (mass transmission which guarantees certainty)—and not the looser, unspecified *istifāḍa*—for any satisfactory transmission of a report.

When Bakhīt arrives at his discussion of this issue,[109] he exploits this discrepancy evident in Ibn ʿĀbidīn. To him, the contradiction is evident, and the unconditioned, literal meaning of al-Ḥalwānī should be thought to be determinative (*iṭlāq al-nuṣūṣ ḥujja*), and therefore given priority over both Ibn al-Humām's exclusive proceduralism and Ibn ʿĀbidīn's attempt to tame the permissiveness evident in al-Ḥalwānī's original quote. For him, there is nothing in the meaning of *istifāḍa* which entails that the content of a report thus conveyed must make reference to the ruling of a *ḥākim*. Nor can he accept the stipulation that what is meant by *istifāḍa* is actually *tawātur*.

On the first count, he makes it a point to disagree with Ibn al-Humām's statement of the *madhhab*, arguing that the case the latter cites as inadmissible—a testimony from a group of people from one town that the people of another town saw, but did not necessarily testify to, a sighting of the new moon—is a perfectly valid method of transmission. Significantly, in the case of fasting, the ruling of a judge is not a necessary component of the way that Bakhīt envisions a modern system of report transmission to work. "It is sufficient to transmit a report in a manner that furnishes a preponderant likelihood (*ghalabat al-ẓann*) that the moon was sighted. *This* is the *ṭarīq mūjib*. . . . *The criterion is a correct report [because] this is what yields preponderance.*"[110] On Bakhīt's understanding, reports of fasting do not depend on a judge at all, and they are to be evaluated for their "correctness." This represents another striking turn away from the long-dominant tradition of Ḥanafī proceduralism toward epistemological criteria. No longer is it the integrity of the material, court-regulated procedure that determines the validity of the report, but rather its correspondence to the truth of the matter.

On the second count, Bakhīt accuses Ibn ʿĀbidīn of taking liberties in relaying the opinion on *istifāḍa* as originally found in the work of al-Raḥmatī—whose condition was not that the threshold be raised to *tawātur*, but rather to signal caution against accepting widespread reports without knowing who spread them. Bakhīt endorses this latter position and interprets

[109] Bakhīt al-Muṭīʿī, *Irshād Ahl al-Milla ilā Ithbāt al-Ahilla*, 144–65.
[110] Bakhīt al-Muṭīʿī, *Irshād Ahl al-Milla ilā Ithbāt al-Ahilla*, 147, emphasis added.

this to mean that "if we know who spread the report, and that he is morally upright, the report is sufficient on its own."[111] As it turns out, it is not so much the quality of being widespread that is solely determinative for Bakhīt, but rather its being related by a trustworthy member of society. In this, he seems to have reversed Ibn ʿĀbidīn's "upgrading" of *istifāḍa* to *tawātur*, instead opting to subject reports, both singular and mass-transmitted, to the full complement of standards of hadith transmission. Having now removed the oversight of the qadis, he concludes, just as he had before, that "the mode of conveying [reports of the new moon of Ramadan] is the same as the mode of relating [Prophetic] reports."[112]

Taken together, these critiques serve again to overthrow the precisely delineated system of procedures and court jurisdiction that had long defined the Ḥanafī position on this issue. In its stead, Bakhīt once more substitutes as the central criterion the truth of the content of the report itself as determined by the norms of hadith scholarship.

The Inert Telegraph: Language and Religion

The motivation behind the aforementioned shift is clear when we recall the original question that motivated the treatise itself, namely how to evaluate reports that arrive via telegraph. Since telegraph reports arrive without testimony of the sort envisioned by the prevailing tradition, they posed a difficult problem for a society in which they had come to feature prominently. This is why Bakhīt is eager to point out that this new manner of dealing with reports applies to correspondence (*mukātaba*) as much as it does to spoken communication (*mushāfaha*, among which he includes phonographs and telephones).[113]

111 Bakhīt al-Muṭīʿī, *Irshād Ahl al-Milla ilā Ithbāt al-Ahilla*, 150.

112 Bakhīt al-Muṭīʿī, *Irshād Ahl al-Milla ilā Ithbāt al-Ahilla*, 151.

113 Bakhīt describes this spoken communication as follows: "As for the report by *mushāfaha*, it is that a morally upright person says to someone else that he saw the new-moon, or that so-and-so upright person informed him that he or another upright person saw the new-moon, or that a large group saw it. Among the class of reports by *mushāfaha* are reports through the phonograph—the instrument well-known today—for that which is heard through it is the speech of the speaker itself, repeated by the instrument such that it relates the voice of the speaker precisely. When the speaker is known to be upright by the listener, and the latter hears the report, fasting is religiously mandatory on him. Similarly, for reports transmitted by the telephone: When the speaker and his voice are known, and his report is trusted, fasting is obligatory." Bakhīt al-Muṭīʿī, *Irshād Ahl al-Milla ilā Ithbāt al-Ahilla*, 151. For his views on the phonograph, see "Fī Aḥkām Qirāʾat al-Fūnūghrāf," in *Thalātha Rasāʾil* (Cairo: Jamʿiyyat al-Azhar al-ʿIlmiyya, 1932), 1–10. For the reservations of previous scholars, including Ḥusayn al-Jisr, see C. Snouck Hurgronje, *Islam und Phonograph* (Batavia, 1900).

> As for the report via correspondence, it is that an upright person (*ʿadl*) writes to someone else that he saw the new moon or that so-and-so upright person informed him that he saw the new moon, and sends this letter with a specific person or through the well-known postal system. When the recipient recognizes the handwriting or the seal of the sender, and knows of his moral probity, fasting is obligatory on [the recipient].
>
> From the species of written reports are telegraphic messages, whether they be by wire or by radio. Just as the informant in spoken reports of all types is the speaker, who possesses the voice, and not the phonograph or telephone, similarly the sender of written messages is the informant. It is of him that moral probity is demanded. So, when the recipient realizes that this message, be it a letter or a telegraph message, issues from the sender, because he is morally upright, it must be acted upon. For correspondence must be acted upon in religious matters, just like spoken communication.
>
> As for the intermediary in messages of this sort, he is not the sender and so no attention is paid to him. It is all the same whether they are upright or not, Muslim or non-Muslim. The postman and the telegraph operator are both [merely] means of sending the message from the sender. They are neither the sender nor the informant.[114]

Technologies, on Bakhīt's understanding, do not in any way impinge on the truth value of reports, whose veracity is established based on the integrity of their sources. The particular means for conveying these reports are separate from, and immaterial to, what is really decisive: the content of the reports.

This tendency of Bakhīt's to conceive of knowledge transmission as independent of all sorts of materiality relies on a specifically modern notion of language as abstract, immaterial, and communicable between otherwise private minds. Just as knowledge itself came to be representational, according to Timothy Mitchell, so too did the language required to transmit that knowledge. The paradigmatic symbol of this conception, according to Mitchell, was the telegraph itself. As evidence, Mitchell quotes Michel Bréal, professor of comparative grammar at the Collège de France arguing in 1897, that "Words are signs. They have no other existence than the signals of the wireless telegraph."[115] What is important for Mitchell's documentation of the representationalist turn is to point out that, on this

[114] Bakhīt al-Muṭīʿī, *Irshād Ahl al-Milla ilā Ithbāt al-Ahilla*, 151–52.
[115] Timothy Mitchell, *Colonising Egypt* (Berkeley: University of California Press, 1991), 140.

understanding, "Linguistic meaning was to be found . . . neither within the material of the words themselves nor simply within the mind of the individual. It lay outside both, as a 'structure' with an 'ideal existence.'"[116] This fits well with the move toward representationalism we identified in chapter 4. What is relevant to us in this chapter, however, are his comments about linguistic representation itself. Because words were no longer "living organisms" as Mitchell understands them to have been on older theories of language, their sole purpose was now to represent the metaphysical linguistic realm proper. The purpose of linguistic representation, in turn, is to enable "communication between speaking subjects."[117] Just as words, then, are mere vehicles by which meaning is conveyed, all the more so for the signals of the telegraph—the symbol of this new conception—or, indeed, any of the emergent communications technologies of the period, such as the telephone or the phonograph. They are all equally inert with respect to the conveying of reports.

Bakhīt is explicit that this is how he envisions legitimate knowledge transmission. It is not that the courts have any role in establishing or regulating actionable knowledge, but rather knowledge is conveyed directly from one individual to another, "whether through spoken communication or through correspondence":[118]

> If a witness reports [a sighting of the new moon] to someone else, and he is morally upright, the truth of the reporter with regards to his report becomes overwhelmingly likely for the recipient. Then, it becomes as if the recipient saw the new moon himself, so fasting becomes obligatory on him. . . . It is not that the report of the witness obliged anyone else, but rather that the witness, based on his sighting of the new moon, is obliged to fast due to the existence of the proof of obligation within him (*ʿindahu*). If he then informs someone else of that, the proof is now also found . . . in this other person. Fasting is therefore obligatory for him. The one who saw the new moon is like the narrator of a hadith who relates the proof of a shariʿa ruling, which then obligates everyone it reaches.[119]

[116] Mitchell, *Colonising Egypt*, 141.
[117] Mitchell, *Colonising Egypt*, 141.
[118] Bakhīt al-Muṭīʿī, *Irshād Ahl al-Milla ilā Ithbāt al-Ahilla*, 151.
[119] Bakhīt al-Muṭīʿī, *Irshād Ahl al-Milla ilā Ithbāt al-Ahilla*, 30.

Because the reports transmitted by telegraph are "religious reports," then, they are to be treated just like Prophetic traditions, according to the same standards of transmission.

But the meaning of religion itself was being recast in Muslim circles at this moment, in a manner that dovetailed well with the focus on abstraction and immateriality evident in the discussion of the telegraph. Encounters between Europe and the Islamic world gave rise to vigorous debates about the nature of religion, its compatibility with the modern sciences, and the status of Islam in particular. An early salvo in this debate was *Refutation of the Materialists* of Jamāl al-Dīn al-Afghānī, the famous itinerant pan-Islamic activist and teacher of ʿAbduh.[120] ʿAbduh translated the work, originally written in Persian, into Arabic so that it could be widely read in Egypt and the Arabic-speaking world. In that work, al-Afghānī positioned himself as a critic of what he thought was a far too concessionary stance taken up by Sir Sayyid Ahmad Khan in British India. Decrying the materialism of what he called the *neicheri* (naturalist) sect, al-Afghānī was interested in reasserting the role of religion in a world that he saw as being dominated by material considerations. A complex figure, whose scattered writings have often given rise to contradictory readings, what is nonetheless clear from al-Afghānī's text is that his notion of religion relies upon the positing of an opposition between it, on the one hand, and the impious focus on nature to the exclusion of the divine, on the other. As Abdulkader Tayob has remarked, for al-Afghānī, "Religion in this regard was the antithesis of naturalism; its essence lay in the existence of a higher reality."[121]

Charles Taylor has commented that the obviousness of the distinction between the natural and supernatural (or worldly and abstract) is a peculiar feature of modern life.[122] This seems to characterize quite well the unspoken background of the debate between al-Afghānī and Khan. That is to say, despite al-Afghānī's condemnation of Khan for what he takes to be a system of thought that effectively alienates Muslim society from the divine, he shares with him an ontology in which the distinction between natural and supernatural is both intelligible and given. As we move into the modern period, then, figures like al-Afghānī provide us with evidence that religion was coming to be increasingly understood among Muslims as that which pertains to a

[120] For a translation of this work, see Nikki R. Keddie, *An Islamic Response to Imperialism* (Berkeley: University of California Press, 1968).
[121] Tayob, *Religion in Modern Islamic Discourse*, 54.
[122] Taylor, *A Secular Age*, 14.

transcendent realm conceptually distinct from the world. Bakhīt himself studied philosophy with al-Afghānī, and though he later expressed opposition to the reformist ideas expressed by al-Afghānī and his disciples ʿAbduh and Riḍā, we have seen that he was far from untouched by the changes in the basic categories of thought that structured Muslims' engagements with their own tradition.

The old *fiqhī* category of "religious matters," then, is reconceptualized by Bakhīt in a manner that reflects this new understanding of religion. On his reading, the *umūr dīniyya* are abstract epistemological entities that circulate from individual to individual, unaffected by the social-material world in which they travel—whether the technologies through which they are conveyed or the stipulated procedures, modes of regulation, and documentation of the courts.

Conclusion

By the time Bakhīt revisited the *umūr dīniyya* in 1910, Egypt had been under British occupation since 1882. Colonial administrators felt a keen responsibility to remake Egypt into a productive, orderly state, a burden that is well captured in their writings. For figures like Lord Cromer, British agent and consul-general from 1883 to 1907, the prevailing legal system was one of the central targets of reform. Cromer was particularly concerned that Islam "crystallises religion and law into one inseparable and immutable whole, with the result that all elasticity is taken away from the social system."[123] The creation of a space in which religion could make its appearance free of legal constraints, then, was a clear desideratum of colonial policy. It is this preoccupation that also underlays and informs Bakhīt's argument in this chapter. Integral to his argument is the insistence that it proceed in line with the provisions set out in Law Number 25, which specifies that courts may only deal with matters in which there is disagreement (*al-nizāʿ*) and opposition (*al-khuṣūma*) between two parties.[124] In other words, recalling Ibn al-Shaṭṭ earlier in our chapter, the courts deal exclusively with matters of *dunyā* and, as our analysis in this chapter shows, have no role to play in matters of

[123] Cromer, *Modern Egypt*, 2:135.
[124] Bakhīt al-Muṭīʿī, *Irshād*, 166.

dīn.[125] Pace Asad, for whom the effect of secularization was to locate religion within the defined space of the shariʿa courts, the domain of religion for Bakhīt is outside of the court system altogether.

It is noteworthy that, for Cromer, the task of the colonial apparatus in Egypt was "to rule without having the appearance of ruling."[126] This meant that the reform of the shariʿa was to be carried out by natives, and it is indeed in the internal discourse among Muslim thinkers on the category of religion that the imprint of the colonial encounter is deeply felt.

The Ḥanafī school had long made room for both epistemological considerations (via references to certainty and truth) and procedural ones.[127] The weight of the tradition, however, placed emphasis on the latter as a mechanism of social regulation. Consider, for example, the case of a person who saw the Ramadan crescent but had his testimony rejected by the judge. Even as the Ḥanafīs held that the witness should himself fast "in consideration of the truth within him," they demanded the judge's ruling be respected by the rest of the community.[128] When it comes to his intervention in the *umūr dīniyya*, Bakhīt's contribution is to eliminate altogether the insistent Ḥanafī concern with court procedure and authority. Importantly, this shift is made natural—and not just possible—because of the underlying transformation in the very conception of *dīn*, which heavily conditioned Bakhīt's understanding of the *umūr dīniyya*. The *umūr dīniyya*, as we have seen, have now been recast as entirely separate from the world, the boundary between "this world" and the "other world" now a solid and impermeable one, at odds with its more complex and hybrid premodern instantiation. This was accomplished by assimilating the *umūr dīniyya* entirely to the class of reports known as *riwāyāt* that included the traditions of the Prophet, in contradistinction to the *shahādāt* which were by necessity subject to the judgment of the qadi. These "religious matters," then, belonged to a domain outside the authority of qadis and their courts. Religion, on this reading, occupied an immaterial realm which was not to be interfered with by non-"religious" (i.e.,

[125] Recall that Ibn al-Shaṭṭ's argument is to distinguish between the *umūr dīniyya* and *shahādāt*, not to deny that the *umūr dīniyya* have any place in the courts.

[126] Cromer, *Modern Egypt*, 2:126.

[127] For a development of this line of argument, see Junaid Quadri, "Correspondence, Constructivism, and Representation: Variant Approaches to Astronomical Knowledge in Islamic Legal Texts," *Comparative Studies of South Asia, Africa and the Middle East* 39, no. 3 (December 1, 2019): 513–27.

[128] Al-Marghīnānī, *al-Hidāya*, 2:320–21.

worldly) institutions and technologies. Instead of a reading on which the *umūr dīniyya* were thought to be "religious" because they were simply oriented toward other-worldly considerations, Bakhīt accepts, and participates in the carving out of, a dichotomy which understands their "religious-ness" to render them entirely ineligible for the worldly adjudication of the courts.

Conclusion

When Muṣṭafā Ṣabrī arrived in Egypt, the intellectual and political scene he found there left him dissatisfied and pining for a lost Istanbul. The former *Shaykh al-Islām* of the Ottoman lands had fled the capital just as the sultanate was being abolished in late 1922, and a year before Mustafa Kemal Atatürk's proclamation of the Turkish republic. Ṣabrī was a star of the learned religious establishment, the *ilmiye*, and advanced rapidly through the ranks, ultimately occupying the highest religious office in the empire. He was also a leading politician and prominent public figure during the years of intrigue that followed the Young Turk revolution, galvanizing the ulama to political activity first in alliance with the Committee of Union and Progress (CUP), and then in a newly formed party of his own that split from the CUP and positioned itself in opposition to them.[1] Despite his talents and achievements, by the end of this period of tumult, Ṣabrī had both lost his office and was forced to leave his homeland. His first port of call was Cairo, but his stay there was short. He quickly moved on to a series of destinations in the Middle East and Europe before ultimately settling in Western Thrace in 1927, some four years after the Treaty of Lausanne.

We do not know the precise reason for Ṣabrī's quick departure from Egypt, but what is clear is that he found it not quite as hospitable a site for his intellectual and political views as he would have liked. His central complaint was that Egypt had been overcome by European culture and thought. The "disease of *taqlīd* of the West . . . which has afflicted Muslims and hastened their demise" was especially widespread in Egypt, equally among those who willingly imitated Westerners without a clear sense of who or what they were imitating as well as those who insistently denied they were being mimics, but nonetheless fell under the sway of their unthinking compatriots without knowing.[2] One particular example that struck him was the prevalence of the

[1] For a detailed reading of Ṣabrī's political career, see Amit Bein, *Ottoman Ulema, Turkish Republic: Agents of Change and Guardians of Tradition* (Stanford, CA: Stanford University Press, 2011), 77–104.

[2] Muṣṭafā Ṣabrī, *Mawqif al-Bashar Taḥta Sulṭān al-Qadar* (Beirut: Dār al-Hijra, 1950), 7.

Transformations of Tradition. Junaid Quadri, Oxford University Press (2021). © Oxford University Press.
DOI: 10.1093/oso/9780190077044.003.0007

European hat. Ṣabrī noted with disdain that even men of religion (*rijāl al-dīn*) downplayed the harms of adopting European dress. When they did object to it, however, they largely did so on nationalist grounds instead of considering it an offence against religion.[3] "They exclude imitation of disbelievers (*tashabbuh bi-l-kuffār*) from the markers of disbelief (*kufr*), despite the proclamation of Islam that 'whoever imitates a people (*qawm*) is one of them.' It is as if they saw the word *qawm* and took the comment to pertain to nationalism (*qawmiyya*) and not Islam."[4]

It is likely that Ṣabrī had in mind two moments in twentieth-century Egypt: first, the Transvaal fatwa in which Muḥammad ʿAbduh had already pronounced on the permissibility of wearing the European hat;[5] and second, the controversies that erupted at the Azhar and the Dār al-ʿUlūm in early 1926, in which students cast off their mandated turbans and robes in favor of the suit and *ṭarbūsh* as a statement of nationalist modernity.[6] There were in fact prominent voices at the time calling for the reinstatement of the dress code, but it is true that the *ṭarbūsh* and suit were adopted as significations of a modern subject. Whether one preferred the hat or the *ṭarbūsh*, however, Ṣabrī considered both of these capitulations—in the first case, to the overt display of European sartoriality and manners on the body of the Egyptian subject and in the Egyptian public sphere; in the second, to a nationalist consciousness he associated with Europe. In Ṣabrī's mind, Europeanization was interchangeable with modernization, and so he explained the cultural changes that had beset Egyptian society by reference to Egyptians' preoccupation with the new and modern. "People are naturally disposed to love innovation, for as the famous saying goes, 'Every new thing has its delight (*li-kulli jadīd ladhdha*).'"[7]

[3] Ṣabrī does admit that some objected to the wearing of European hats on Islamic grounds, but they were too ambivalent for his liking, vacillating between considering it forbidden (*ḥarām*) or simply discouraged (*makrūh*). Ṣabrī, *Mawqif al-Bashar Taḥta Sulṭān al-Qadar*, 7.

[4] Ṣabrī, *Mawqif al-Bashar Taḥta Sulṭān al-Qadar*, 7. For the history of the "proclamation" quoted by Ṣabrī, actually a hadith, see Youshaa Patel, "'Whoever Imitates a People Becomes One of Them': A Hadith and Its Interpreters," *Islamic Law and Society* 25, no. 4 (October 19, 2018): 359–426.

[5] A translation of the fatwa has been published in Charles C. Adams, "Muḥammad ʿAbduh and the Transvaal Fatwā," in *The Macdonald Presentation Volume, a Tribute to Duncan Black Macdonald, Consisting of Articles by Former Students, Presented to Him on His Seventieth Birthday, April 9, 1933* (Princeton, NJ: Princeton University Press, 1933). See also Jakob Skovgaard-Petersen, *Defining Islam for the Egyptian State: Muftis and Fatwas of the Dār al-Iftā* (Leiden: Brill, 1997), 123–33.

[6] This episode has been analyzed in Wilson Chacko Jacob, *Working Out Egypt: Effendi Masculinity and Subject Formation in Colonial Modernity, 1870–1940* (Durham, NC: Duke University Press, 2011), 205–15.

[7] Ṣabrī, *Mawqif al-Bashar Taḥta Sulṭān al-Qadar*, 7–8.

This applied as much to what was in Egyptians' heads as to what was on them. Ṣabrī was dismayed at not only the hold that nationalism had on Egyptian minds but also the widespread interest in the thought of Darwin in the country that has been so ably documented by Marwa Elshakry.[8] He considered attempts to reconcile the Qurʾan to Darwinism, in the spirit of the *tafsīr ʿilmī* genre discussed in chapter 3, blatant misappropriations of Qurʾanic verses that stretched their semantic ranges beyond acceptable boundaries.[9] But the topic that most exercised him was the theological question of free will and predestination. Upon arriving in Egypt, Ṣabrī came across a three-volume work titled *The Question of Free Will and Predestination, or The Secret of the Backwardness of the Muslims* (Ar. *ʿIlm al-Qaḍāʾ wa-l-Qadar aw Sirr Taʾakhkhur al-Muslimīn*), which argued, as the title suggests, that Islamic civilization lagged behind Europe in large part due to the prevailing Muslim belief in divine determinism. Ṣabrī quotes from the following offending passage from the text:

> Perhaps the reason for [Europeans' advancement] is that their hearts have not been dominated by a belief in fate the way Muslims' have . . . When one observes the various Muslim nations, one sees in most cases only division, mutual enmity, jealousy, and backwardness. One also finds that every person suffering from a sickness becomes chronically ill, a cure scarcely to be found. And so, man gives up on the possibility that there could be a cure for his disease. The reason for this is the lethargy that is a product of their upside-down understanding of fate.[10]

This was, of course, a reductive reading of Islamic (and, for that matter, Christian) theology, but it facilitated the setting up of a civilizational opposition that was a hallmark of this discourse, whose tone and parameters were set by French authors who came to be widely read in Egypt. The most egregious example is that of Daniel Kimon whose book *La Pathologie de l'Islam et les Moyens de le Détruire* was quoted in the three-volume work Ṣabrī found as saying, "The Muḥammadan religion is a leprosy that has spread among

[8] Marwa Elshakry, *Reading Darwin in Arabic, 1860–1950* (Chicago: University of Chicago Press, 2014).

[9] Ṣabrī, *Mawqif al-Bashar Taḥta Sulṭān al-Qadar*, 7–8.

[10] Ṣabrī, *Mawqif al-Bashar Taḥta Sulṭān al-Qadar*, 13–14. An excerpt containing this quote is also found in Hanotaux's article. The Arabic translation of Hanotaux's article is reproduced in Muḥammad Rashīd Riḍā, *Tārīkh al-Ustādh al-Imām al-Shaykh Muḥammad ʿAbduh* (Cairo: Dār al-Faḍīla, 2006), 2:401–414, immediately followed by ʿAbduh's responses.

people, decimating them. Or, rather, it is a proliferating disease, a paralysis, and a stupefying madness that induces man to laziness and lethargy."[11] But even the relatively more even-handed Gabriel Hanotaux, a former French Minister of Foreign Affairs, engaged in a civilizational discourse transparently positioned in the service of French colonial interests in North Africa. Just as Ernest Renan had done a decade and a half earlier in "L'Islamisme et la Science," Hanotaux's 1900 article in *Le Journal* posited a stark contrast between Europe, represented as Aryan and Christian, and the Muslim World, represented as Semitic and Islamic. The contrast he drew, though, was more explicitly theological than Renan's. For Hanotaux, whereas Christianity valued the human—through the doctrine of the Trinity which provides room for God's immanence, and the belief in man's free will—Islam stressed instead God's Transcendence and Omnipotence.[12]

Both provocations drew strong responses in Egypt, but the Hanotaux piece was clearly the principal work of interest.[13] ʿAbduh read it on his commute home the very day the Arabic translation was published in the daily *al-Muʾayyad*. He spent the rest of the evening penning a rejoinder that was immediately published in three consecutive instalments of the journal.[14] In his response, ʿAbduh refuted Hanotaux's identification of Islam with determinism by referring to the Qurʾan. He pointed in particular to the Qurʾanic verse that responds harshly to idolaters who evade responsibility for their idolatry by pointing to God's Omnipotence, protesting, "Had God willed, we would not have ascribed partners unto God."[15] To the contrary, ʿAbduh says, the Qurʾan supports the doctrine of acquisition (*al-kasb*) and free will (*al-ikhtiyār*) in some sixty-four places. Those passages that appear deterministic do not apply to human responsibility, but should instead be thought of as general "laws of existence (*nawāmīs al-kawn*)," as for example the verse, "Had thy Lord willed, He would have made mankind one community."[16]

[11] Ṣabrī, *Mawqif al-Bashar Taḥta Sulṭān al-Qadar*, 13.

[12] Charles C. Adams, *Islam and Modernism in Egypt: A Study of the Modern Reform Movement Inaugurated by Muḥammad ʿAbduh* (London: Oxford University Press, 1933), 86–90.

[13] For a careful and comprehensive reading of the entire affair, see Ammeke Kateman, *Muḥammad ʿAbduh and His Interlocutors: Conceptualizing Religion in a Globalizing World* (Leiden: Brill, 2019), 163–85. Kimon's article drew only subsidiary attention, mostly of interest in Egypt because Hanotaux had cited it. Many Egyptians construed Hanotaux's citation of Kimon as an approval of his views, a misreading that Hanotaux was at pains to deny in follow-up responses.

[14] Riḍā, *Tārīkh al-Ustādh al-Imām*, 2:400.

[15] Riḍā, *Tārīkh al-Ustādh al-Imām*, 2:422. The translation of the verse (*al-Anʿām* 6:148) is from Seyyed Hossein Nasr, ed., *The Study Quran: A New Translation and Commentary* (New York: HarperOne, 2017), 396.

[16] *Hūd* 11:118; Nasr, *The Study Quran*, 587.

As one might expect, Ṣabrī was strongly opposed to what he took to be the concessions ʿAbduh made to the libertarian position, concluding that the Egyptian mufti had effectively adopted the Muʿtazilī position that was heterodox to those working within latter-day Sunnism.[17] Recourse to Muʿtazilism was seen by Ṣabrī as a strategy adopted by some Muslims to stem the critique of Islamic theology advanced by the likes of Hanotaux, a critique whose force was second only to European objections on women's issues.[18] For Ṣabrī, then, this was simply further evidence that Egypt was overrun by a desire to prove Islam's compatibility with European demands.

Ṣabrī, of course, was not inclined to look favorably on ʿAbduh, but when he came across the printed version of a lecture Bakhīt had delivered in Cairo, he had higher hopes. Referring to him as the "teacher of teachers in Egypt," Ṣabrī read Bakhīt's lecture with the expectation that it would offer both clarification on an issue that remained a point of controversy for Muslim scholars and a riposte to "the negative opinion of the ancient Islamic doctrine of predestination that is virtually implanted in the minds of moderns."[19] He would, however, come away disappointed on both counts, finding Bakhīt's argumentation both unconvincing and far too conciliatory to the fashions of the day. Bakhīt's basic point was that there is room for human agency if one understands it in a more limited way that did not transgress divine omnipotence, namely by conceptualizing free choice in terms of the connection between human capability (*qudra*, *irāda*) and human action (*afʿāl al-ʿibād*).[20] Ṣabrī attributed this position to the Māturīdī school's notion of "partial will (*irāda juzʾiyya*)." Māturīdism was generally a safe orthodox theological option for latter-day Sunnis—indeed, Ṣabrī says so himself at the outset of his treatise[21]—but Bakhīt's decision to stress this aspect of Māturīdism was read by the Turkish exile as a failure to "dispel the accusation leveled by our modern enemies against the long-transmitted Islamic belief in God's decree."[22] Bakhīt had also suggested that a proper belief in the Islamic doctrine of predestination (*al-qaḍāʾ wa-l-qadar*) supports active human participation

[17] Ṣabrī, *Mawqif al-Bashar Taḥta Sulṭān al-Qadar*, 35, 44–46. Ṣabrī bases his comments not on ʿAbduh's response to Hanotaux, but on his reading of ʿAbduh's famous work, *Risālat al-Tawḥīd*. A translation of that work has been published as Muḥammad ʿAbduh, *The Theology of Unity* (London: Allen and Unwin, 1966).

[18] Ṣabrī, *Mawqif al-Bashar Taḥta Sulṭān al-Qadar*, 22.

[19] Ṣabrī, *Mawqif al-Bashar Taḥta Sulṭān al-Qadar*, 20.

[20] Muḥammad Bakhīt al-Muṭīʿī, "al-Qaḍāʾ wa-l-Qadar," *Al-Hidāya al-Islāmiyya* 2, no. 8 (Muḥarram 1349H): 402; cf. Ṣabrī, *Mawqif al-Bashar Taḥta Sulṭān al-Qadar*, 21.

[21] Ṣabrī, *Mawqif al-Bashar Taḥta Sulṭān al-Qadar*, 6.

[22] Ṣabrī, *Mawqif al-Bashar Taḥta Sulṭān al-Qadar*, 21.

in the world, though some are "ignorant of the reality of divine legislation, fashioning it instead so as to impede human ambition and spread a spirit of laziness and withdrawal from meritorious activity."[23] Ṣabrī read this as a veiled criticism of the prevailing orthodoxy of Ashʿarism, which proposed an "intermediate determinism (*al-jabr al-mutawassiṭ*)"[24] but also as an affirmation of European critics like Hanotaux and Kimon who had used language reminiscent of Bakhīt's to attribute Islam's supposed backwardness to its supposed fatalism.

For his part, Bakhīt positioned his intervention as a point of agreement among all Muslim theological schools. Key to his thinking, however, is the influence of Shihāb al-Dīn al-Ālūsī, the complex nineteenth-century figure who was at once the Ḥanafī mufti of Baghdad and a forerunner of the modernist Salafism of figures like ʿAbduh and Riḍā.[25] As it turns out, Bakhīt had written on this topic already in his commentary on the famous *Kharīda* of al-Dardīr, a theological primer that was a staple of the Azharī curriculum. There, too, he had made reference to al-Ālūsī by citing the Iraqi exegete's understanding of *istiṭāʿa* (human capacity), as presented in his commentary on the Qurʾanic verse that mandated the *ḥajj* pilgrimage on "those who are able."[26] Al-Ālūsī's impact on Bakhīt becomes all the more evident from the latter's citation of two of al-Ālūsī's most important influences: the seventeenth-century hadith scholar and revivalist Ibrāhīm b. Ḥasan al-Kūrānī, and the later doctrine of al-Ashʿarī—the eponym of the Ashʿarī school Ṣabrī was so keen to defend—as expressed in his *al-Ibāna*.[27] The *Ibāna*, generally considered al-Ashʿarī's final work, was praised for its fidelity to scripture by none other

[23] Bakhīt al-Muṭīʿī, "al-Qaḍāʾ wa-l-Qadar," 407; Ṣabrī, *Mawqif al-Bashar Taḥta Sulṭān al-Qadar*, 21. Ṣabrī's excerpt of Bakhīt actually conjoins two separate quotations from Bakhīt. The first half can be found at Bakhīt al-Muṭīʿī, "al-Qaḍāʾ wa-l-Qadar," 395.

[24] Indeed, in his commentary on the *Kharīda* of al-Dardīr, Bakhīt had counterposed the *irāda juzʾiyya* of the Māturīdīs to Ashʿarism. Muḥammad Bakhīt al-Muṭīʿī, *Ḥāshiyat ʿalā Kharīdat al-Tawḥid* (Cairo: Maṭbaʿat al-Islām, 1314H), 66.

[25] For an attempt to make sense of al-Ālūsī's intellectual genealogy and the diverse influences on him, see Basheer M. Nafi, "Abu al-Thanaʾ al-Alusi: An Alim, Ottoman Mufti, and Exegete of the Qurʾan," *International Journal of Middle East Studies* 34, no. 3 (2002): 465–94.

[26] Bakhīt al-Muṭīʿī, *Ḥāshiyat ʿalā Kharīdat al-Tawḥid*, 66.

[27] On al-Kūrānī, see Basheer M. Nafi, "Taṣawwuf and Reform in Pre-Modern Islamic Culture: In Search of Ibrāhīm al-Kūrānī," *Die Welt des Islams* 42, no. 3 (2002): 307–55; John O. Voll, "ʿAbdallah ibn Salim al-Basri and 18th Century Hadith Scholarship," *Die Welt des Islams* 42, no. 3 (2002): 356–72. Al-Kūrānī was associated with a circle of hadith-centric revivalists first studied in detail by John Voll. John Voll, "Muḥammad Ḥayyā al-Sindī and Muḥammad ibn ʿAbd al-Wahhāb: An Analysis of an Intellectual Group in Eighteenth-Century Madīna," *Bulletin of the School of Oriental and African Studies, University of London* 38, no. 1 (1975): 32–39; John O. Voll, "Hadith Scholars and Tariqahs: An Ulama Group in the 18th Century Haramayn and Their Impact in the Islamic World," *Journal of Asian and African Studies* 15, no. 3 (January 1, 1980): 264–73.

than Ibn Taymiyya who, recall from chapter 1, was an important inspiration for twentieth-century Egyptian reformists.[28] In just the way he leaned on al-Marjānī and al-Laknawī, then, Bakhīt once more evinces his propensity to rely on acclaimed senior Ḥanafī authorities who, though they identified as Ḥanafīs, occupied a complex liminal identity, often advancing maverick opinions that coincided with the concerns of revivalists and reformists. As we saw in chapters 1, 2, and 4, Bakhīt draws on the protocols and authority of the transregional "social *madhhab*" to further intensify and entrench these maverick approaches within his modern context.

Francis Robinson has noted that among the commitments shared by the numerous modern reformist trends in India was a "new emphasis on human will [that] heightened ideas of human instrumentality in the world."[29] This seems to have been the case in Egypt as well. Ṣabrī thought that the "general scholarly view" ever since ʿAbduh had coalesced around an emphasis on man's free will.[30] Robinson views this change in emphasis in India as a natural outcome of the soul searching that accompanied the loss of political power, but in Egypt, the question seems to have been motivated by the comments of outside observers seeking to understand—or indeed, denigrate—the Muslim world in the service of their country's colonial interests. The question emerges in Egypt, then, not in a vacuum, but in a climate of civilizational competition and scrutiny. When Bakhīt broaches the topic, he characteristically gives a response that draws on the contributions of nineteenth-century Ḥanafī predecessors and entrenches their views in the venerable language and concepts of medieval theological schools. But he does so under the specter of European dominance, at pains to show, against European accusations, that belief in *qaḍāʾ* and *qadar* actually encouraged virtuous activity, not fatalism.[31] Just as we saw in chapter 3, Bakhīt's response to a discourse delimited by the parameters of colonial powers was to work "through empire rather than against it," drawing on Arab-Islamic traditions to assert a norm that was nonetheless always conditioned by the constant and ever-looming presence of European values and discourses. Equally part

[28] Taqī al-Dīn Aḥmad Ibn Taymiyya, *Darʾ Taʿāruḍ al-ʿAql wa-l-Naql* (Riyadh: Dār al-Kunūz al-Adabiyya, 1979), 2:16–17. The *Ibāna* was also an important reference point for al-Kūrānī, as it came to him mediated by the work of the twelfth-century Ashʿarite Ibn ʿAsākir, who as it turns out also appears in Bakhīt's citations. Nafi, "Taṣawwuf and Reform in Pre-Modern Islamic Culture," 332–33.

[29] Francis Robinson, "Islamic Reform and Modernities in South Asia," *Modern Asian Studies* 42, no. 2/3 (2008): 270.

[30] Ṣabrī, *Mawqif al-Bashar Taḥta Sulṭān al-Qadar*, 44.

[31] Bakhīt al-Muṭīʿī, "al-Qaḍāʾ wa-l-Qadar," 411.

of the background of Bakhīt's response, though, is the need to vie with the growing influence of Reformists like ʿAbduh that defined the field of play for "traditional" scholars in the early twentieth century (chapter 1). In at least Ṣabrī's view, ʿAbduh's early response to Hanotaux set the tenor of debate; his tendency toward upholding free will came to constitute the "general scholarly view" of Egypt's Islamic intelligentsia after him.

Ṣabrī's account should be taken with a grain of salt. His close colleague, Muḥammad Zāhid al-Kawtharī, suggests that the former *Shaykh al-Islām*'s strongly deterministic take on the issue was overdetermined by his own personal experience with loss and exile.[32] And yet his observations on the contours of the religious field in Egypt are instructive, helpfully providing an outsider's vantage point on a set of questions that have tended to be examined in the secondary scholarship with a view to domestic questions and concerns. Those who have considered the emergence of modern forms and subjectivities in Egypt have largely done so from the point of view of new political and cultural elites, and governmental and colonial powers interested in state building and large-scale institutional change. In this framing, the ulama have often been regarded as reactionary conservatives opposed to reform and modernization. The clearest example of such sentiment can be found in the work of Daniel Crecelius, who argues that, faced with their increasing irrelevance, the ulama engaged in a series of strategies: their primary preference was "a staunch opposition to modernization";[33] where that was not possible, the ulama chose to "[withdraw] around their own institutions in an effort to preserve them from contamination through contact with the modernizing elements in society";[34] and finally, when reform of the curriculum and organizational structure of the Azhar came to be imposed on them in due course, the marginalization of the ulama from circles of power meant that they were forced to make use of "the last weapon in their arsenal of defense, obstructionism":[35]

> Obstructionism was often simple overt opposition to reform and the obstinate refusal to implement it, but as the ulama's political influence continued

[32] Muḥammad Zāhid al-Kawtharī, *al-Istibṣār fī al-Taḥadduth ʿan al-Jabr wa-l-Ikhtiyār*, Min Turāth al-Kawtharī 40 (Cairo: al-Maktabat al-Azhariyya li-l-Turāth, 2005), 4.

[33] Daniel Crecelius, "Nonideological Responses of the Egyptian Ulama to Modernization," in *Scholars, Saints, and Sufis: Muslim Religious Institutions in the Middle East Since 1500* (Berkeley: University of California Press, 1972), 186.

[34] Crecelius, "Nonideological Responses of the Egyptian Ulama to Modernization," 186.

[35] Crecelius, "Nonideological Responses of the Egyptian Ulama to Modernization," 206.

> to worsen relative to other groups obstructionism took far more devious forms. Obstructionism goes beyond passive resistance. It has been the ulama's special ability seemingly to accept reform while working against it, to admit the necessity for change while restricting, isolating, and smothering it, to welcome outsiders into their institutions while preparing the means for their expulsion, to publicly countenance new ideas while privately preaching against them, to maintain cordial public relations with the government while privately struggling against its interference in religious affairs.[36]

Given their resolute opposition, Crecelius concludes, the ulama were entirely alienated from the regime and, as a result, "could not play a role similar to that of their counterparts in Istanbul, where the Ottoman ulama helped formulate and implement the reform programs of their Sultans."[37]

This thesis has come under direct challenge from an important recent intervention in the debate. In a carefully researched work looking at the very same issue of curricular reform, Indira Falk Gesink has argued that "a close look at the process of al-Azhar's reforms suggests that conservatives actually accomplished them."[38] This constitutes a marked departure from the settled opinion of the scholarship. Gesink explains, "The reform of religious education in Egypt . . . did not just happen. It was—and had to be—a negotiated product that both preserved key elements of the existing system of knowledge transmission and allowed reformers and their opponents to participate equally."[39] Drawing on a wide range of sources, including contemporary journals and newspapers, to show how the "conservative" ulama have been discarded from the story of reform, Gesink adeptly shows that their participation was in fact crucial to the process, lending it a legitimacy that the likes of ʿAbduh (whom she considers, inspired by Gramsci, to have been a "failed intellectual"[40]) did not, and perhaps could not, provide.

Gesink's is a sophisticated argument which draws on thorough research. In this book, however, I have chosen to decenter controversies of political prominence within Egypt like the reform of the Azhar curriculum, the shariʿa courts, and the laws on endowments and divorce in favor

[36] Crecelius, "Nonideological Responses of the Egyptian Ulama to Modernization," 206.
[37] Crecelius, "Nonideological Responses of the Egyptian Ulama to Modernization," 183.
[38] Indira Falk Gesink, *Islamic Reform and Conservatism: Al-Azhar and the Evolution of Modern Sunni Islam* (London: Tauris Academic Studies, 2010), 2.
[39] Gesink, *Islamic Reform and Conservatism*, 3.
[40] Gesink, *Islamic Reform and Conservatism*, 229.

of examining debates and departures found within seemingly ritualistic aspects of *fiqh*. It is not that these latter sorts of questions evade politics because they concern ritual, but rather that because of their relative remoteness from the charged political debates that were conducted squarely within the public sphere, we are better able to discern and track the intellectual shifts that animated what may otherwise strike as unremarkable changes to ritual law. This book has sought to track these changes in legal reasoning to show how significant epistemological shifts widely thought to be associated with colonial modernity—new conceptions of time, science, and religion—implanted themselves within the thought-world of the Ḥanafī school.

When viewed from the perspective of *fiqh*, then, Gesink's portrayal of conservatives and modernists "work[ing] together as agents of hybridization, sculptors of the new cultural forms Islam would inhabit in the twentieth century" merits reconsideration.[41] Of course, it is not inappropriate to argue that Bakhīt making arguments from within the languages and discourses of the tradition of the *madhhab*, as opposed to the unconstrained writing of the Reformists, added a certain force to the articulation and especially justification of central ideals of modernity. Yet my reading of Bakhīt's intellectual output in this book casts doubt on the proposition that this is the whole story. In view of the fundamental shifts in the direction of central modernist ideals that were effected through his argumentation, it would be difficult to characterize his engagement with the *madhhab* as being as agentive as Gesink finds to be the case in her study.

Gesink is correct in saying that "it is too simple to describe the debaters as mere agents of conceptual colonization or defenders of tradition." But this is perhaps not the right way to frame the question. Colonial discourse, as we saw in chapter 3, countenanced participants who cannot simply be reduced to agents of the colonial order, but nonetheless contributed to the entrenching of its logics and norms. I am in agreement with Asad that the colonial enterprise ought not to be studied as a game "whose stakes are familiar to all participants, and whose rules are accepted by them," but rather as "the totality of forces that converge to create (largely contingently) a new moral landscape."[42] These forces were much more powerful and pervasive than is generally allowed for by claims of hybridization, especially when such

[41] Gesink, *Islamic Reform and Conservatism*, 5.

[42] Talal Asad, *Formations of the Secular: Christianity, Islam, Modernity* (Stanford, CA: Stanford University Press, 2003), 216.

arguments proceed without a careful accounting of the relative strength of the forces that form the resultant hybrid. As Asad says elsewhere of the colonial experience, the very act of reinvention and resistance was structured and defined by "a new scheme of things—new forms of power, work and knowledge" which resulted in "an irrevocable process of transmutation, in which old desires and ways of life were destroyed and new ones took their place."[43] On this view, what is worthy of our attention, as I argued at the outset of the Introduction, is to determine the contours of that new transmutated landscape and "the degree to which the languages, behaviors, and institutions it makes possible come to resemble those that obtain in the West-European nation-states."[44]

This new landscape was a result of not only the politics of reform and resistance but also a range of factors such as the emergence of new technologies, the rearrangement of political institutions, exposure to a wider variety of intellectual currents, shifts in the sensibilities of the educated classes, and the creation of new reading publics. Bakhīt's biography does indicate that he was ill at ease with some of the more sensational instances of reforming the old order, like divorce laws, the system of endowments, and the Azhar curriculum. However, our reading of the *Irshād* and related works throughout the previous chapters makes clear that, once we turn our attention away from these controversial, politically charged episodes—which have too often been used in the literature as "litmus tests" by which to identify individuals as either reformist or conservative—and the turf battles to which they gave rise, we find that fundamental components of a modern episteme were made to seem natural and irresistible to even those, like Bakhīt, who opposed the Reformist movement of ʿAbduh and Riḍā and have always been remembered as "traditionalists."

As the case of Bakhīt shows, however, this was not a phenomenon that proceeded entirely on Egyptian ground. Bakhīt's connections with the larger Muslim world were no less widespread and varied as Riḍā's. Drawing inspiration from the centuries-old protocols of the Ḥanafī *madhhab*, transregionalism was instead a key feature of how he conducted intellectual work. His interlocutors were other Ḥanafīs, and his opposition to Riḍā only cemented his links to others he considered as belonging to an

[43] Talal Asad, "From the History of Colonial Anthropology to the Anthropology of Western Hegemony," in *Colonial Situations: Essays on the Contextualization of Ethnographic Knowledge*, ed. George W. Stocking, History of Anthropology 7 (Madison: University of Wisconsin Press, 1991), 314.

[44] Asad, *Formations of the Secular*, 217.

older order, and therefore opposed to Reformism. This feature pushes us to think of the nature of his interventions as not just an Egyptian development but as a transformation of Ḥanafī tradition, or more precisely a shift from a tradition, in the MacIntyrean sense, to a thoroughly modern stream of thought.

Bibliography

Archival Sources

ʿAbbās Ḥilmī II Papers [HIL]. Palace Green Library, Durham University, UK.
Dār al-Iftāʾ al-Miṣriyya [DIM]. Cairo.
Dār al-Wathāʾiq al-Qawmiyya [DWQ]. Cairo.
Foreign Office [FO]. The National Archives, Kew, UK.

Published Sources

ʿAbd al-Rāziq, ʿAlī. *Al-Islām wa-Uṣūl al-Ḥukm: Baḥth fī al-Khilāfa wa-l-Ḥukūma fī al-Islām*. 2nd ed. Cairo: Maṭbaʿat Miṣr, 1925.

ʿAbd al-Rāziq, ʿAlī. *L'Islam et Les Fondements Du Pouvoir*. Translated by Abdou Filali-Ansary. Paris: Éditions La Découverte, 1994.

ʿAbduh, Muḥammad. *Al-Iḥtifāl bi-Iḥyāʾ Dhikrā al-Ustādh al-Imām al-Shaykh Muḥammad ʿAbduh bi-Dār al-Jāmiʿa al-Miṣriyya fī 11 Yūlyū 1922*. Miṣr: Maṭbaʿat al-Manār, 1340H.

ʿAbduh, Muḥammad. *Al-Islām wa-l-Naṣrāniyya*. Edited by Muḥammad Rashīd Riḍā. Cairo: Maṭbaʿat Majallat al-Manār, 1323H.

ʿAbduh, Muḥammad. *The Theology of Unity*. London: Allen and Unwin, 1966.

Adams, Charles C. *Islam and Modernism in Egypt: A Study of the Modern Reform Movement Inaugurated by Muḥammad ʿAbduh*. London: Oxford University Press, 1933.

Adams, Charles C. "Muḥammad ʿAbduh and the Transvaal Fatwā." In *The Macdonald Presentation Volume, a Tribute to Duncan Black Macdonald, Consisting of Articles by Former Students, Presented to Him on His Seventieth Birthday, April 9, 1933*. Princeton, NJ: Princeton University Press, 1933.

Adorno, Theodor W. "On Tradition." *Telos* 94 (December 21, 1992): 75–82.

ʿAlawī, Sayyid ʿUthmān b. ʿAbd Allāh b. ʿAqīl al-. *Ṭulūʿ Badr al-ʿIlm al-Murtafaʿ wa-Ẓuhūr Najm al-Ṣidq al-Muntafaʿ ʿalā Ṣiḥḥat Jawāb Ḥukm al-Ṣawt al-Mukhtaraʿ*. Batavia, 1899.

Ali, Aun Hasan. "The Beginnings of the School of Ḥillah: A Bio-Bibliographical Study of Twelver Shīʿism in the Late ʿAbbāsid and Early Ilkhānid Periods." PhD diss., McGill University, 2016.

Ali, Souad T. *A Religion, Not a State: Ali ʿAbd Al-Raziq's Islamic Justification of Political Secularism*. Salt Lake City: University of Utah Press, 2009.

ʿAlūba Pāshā, ʿAlī. *Muḥāḍara fī al-Waqf*. Cairo: Maṭbaʿa al-Qāhira, n.d.

Arendt, Hannah. *The Human Condition*. 2nd ed. Chicago: The University of Chicago Press, 1998.

Asad, Talal. *Formations of the Secular: Christianity, Islam, Modernity*. Stanford, CA: Stanford University Press, 2003.

Asad, Talal. "From the History of Colonial Anthropology to the Anthropology of Western Hegemony." In *Colonial Situations: Essays on the Contextualization of Ethnographic Knowledge*, edited by George W. Stocking. History of Anthropology 7. Madison: University of Wisconsin Press, 1991.

Asad, Talal. *Genealogies of Religion: Discipline and Reasons of Power in Christianity and Islam*. Baltimore: Johns Hopkins University Press, 1993.

Asad, Talal. "The Idea of an Anthropology of Islam." Occasional Papers Series. Washington, DC: Georgetown University Center for Contemporary Arab Studies, 1986.

Asad, Talal. "Reading a Modern Classic: W. C. Smith's 'The Meaning and End of Religion.'" *History of Religions* 40, no. 3 (February 1, 2001): 205–22.

Asad, Talal. "Thinking About Tradition, Religion, and Politics in Egypt Today." *Critical Inquiry* 42, no. 1 (September 1, 2015): 166–214.

ʿAsqalānī, Ibn Ḥajar al-. *Talkhīṣ al-Ḥabīr*. Vol. 2. Mecca: Muʾassasat al-Qurṭuba, 1995.

ʿAṭiyyat Allāh, Aḥmad. *Al-Qāmūs al-Islāmī*. Cairo: Maktabat al-Nahḍa al-Miṣriyya, 1963.

Ayalon, Ami. *The Arabic Print Revolution: Cultural Production and Mass Readership*. Cambridge, UK: Cambridge University Press, 2016.

Ayoub, Samy A. *Law, Empire, and the Sultan: Ottoman Imperial Authority and Late Ḥanafī Jurisprudence*. Oxford Islamic Legal Studies. New York: Oxford University Press, 2020.

Al-Azem, Talal. *Rule-Formulation and Binding Precedent in the Madhhab-Law Tradition: Ibn Qutlubugha's Commentary on the Compendium of Quduri*. Islamicate Intellectual History. Leiden: Brill, 2016.

Bakhīt al-Muṭīʿī, Muḥammad. *Al-Jawāb al-Shāfī fī Ibāḥat al-Taṣwīr al-Fūtūghrāfī*. Cairo: al-Maṭbaʿa al-Khayriyya, n.d.

Bakhīt al-Muṭīʿī, Muḥammad. *Al-Murhafāt al-Yamāniyya fī ʿUnq Man Qāla bi-Buṭlān al-Waqf ʿalā al-Dhurriyya*. Cairo: al-Maṭbaʿa al-Salafiyya, 1344H.

Bakhīt al-Muṭīʿī, Muḥammad. "Al-Qaḍāʾ wa-l-Qadar." *Al-Hidāya al-Islāmiyya* 2, no. 8 (Muḥarram 1349H): 395–411.

Bakhīt al-Muṭīʿī, Muḥammad. "Fī Aḥkām al-Sūkūrtāh." In *Thalātha Rasāʾil*. Cairo: Jamʿiyyat al-Azhar al-ʿIlmiyya, 1932.

Bakhīt al-Muṭīʿī, Muḥammad. "Fī Aḥkām Qirāʾat al-Fūnūghrāf." In *Thalātha Rasāʾil*. Cairo: Jamʿiyyat al-Azhar al-ʿIlmiyya, 1932.

Bakhīt al-Muṭīʿī, Muḥammad. *Ḥaqīqat al-Islām wa-Uṣūl al-Ḥukm*. Cairo: al-Maṭbaʿa al-Salafiyya, 1925.

Bakhīt al-Muṭīʿī, Muḥammad. *Ḥāshiyat ʿalā Kharīdat al-Tawḥid*. Cairo: Maṭbaʿat al-Islām, 1314H.

Bakhīt al-Muṭīʿī, Muḥammad. *Irshād Ahl al-Milla ilā Ithbāt al-Ahilla*. Edited by Ḥasan Aḥmad Isbir. Beirut: Dār Ibn Ḥazm, 2000.

Bakhīt al-Muṭīʿī, Muḥammad. "Izāḥat al-Wahm wa-l-Ishtibāh ʿan Risālatay al-Fūnūghrāf wa-l-Sūkūrtāh." In *Thalātha Rasāʾil*. Cairo: Jamʿiyyat al-Azhar al-ʿIlmiyya, 1932.

Bakhīt al-Muṭīʿī, Muḥammad. *Kitāb Irshād Ahl al-Milla ilā Ithbāt al-Ahilla*. Miṣr: Maṭbaʿat al-Kurdistān al-ʿIlmiyya, 1329H.

Bakhīt al-Muṭīʿī, Muḥammad. *Kitāb Tawfīq al-Raḥmān li-l-Tawfīq bayna mā Qālahu ʿUlamāʾ al-Hayʾa wa-bayna mā Jāʾa fī al-Aḥādīth al-Ṣaḥīḥa wa-Āyāt al-Qurʾān*. Cairo: Maṭbaʿat al-Saʿāda, 1341H.

Bakhīt al-Muṭīʿī, Muḥammad. *Muḥāḍara fī Niẓām al-Waqf*. Cairo: al-Maṭbaʿa al-Salafiyya, 1345H.

Bakhīt al-Muṭīʿī, Muḥammad. *Muḥāḍara fī Niẓām al-Waqf*. Cairo: al-Maṭbaʿa al-Salafiyya, 1346H.

Bakhīt al-Muṭīʿī, Muḥammad. *Tanbīh al-ʿUqūl al-Insāniyya li-mā fī Āyāt al-Qurʾān min al-ʿUlūm al-Kawniyya wa-l-ʿUmrāniyya*. Maṭbaʿat al-Saʿāda, 1923.

Bakhīt al-Muṭīʿī, Muḥammad. *Taṭhīr al-Fuʾād min Danas al-Iʿtiqād*. Būlāq: al-Maṭbaʿa al-Kubrā al-Amīriyya, 1318H.

Barak, On. *On Time: Technology and Temporality in Modern Egypt*. Berkeley: University of California Press, 2013.

Bashkin, Orit. "The Iraqi Afghanis and ʿAbduhs: Debate over Reform among Shiʿite and Sunni ʿUlamaʾ in Interwar Iraq." In *Guardians of Faith in Modern Times: ʿUlamaʾ in the Middle East*, edited by Meir Hatina, 141–70. Leiden: Brill, 2008.

Bein, Amit. *Ottoman Ulema, Turkish Republic: Agents of Change and Guardians of Tradition*. Stanford, CA: Stanford University Press, 2011.

Benite, Zvi Ben-Dor. "Taking ʿAbduh to China: Chinese-Egyptian Intellectual Contact in the Early Twentieth Century." In *Global Muslims in the Age of Steam and Print*, edited by James L. Gelvin and Nile Green, 249–67. Berkeley: University of California Press, 2014.

Berque, Jacques. *Egypt: Imperialism & Revolution*. London: Faber, 1972.

Bhabha, Homi. "Of Mimicry and Man: The Ambivalence of Colonial Discourse." *October* 28 (1984): 125–33.

Block, David, and Ken Freeman. *Shrouds of the Night: Masks of the Milky Way and the Awesome New View of Galaxies*. New York: Springer, 2008.

Boer, T. J. de. *Geschichte Der Philosophie Im Islam*. Stuttgart: F. Frommanns Verlag (E. Hauff), 1901.

Boer, T. J. de. *The History of Philosophy in Islam*. New York: Dover, 1967.

Bright, Charles. *Submarine Telegraphs: Their History, Construction, and Working*. London: C. Lockwood and Son, 1898.

Broucek, James. "The Controversy of Shaykh ʿAli ʿAbd al-Raziq." PhD diss., The Florida State University, 2012.

Brown, Jonathan A. C. "Even If It's Not True It's True: Using Unreliable Hadiths in Sunni Islam." *Islamic Law and Society* 18, no. 1 (2011): 1–52.

Brown, Nathan. "Law and Imperialism: Egypt in Comparative Perspective." *Law and Society Review* 29, no. 1 (1995): 103–26.

Brown, Nathan. *Rule of Law in the Arab World*. New York: Cambridge University Press, 1997.

Burak, Guy. *The Second Formation of Islamic Law: The Hanafi School in the Early Modern Ottoman Empire*. New York: Cambridge University Press, 2015.

Calder, Norman. "Al-Nawawī's Typology of Muftīs and Its Significance for a General Theory of Islamic Law." *Islamic Law and Society* 3, no. 2 (January 1, 1996): 137–64.

Calder, Norman. "The ''Uqūd Rasm Al-Muftī' of ibn ʿĀbidīn." *Bulletin of the School of Oriental and African Studies, University of London* 63, no. 2 (January 1, 2000): 215–28.

Casanova, José. *Public Religions in the Modern World*. Chicago: University of Chicago Press, 1994.

Casanova, José. "Public Religions Revisited." In *Religion: Beyond a Concept*, edited by Hent de Vries, 101–19. New York: Fordham University Press, 2008.

Casanova, José. "The Secular, Secularizations, Secularisms." In *Rethinking Secularism*, edited by Craig J. Calhoun, Mark Juergensmeyer, and Jonathan VanAntwerpen. New York: Oxford University Press, 2011.

Choueiri, Youssef M. *Modern Arab Historiography: Historical Discourse and the Nation-State*. London: RoutledgeCurzon, 2003.

Commins, David Dean. "Guiding Mankind to Act on the Basis of Telegraphic Messages." In *Modernist Islam: 1840–1940*, edited by Charles Kurzman, 181–87. New York: Oxford University Press, 2002.

Commins, David Dean. *Islamic Reform: Politics and Social Change in Late Ottoman Syria*. New York: Oxford University Press, 1990.

Costet-Tardieu, Francine. *Un Réformiste à l'université Al-Azhar: Œuvre et Pensée de Mustafâ al-Marâghî, 1881–1945*. Paris: Centre d'études et de documentation économiques juridiques et sociales, 2005.

Crecelius, Daniel. "Nonideological Responses of the Egyptian Ulama to Modernization." In *Scholars, Saints, and Sufis: Muslim Religious Institutions in the Middle East Since 1500*, 167–210. Berkeley: University of California Press, 1972.

Crecelius, Daniel Neil. "The Ulama and the State in Modern Egypt." PhD diss., Princeton University, 1967.

Cromer, Evelyn Baring. *Modern Egypt*. Vol. 2. 2 vols. New York: The Macmillan Company, 1908.

Crone, Patricia. "Zoroastrian Communism." *Comparative Studies in Society and History* 36, no. 3 (1994): 447–62.

Crozet, Pascal. *Les Sciences Modernes en Égypte: Transfert et Appropriation, 1805–1902*. Paris: Geuthner, 2008.

Cuno, Kenneth M. "Reorganization of the Sharia Courts of Egypt: How Legal Modernization Set Back Women's Rights in the Nineteenth Century." In *Law and Legality in the Ottoman Empire and Republic of Turkey*, ed. Kent F. Schull, M. Safa Saraçoğlu, and Robert Zens, 92–107. Bloomington: Indiana University Press, 2016.

Dallal, Ahmad. "Appropriating the Past: Twentieth-Century Reconstruction of Pre-Modern Islamic Thought." *Islamic Law and Society* 7, no. 3 (2000): 325–58.

Dallal, Ahmad S. *Islam, Science, and the Challenge of History*. New Haven, CT: Yale University Press, 2010.

Dallal, Ahmad. "The Origins and Objectives of Islamic Revivalist Thought, 1750–1850." *Journal of the American Oriental Society* 113, no. 3 (1993): 341–59.

Dasūqī, Muḥammad al-. *Muḥammad Bakhīt al-Muṭīʿī: Shaykh al-Islām wa-l-Muftī al-ʿĀlamī*. Damascus: Dār al-Qalam, 2011.

Davidson, Garrett A. *Carrying on the Tradition: A Social and Intellectual History of Hadith Transmission across a Thousand Years*. Boston: Brill, 2020.

Deeb, Marius. *Party Politics in Egypt: The Wafd & Its Rivals, 1919–1939*. St. Antony's Middle East Monographs, no. 9. London: Ithaca Press for the Middle East Centre, St Antony's College, Oxford, 1979.

Delanoue, Gilbert. *Moralistes et Politiques Musulmans Dans l'Égypte Du XIXe Siècle (1798–1882)*. 2 vols. Paris: Institut français d'archéologie orientale du Caire, 1982.

Depont, Octave, and Xavier Coppolani. *Les Confréries Religieuses Musulmanes*. Alger: Jourdan, 1897.

Di-Capua, Yoav. *Gatekeepers of the Arab Past: Historians and History Writing in Twentieth-Century Egypt*. Berkeley: University of California Press, 2009.

Dijwī, Yūsuf al-. *Radd Ḥaḍrat Ṣāḥib al-Faḍīla al-Ustādh al-Kabīr al-Shaykh Yūsuf al-Dijwī ʿalā Kitāb al-Shaykh ʿAlī ʿAbd al-Rāziq al-Islām wa-Uṣūl al-Ḥukm*. Miṣr: Maṭbaʿat al-Samāḥ, n.d.

Doğan, Mehmet Ali, and Heather J. Sharkey, eds. *American Missionaries and the Middle East: Foundational Encounters*. Salt Lake City: University of Utah Press, 2011.

Dreyfus, Hubert L. "Taylor's (Anti-) Epistemology." In *Charles Taylor*, edited by Ruth Abbey. Contemporary Philosophy in Focus, 52–83. Cambridge, UK: Cambridge University Press, 2004.

Dreyfus, Hubert, and Charles Taylor. *Retrieving Realism*. Cambridge, MA: Harvard University Press, 2015.

El Shamsy, Ahmed. *Rediscovering the Islamic Classics: How Editors and Print Culture Transformed an Intellectual Tradition*. Princeton, NJ: Princeton University Press, 2020.

El Shamsy, Ahmed. "Rethinking Taqlīd in the Early Shāfiʿī School." *Journal of the American Oriental Society* 128, no. 1 (January 2008): 1–23.

Elshakry, Marwa. "The Exegesis of Science in Twentieth-Century Arabic Interpretations of the Qurʾān." In *Nature and Scripture in the Abrahamic Religions: 1700–Present*, edited by Jitse M. van der Meer and Scott Mandelbrote, 1:491–523. Leiden: Brill, 2008.

Elshakry, Marwa. "The Gospel of Science and American Evangelism in Late Ottoman Beirut." *Past & Present* 196, no. 1 (August 1, 2007): 173–214.

Elshakry, Marwa. *Reading Darwin in Arabic, 1860–1950*. Chicago: University of Chicago Press, 2014.

Elshakry, Marwa. "When Science Became Western: Historiographical Reflections." *Isis* 101, no. 1 (March 2010): 98–109.

Enayat, Hamid. *Modern Islamic Political Thought: The Response of the Shīʿī and Sunnī Muslims to the Twentieth Century*. New ed. London: I.B. Tauris, 2005.

Ephrat, Eliza. *Mabādiʾ ʿIlm al-Hayʾa*. Beirut, 1875.

Fadel, Mohammad. "The Social Logic of Taqlīd and the Rise of the Mukhtaṣar." *Islamic Law and Society* 3, no. 2 (January 1, 1996): 193–233.

Fahmī, Zakī. *Ṣafwat al-ʿAṣr fī Tārīkh wa-Rusūm Mashāhīr Rijāl Miṣr Min ʿAhd Sākin al-Jinān Muḥammad ʿAlī Bāshā al-Kabīr*. Reprint of the 1926 edition. Ṣafaḥāt Min Tārīkh Miṣr 23. Cairo: Maktabat Madbūlī, 1995.

Fahmy, Khaled. *In Quest of Justice: Islamic Law and Forensic Medicine in Modern Egypt*. Oakland: University of California Press, 2018.

Farag, Nadia. "The Lewis Affair and the Fortunes of Al-Muqtataf." *Middle Eastern Studies* 8, no. 1 (January 1, 1972): 73–83.

Feener, R. Michael. *Muslim Legal Thought in Modern Indonesia*. Cambridge, UK: Cambridge University Press, 2007.

Fikrī, ʿAbd Allāh. *Risāla fī Muqāranat Baʿḍ Nuṣūṣ al-Hayʾa bi-l-Wārid fī al-Nuṣūṣ al-Sharʿiyya*. Cairo: Maṭbaʿat al-Madāris, 1876.

Fīrūzābādī, Muḥammad ibn Yaʿqūb. "Danā." *Al-Qāmūs al-Muḥīṭ*. Miṣr: Maṭbaʿat al-Saʿāda, n.d.

Fīrūzābādī, Muḥammad ibn Yaʿqūb. "Dīn." *Al-Qāmūs al-Muḥīṭ*. Miṣr: Maṭbaʿat al-Saʿāda, n.d.

Fīrūzābādī, Muḥammad ibn Yaʿqūb. "Al-Jadd." *Al-Qāmūs al-Muḥīṭ*. Miṣr: Maṭbaʿat al-Saʿāda, n.d.

Gadamer, Hans-Georg. *Truth and Method*. Translated by Joel Weinsheimer and Donald G. Marshall. Second, rev. ed. New York: Continuum, 2006.

Gershoni, I., and James P. Jankowski. *Egypt, Islam, and the Arabs: The Search for Egyptian Nationhood, 1900–1930*. Studies in Middle Eastern History. New York: Oxford University Press, 1986.

Gershoni, Israel. "The Evolution of National Culture in Modern Egypt: Intellectual Formation and Social Diffusion, 1892–1945." *Poetics Today* 13, no. 2 (July 1, 1992): 325–50.

Gesink, Indira Falk. *Islamic Reform and Conservatism: Al-Azhar and the Evolution of Modern Sunni Islam*. London: Tauris Academic Studies, 2010.

Gesink, Indira Falk. "Beyond Modernisms: Opposition and Negotiation in the Azhar Reform Debate in Egypt, 1870–1911." PhD diss., Washington University in St. Louis, 2000.

Ghazal, Amal N. *Islamic Reform and Arab Nationalism: Expanding the Crescent from the Mediterranean to the Indian Ocean (1880s–1930s)*. London: Routledge, 2010.

Ghumārī, Aḥmad al-. *Tawjīh al-Anẓār li-Tawḥīd al-Muslimīn fī al-Ṣawm wa-l-Ifṭār*. Amman: Dār al-Nafā'is & Dār al-Bayāriq, 1999.

Ghumārī, Aḥmad ibn al-Ṣiddīq al-. *Al-Baḥr al-ʿAmīq fī Marwiyyāt Ibn al-Ṣiddīq*. Vol. 1. Cairo: Dār al-Kutubī, 2007.

Gibb, H. *Whither Islam?: A Survey of Modern Movements in the Moslem World*. London: V. Gollancz, 1932.

Gibb, H. A. R. *Modern Trends in Islam*. Chicago: University of Chicago Press, 1947.

Gilliot, Cl. "Ṭabaḳāt." Edited by P. J. Bearman, Th. Bianquis, C. E. Bosworth, E. van Donzel, and W. P. Heinrichs. *Encyclopaedia of Islam 2*. Leiden: Brill, 2000.

Goldschmidt, Arthur. "The Butrus Ghali Family." *Journal of the American Research Center in Egypt* 30 (1993): 183–88.

Goldziher, Ignác. *Die Richtungen Der Islamischen Koranauslegung*. Leiden: E.J. Brill, 1970.

Gran, Peter. *Islamic Roots of Capitalism: Egypt, 1760–1840*. Austin: University of Texas Press, 1979.

Griffel, Frank. "What Do We Mean By 'Salafī'? Connecting Muḥammad ʿAbduh with Egypt's Nūr Party in Islam's Contemporary Intellectual History." *Die Welt des Islams* 55, no. 2 (June 2015): 186–220.

Griffel, Frank. "What Is the Task of the Intellectual (Contemporary) Historian?—A Response to Henri Lauzière's 'Reply.'" *Die Welt des Islams* 56, no. 2 (June 2016): 249–55.

Gutas, Dimitri. "The Study of Arabic Philosophy in the Twentieth Century: An Essay on the Historiography of Arabic Philosophy." *British Journal of Middle Eastern Studies* 29, no. 1 (May 1, 2002): 5–25.

Haddad, Mohamed. "ʿAbduh et ses Lecteurs: Pour une Histoire Critique des 'Lectures' de M. ʿAbduh." *Arabica* 45, no. 1 (1998): 22–49.

Haj, Samira. *Reconfiguring Islamic Tradition: Reform, Rationality, and Modernity*. Cultural Memory in the Present. Stanford, CA: Stanford University Press, 2009.

Halevi, Leor. *Modern Things on Trial: Islam's Global and Material Reformation in the Age of Rida, 1865–1935*. New York: Columbia University Press, 2019.

Hallaq, Wael B. *Authority, Continuity, and Change in Islamic Law*. Cambridge, UK: Cambridge University Press, 2001.

Hallaq, Wael B. "From Fatwās to Furūʿ: Growth and Change in Islamic Substantive Law." *Islamic Law and Society* 1, no. 1 (1994): 29–65.

Hallaq, Wael B. *A History of Islamic Legal Theories: An Introduction to Sunnī Uṣūl al-Fiqh*. New York: Cambridge University Press, 1997.

Hallaq, Wael B. "A Prelude to Ottoman Reform: Ibn ʿAbidin on Custom and Legal Change." In *Histories of the Modern Middle East: New Directions*, 37–61. Boulder, CO: Lynne Rienner, 2002.

Hallaq, Wael B. "Qāḍīs Communicating: Legal Change and the Law of Documentary Evidence." *Al-Qanṭara* XX, no. 2 (1999): 437–66.

Hallaq, Wael B. "Was the Gate of Ijtihad Closed?" *International Journal of Middle East Studies* 16, no. 1 (March 1, 1984): 3–41.

Hamzah, Dyala. "From *ʿilm* to *Ṣiḥāfa* or the Politics of the Public Interest (*Maṣlaḥa*): Muḥammad Rashīd Riḍā and His Journal *al-Manār* (1898–1935)." In *The Making of the Arab Intellectual: Empire, Public Sphere and the Colonial Coordinates of Selfhood*, edited by Dyala Hamzah, 90–127. London: Routledge, 2013.

Ḥasanī, ʿAbd al-Ḥayy b. Fakhr al-Dīn al-. *Nuzhat al-Khawāṭir wa-Bahjat al-Masāmiʿ wa-l-Nawāẓir*. 8 vols. Beirut: Dār Ibn Ḥazm, 1999.

Hatina, Meir, ed. *Guardians of Faith in Modern Times: ʿUlamaʾ in the Middle East*. Leiden: Brill, 2009.

Heidegger, Martin. "The Age of the World Picture." In *Off the Beaten Track*, edited by Julian Young and Kenneth Haynes, 57–85. Cambridge, UK: Cambridge University Press, 2002.

Hermansen, Marcia. *Shāh Walī Allāh's Treatises on Islamic Law*. Louisville, KY: Fons Vitae, 2010.

Heyworth-Dunne, J. "Rifāʿah Badawī Rāfiʿ aṭ-Ṭahṭāwī: The Egyptian Revivalist." *Bulletin of the School of Oriental Studies, University of London* 9, no. 4 (1939): 961–67.

Hilāl, ʿImād Aḥmad. *Al-Iftāʾ al-Miṣrī min al-Ṣaḥābī ʿUqba ibn ʿĀmir ilā al-Duktūr ʿAlī Jumʿa*. 6 vols. Cairo: Maṭbaʿat Dār al-Kutub wa-l-Wathāʾiq al-Qawmiyya, 2010–2020.

Hodgson, Marshall G. S. *The Venture of Islam*. Vol. 3. Chicago: University of Chicago Press, 1977.

Hoskins, Halford Lancaster. *British Routes to India*. New York: Longmans, Green and Co., 1928.

Hourani, Albert. *Arabic Thought in the Liberal Age, 1798–1939*. London: Oxford University Press, 1970.

Ḥukm al-Sharīʿa al-Islāmiyya fī al-Waqf al-Khayrī wa-l-Ahlī: Bayān Min al-ʿUlamāʾ. Cairo: al-Maṭbaʿa al-Salafiyya wa-Maktabatuhā, 1927.

Ḥukm Hayʾat Kibār al-ʿUlamāʾ ʿalā Kitāb al-Islām wa-Uṣūl al-Ḥukm. al-Maṭbaʿa al-Salafiyya, 1344H.

Ḥusayn, Muḥammad al-Khiḍr. *Naqḍ Kitāb al-Islām wa-Uṣūl al-Ḥukm*. Cairo: al-Maṭbaʿa al-Salafiyya wa-Maktabatuhā, 1344H.

Ibn ʿĀbidīn, Muḥammad Amīn. *Ḥāshiyat Radd al-Muḥtār*. Vol. 3. 8 vols. Riyadh: Dār ʿĀlam al-Kutub, 2003.

Ibn ʿĀbidīn, Muḥammad Amīn. "Nashr al-ʿArf fī Bināʾ Baʿḍ al-Aḥkām ʿalā al-ʿUrf." In *Majmūʿat Rasāʾil Ibn ʿĀbidīn*, 2:114–47. Damascus: al-Maktaba al-Hāshimiyya, 1325H.

Ibn ʿĀbidīn, Muḥammad Amīn. "Sharḥ al-Manẓūma al-Musammāt bi-ʿUqūd Rasm al-Muftī." In *Majmūʿat Rasāʾil Ibn ʿĀbidīn*, 1:9–52. Damascus: al-Maktaba al-Hāshimiyya, 1325H.

Ibn ʿĀbidīn, Muḥammad Amīn. "Tanbīh al-Ghāfil wa-l-Wasnān ʿalā Aḥkām Hilāl Ramaḍān." In *Arbaʿa Rasāʾil fī Hilāl Khayr al-Shuhūr*, 63–110. Beirut: Dār Ibn Ḥazm, 2000.

Ibn al-Humām, Kamāl al-Dīn. *Fatḥ al-Qadīr*. Vol. 2. Cairo: al-Maṭbaʿa al-Kubrā al-Amīriyya, 1315H.

Ibn al-Humām, Kamāl al-Dīn. *Fatḥ al-Qadīr*. Vol. 2. Beirut: Dār al-Fikr, n.d.
Ibn Daqīq al-ʿĪd, Taqī al-Dīn. *Iḥkām al-Aḥkām* ed. Aḥmad Shākir. Vol. 2. Beirut: ʿĀlam al-Kutub, 1987.
Ibn Nujaym, Zayn al-Dīn b. Ibrāhīm. *Al-Baḥr al-Rāʾiq*. Vol. 2. Beirut: Dār al-Kutub al-ʿIlmiyya, 1997.
Ibn Taymiyya, Taqī al-Dīn Aḥmad. *Al-Wāsiṭa bayna al-Khalq wa-l-Ḥaqq*. Cairo: Maṭbaʿat al- Ādāb, 1318H.
Ibn Taymiyya, Taqī al-Dīn Aḥmad. *Darʾ Taʿāruḍ al-ʿAql wa-l-Naql*. 11 vols. Riyadh: Dār al-Kunūz al-Adabiyya, 1979.
Ibrahim, Ahmed Fekry. "Al-Shaʿrānī's Response to Legal Purism: A Theory of Legal Pluralism." *Islamic Law & Society* 20, no. 1/2 (February 2013): 110–40.
Ibrahim, Ahmed Fekry. *Pragmatism in Islamic Law: A Social and Intellectual History*. Syracuse, NY: Syracuse University Press, 2015.
Ibrahim, Ahmed Fekry. "Rethinking the *Taqlīd* Hegemony: An Institutional, *Longue-Durée* Approach." *Journal of the American Oriental Society* 136, no. 4 (2016): 801–16.
Ihde, Don. "The Structure of Technology Knowledge." *International Journal of Technology and Design Education* 7, no. 1–2 (1997): 73–79.
"Ilā Raḥmat Allāh." *Majallat Al-Azhar* 6, no. 8 (1354H).
ʿIllīsh, Muḥammad. *Fatḥ al-ʿAlī al-Mālik*. Cairo: Maṭbaʿat Muṣṭafā al-Bābī al-Ḥalabī, 1958.
ʿImāra, Muḥammad. *Maʿrikat al-Islām wa-Uṣūl al-Ḥukm*. Cairo: Dār al-Shurūq, 1997.
Ingalls, Matthew B. "Subtle Innovation Within Networks of Convention: The Life, Thought, and Intellectual Legacy of Zakariyyā Al-Anṣārī (d. 926/1520)." PhD diss., Yale University, 2011.
Ismael, Tareq Y. *The Communist Movement in Egypt, 1920–1988*. 1st ed. Syracuse, NY: Syracuse University Press, 1990.
Jābī, Bassām. *Muʿjam al-Aʿlām: Muʿjam Tarājim li-Ashhar al-Rijāl wa-l-Nisāʾ Min al-ʿArab wa-l-Mustaʿribīn wa-l-Mustashriqīn*. Limassol, Cyprus: al-Jaffān wa-l-Jābī, 1987.
Jackson, Peter. "Retracing the Path: Gesture, Memory, and the Exegesis of Tradition." *History of Religions* 45, no. 1 (2005): 1–28.
Jackson, Sherman A. "*Taqlīd*, Legal Scaffolding and the Scope of Legal Injunctions in Post-Formative Theory *Muṭlaq* and *ʿĀmm* in the Jurisprudence of Shihāb al-Dīn al-Qarāfī." *Islamic Law and Society* 3, no. 2 (January 1, 1996): 165–92.
Jacob, Wilson Chacko. *Working Out Egypt: Effendi Masculinity and Subject Formation in Colonial Modernity, 1870–1940*. Durham, NC: Duke University Press, 2011.
Jankowski, James. "The Eastern Idea and the Eastern Union in Interwar Egypt." *The International Journal of African Historical Studies* 14, no. 4 (January 1, 1981): 643–66.
Johansen, Baber. *Contingency in a Sacred Law: Legal and Ethical Norms in the Muslim Fiqh*. Studies in Islamic Law and Society, vol. 7. Leiden: Brill, 1998.
Johansen, Baber. *The Islamic Law on Land Tax and Rent: The Peasants' Loss of Property Rights as Interpreted in the Hanafite Legal Literature of the Mamluk and Ottoman Periods*. London: Croom Helm, 1988.
Jomier, Jacques. *Le Commentaire Coranique Du Manâr: Tendances Modernes de l'Exégèse Coranique En Égypte*. Paris: G.-P. Maisonneuve, 1954.
Jong, F. de. "Bakhīt al-Muṭīʿī, Muḥammad." *Encyclopaedia of Islam 2*. Leiden: Brill, n.d.
Jurjānī, ʿAlī b. Muḥammad al-Sharīf al-. *Al-Taʿrīfāt*. Beirut: Maktabat Lubnān, 1985.
Kaḥḥāla, ʿUmar. *Muʿjam al-Muʾallifīn: Tarājim Muṣannifī al-Kutub al-ʿArabiyya*. Vol. 9. Beirut: Dār Iḥyāʾ al-Turāth al-ʿArabī, n.d.

Kallek, Cengiz. "Bahît, Muhammed." *İslâm Ansiklopedisi*. Üsküdar, İstanbul: Türkiye Diyanet Vakfı, 1991.

Kanlidere, Ahmet. "Reform Within Islam: The Tajdid (Reform) Movement among the Kazan Tatars (1850–1917): Conciliation or Conflict?" PhD diss., Columbia University, 1995.

Kaptein, Nico J. G. *Islam, Colonialism and the Modern Age in the Netherlands East Indies: A Biography of Sayyid ʿUthman (1822–1914)*. Leiden: Brill, 2014.

Karamustafa, Ahmet T. "Islamic *Dīn* as an Alternative to Western Models of Religion." In *Religion, Theory, Critique: Classic and Contemporary Approaches and Methodologies*, edited by Richard King. New York: Columbia University Press, 2017.

Kāsānī, ʿAlāʾ al-Dīn al-. *Badāʾiʿ al-Ṣanāʾiʿ fī Tartīb al-Sharāʾiʿ*. Vol. 2. Beirut: Dār al-Kutub al-ʿIlmiyya, n.d.

Kateman, Ammeke. *Muḥammad ʿAbduh and His Interlocutors: Conceptualizing Religion in a Globalizing World*. Leiden: Brill, 2019.

Kawtharī, Muḥammad Zāhid al-. *Al-Istibṣār fī al-Taḥadduth ʿan al-Jabr wa-l-Ikhtiyār*. Cairo: al-Maktabat al-Azhariyya li-l-Turāth, 2005.

Kawtharī, Muḥammad Zāhid al-. *Maqālāt al-Kawtharī*. Cairo: al-Maktaba al-Azhariyya li-l-Turāth, 2009.

Kaya, Eyyup Said. "Continuity and Change in Islamic Law: The Concept of Madhhab and the Dimensions of Legal Disagreement in Hanafi Scholarship of the Tenth Century." In *The Islamic School of Law: Evolution, Devolution, and Progress*, edited by Peri J. Bearman, Rudolph Peters, and Frank E. Vogel, 26–40. Cambridge, MA: Harvard University Press, 2005.

Keddie, Nikki R. *An Islamic Response to Imperialism: Political and Religious Writings of Sayyid Jamāl ad-Dīn "al-Afghānī."* Berkeley: University of California Press, 1968.

Keddie, Nikki R. "Islamic Philosophy and Islamic Modernism: The Case of Sayyid Jamāl ad-Dīn al-Afghānī." *Iran* 6 (January 1, 1968): 53–56.

Keddie, Nikki R. *Sayyid Jamāl ad-Dīn "Al-Afghānī": A Political Biography*. Berkeley: University of California Press, 1972.

Kedourie, Elie. *Afghani and ʿAbduh: An Essay on Religious Unbelief and Political Activism in Modern Islam*. New York: Humanities Press, 1966.

Kenny, L. M. "East versus West in Al-Muqtaṭaf, 1875–1900: Image and Self-Image." In *Essays on Islamic Civilization: Presented to Niyazi Berkes*, edited by Donald P. Little, 140–54. Leiden: Brill, 1976.

Kerr, Malcolm. *Islamic Reform: The Political and Legal Theories of Muḥammad ʿAbduh and Rashīd Riḍā*. Berkeley: University of California Press, 1966.

"Khabar." *Al-Mawsūʿa al-Fiqhiyya*. Kuwait: Wizārat al-Awqāf wa-l-Shuʾūn al-Islāmiyya, 1990.

Khalid, Adeeb. *The Politics of Muslim Cultural Reform: Jadidism in Central Asia*. Berkeley: University of California Press, 1988.

Khan, Fareeha. "Traditionalist Approaches to Sharīʿah Reform: Mawlana Ashraf ʿAli Thānawi's Fatwa on Women's Right to Divorce." PhD diss., University of Michigan, 2008.

King, David A. "Science in the Service of Religion: The Case of Islam." In *Astronomy in the Service of Islam*, 245–62. Aldershot, UK: Variorum, 1993.

Koselleck, Reinhart. *Futures Past: On the Semantics of Historical Time*. Translated by Keith Tribe. Reprint ed. Cambridge, MA: The MIT Press, 1990.

Laknawī, ʿAbd al-Ḥayy al-. *Al-Fawāʾid al-Bahiyya fī Tarājim al-Ḥanafiyya*. Cairo: Maṭbaʿat al-Saʿāda, 1324H.

Laknawī, ʿAbd al-Ḥayy al-. *Al-Nāfiʿ al-Kabīr li-man Yuṭāliʿ al-Jāmiʿ al-Ṣaghīr*. Karachi: Idārat al-Qurʾān, 1990.

Laknawī, ʿAbd al-Ḥayy al-. "Al-Qawl al-Manshūr fī Hilāl Khayr al-Shuhūr." In *Arbaʿa Rasāʾil fī Hilāl Khayr al-Shuhūr*, 145–56. Beirut: Dār Ibn Ḥazm, 2000.

Laoust, Henri. "Le Réformisme Orthodoxe des Salafiyyah et les Caractères Généraux de son Orientation Actuelle." *Revue Des Études Islamiques* 6 (1932): 175–224.

Lauzière, Henri. "The Construction of Salafiyya: Reconsidering Salafism from the Perspective of Conceptual History." *International Journal of Middle East Studies* 42, no. 3 (2010): 369–89.

Lauzière, Henri. "What We Mean Versus What They Meant by 'Salafi': A Reply to Frank Griffel." *Die Welt des Islams* 56, no. 1 (April 19, 2016):-89–96.

Layish, Aharon. "The Contribution of the Modernists to the Secularization of Islamic Law." *Middle Eastern Studies* 14, no. 3 (October 1, 1978): 263–77.

Lee, David C. J. *Ernest Renan: In the Shadow of Faith*. London: Duckworth, 1996.

Livingston, John W. "Western Science and Educational Reform in the Thought of Shaykh Rifaʿa al-Tahtawi." *International Journal of Middle East Studies* 28, no. 4 (November 1, 1996): 543–64.

Loimeier, Roman. *Islamic Reform in Twentieth-Century Africa*. Edinburgh: Edinburgh University Press, 2018.

Machamer, Peter. "Introduction." In *The Cambridge Companion to Galileo*, edited by Peter Machamer, 1–26. Cambridge, UK: Cambridge University Press, 1998.

MacIntyre, Alasdair. *After Virtue: A Study in Moral Theory*. 3rd ed. Notre Dame, IN: University of Notre Dame Press, 2007.

MacIntyre, Alasdair. *Three Rival Versions of Moral Enquiry: Encyclopaedia, Genealogy, and Tradition*. Paperback edition. Notre Dame, IN: University of Notre Dame Press, 1991.

MacIntyre, Alasdair. *Whose Justice? Which Rationality?* Notre Dame, IN: University of Notre Dame Press, 1988.

Makdisi, Ussama. *Artillery of Heaven: American Missionaries and the Failed Conversion of the Middle East*. Ithaca, NY: Cornell University Press, 2009.

Makhlūf, Muḥammad b. Ḥasanayn b. Muḥammad. *Manhaj al-Yaqīn fī Bayān Anna al-Waqf al-Ahlī Min al-Dīn*. Cairo: Maṭbaʿa Muṣṭafā al-Ḥalabī, 1347H.

Mardanova, Dinara. "Debates around Ibādah between Shihab Ad-Din Mardjani and His Opponents." *Islamology* 7, no. 1 (2017): 180–93.

Marghīnānī, Burhān al-Dīn ʿAli b. Abū Bakr al-. *Al-Hidāya*. Vol. 2. Beirut: Dār al-Fikr, n.d.

Marghīnānī, Burhān al-Dīn ʿAli b. Abū Bakr al-. *Al-Hidāyah: The Guidance: A Translation of Al-Hidāyah Fī Sharḥ Bidāyat Al-Mubtadī, a Classical Manual of Ḥanafī Law*. Translated by Imran Ahsan Khan Nyazee. Bristol, UK: Amal Press, 2006.

Marghīnānī, Burhān al-Dīn ʿAli b. Abū Bakr al-. *The Hedaya, or Guide: A Commentary on the Mussulman Laws*. Translated by Charles Hamilton. Lahore: Premier Book House, 1963.

Marjānī, Shihāb al-Dīn al-. *Nāẓūrat al-Ḥaqq fī Farḍiyyat al-ʿIshāʾ wa in lam Yaghib al-Shafaq*. Edited by Ūrkhān ibn Idrīs Anjaqār and ʿAbd al-Qādir ibn Saljūq Yīlmāz. Amman: Dār al-Fatḥ, 2012.

Masud, Muhammad Khalid. "Apostasy and Judicial Separation in British India." In *Islamic Legal Interpretation: Muftis and Their Fatwas*, edited by Muhammad Khalid Masud, Brinkley Messick, and David S. Powers, 193–203. Harvard Studies in Islamic Law. Cambridge, MA: Harvard University Press, 1996.

Masud, Muhammad Khalid, Brinkley Morris Messick, and David Stephan Powers, eds. *Islamic Legal Interpretation: Muftis and Their Fatwas*. Harvard Studies in Islamic Law. Cambridge, MA: Harvard University Press, 1996.

McGregor, Richard, Adam Sabra, and Mireille Loubet, eds. *The Development of Sufism in Mamluk Egypt/La Développement Du Soufisme En Egypte à l'époque Mamelouke*. Cairo: Institut Français d'Archéologie Orientale, 2006.

Meïer, Olivier. *Al-Muqtataf et le Débat sur le Darwinisme: Beyrouth, 1876–1885*. Le Caire: CEDEJ, 1996.

Messick, Brinkley. "Madhhabs and Modernities." In *The Islamic School of Law: Evolution, Devolution, and Progress*, edited by P. Bearman, R. Peters, and F. Vogel, 159–74. Cambridge, MA: Harvard University Press, 2005.

Mian, Ali Altaf. "Troubling Technology: The Deobandī Debate on the Loudspeaker and Ritual Prayer." *Islamic Law and Society* 24, no. 4 (October 3, 2017): 355–83.

Mitchell, Timothy. *Colonising Egypt*. Berkeley: University of California Press, 1991.

Mitchell, Timothy, ed. *Questions of Modernity*. Contradictions of Modernity, vol. 11. Minneapolis: University of Minnesota Press, 2000.

Moosa, Ebrahim. "Shaykh Aḥmad Shākir and the Adoption of a Scientifically-Based Lunar Calendar." *Islamic Law and Society* 5, no. 1 (1998): 57–89.

Moumtaz, Nada. "'Is the Family Waqf a Religious Institution?' Charity, Religion, and Economy in French Mandate Lebanon." *Islamic Law and Society* 25, no. 1–2 (April 3, 2018): 37–77.

Mubārak, ʿAlī. *Al-Khiṭaṭ al-Tawfīqiyya al-Jadīda*. Vol. 14. 20 vols. Būlāq: al-Maṭbaʿa al-Kubrā al-Amīriyya, 1305.

Muḥammad Ḥusayn Haykal. *Tarājim Miṣriyya wa-Gharbiyya*. Cairo: Dār al-Maʿārif, n.d.

Mujīb al-Raḥmān, Qāḍī. "Al-Shaykh ʿAbd al-Ḥayy al-Laknawī." PhD diss., Al-Azhar University, Faculty of Shariʿa, 1964.

Nafi, Basheer M. "Abu al-Thanaʾ al-Alusi: An Alim, Ottoman Mufti, and Exegete of the Qurʾan." *International Journal of Middle East Studies* 34, no. 3 (2002): 465–94.

Nafi, Basheer M. "Taṣawwuf and Reform in Pre-Modern Islamic Culture: In Search of Ibrāhīm al-Kūrānī." *Die Welt des Islams* 42, no. 3 (2002): 307–55.

Nasr, Seyyed Hossein, ed. *The Study Quran: A New Translation and Commentary*. New York: HarperOne, 2017.

Noam, Eli M. *Telecommunications in Africa*. Oxford: Oxford University Press, 1999.

Ogle, Vanessa. *The Global Transformation of Time: 1870–1950*. Cambridge, MA: Harvard University Press, 2015.

Opwis, Felicitas. "Maṣlaḥa in Contemporary Islamic Legal Theory." *Islamic Law and Society* 12, no. 2 (2005): 182–223.

Owen, Roger. *Lord Cromer: Victorian Imperialist, Edwardian Proconsul*. Oxford: Oxford University Press, 2004.

Pagani, Samuela. "The Meaning of the *Ikhtilāf al-Madhāhib* in ʿAbd al-Wahhāb al-Shaʿrānī's *al-Mīzān al-Kubrā*." *Islamic Law and Society* 11, no. 2 (2004): 177–212.

Palmer, Richard E. *Hermeneutics: Interpretation Theory in Schleiermacher, Dilthey, Heidegger, and Gadamer*. Northwestern University Studies in Phenomenology & Existential Philosophy. Evanston, IL: Northwestern University Press, 1969.

Patel, Youshaa. "'Whoever Imitates a People Becomes One of Them': A Hadith and Its Interpreters." *Islamic Law and Society* 25, no. 4 (October 19, 2018): 359–426.

Peters, Rudolph. "Idjtihād and Taqlīd in 18th and 19th Century Islam." *Die Welt des Islams*, New Series, 20, no. 3/4 (January 1, 1980): 131–45. https://doi.org/10.2307/1569501.

Peters, Rudolph. "Muḥammad al-ʿAbbāsī al-Mahdī (d. 1897), Grand Muftī of Egypt, and His *al-Fatāwā al-Mahdiyya*." *Islamic Law and Society* 1, no. 1 (January 1, 1994): 66–82.

Pieper, Josef. *Tradition: Concept and Claim*. Translated by E. Christian Kopff. South Bend, IN: St. Augustine's Press, 2010.

Porter, Jean. "Openness and Constraint: Moral Reflection as Tradition-Guided Inquiry in Alasdair MacIntyre's Recent Works." *The Journal of Religion* 73, no. 4 (1993): 514–36.

Qarāfī, Aḥmad ibn Idrīs al-. *Al-Furūq, aw Anwār al-Burūq fī Anwāʾ al-Furūq*. Al-Ṭabʿa 1. Beirut: Dār al-Kutub al-ʿIlmiyya, 1998.

Qāsimī, Muḥammad Jamāl al-Dīn al-. *Irshād al-Khalq ilā al-ʿAmal bi-Khabar al-Barq*. Maṭbaʿat al-Muqtabas, 1329H.

Quadri, Junaid. "Correspondence, Constructivism, and Representation: Variant Approaches to Astronomical Knowledge in Islamic Legal Texts." *Comparative Studies of South Asia, Africa and the Middle East* 39, no. 3 (December 1, 2019): 513–27.

Queysanne, Bruno. "Tradition and Modernity in the Face of Time." *Traditional Dwellings and Settlements Review* 1, no. 1 (1989): 3–6.

Qurashī, Abū al-Wafāʾ al-. *Al-Jawāhir al-Muḍīʾa*. 2 vols. Hyderabad: Maṭbaʿat Majlis Dāʾirat al-Maʿārif al-Niẓāmiyya, n.d.

Qūrṣāwī, Abū Naṣr al-. *Nastavlenie Li͡udeĭ Na Put' Istiny: Al-Irshād li-l-ʿIbād*. Kazan: Tatarskoe knizhnoe izd-vo, 2005.

Radtke, Bernd, John O'Kane, Knut S. Vikør, and R. S. O'Fahey. *The Exoteric Ahmad Ibn Idris: A Sufi's Critique of the Madhahib and the Wahhabis: Four Arabic Texts With Translation and Commentary*. Leiden: Brill, 1999.

Ragep, F. Jamil. "Copernicus and His Islamic Predecessors: Some Historical Remarks." *History of Science* 45, no. 1 (2007): 65–81.

Rahbar, Muhammad Daüd. "Shāh Walī Ullāh and Ijtihād." *The Muslim World* 45, no. 4 (October 1, 1955): 346–58.

Rahman, Fazlur. "Internal Religious Developments in the Present Century Islam." *Cahiers d'histoire Mondiale/Journal of World History* 2 (1955): 862–79.

Rahman, Fazlur. *Islam & Modernity: Transformation of an Intellectual Tradition*. Publications of the Center for Middle Eastern Studies, no. 15. Chicago: University of Chicago Press, 1982.

Reid, Donald Malcolm. *Cairo University and the Making of Modern Egypt*. Cambridge, UK: Cambridge University Press, 2002.

Reid, Donald Malcolm. "Cairo University and the Orientalists." *International Journal of Middle East Studies* 19, no. 1 (February 1, 1987): 51–75.

Renan, Ernest. "Islamism and Science." In *The Poetry of the Celtic Races, and Other Essays*, translated by William G. Hutchison. London: W. Scott, 1896.

Renan, Ernest. *L'Islam et la Science: Avec la Réponse d'Afghâni*. Montpellier: Archange minotaure, 2003.

Renan, Ernest. "L'Islamisme et la Science." *Journal des Débats Politiques et Littéraires*. March 30, 1883.

Riḍā, Muḥammad Rashīd. *Al-Khilāfa aw al-Imāma al-ʿUẓmā*. Cairo: Maṭbaʿat al-Manār, 1923.

Riḍā, Muḥammad Rashīd. *Al-Manār wa-l-Azhar*. Cairo: Maṭbaʿat al-Manār, 1353H.

Riḍā, Muḥammad Rashīd. "Bāb al-Murāsala wa-l-Munāẓara." *Al-Manār* 9, no. 9 (1906): 694.

Riḍā, Muḥammad Rashīd. *Maqālāt al-Shaykh Rashīd Riḍā al-Siyāsiyya*. Edited by Yūsuf Ībish and Yūsuf Q. Khūrī. 5 vols. Beirut: Dār Ibn ʿArabī, 1994.

Riḍā, Muḥammad Rashīd.*Muḥāwarāt al-Muṣliḥ wa-l-Muqallid wa-l-Waḥda al-Islāmiyya*. Cairo: Maṭbaʿat Majallat al-Manār al-Islāmiyya, 1324H.

Riḍā, Muḥammad Rashīd.*Muḥāwarāt al-Muṣliḥ wa-l-Muqallid wa-l-Waḥda al-Islāmiyya*. Cairo: Dār al-Nashr; Dār al-Manār, 2008.

Riḍā, Muḥammad Rashīd. "Risālatān fī Qirāʾat al-Fūnughrāf wa-l-Sukūrtah." *Al-Manār* 9, no. 2 (1906): 153–54.

Riḍā, Muḥammad Rashīd. *Tārīkh al-Ustādh al-Imām al-Shaykh Muḥammad ʿAbduh*. 2 vols. Cairo: Dār al-Faḍīla, 2006.

Robinson, Francis. "Islamic Reform and Modernities in South Asia." *Modern Asian Studies* 42, no. 2/3 (2008): 259–81.

Ryad, Umar. "A Printed Muslim 'Lighthouse' in Cairo: *al-Manār*'s Early Years, Religious Aspiration and Reception (1898–1903)." *Arabica* 56, no. 1 (2009): 27–60.

Sabra, A. I. "The Appropriation and Subsequent Naturalization of Greek Science in Medieval Islam: A Preliminary Statement." *History of Science* 25 (1987): 223–43.

Ṣabrī, Muṣṭafā. *Mawqif al-Bashar Taḥta Sulṭān al-Qadar*. Beirut: Dār al-Hijra, 1950.

Sadeghi, Behnam. *The Logic of Law Making in Islam: Women and Prayer in the Legal Tradition*. New York: Cambridge University Press, 2013.

Saʿdi, Lutfi M., George Sarton, and W. T. Van Dyck. "Al-Hakîm Cornelius Van Alen Van Dyck (1818–1895)." *Isis* 27, no. 1 (May 1, 1937): 20–45.

Saliba, George. *Islamic Science and the Making of the European Renaissance*. Transformations. Cambridge, MA: MIT Press, 2007.

Sanūsī, Muḥammad ibn ʿAlī al-. *al-Majmūʿa al-Mukhtāra min Muʾallafāt Muḥammad ibn ʿAlī al-Sanūsī*. Manchester, UK, 1990.

Sarakhsī, Shams al-Dīn al-. *Al-Mabsūṭ*. Vol. 3. Beirut: Dār al-Maʿrifa, n.d.

Sayyid-Marsot, Afaf Lutfi. *Egypt's Liberal Experiment, 1922–1936*. Berkeley: University of California Press, 1977.

Schacht, Joseph. *An Introduction to Islamic Law*. Oxford: Clarendon Press, 1982.

Schayegh, Cyrus. *Who Is Knowledgeable Is Strong: Science, Class, and the Formation of Modern Iranian Society, 1900–1950*. Berkeley: Univerity of California Press, 2009.

Schulze, Reinhard. *Islamischer Internationalismus Im 20. Jahrhundert: Untersuchungen Zur Geschichte Der Islamischen Weltliga*. Leiden: Brill, 1990.

Schwartz, Kathryn A. "The Political Economy of Private Printing in Cairo as Told from a Commissioning Deal Turned Sour, 1871." *International Journal of Middle East Studies* 49, no. 1 (February 2017): 25–45.

Scott, David, and Charles Hirschkind, eds. *Powers of the Secular Modern: Talal Asad and His Interlocutors*. Cultural Memory in the Present. Stanford, CA: Stanford University Press, 2006.

Sedgwick, Mark J. *Muhammad Abduh: A Biography*. Cairo: The American University in Cairo Press, 2009.

Shafīq, Aḥmad. *Mudhakkirātī fī Niṣf Qarn*. Vol. 2. 2 vols. Cairo: Maṭbaʿat Miṣr, 1936.

Shaham, Ron. *Family and the Courts in Modern Egypt: A Study Based on Decisions by the Sharīʿa Courts, 1900-1955*. Leiden: Brill, 1997.

Shaham, Ron. "Judicial Divorce at the Wife's Initiative: The Sharīʿa Courts of Egypt, 1920–1955." *Islamic Law and Society* 1, no. 2 (January 1, 1994): 217–57.

Shahrastānī, Muḥammad b. ʿAbd al-Karīm. *Al-Milal wa-l-Niḥal*. Beirut: Dār al-Kutub al-ʿIlmiyya, 1992.

Shākir, Usāma Muḥammad, ed. *Min Aʿlām al-ʿAṣr*. Cairo, 2001.

Shapin, Steven. *The Scientific Revolution*. Chicago: University of Chicago Press, 1996.

Sharabi, Hisham. *Arab Intellectuals and the West: The Formative Years, 1875–1914*. Baltimore: Johns Hopkins Press, 1970.

Sharkey, Heather J. *American Evangelicals in Egypt: Missionary Encounters in an Age of Empire*. Princeton, NJ: Princeton University Press, 2008.

Shaʿrānī, ʿAbd al-Wahhāb al-. *Al-Mīzān*. Cairo: Maṭbaʿat al-Kastaliyya, 1279H.

Shils, Edward. *Tradition*. Chicago: University of Chicago Press, 2006.

Sirriyeh, Elizabeth. "Rashid Rida's Autobiography of the Syrian Years, 1865–1897." *Arabic & Middle Eastern Literature* 3, no. 2 (July 1, 2000): 179–94. https://doi.org/10.1080/13666160008718238.

Skovgaard-Petersen, Jakob. *Defining Islam for the Egyptian State: Muftis and Fatwas of the Dār al-Iftā*. Leiden: Brill, 1997.

Smith, Wilfred Cantwell. "The Azhar Journal: Survey and Critique." PhD diss., Princeton University, 1948.

Smith, Wilfred Cantwell. *Islam in Modern History*. Princeton, NJ: Princeton University Press, 1957.

Smith, Wilfred Cantwell. *The Meaning and End of Religion: A New Approach to the Religious Traditions of Mankind*. New York: Macmillan, 1962.

Snouck Hurgronje, C. "Islam and the Phonograph." *The Muslim World* 5, no. 2 (April 1, 1915): 159–65.

Snouck Hurgronje, C. *Islam und Phonograph*. Batavia, 1900.

Spannaus, Nathan. *Preserving Islamic Tradition: Abū Naṣr Qūrṣāwī and the Beginnings of Modern Reformism*. New York: Oxford University Press, 2019.

Spannaus, Nathan. "The Ur-Text of Jadidism: Abū Naṣr Qūrṣāwī's *Irshād* and the Historiography of Muslim Modernism in Russia." *Journal of the Economic and Social History of the Orient* 59, no. 1–2 (2016): 93–125.

Stolz, Daniel A. *The Lighthouse and the Observatory: Islam, Science, and Empire in Late Ottoman Egypt*. Cambridge, UK: Cambridge University Press, 2018.

Subkī, Taqī al-Dīn al-. *Al-ʿAlam al-Manshur fī Ithbāt al-Shuhūr*. Cairo: Matbaʿat Kurdistān al-ʿIlmiyya, 1911.

Subkī, Taqī al-Dīn al-. "Al-ʿAlam al-Manshūr fī Hilāl Khayr al-Shuhūr." In *Arbaʿa Rasāʾil fī Hilāl Khayr al-Shuhūr*. Beirut: Dār Ibn Ḥazm, 2000.

Subkī, Taqī al-Dīn al-. *Shifāʾ al-Saqām fī Ziyārat Khayr al-Anām*. Būlāq: al-Maṭbaʿa al-Kubrā al-Amīriyya, 1318H.

Ṭaḥṭāwī, Aḥmad b. Muḥammad al-. *Hāshiyat al-Ṭaḥṭāwī ʿalā al-Durr al-Mukhtār*. 4 vols. Cairo: Maṭbaʿat Būlāq, 1254H.

"Taqlīd." *Al-Mawsūʿa al-Fiqhiyya*. Kuwait: Wizārat al-Awqāf wa-l-Shuʾūn al-Islāmiyya, 1988.

Tageldin, Shaden M. *Disarming Words: Empire and the Seductions of Translation in Egypt*. Berkeley: University of California Press, 2011.

Taylor, Charles. *Philosophical Arguments*. Cambridge, MA: Harvard University Press, 1995.

Taylor, Charles. *A Secular Age*. Cambridge, MA: Belknap Press of Harvard University Press, 2007.

Tayob, Abdulkader. *Religion in Modern Islamic Discourse*. New York: Columbia University Press, 2009.

Tibawi, A. L. "The Genesis and Early History of the Syrian Protestant College: Part I." *Middle East Journal* 21, no. 1 (January 1, 1967): 1–15.

Tibawi, A. L. "The Genesis and Early History of the Syrian Protestant College: Part II." *Middle East Journal* 21, no. 2 (April 1, 1967): 199–212.

Trimingham, J. Spencer. *The Sufi Orders in Islam*. Oxford: Clarendon Press, 1971.

Tucker, Judith E. *In the House of the Law: Gender and Islamic Law in Ottoman Syria and Palestine*. Berkeley: University of California Press, 2000.

ʿUthmānī, Muḥammad Taqī al-. *Uṣūl al-Iftāʾ wa-Ādābuhu*. Karachi: Maktabat Maʿārif al-Qurʾān, 2011.

Van Dyck, Cornelius. *Uṣūl ʿIlm al-Hayʾa*. Beirut, 1874.

Vatikiotis, P. J. *The History of Modern Egypt: From Muhammad Ali to Mubarak*. 4th ed. Baltimore: The Johns Hopkins University Press, 1991.

Vikør, Knut. *Sufi and Scholar on the Desert Edge: Muḥammad b. ʿAlī al-Sanūsī and His Brotherhood*. Evanston, IL: Northwestern University Press, 1995.

Voll, John. "ʿAbdallah ibn Salim al-Basri and 18th Century Hadith Scholarship." *Die Welt des Islams* 42, no. 3 (2002): 356–72.

Voll, John. "Hadith Scholars and Tariqahs: An Ulama Group in the 18th Century Haramayn and Their Impact in the Islamic World." *Journal of Asian and African Studies* 15, no. 3 (January 1, 1980): 264–273.

Voll, John. "Muḥammad Ḥayyā al-Sindī and Muḥammad ibn ʿAbd al-Wahhāb: An Analysis of an Intellectual Group in Eighteenth-Century Madīna." *Bulletin of the School of Oriental and African Studies, University of London* 38, no. 1 (1975): 32–39.

Voll, John. "The Sudanese Mahdi: Frontier Fundmentalist." *International Journal of Middle East Studies* 10, no. 2 (1979): 145–66.

von Grunebaum, G. E. "Muslim World View and Muslim Science." *Dialectica* 17, no. 4 (1963): 353–367.

Weinberg, Steven. *To Explain the World: The Discovery of Modern Science*. 1st ed. New York: Harper, 2015.

Wheeler, Brannon M. *Applying the Canon in Islam: The Authorization and Maintenance of Interpretive Reasoning in Ḥanafī Scholarship*. Toward a Comparative Philosophy of Religions. Albany: State University of New York Press, 1996.

Winter, Michael. *Society and Religion in Early Ottoman Egypt: Studies in the Writings of ʿAbd al-Wahhāb al-Shaʿrāni*. Studies in Islamic Culture and History, vol. 4. New Brunswick, NJ: Transaction Books, 1982.

Yalçınkaya, M. Alper. *Learned Patriots: Debating Science, State, and Society in the Nineteenth-Century Ottoman Empire*. Chicago: The University of Chicago Press, 2015.

Zaman, Muhammad Qasim. *Modern Islamic Thought in a Radical Age: Religious Authority and Internal Criticism*. Cambridge, UK: Cambridge University Press, 2012.

Zaman, Muhammad Qasim. *The Ulama in Contemporary Islam: Custodians of Change*. Princeton Studies in Muslim Politics. Princeton, NJ: Princeton University Press, 2002.

Zaydān, Jurjī. *Tarājim Mashāhīr al-Sharq fī al-Qarn al-Tāsiʿ ʿAshar*. Al-Ṭabʿa 3. Cairo: Maṭbaʿat al-Hilāl, 1922.

Zebiri, Kate. *Maḥmūd Shaltūt and Islamic Modernism*. Oxford: Oxford University Press, 1993.

Zeghal, Malika. *Gardiens De l'Islam: Les Oulémas d'Al Azhar Dans l'Egypte Contemporaine*. Paris: Presses de la Fondation nationale des sciences politiques, 1996.

Ziadeh, Farhat. *Lawyers, the Rule of Law and Liberalism in Modern Egypt*. Stanford, CA: Hoover Institution on War Revolution and Peace, Stanford University, 1968.

Ziadeh, Nicola. *Sanūsīyah: A Study of a Revivalist Movement in Islam*. Leiden: E.J. Brill, 1958.

Ziriklī, Khayr al-Dīn al-. *al-Aʿlām: Qāmūs Tarājim li-Ashhar al-Rijāl wa-l-Nisāʾ min al-ʿArab wa-l-Mustaʿribīn wa-l-Mustashriqīn*. 15th ed. Beirut: Dār al-ʿIlm li-l-Malāyīn, 2002.

Zuckert, Catherine H. "Hermeneutics in Practice: Gadamer on Ancient Philosophy." In *The Cambridge Companion to Gadamer*, edited by Robert J Dostal. Cambridge, UK: Cambridge University Press, 2002.

Zysow, Aron. *The Economy of Certainty: An Introduction to the Typology of Islamic Legal Theory*. Atlanta, GA: Lockwood Press, 2013.

Index

For the benefit of digital users, indexed terms that span two pages (e.g., 52–53) may, on occasion, appear on only one of those pages.

ʿAbbās Ḥilmī II (Khedive of Egypt), 1, 3–4, 37–40, 41–42
ʿAbbāsī al-Mahdī, Muḥammad al-, 25, 37–38, 70
ʿAbd Allāh b. ʿAbbās, 3–4, 197
ʿAbd al-Rāziq, ʿAlī, 28–29, 35–36, 165–66
ʿAbduh, Muḥammad, 12, 16–17, 18–19, 28n.82, 31, 33, 37–43, 60–61, 114–15, 210, 217
  run-ins with Muḥammad ʿIllīsh, 68–70
  response to Hanotaux, 212–13
Abū Ḥanīfa, 79–80, 88–89, 94–95, 96, 176, 177, 181, 186–87, 189
Abū Yūsuf, 79–80, 88–89, 178, 186–87, 189
Aden, 48–49, 102
Afghānī, Jamāl al-Dīn al-, 60–61, 205–6
  debate with Renan, 116–19
Aḥmad b. Idrīs, 70–71
al-ʿAlam al-Manshūr fī Ithbāt al-Shuhūr (al-Subkī), 145–53
Alasdair MacIntyre, 9–18
ʿAlawī, Sayyid ʿUthmān b. ʿAbd Allāh b. ʿAqīl al-, 133–34
Alexandria, 4–5, 37
ʿAlī, Muḥammad (Mehmed Ali), 27n.78, 112–13, 168–69
Ālūsī, Shihāb al-Dīn al-, 57, 214–15
ambivalence, 106–7
Amīn, Aḥmad, 118
Amīn, Qāsim, 31, 45
Anas b. Mālik, 178–79
Andalusia, 114–15
Anṣārī, Zakariyyā al-, 72–74, 75
Arendt, Hannah, 162–64
Asad, Talal, 9–18, 19, 100, 168–69, 170–71, 172, 181–82, 185–86, 218–19
Ashʿarism, 68–70
astronomy
  astronomical calculations, 35, 140–45
  premodern Ḥanafī attitudes, 140–45
Aswan, 1, 4
ʿAṭṭār, Ḥasan al-
  Maqāmāt al-Faransīs, 130
  on *ijtihād* and *taqlīd*, 70–71
authority
  juristic authority, 9, 34–35
Avicenna. *See* Ibn Sīnā
ʿayn al-sharīʿa, 75–76, 78
ʿAynī, Badr al-Dīn al-, 151–52
Azhar, 21, 24–26, 60–61, 68–70
  Azhar journal, 30–31
  competing institutions in the modern period, 112–13
  controversy over clothing, 210
  curricular reform, 216–18, 219
  curriculum, 52n.45, 60–61, 214–15
  students' views of Bakhīt, 58, 105

Badāʾiʿ al-Ṣanāʾiʿ (al-Kāsānī), 184, 192n.83
Baghdad, 22–23, 102, 214–15
Bakhīt al-Muṭīʿī, Muḥammad
  biography, 24–33
  as commentator, 29–30
  confiding in al-Ghumārī, 40–41
  on conformity of Islam and astronomical knowledge, 119–21
  criticisms of later Ḥanafī scholars, 186–87, 190–91, 193
  debate with Riḍā, 43–46
  in the eyes of Azharī students, 58
  fatwa on Bolshevism, 25–26, 101–4, 105
  fatwa on insurance, 50–51

Bakhīt al-Muṭīʿī, Muḥammad (*cont.*)
on free will and predestination (*al-qaḍāʾ wa-l-qadar*), 213–15
historical consciousness, 96–98
history of astronomy, 123–28, 131–32
on *ijtihād,* 66–68, 82–90
on *ʿilm* (knowledge) and *ruʾya* (sighting), 149–52
influence of European tastes and manners, 106
ontology of objectivity, 154–59
opponent of Reformists, 31–33, 34, 40–43
on the phonograph, 135–38
as producer of colonial discourse, 132
reason for writing the *Irshād,* 1–4
on relying on astronomical calculations to determine Ramadan, 145–62
on Renan-Afghānī debate, 116–19
representationalism, 159–62
response to ʿAlī ʿAbd al-Rāziq, 165–67
scientific realism, 136–38, 159–60
on the speech of God, 136–37
technological optimism, 135–38
on the telegraph, 195–96, 202–6
on the *umūr dīniyya,* 186–202
on using a telescope to sight the new moon, 159–61
al-Barq al-Wamīḍ (al-Marjānī), 53, 54
Bazdawī, Abū al-Yusr al-, 79–80
Beirut, 115, 121, 124
Bhabha, Homi, 35, 106–8, 130, 131–32
Bourdieu, Pierre, 46
Bukhara, 180
Būlāqī, Muṣṭafā al-, 71–72
Burak, Guy, 84–85
al-Burda (al-Būṣīrī), 130

Cairo, 4–5, 22–23, 37, 78–79, 115, 209
Calder, Norman, 83, 99–100
Casanova, José, 171–72, 184–85
colonial modernity, 7–8, 9–18, 35
colonialism, 4–5, 102–3, 129–32, 155–56, 206–7, 215–16, 218–19
Copernicus, 122–23, 125–27, 131, 139–40
Crecelius, Daniel, 27n.78, 109n.27, 216–17
crescent. See *hilāl*
Cromer, Lord (Evelyn Baring), 4–5, 19n.57, 206–7
cultural imperialism, 129–32

Dabbūsī, Abū Zayd al-, 157–58
Dallal, Ahmad, 85–87, 140n.23
Damascus, 145, 146
Delanoue, Gilbert, 74–75
Delhi Sultanate, 6–7
democracy, 167
Di-Capua, Yoav, 98
dīn. See religion, concept of
divorce law, 8–9, 29–30, 217–18, 219
dunyā, 183–85
al-Durr al-Mukhtār (al-Ḥaṣkafī), 79–80

Egyptian state, 4
Eid, 1
Elshakry, Marwa, 113–15, 120–21, 211
endowments, 8–9, 27n.78, 29–30, 217–18, 219
Ephrat, Eliza 122
epistemological approach to law, 35, 149–52, 187, 190, 201

Fahmy, Khaled, 169–70
Fārābī, Abū Naṣr al-, 125–27
Fatḥ al-Qadīr (Ibn al-Humām), 181, 196–99
fatwas, 2–3, 21
Fikrī, ʿAbd Allāh, 114–16, 119–20, 124
France, 112–13
free will. See *al-qaḍāʾ wa-l-qadar*
al-Furūq (al-Qarāfī), 182n.50, 183–84

Gadamer, Hans-Georg, 74, 98, 99–100
Galileo, 122–23, 124–27, 131, 139–40
Gesink, Indira Falk, 11n.26, 64–66, 217–19
Ghālī, Buṭrus, 38–39
Ghazālī, Abū Ḥāmid al-, 109–10
Ghumārī, Aḥmad b. Ṣiddīq al-
biographical details of Bakhīt in *al-Baḥr al-ʿAmīq,* 25n.71, 26, 28n.82, 31, 58, 104n.17, 105, 106, 136
relationship with Bakhīt, 40–41
on relying on astronomical calculations to determine Ramadan, 141n.25
Gutas, Dimitri, 110

hadith
  hadith criticism, 52–54
  positioned in opposition to juristic opinions, 84
Hallaq, Wael B., 78, 89
Ḥalwānī, Shams al-A'imma al-, 79–80, 143, 199–201
Ḥanafism, 6–7, 8–9, 12–13, 17–18, 78–82, 99–100, 167–68
  on astronomy and astronomical calculations, 140–45
  dissident forms of Ḥanafism, 85–87
  on the *umūr dīniyya*, 173–86
Hanotaux, Gabriel, 211–14
Ḥaqīqat al-Islām wa-Uṣūl al-Ḥukm (Bakhīt), 28–29, 165–67
Ḥasan Bāshā Madkūr, 2, 5
Ḥāshiyat Radd al-Muḥtār (Ibn ʿĀbidīn), 78–79, 81, 95
Ḥaṣkafī, ʿAlā' al-Dīn al-, 81, 143
Hay'at Kibār al-ʿUlamā' (Council of Senior Ulama), 27, 28–29, 165
Heidegger, Martin, 98, 100, 139
heliocentrism, 122–23, 124–27, 131, 157–58
Helwan Observatory, 138–39, 159
al-Hidāya (al-Marghīnānī), 143, 175–77, 180
hijrī calendar, 1n.1, 141n.24
hilāl, 1n.1
  disagreements over sightings, 3–4
Hilmiyyat al-Zaytun. *See* Zaytun
historical consciousness, 9, 34–35, 93–94, 96–100
history of science, 121–28
Hourani, Albert, 22n.66, 165–67

al-Ibāna (al-Ashʿarī), 214–15
Ibn ʿĀbidīn, Muḥammad Amīn, 78–79, 81, 89–90, 94–95
  on "difference in horizons" (*ikhtilāf al-maṭāliʿ*), 196
  on *istifāḍa*, 199–201
  on new moon sightings from outside the city or an elevated altitude, 189–91
  on relying on astronomical calculations to determine Ramadan, 142–45
Ibn Battuta, 6–7
Ibn Daqīq al-ʿĪd, 151–52
Ibn Ḥajar al-ʿAsqalānī, 151–52
Ibn Ḥajar al-Haytamī al-Makkī, 85–87
Ibn al-Humām, Kamāl al-Dīn, 181, 196–99
Ibn Kamāl Pāshā (Kemalpaşazade), 78–82, 84–85, 87–88
Ibn Nujaym, Zayn al-Dīn b. Ibrāhīm, 143
Ibn Rushd, 141n.25
Ibn al-Shāṭṭ, 183–84
Ibn Sīnā, Abū ʿAlī, 125–27
Ibn Surayj, 141n.25
Ibn Taymiyya, Taqī al-Dīn Aḥmad, 31, 43–46
Ījī, ʿAḍud al-Dīn al-, 125–27, 131
Ihde, Don, 159–60
ijmāʿ (consensus), 45
ijtihād, 34–35, 63–64
  Bakhīt on *ijtihād*, 66–68, 90–91
  ijtihād as unifying and egalitarian, 76–77, 92
  prevailing views before Bakhīt, 67–82
  Riḍā's advocacy of *ijtihād*, 63–64
  in secondary scholarship, 64–66
ʿIllīsh, Muḥammad, 25
  defense of *taqlīd*, 70–78
  opposition to ʿAbduh, 68–70
  on telegraph reports, 195–96
ʿilm (knowledge)
  vs. *ru'ya* (sighting), 143–45
ʿImāra, Muḥammad, 165
India, 2, 4–6, 19, 102, 114–15, 205
insurance (*sūkūrtāh*), 29–30, 48–50
Irshād Ahl al-Milla ilā Ithbāt al-Ahilla (Guidance to the Muslims on Determining the New Moons) (Bakhīt), 2, 8–9, 33–34
  discussion of *ijtihād* and *taqlīd*, 82–90
  on relying on astronomical calculations to determine Ramadan, 145–62
  on the *umūr dīniyya*, 186–202
Irshād al-Khalq ilā al-ʿAmal bi-Khabar al-Barq (al-Qāsimī), 195–96
al-Islām wa-Uṣūl al-Ḥukm (ʿAbd al-Rāziq), 28–29, 165–66
Ismāʿīl Pāshā (Khedive of Egypt), 4–5
Istanbul, 78–79, 102, 115
istifāḍa, 199–202
Iyās b. Muʿāwiya, 178–79

Jadidism, 46, 85–87
al-Jawāhir al-Muḍīʾa (al-Qurashī), 78–79
Jawharī, Ṭanṭāwī al-, 114–15
Jisr, Ḥusayn al-, 33, 60–61
on the phonograph, 133–34
juristic typology, 34–35, 78–90

Kaflaytwī, ʿAbd al-Ḥayy al-, 6–7
kalām, 124–25, 127, 140n.23
Kanz al-Daqāʾiq (al-Nasafī), 79–80, 142–43
Karkhī, Abū al-Ḥasan al-, 79–80
Kāsānī, ʿAlāʾ al-Dīn al-, 184, 192n.83
Kattānī, ʿAbd al-Ḥayy al-, 55–57
Kawtharī, Muḥammad Zāhid al-, 30, 216
Kaya, Eyyup Said, 99–100
Kazan, 22–23
Keddie, Nikki R., 117
Khalid, Adeeb, 46
Khan, Sir Sayyid Ahmad, 205–6
Khaṣṣāf, Aḥmad al-, 79–80
Khawwāṣ, ʿAlī al-, 72–74
Kimon, Daniel, 211–14
King, David A., 110
Koselleck, Reinhart, 93–94
Kūrānī, Ibrāhīm b. Ḥasan al-, 214–15
Kurayb
hadith of, 3n.7, 197

Laknawī, ʿAbd al-Ḥayy al-, 57, 85–89, 97, 214–15
Laknawī, Baḥr al-ʿUlūm al-, 85–87
Liberal Constitutionalist Party, 28–29, 104
Lucknow, 22–23

Mabādiʾ ʿIlm al-Hayʾa (Ephrat), 122
al-Mabsūṭ (al-Sarakhsī), 142, 176–77, 189
madhhab, 21–24, 141
differences between *madhhabs*, 16
as historical decline, 76, 77, 81–82
"social *madhhab*," 21–24, 46–57, 85, 214–15
Majmaʿ al-Baḥrayn (al-Baʿlabakī), 79–80
Mālikism, 24, 37–38, 68–70, 71–72, 83, 177n.37, 182n.50, 183–84
al-Manār (journal), 37, 43–44n.20, 46–48, 114–15
dialogue between *muṣliḥ* and *muqallid*, 59–61
Maqarrī, Aḥmad al-, 54
Marghīnānī, Burhān al-Dīn ʿAlī b. Abū Bakr al-, 79–80, 143, 175–76, 180
Marjānī, Shihāb al-Dīn al-, 53, 54–55, 57, 145–46, 214–15
on *ijtihād* and *taqlīd*, 85–89
on prayers in extreme latitudes, 153–54
maṣlaḥa, 64
Māturīdism, 213–14
Medina, 2, 3–4, 5, 105, 197
Messick, Brinkley, 48
al-Milal wa-l-Niḥal (al-Shahrastānī), 96
Milner Commission, 104
mimicry, 35, 106–8, 130, 131–32
Mirghānī, Muḥammad ʿUthmān al-. *See* Mirghāniyya
Mirghāniyya, 70–71
Mitchell, Timothy, 10n.24, 11n.26, 35, 154–56, 161, 203–4
Modernist, 8–9, 11n.25
modernity. *See* colonial modernity
Muʿāwiya b. Abū Sufyān, 197
al-Muʾayyad (journal), 41–42
mudhabdhab, 105–6
mujmal, 73–74
al-Mukhtār (al-Mawṣilī), 79–80
Muqāranat Baʿḍ Nuṣūṣ al-Hayʾa bi-l-Wārid fī al-Nuṣūṣ al-Sharʿiyya (Fikrī), 114–16
al-Muqtaṭaf (journal), 112–13, 121, 124, 135–37
Muṭarrif b. ʿAbd Allāh b. al-Shikhkhīr, 141n.25
Muʿtazilism, 68–70

al-Nāfiʿ al-Kabīr (al-Laknawī), 85–89
Nallino, Carlo, 118
Napoleon, 128–30, 131
narrations. See *riwāya*
Nashr al-ʿArf (Ibn ʿĀbidīn), 94–95
nationalism, 26, 28, 40–41, 209–10
Nayl al-Awṭār (al-Shawkānī), 54
Nāẓūrat al-Ḥaqq (al-Marjānī), 85–89, 97
new moon. See *hilāl*

objectivity, 9, 139, 153–59
Ottoman
abolition of caliphate, 28–29, 165–66, 209
Young Ottomans, 114–15

phonograph, 7–8, 29–30, 133–38
photography, 7–8, 29–30
predestination. See *al-qaḍāʾ wa-l-qadar*
print, 6–7
  comparison to phonograph, 134–35
  use by Reformists, 46–48, 82–83
proceduralism (legal), 35–36, 54, 172–73, 196–99, 200–1
Ptolemy, 122–23, 124–27
Pythagoras, 122–23, 124–27, 131

al-qaḍāʾ wa-l-qadar, 211–16
qadi (judge), 1, 4, 6–7, 176–81
Qāḍīkhān, Ḥasan b. Manṣūr, 79–80, 84n.87, 193
Qarāfī, Shihāb al-Dīn Aḥmad b. Idrīs, 182n.50, 183–84
Qārī, Mullā ʿAlī al-, 78–79
Qāsim b. Quṭlūbughā, 83n.82
Qāsimī, Jamāl al-Dīn al-, 195–96
qibla, 42
Qubba Palace, 39
Qudūrī, Aḥmad b. Muḥammad al-, 79–80
Qūrṣāwī, Abū Naṣr al-, 85–87
Qushayrī, al-, 149–50, 151–52

al-Rābiṭa al-Sharqiyya, 28–29
Radd al-Muḥtār. See *Ḥāshiyat Radd al-Muḥtār*
al-Raḥma al-Mursala (al-Kattānī), 55–56
Ramlī, Shihāb al-Dīn, 141–42n.26, 143–44
Rangoon, 6–7
Rawḍat al-Madāris (journal), 114–15
Rāzī, Aḥmad b. ʿAlī al- (al-Jaṣṣāṣ), 79–80
al-Rāzī, Muḥammad b. Muqātil, 141n.25, 142
Reformist movement, 8–9, 10, 21, 31, 112–13
religion
  concept of, 9, 35–36, 168–69, 170–71, 172–73, 181–86, 205–6
  religious matters (*umūr dīniyya*), 35–36, 168–69, 170–71, 172–202
Renan, Ernest, 116–19, 211–12
representationalism, 10n.24, 35, 138, 139–40, 145–62
revolution
  Egyptian revolution of 1919, 28, 104
Reynolds, John, 138–39
Riḍā, Muḥammad Rashīd, 12, 16–17, 31–32, 33, 34, 114–15
  on Azharīs' unfamiliarity with geography, 51
  criticisms of Bakhīt, 43–46, 103–4
  historical progressivism, 91–93
  on *ijtihād* and *taqlīd*, 59–64
  on insurance, 48–50
  intrigues against, 38–39
ritual (*ʿibāda*), 9, 182–83, 184–85
  ritual law, 8–9
riwāya, 173–95
Robinson, Francis, 215–16
Russia, 102, 114–15
ruʾya (sighting)
  vs. *ʿilm* (knowledge), 143–45

Sabra, A. I., 109n.28, 110–11
Ṣabrī, Muṣṭafā, 209–14, 216
Saliba, George, 110
al-Sanūsī, 70–72
Sanūsiyya. *See* al-Sanūsī
Saqqāf, ʿAlawī b. Aḥmad al-, 49
Sarakhsī, Shams al-Aʾimma al-, 79–80, 142, 143, 176–77, 189
Sarton, George, 113–14
science
  modern science, 60–61, 134–35, 139
  "new science" in modern Egypt, 112–29
  scientific optimism, 9
  scientism, 35, 123–24
  secondary scholarship on Muslim contributions, 108–11
secularism, 165–67
  concept of the secular, 167, 170–71, 184–86
  secularity, 9, 167
  secularization, 35–36, 168–73
seduction. *See* translational seduction
Shāfiʿism, 16, 49, 72–73, 83, 85–87, 141n.25, 141–42n.26, 142–43, 145–46, 148, 151–52, 151n.48, 189, 197
Shafīq, Aḥmad, 40n.11, 41–42
Shāh Walī Allāh. *See* Walī Allāh, Shāh
shahāda, 173–95
Shahrastānī, ʿAbd al-Karīm al-, 96
Shākir, Muḥammad, 37–40, 41–42, 58
Shaʿrānī, ʿAbd al-Wahhāb al-
  on following the *mujtahid* imams, 72–76

shariʿa courts, reorganization or reform of, 25–26, 37–38, 105, 168–69, 217–18
Shawkānī, Muḥammad al-, 54
Shaybānī, Muḥammad b. Ḥasan al-, 79–80, 88–89, 178, 186–87, 189–90
Shaykh al-Azhar (Rector of al-Azhar), 27, 133
Shirbīnī, ʿAbd al-Raḥmān al-, 133
Ṣidqī, Tawfīq, 114–15
Singapore, 48
Sinnar, 70–71
al-Siyāsa al-Usbūʿiyya (weekly), 29n.89, 118
Skovgaard-Petersen, Jakob, 26n.74, 27n.80, 34, 46–48
Smith, Wilfred Cantwell, 181–82
Snouck Hurgronje, C., 134–35
Spannaus, Nathan, 85–87
Stolz, Daniel A., 114–16
Subkī, Taqī al-Dīn al-, 31, 43–44
  on Ḥanafī conceptualizations of reports of new moon sightings, 177–80, 181–82
  on relying on astronomical calculations to determine Ramadan, 145–53
Sudan, 102
Suez, 4–5
Syria, 3–4, 197

al-Ṭabaqāt al-Saniyya (al-Tamīmī), 88
tafsīr ʿilmī ("scientific exegesis" of the Qurʾan), 114–15, 116–29
Tageldin, Shaden, 107–8, 129–32
Ṭaḥāwī, Abū Jaʿfar al-, 79–80, 188–90
Ṭahṭāwī, Aḥmad b. Muḥammad al-, 95
Ṭahṭāwī, Rifāʿa al-, 112–13
  on modern science, 128–29
tajaddud, 96
Tamīmī, Taqī al-Dīn al-, 88
Tanbīh al-ʿUqūl al-Insāniyya li-mā fī Āyāt al-Qurʾān min al-ʿUlūm al-Kawniyya wa-l-ʿUmrāniyya (Bakhīt), 116–19
Tangier, 6–7
taqlīd
  ʿIllīsh on *taqlīd*, 70–78
  Riḍā's criticism of *taqlīd*, 61–64
  taqlīd as divisive and hierarchical, 76–77
Tārīkh al-Falak ʿinda al-ʿArab (Nallino), 118
Tārīkh al-Ustādh al-Imām (Riḍā), 28n.82, 37, 38–39
ṭarīq mūjib, 199
Taṭhīr al-Fuʾād min Danas al-Iʿtiqād (Bakhīt), 44–45
Tawfīq al-Raḥmān li-l-Tawfīq bayna mā Qālahu ʿUlamāʾ al-Hayʾa wa-bayna mā jāʾa fī al-Aḥādīth al-Ṣaḥīḥa wa-Āyāt al-Qurʾān (Bakhīt), 119–21, 123–28
Taylor, Charles, 139–40, 160–61, 205–6
Tayob, Abdulkader, 205
telegraph, 1–2, 3–5, 7–8, 29–30, 35–36, 138–39
  telegraphic infrastructure, 4–5
  telegraphic reports, 1, 4, 195–96
telescope, 7–8, 138–39, 159–61, 162–63
testimonies. See *shahāda*
tradition
  concept of, 9–18
  Islamic law as, 7
  the *madhhab* as, 14–16
  traditional view of *fiqh*, 74–75, 77
translational seduction, 107–8, 129–32
transregionalism, 4, 21–24, 34, 50, 219–20
Transvaal fatwa, 38–39, 210
Treaty of Lausanne, 209
Tripoli, 60–61

ulama, 6–7, 10–11, 18–21
  ʿulamāʾ al-sūʾ, 44–45
Umm al-Faḍl, 197
umma, 61
ʿUqūd Rasm al-Muftī (Ibn ʿĀbidīn), 78–79
al-ʿUrwa al-Wuthqā (journal), 46–48
Uṣūl ʿIlm al-Hayʾa (Van Dyck), 122–23, 124, 131

Van Dyck, Cornelius, 121–23, 124–25

Wādī al-Nīl (journal), 114–15
Wajdī, Farīd, 114–15
Walī Allāh, Shāh, 85–87, 97
al-Waqāʾiʿ al-Miṣriyya (newspaper), 46–48
al-Wāsiṭā bayna al-Khalq wa-l-Ḥaqq (Ibn Taymiyya), 43–46

Western Thrace, 209
Wheeler, Brannon, 54–55, 77–78, 99–100
al-Wiqāya (Tāj al-Sharīʿa), 79–80, 188

Zaghlūl, Saʿd, 28, 104
ẓāhir al-riwāya, 94–95, 186–87, 188, 189–91, 196
Zaman, Muhammad Qasim, 14–15, 19–20
Zaytun (Hilmiyyat al-Zaytun), 30, 104
Ziadeh, Farhat, 19n.58, 168–69
Ziriklī, Khayr al-Dīn al-, 31, 42–43
Zoroastrianism, 101–3
Zufar b. al-Hudhayl, 88–89
Zysow, Aron, 75